Human Development from Early Childhood to Early Adulthood

WITHDRAWN

WITHDRAWN

Human Development from Early Childhood to Early Adulthood

Findings from a 20 Year Longitudinal Study

TOURO COLLEGE LIBRARY
Kings Hwy

Edited by

Wolfgang Schneider
University of Wuerzburg
Wuerzburg, Germany

Merry Bullock
American Psychological Association
Washington DC, United States

 Psychology Press
Taylor & Francis Group

New York   Hove

KH

Psychology Press
Taylor & Francis Group
270 Madison Avenue
New York, NY 10016

Psychology Press
Taylor & Francis Group
27 Church Road
Hove, East Sussex BN3 2FA

© 2009 by Taylor & Francis Group, LLC
Psychology Press is an imprint of Taylor & Francis Group, an Informa business

Printed in the United States of America on acid-free paper
10 9 8 7 6 5 4 3 2 1

International Standard Book Number-13: 978-0-8058-6108-2 (Softcover) 978-0-8058-6107-5 (Hardcover)

Except as permitted under U.S. Copyright Law, no part of this book may be reprinted, reproduced, transmitted, or utilized in any form by any electronic, mechanical, or other means, now known or hereafter invented, including photocopying, microfilming, and recording, or in any information storage or retrieval system, without written permission from the publishers.

Trademark Notice: Product or corporate names may be trademarks or registered trademarks, and are used only for identification and explanation without intent to infringe.

Library of Congress Cataloging-in-Publication Data

Human development from early childhood to early adulthood : findings from a 20 year
  longitudinal study / [edited by] Wolfgang Schneider and Merry Bullock.
       p. cm.
    Includes bibliographical references.
    ISBN 978-0-8058-6107-5 (hardcover : alk. paper) – ISBN 978-0-8058-6108-2 (pbk. :
    alk. paper) -- ISBN 978-0-203-88854-4 (e-book : alk. paper)
    1. Child psychology. 2. Developmental psychology. I. Schneider, Wolfgang, 1950
  June 19- II. Bullock, Merry.

    BF721.H798 2008
    155--dc22   2008019694

Visit the Taylor & Francis Web site at
http://www.taylorandfrancis.com

and the Psychology Press Web site at
http://www.psypress.com

7/5/11

Contents

Contributors

Dr. Jutta Ahnert
Institute of Psychotherapy and Medical Psychology
University of Würzburg
Würzburg, Germany

Prof. Dr. Jens Asendorpf
Psychology Institute
Humboldt University
Berlin, Germany

Prof. Dr. Klaus Bös
Institute of Sports Science
Karlsruhe University
Karlsruhe, Germany

Merry Bullock, PhD
Office of International Affairs
American Psychological Association
Washington, DC

Prof. Dr. Jaap Denissen
Psychology Institute
Humboldt University
Berlin, Germany

Prof. Dr. Andreas Helmke
Department of Psychology
University of Koblenz-Landau
Landau, Germany

Prof. Dr. Monika Knopf
Psychology Institute
U.W. Goethe University
Frankfurt/Main, Germany

Dipl.-Psych. Frank Niklas
Department of Psychology
University of Würzburg
Würzburg, Germany

Susanne Koerber
Department of Psychology
Ludwig Maximillian Universtiy
Munich, Germany

PD Dr. Gertrud Nunner-Winkler
Max Planck Institute for Cognition and Neuroscience
Department of Psychology/Ethics
Leipzig, Germany

Dr. Wolfgang Schneider
Department of Psychology
University of Würzburg
Würzburg, Germany

Dr. Friedrich-Wilhelm Schrader
Department of Psychology
University of Koblenz-Landau
Landau, Germany

Prof. Dr. Beate Sodian
Department of Psychology
Ludwig Maximillian University
Munich, Germany

Jan Stefanek, M.A.
Consultant
Munich, Germany

Prof. Dr. Elsbeth Stern
ETH Zürich
Research on Learning and Instruction
Zürich, Switzerland

Prof. Dr. Marcel van Aken
Department of Psychology
Utrecht University
Utrecht, The Netherlands

Preface

The Munich Longitudinal study on the Ontogenesis of Individual Competencies (LOGIC) traced developmental pathways in cognitive, social and motor domains from preschool to young adulthood in a sample of German children who grew up during the 1980s and 1990s in Munich, Germany. The goal of the study was to investigate the development of individual differences and to ask whether it is possible to understand and predict later competencies from earlier ones. This book is the second collected volume to provide a comprehensive look at developmental issues in most of the domains studied. The first volume (Weinert and Schneider, 1999) traced development from ages 3 to 12. This volume extends the overview through young adulthood, and provides a rich description of developmental trends and the stability of individual differences. In each chapter the authors provide an overview of current research for their specific domain and then address how their data help us better understand the presence and developmental effects of individual differences. The findings reported in this volune – from relative stability of basal cognitive competencies to long term effects of shyness or aggression, to relations between moral understanding and action, to investigations of the role of education in the development or maintenance of performance differences – will be of interest to researchers in cognitive, social, moral, motor, personality and educational domains, and to educators and practitioners.

Such a project requires the participation, collaboration and dedication of a large number of people without whom it could not have progressed. We want to thank all those who contributed to this two-decades-long effort. These include:

- Franz Weinert, whose vision set the stage and inspired the questions, and whose stewardship allowed LOGIC to flourish;
- The Max Planck Society, Volkswagen Foundation, and Jacobs Foundation who supported the development, implementation and dissemination of LOGIC;
- The research team, including the researchers whose work is reported in these pages and the many LOGIC publications; the professional research assistants who dedicated their careers to keeping the LOGIC sample intact and who rigorously conducted the measurements; the many students who helped collect and analyze LOGIC data; the graduate students, postdocs and visiting colleagues who brought a richness of perspectives in the planning, designing and analyses of LOGIC tasks and data;
- The technical and administrative staff of the Max Planck Institute who provided the infrastructure, equipment and technical support over a sustained 20-year period;

- And of course, the participants and their families who dedicated many hours over two decades of testing throughout the course of LOGIC. We hope you will all benefit from your generous contribution.

For the preparation of this volume we especially wish to thank Michaela Pirkner from the Department of Psychology, University of Würzburg, who managed the lengthy and copious task of coordinating the editing, formatting and checking of each chapter comprising the manuscript.

1 Introduction and Overview

Goals and Structure of LOGIC

Merry Bullock and Wolfgang Schneider

1.1 INTRODUCTION AND OVERVIEW

Many of the essential human questions—who we are; how much of what we are is due to our personal history, education, and experiences; how we change; how much our essential characteristics can change; and what happens during growth and childhood—are among the questions that underlie developmental psychology. Although everyday folk psychology provides potential answers to these questions—such as "The child is father to the man"; "As the twig is bent, so grows the tree"; "The child is a blank slate"; and "From little acorns grow mighty oaks"—the answers are often contradictory, some implying that our essential characteristics are independent of experience, and others that we are molded by our own specific life trajectories.

The contributions of nature (inherent characteristics) and nurture (experience) to development comprise one issue that motivates developmental psychology. Another is the nature of change itself. Is the development of new skills and competencies gradual and even throughout development? Are there spurts and stops? Do all children progress through the same sequence at the same time? Another question is individual differences. Does relative standing in memory ability or language skill early in life remain stable later on? Does personality remain the same? What characteristics of childhood predict who we are as adults?

Although the goal of developmental psychology is to understand change in behavior across the life span, most empirical work provides only a short snapshot view of behavioral change, because most developmental research infers change by comparing *different* people of *different* ages (cross-sectional studies) rather than attempting to follow change within the same people over time (longitudinal studies).

Why does a science of change base its theories on the indirect evidence provided by cross-sectional data? One reason is pragmatic: Longitudinal studies require investment of long periods of time and resources, and commitment to a single sample and set of questions. It is difficult to find funding for such projects, and this represents one of the major reasons for the overall lack of longitudinal studies, despite the fact that calls for longitudinal studies are frequent in the literature (see Block & Block, 2006; Harway, Mednick, & Mednick, 1984; Schneider, 1989). Another reason is more conceptual: There has been an assumption in much of psychology that the basic processes governing human behavior are universal in nature, sequence, and scope, with variation primarily in rate of change, not kind of change. Given this assumption, cross-sectional studies make sense, as one can look at the "prototypical" child to predict the "prototypical" adolescent or adult.

As longitudinal studies have proliferated from a few hundred in the 1980s to many thousands today, it has become clear that the data they generate provide crucial windows into change that paint a rich and varied picture of development, and that allow researchers to understand more deeply how context and experience interact with stable characteristics of the developing person. The goal of this volume is to contribute to the growing body of information about stability, change, and development in individuals over time.

1.1.2 The LOGIC Study

1.1.2.1 The Original Plan

At the time of its conception, the Munich Longitudinal Study on the Ontogenesis of Individual Competencies (the LOGIC study) was rather unique in its approach. First, it was begun with a commitment for stable funding for the entire longitudinal span tracing development from preschool until high school. Such a commitment could not be carried out through a university system, but was assured through the founding of the Max Planck Institute for Psychological Research in 1982, directed by Franz Weinert. At that time, one reason for founding a Max Planck Institute (to provide context, there were 62 institutes, including three in psychology, in 1982) was to support research programs that were too comprehensive, too costly, or too resource intensive to be feasible within a university system and its shorter term funding commitments. Franz Weinert's vision was to design and carry out a longitudinal study covering a variety of domains of cognitive and social and personality development, with a strong focus on the genesis and growth of individual differences, and on the prediction of school achievement, which he carried out through a parallel study that matched the LOGIC participants with their school classmates (the SCHOLASTIC study; see Weinert & Helmke, 1997).

The team that Franz Weinert assembled included a group of young scientists interested in development from multiple standpoints—cognition, personality, intelligence, memory, moral development, motor abilities and action development, and schooling. His vision was to combine investigation of development from ages 3–4 through grammar school with an intense look at individual differences that moved beyond the traditional concerns of differential psychology. Weinert was interested in patterns of development—and in asking whether there were important interindividual differences in intraindividual change (for more details, see Weinert, Schneider, Stefanek, & Weber, 1999). Results from this period of LOGIC have been reported extensively in the literature (see the list of publications in the Bibliography) and in an earlier volume, *Individual Development from 3 to 12* (Weinert & Schneider, 1999).

1.2.2   LOGIC—Revised

Although the original plan was for LOGIC data collection to stop at the end of grammar school, this was extended as it became clear that there were important questions stemming from LOGIC that could only be addressed by looking at adolescent development and beyond. LOGIC was thus extended two times—in 1998, when participants averaged 18 years of age, and in 2003, when participants averaged 23 years of age. These extensions were made possible by a commitment from the Max Planck Institute for funding until Wave 10 and for the use of Max Planck facilities for testing and analyses for Wave 11, by funding from the Volkswagen Foundation for data collection and transcription for Wave 11, and by funding from the Jacobs Foundation for the final period of data reduction and archiving.

There are some noteworthy features about the LOGIC study that bear recognition, including characteristics of its sample, its research team, and the context (Bavaria, Germany) in which it took place.

1.2.2.1   The Sample

The LOGIC sample remained remarkably stable over the 20 year period of data collection. When the study began, the sample of around 200 children was representative for the Munich area in Germany. The sample was those children who attended one of 10 preschools in the greater Munich area and were German speakers. Over the next almost 20 years, attrition remained low, at least until adulthood, as indicated in Table 1.1.

1.2.2.2   The Research Team

Another remarkable feature of LOGIC was the research team. Of the initial research team of nine scientists and students who were part of the first planning, five remained actively involved in each assessment wave throughout the LOGIC study. Three new domains (mathematics, moral reasoning, and logical and scientific reasoning) were added during subsequent waves as children entered school, and the researchers for those domains remained engaged throughout the remainder of the study. In addition to the core team (researchers, graduate students, and postdocs) a number of national and international colleagues remained engaged with the LOGIC study, participating in planning seminars and regular evaluations.

Data collection was carried out by a core team of four research assistant professionals, two of whom also remained with LOGIC until the end of the study. These core professionals were the liaisons with the researchers, and trained and maintained reliability with student research assistants who participated in the data collection. Coding was carried out by each researcher and his or her research assistants. This stability is not trivial. It meant that the questions asked and, perhaps more importantly, the individuals responsible for administering and measuring the constructs remained stable over the course of the study.

1.2.2.3   The Context

At the time that the LOGIC study was carried out, the German school system had some unique characteristics. All children attended grammar school from grades 1 to 4. At the end of grade 4, school tracking began. School tracking was of several sorts. The *preuniversity track* began with entrance in grade 5 in the gymnasium, a school that spanned grades 5–13 and that focused on a more academic course of studies. The *preprofessional* and *prevocational* tracks began with Hauptschule in grades 5 and 6, and then a further bifurcation after grade 6 into *preprofessional* training in Realschule for the next 4 years (through grade 10) or *prevocational* training in Hauptschule, ending in grade 9. This tracking system allowed LOGIC researchers to ask about the effects of schooling in cognitive, social, and moral domains.

Table 1.1 shows the overall data collection timetable for LOGIC for the period 1984–2004—a span of 20 years. Each "year" in the table represents three data collection points of 3 hours each—for a total of 9 hours testing time per year (each year's measurement was labeled as one measurement wave in LOGIC). Participants came to the Max Planck Institute for testing sessions, and participants and families were contacted several times over the course of the year to maintain motivation and interest.

As noted in Table 1.1, there was only modest attrition between Waves 1 and 9. In Wave 10, dropout was 8% of the Wave 9 participants; and in Wave 11, it was 10% of the Wave 10 sample. These attrition rates are expected, as in Waves 10 and 11 participants were no longer necessarily in the school system or in the same geographical area. Preliminary results suggested no substantial differences among those who remained in the LOGIC sample except that the proportion of participants in Wave 11 who were in the higher educational tracks was higher (and probably related to ease of follow-up and recruitment).

These attrition rates are an issue for those analyses that are used to make general comments about developmental patterns. However, given the interest in differential prediction and individual differences, the attrition rates may affect overall generalizability but do not affect our conclusions about early to late patterns and predictions.

1.3   THIS VOLUME

This volume, published more than 25 years after the onset of the Munich Longitudinal Study, is the second book that presents an overview of findings from LOGIC. The first looked at the period that was originally the extent of the study—from age

TABLE 1.1
Selected Demographics: LOGIC Sample

	Wave 1: 1984	Wave 2: 1985	Wave 3: 1986	Wave 4: 1987	Wave 5: 1988	Wave 6: 1989	Wave 7: 1990	Wave 8: 1991	Wave 9: 1992	Wave 10: 1998	Wave 11: 2003
N	205	217	213	204	200	195	194	189	186	176	152
Average age	4	5	6	7	8	9	10	11	12	18	23
% male	51	52	52	51	52	52	52	53	53	53	54
Schooling											

Note: There was some change from Waves 1 to 2; a new sample of 25 was added in Wave 2 to accommodate the initial dropout of 13 participants after Wave 2. There were no differences between the new subsample and the entire sample.

3 to age 12. This volume continues the story, integrating these early findings with results from the next two developmental phases—adolescence (measurements at ages 13 and 18) and young adulthood (measurements at age 23).

Each of the chapters provides a summary of the state of the literature and a set of answers to some common questions—was development stable, and was it possible to predict later variables from earlier ones? The topics covered include core variables reflecting basic cognitive and motor skills (intelligence, memory, and motor skills), social-cognitive competencies (moral thinking, personality, and self-concept), and school-related competencies (scientific reasoning, spelling, and mathematics). Each author summarizes developmental trends within his or her specific domain, and addresses issues of individual development—its stability over time, and the extent to which earlier performance predicts later competencies.

The size of the LOGIC sample allows comparison of subgroups and subgroup analyses, defined by early personality characteristics (Asendorpf et al., chap. 6) or educational track (Bullock et al., chap. 8; Stern, chap. 10) or adult sociocognitive variables (Nunner-Winkler, chap. 5).

The chapters in this volume provide a general overview of some of the LOGIC results. They cannot begin to capture the richness of the data, however. In presenting this work, it is the hope of the LOGIC researchers and authors that the study data, scope, and results will inspire others to experimentally test some of the many ideas that can only be presented as viable hypotheses, and inspire yet others to use the LOGIC data to answer new questions about individuals and how they develop.

REFERENCES

Block, J., & Block, J. H. (2006). Venturing a 30-year longitudinal study. *American Psychologist, 61,* 315–327.

Harway, M., Mednick, S. A., & Mednick, B. (1984). Research strategies: Methodological and practical problems. In S. A. Mednick, M. Harway, & K. M. Finello (Eds.), *Handbook of longitudinal research. Vol. 1: Birth and childhood cohorts.* New York: Praeger.

Schneider, W. (1989). Problems of longitudinal studies with children: Practical, conceptual, and methodological issues. In M. Brambring, F. Lösel, & H. Skowronek (Eds.), *Children at risk: Assessment, longitudinal research, and intervention* (pp. 313–335). New York: de Gruyter.

Weinert, F. E., & Helmke, A. (Eds.). (1997). *Entwicklung in der Grundschule* [Development in elementary school]. Weinheim, Germany: Beltz.

Weinert, F. E., & Schneider, W. (Eds.). (1999). *Individual development from 3 to 12: Findings from the Munich Longitudinal Study.* Cambridge: Cambridge University Press.

Weinert, F. E., Schneider, W., Stefanek, J., & Weber, A. (1999). LOGIC: Introduction and overview. In F. E. Weinert & W. Schneider (Eds.), *Individual development from 3 to 12: Findings from the Munich Longitudinal Study* (pp. 1–8). Cambridge: Cambridge University Press.

2 Development of Intelligence and Thinking

Wolfgang Schneider, Jan Stefanek, and Frank Niklas

2.1 INTRODUCTION

This chapter is concerned with developmental changes in various aspects of intelligence and thinking observed in the Munich Longitudinal Study on the Ontogenesis of Individual Competencies (the LOGIC study) from preschool age to early adulthood, and updates a previous review chapter (Schneider, Perner, Bullock, Stefanek, & Ziegler, 1999). When the LOGIC study was started in 1984, two important issues were to assess interindividual differences in intelligence and to assess developmental changes in these differences over the course of the study. Including intelligence measures also allowed us to assess practice effects, that is, the degree to which repeated exposure to intelligence measures increases test performance. As will be apparent from the description of test instruments given below, the majority of intelligence measures used in the study was based on a psychometric approach. However, some of the measures were derived from the assessment of constructs typical of a cognitive developmental approach. The major purpose of adding these tasks was to be able to relate changes in cognitive development assessed by Piagetian-type instruments with changes in psychometric intelligence at different time points, thus exploring the interrelationships among these variables for different ages. Because of time constraints, the design used to investigate this issue was not as systematic as that of many longitudinal studies focusing solely on intellectual development (e.g., Schaie, 1994). In contrast to those studies, however, developmental trends in intelligence assessed in our longitudinal study could be systematically related to developmental changes in other psychological constructs such as memory, motivation, personality, and academic achievement. Before we present the measures and the results in more detail, we begin with a short overview of the existing literature on developmental changes in intelligence and thinking.

2.1.1 THE STARTING POINT: PSYCHOMETRIC PERSPECTIVES
ON THE DEVELOPMENT OF INTELLECTUAL ABILITY

The study of the development of mental abilities has a long tradition in the field of psychology. Psychometric theories of intelligence are based on the belief that intelligence can be described in terms of mental factors, and that tests can be constructed that reveal individual differences in these factors (see Bjorklund, 2005). Since the 1880s, numerous tests of psychometric intelligence have been used worldwide to explore children's cognitive abilities and to characterize the structure of these abilities. From the very beginning, the definition of the term *intelligence* aroused controversy, because there were diverse views of the structure and organization of intelligence (see Berg, 1992; Sternberg & Detterman, 1986). However, despite problems in agreeing on a narrow definition of intelligence, most researchers dedicated to the psychometric approach do agree that the nature of intelligence and intellectual development can be fruitfully studied by examining individual differences in performance on tests of mental abilities (see Kail & Pellegrino, 1985; Siegler & Richards, 1982; Sternberg & Powell, 1983). From this perspective, the primary developmental interest has been in assessing the stability of individual differences over time.

It is, however, important to note that the study of individual differences is only one aspect of the overall picture of the development of psychometric intellectual ability (see Gardner & Clark, 1992). Focusing exclusively on individual differences and their stability overlooks the fact that change or stability in individual differences (indicated by correlations across various intelligence tests) is logically independent of growth in the average level of mental ability (see McCall, 1981; Schneider, 1989). Ignoring this difference can yield misleading conclusions. One famous example concerns Bloom's (1964) claim that 50% of an individual's adult intelligence is already developed by the age of 4. This claim was based on the finding from previous studies that the correlations among IQs assessed at age 4 and at age 18 average around .7, which means that they share about 50% variance. The reason that this conclusion is misleading is that Bloom's claim is based solely on the stability of individual differences and not on the absolute level of mental abilities. Undoubtedly, a 4 year old's performance level is far less than 50% of an 18 year old's.

Both individual differences and overall growth were assessed in several famous longitudinal studies conducted during the first half of the 20th century at different places in the United States (for overviews, see Bayley, 1970; Gardner & Clark, 1992; Goodenough, 1946). Although most of these studies focused on individual difference questions such as stability over time, some studies also explored the question of developmental changes in mental growth rates. Typically, participants in these studies were recruited at an early age (during infancy or the preschool years) and followed until adolescence or adulthood.

Findings regarding the *stability* issue can be summarized with three points: Infant tests of intelligence do not predict later intelligence levels, IQ can be predicted from age 3 onward, and temporal stability does not indicate lack of change.

2.1.1.1 Infant Tests of Intelligence Do Not Predict Later Intelligence Levels

Researchers (Bayley, 1949, 1970; McCall, Hogarty, & Hurlburt, 1972) have noted that there is no correlation between infant intelligence assessments and later measured IQ. McCall et al. pointed out that the lack of a correlation is not due to poor infant test reliability. Rather, they give the plausible explanation that the competencies measured in infancy are different from those measured in the preschool years and later.

2.1.1.2 Later Intelligence Levels Can Be Predicted with Sufficient Accuracy from Age 3 Onward

In contrast to infant assessments, IQ measured as early as age 3 does correlate with later IQ levels (Bayley, 1949; Honzik, MacFarlane, & Allen, 1948; Sontag, Baker, & Nelson, 1958). Stable patterns were found in an 11 year follow-up study by Yule, Gold, and Busch (1982), who tested a sample of 85 children on the Wechsler Preschool and Primary Scale of Intelligence (WPPSI; Eggert, 1978) at about 5 years and then on the Wechsler Intelligence Scale for Children (WISC; Tewes, 1983) at about 16 years. Long-term predictive validity of the WPPSI was high, with an intercorrelation between the full-scale IQs on the two tests of .86. Generally, correlations between IQ scores across different ages show the familiar simplex pattern, with values increasing as the intervals between tests decrease. For instance, Hindley and Owen (1978) reported a test–retest correlation of .53 for IQ scores assessed at the ages of 3 and 17 years, compared with .74 for scores assessed at ages 8 and 17 and .87 for scores assessed at ages 14 and 17.

2.1.1.3 Temporal Stability Does Not Indicate Lack of Change

Although most longitudinal studies on intellectual development showed high temporal stability between the preschool period and adolescence, they do not support the notion of a "constant IQ." Most longitudinal researchers noted considerable intraindividual change in the level of IQ (e.g., Bayley, 1955; Honzik et al., 1948; Sontag et al., 1958). For instance, IQ changes of 20 points and more between the ages of 6 and 18 occurred in about 35% of the participants in the Honzik et al. study. The patterns of intraindividual change observed in most studies were typically quite idiosyncratic, including periods of loss in IQ followed by a gain, periods of gain followed by little change, and so on.

Sontag et al. (1958) reported larger increments of change during the preschool years than during the school years. This finding was also confirmed by Bayley (1949), who used "intelligence lability scores" for the Berkeley Growth Study children. Whereas the use of IQs or standard scores seems suited for assessing a child's shift in status relative to the norm, a child's progress in relation to his or her own past is better represented by lability scores indicating the degree of variation from his or her own central tendency over time. More precisely, a lability score represents a child's standard deviation from his or her own mean standard score averaged across all testing points. Bayley (1949) found that lability scores decreased consistently as a function of testing age: Lability scores were highest for infancy, lower for the preschool period, and lowest for the school-age period. Accordingly, it appears that children are more likely to maintain their own relative status as they grow older. However, Bayley also emphasized the considerable individual differences in lability at all ages. Overall, these and a variety of other findings demonstrate that patterns of mental growth differ widely across individual children.

Results from a more recent longitudinal study (Moffitt, Caspi, Harkness, & Silva, 1993) based on an analysis of profiles of IQ changes basically support this view. Moffitt et al. studied the reliability, magnitude, and meaning of IQ change using scores on the Revised WISC (WISC-R) obtained from a representative sample of more than 1,000 children at ages 7, 9, 11, and 13. The authors interpreted their findings to show that changes in intellectual performance during the period from childhood to adolescence may reflect several distinct phenomena. Overall, long-term stability in IQ scores tended to be high, ranging between .74 and .85 for different measurement points. Whereas IQ change was negligible in amount, unreliable, or both in the majority of children, it was quite marked and reliable in a nontrivial minority (about 14%) of their participants. One of the most intriguing aspects of Moffitt et al.'s data was that there did not seem to be any differences in intellectual ability between stable and labile children. The question regarding "who changes" could not be answered in this study because no reliable correlates of IQ change were found.

Taken together, the findings from psychometric studies of intelligence indicate that intellectual development is highly stable between the preschool years and adolescence. Although interindividual differences in intraindividual change decrease with age, patterns of mental growth differ more widely across individual children than has been assumed in the classic literature.

2.1.2 COGNITIVE-DEVELOPMENTAL AND DOMAIN-SPECIFIC PERSPECTIVES ON INTELLECTUAL DEVELOPMENT

It is well known that Jean Piaget's perspective on intellectual development was formed during his early psychological studies in Alfred Binet's psychometric laboratory (Piaget, 1952). Piaget was particularly critical of the scoring procedure (pass versus fail) used in all psychometric instruments. This dissatisfaction led him to develop the *clinical method*, which explores the reasoning behind a child's answer. The tasks and methods that Piaget subsequently used and his basic theory of intelligence differed considerably from theoretical approaches and test procedures used within the psychometric tradition. The central questions that guided Piaget's perspective on intellectual development were the description and explanation of universal changes in mental functioning that take place from infancy to adolescence. Piaget viewed the child as similar to a young scientist, constructing theories of the world, and he defined intelligence as an interactive instrument that achieved an equilibrium between a child's internal cognitive structures and the environment. Piaget identified four broad stages of intellectual development, characterized by the types of cognitive structures used to interact with the environment: the (a) sensorimotor stage, (b) preoperational stage, (c) concrete operational stage, and (d) formal operational stage. Unlike the psychometric approach, which characterized intellectual development as continuous change, the Piagetian approach characterized intellectual development as a sequence of qualitatively different stages and emphasized the similarity in cognitive structures among children at a given developmental period or stage. As noted by Bidell and Fischer (1992), the Piagetian focus on similarities among children of a given age has drawn attention away from the extensive literature illustrating variability in cognitive development.

New perspectives on cognitive development ("neo-Piagetian" perspectives with an information-processing component as well as other perspectives that focus on concept structure and content) evolved during the 1970s, as an increasing number of concerns were raised about Piaget's theory. For example, Piaget's theory was formulated in a way that was difficult to test in any straightforward empirical fashion (see Brainerd, 1978), and when it was tested it revealed data that were not easily reconciled with its underlying theoretical claims. Although many of the post-Piagetian perspectives on cognitive development preserve central ideas of Piaget's perspective on intellectual development (e.g., the concept of cognitive structures), several underlying claims have been modified. In particular, current cognitive developmental theorists seem to be interested in (a) exploring the basic mechanisms of developmental change, (b) understanding individual differences, (c) investigating cognitive structures more locally within a given domain and not universally across domains, and (d) investigating the role of specifiable biological factors that regulate cognitive development and determine the possible upper limits to be achieved (see Case, 1992, 1998; Demetriou, 1988; Demetriou & Kazi, 2001; Fischer, 1987; Fischer & Bidell, 1998).

Although Piaget was not interested in the issue of individual differences and differential development, several researchers have demonstrated that individual differences on Piagetian tasks predict academic performance. For example, performance on batteries of Piagetian tasks has been shown to predict early academic skills as well as or even better than standardized IQ tests (Kingma, 1984). In other research, Humphreys and his colleagues (Humphreys, 1980; Humphreys, Rich, & Davey, 1985) examined the relationship between Piagetian tasks, IQ tests, and academic performance for children of varying intellectual abilities and ages. The Piagetian tasks ranged from those that assessed early concrete operational abilities to those evaluating formal operational skills. Correlations between children's performance on Piagetian tasks and on IQ tests were generally high, in most cases exceeding .80. Interestingly, correlations between performance on the Piagetian tasks and academic performance were only slightly lower than those found with verbal IQ (r's > .70). However, the evidence is not consistent. Deanna Kuhn (1976) tested middle-class children from the first through the seventh grades and failed to find a significant relationship between Piagetian measures and IQ for her older groups of children approaching formal operations. A significant correlation ($r =$ .69) was only found for the younger group of children, that is, 6- to 8-year-olds. See Bjorklund (2005) for a more detailed discussion of these findings.

2.2 THE CONTRIBUTION OF THE LOGIC STUDY TO THE UNDERSTANDING OF INTELLECTUAL DEVELOPMENT

The LOGIC study provided assessments of children's intellectual level from ages 4 to 23. It should be noted that there are several constraints in the LOGIC study that limit the scope of our analyses. First, the development of children's intellectual competencies was not a core issue of the LOGIC project. This does not mean that the available database is scarce. Psychometric tests of mental ability were regularly given throughout the study, and tasks assessing various areas of conceptual growth were applied in both early and later phases of the study (see Table 2.1). Thus, we do possess longitudinal data that can be used for the assessment of developmental changes in intellectual competencies. However, unlike other domains such as social inhibition, memory, or mathematical thinking, intelligence measures were included primarily for pragmatic rather than theory-based considerations. There were two main reasons for including psychometric tests of intelligence in the LOGIC study. First, they provided information on how representative the sample was at the beginning of the study

TABLE 2.1
Overview of Intelligence Assessments in the LOGIC Study

Test	Chronological Age										
	4	5	6	7	8	9	10	11	12	18	23
Verbal IQ											
HAWIVA (WPPSI)	x	x									
HAWIK (WISC)					x		x		x	x	x
Nonverbal IQ											
CMMS	x		x		x						
CFT							x		x	x	x
Piagetian tasks											
False belief	x	x									
Number conservation	x		x								
Arlin test								x	x	x	

and in the time periods thereafter. Most longitudinal studies investigating intellectual development have not been representative because the IQ levels of their participants were high, that is, 120 and above (see Bayley, 1949, 1970; Hilden, 1949; Sontag et al., 1958). Needless to say, such lack of representativeness can seriously bias the conclusions concerning important developmental issues such as the general growth of intelligence or the stability of individual differences over time.

As noted above, another reason to include IQ tests was to assess practice effects. Although classic longitudinal studies (e.g., Sontag et al., 1958) reported only minimal effects of repeated testing on IQ, we wanted to explore whether this finding would generalize to the LOGIC study. Compared to most longitudinal studies on intellectual development, the amount of testing time per child in the LOGIC study was immense, and we could not exclude the possibility of significant practice effects for our sample. Thus, tests of verbal and nonverbal intelligence were administered at least once a year to control for changes in overall IQ level.

Although this pragmatic orientation restricts the range of meaningful data analyses, it still allows us to investigate topics not sufficiently covered in the available literature. In the analyses to be discussed here, we focus on four major questions. The first two questions concern replications and extensions of traditional research on psychometric intelligence, whereas the next two questions explore possible links between psychometric and cognitive perspectives.

Specifically, we addressed the following issues:

1. Are there changes in the intercorrelations of verbal and nonverbal intelligence over development? Other longitudinal studies have focused on general intelligence (e.g., as assessed by the Stanford-Binet test) but have not addressed verbal (see Burt's verbal: educational) and nonverbal (kinesthetic: mechanical) components separately.

2. Is IQ test performance assessed in preschool related to IQ performance in the later school years and beyond? If so, does the quality of prediction differ for verbal and nonverbal IQ components? Although an abundance of evidence from American longitudinal studies indicates that mental ability assessed in the preschool years predicts later IQ scores rather well (see above), most of this evidence dates back to the first half of the 20th century and may be methodologically biased in that several measurement points per year were aggregated into a single score (see Bayley, 1949).

3. Are there any significant relationships between measures of psychometric intelligence and indicators of cognitive performance as assessed by Piagetian and other cognitive tasks, and do these relationships change with age? The issue of interrelationships between psychometric intelligence and other cognitive variables was explored to some extent in the 1970s and early 1980s (e.g., Hunt, 1980). However, most of this research was conducted with adults and did not consider longitudinal evidence.

4. Does the growth of mental ability between ages 7 and 23 show a linear pattern, or are first signs of the eventual leveling off at asymptote already discernible at an earlier age? Whereas the first three research questions listed above focus on interindividual differences in cognitive ability, this last issue deals with intraindividual changes over time and explores the topic of cognitive variability, which has been ignored in most models of cognitive development (see Siegler, 1994).

2.3 DESCRIPTIONS OF TASKS

2.3.1 INDICATORS OF INTELLIGENCE AND LOGICAL THINKING

An overview of the psychometric intelligence tests and experimental tasks assessing logical thinking used in the LOGIC study is given in Table 2.1. As is seen, different psychometric tests were administered during the preschool and kindergarten years as well as later on.

2.3.1.1 Verbal Intelligence

The Hannover-Wechsler Intelligence Scale for Preschool Children (HAWIVA; Eggert, 1978) was administered twice at the beginning of the study. This test is roughly comparable to the WPPSI used in most English-speaking countries. Because of time constraints, only the verbal part of the test was administered during the first year of the study. This part consists of three subtests: General Knowledge, Vocabulary, and General Comprehension. One year later, both the verbal and nonverbal ("performance") parts of the HAWIVA were administered. Because the nonverbal component of the HAWIVA is not considered in our analyses, we report only the means and standard deviations of the verbal component of the HAWIVA obtained at Waves 1 and 2.

From Wave 4 onward, the Hamburg-Wechsler Intelligence Scale for School Children (HAWIK) replaced the HAWIVA, which was no longer applicable because the oldest children in the normative sample were younger than the LOGIC children (who averaged 7 years of age in Wave 4 and had just entered elementary school). The HAWIK test (equivalent to the WISC) can be used for children between 6 and 16 years of age. Only performance on the verbal part of the test is considered in the present analyses. This part consisted of the following subtests: General Knowledge, Vocabulary, General Comprehension, Commonalities, Numerical Thinking, and Digit Span. The HAWIK was administered in Waves 4, 6, and 9, that is, in Grades 1, 3, and 6. In the two subsequent waves, the Vocabulary subtest of the Hamburg-Wechsler Intelligence Scale for Adults (HAWIE) was used to assess a core aspect of verbal intelligence. Because of time constraints, it was impossible to include more HAWIE subtests in the study.

2.3.1.2   Nonverbal Intelligence

The Columbia Mental Maturity Scale (CMMS; Burgemeister, Blum, & Lorge, 1972) was chosen to assess children's nonverbal intellectual skills during the early stages of the study. This test is designed to tap general reasoning abilities of children aged 3 years 6 months to 9 years. Test items consisted of picking out the odd item in a group (i.e., selecting the picture that is different from or unrelated to all the others in a series of three to five drawings). The number of correct answers gives the sum raw score, which is then used to calculate a standardized score. Depending on children's age level, an increasing number of items were administered. Because the raw scores for children of different ages are derived from different numbers of items, the standardized age deviation scores, comparable to IQ scores, were used. The results obtained in Waves 1, 3, and 5 were used for the present analyses.

The CMMS measure was no longer appropriate after children entered grade 4. We replaced it with the German version of the Culture Fair Intelligence Test (CFT), first developed by Cattell and Horn (Weiss, 1976) as a measure of nonverbal intelligence from grade 4 onward. According to the test authors, the CFT assesses children's fluid intelligence. The test consists of two parallel forms (A and B), each containing four different subtests: The first subtest (Series) requires the identification and completion of a series of geometric figures, the second subtest (Classification) requires the classification and differentiation of geometric figures, the third (Matrices) requires children to complete matrix figures, and the fourth (Topologies) requires the identification of proportions and relations of geometric areas. The speed version of the test was used on four occasions (i.e., in Waves 7, 9, 10, and 11).

Different test procedures were used to assess operational reasoning in the preschool and school years. In Waves 1 and 3, children were given a *number invariance test* that consisted of 14 problems assessing number invariance as defined by Piaget and generally used to assess preoperational level. Children were required to judge whether the number of items in item sets changed when they were transformed (i.e., either stretched out or compressed). The total number of items correctly answered was used as the dependent measure for the present analyses.

During the advanced elementary years and beyond (i.e., in Waves 8, 9, and 10), children's operational level was tested with the German version of the Arlin Test of Formal Reasoning (the ATFR, or the Arlin test; Arlin, 1984). The Arlin measure was first used in Wave 8, when children were about 11 years old, and then repeated at the ages of 12 and 18. This standardized paper-and-pencil test of operational reasoning skills focuses on the transition between concrete and formal operations. According to Arlin, validation studies have shown that the test is a reliable alternative to the much more time-consuming clinical interview. The original test consists of 32 questions, arranged into eight subtests with four multiple-choice questions. The questions pertaining to two formal schemes (forms of conservation beyond direct verification and mechanical equilibrium) were omitted from the German version because they were judged to be especially difficult. Thus, the resulting test contained 24 items arranged into six subtests:

- Multiplicative Compensations (conservation of water displacement with changes in size and/or shape)
- Correlations (between variables in two dimensions)
- Probability (of different outcomes in games of chance)
- Combinatory Reasoning (the ability to produce exhaustive combinations of five items)
- Proportional Reasoning (balance beam and amount of paper to cover different proportionally sized objects)
- Coordination of Two or More Frames of Reference (relative position of objects moving in different directions)

This test provided an overall score of the total number of questions answered correctly, and allowed a qualitative classification into operational level (i.e., concrete, high concrete, transitional, low formal, and formal operational).

2.4   MAIN RESULTS

The means and standard deviations for each of the psychometric tests as well as those obtained for the number conservation and Arlin test measures are listed in Table 2.2. The data obtained for the standardized IQ tests provide valuable information on the degree to which the LOGIC sample was representative and on practice effects. First of all, mean IQ scores ranged between 106 and 110 points for most measurement points and test procedures. The only exception was the CFT assessments at Waves 9 and 10, with mean IQ scores clearly above this mean. Overall, then, the IQ scores obtained in our study were not as high as those reported for the different American and British longitudinal studies described above, even though the IQ scores of the LOGIC participants were slightly above average (which could be due to a cohort effect). Thus, our sample seems at least as representative as most other samples used to explore the development of psychometric intelligence from early childhood to adulthood.

Overall, the pattern of results obtained in our study is basically in accord with others reported in the relevant literature (e.g., Sontag et al., 1958), which found no substantial practice effects in longitudinal studies on the development of intelligence.

It is important to note that the verbal IQ measures from Waves 10 and 11 could not be compared to verbal IQ measures assessed at previous measurement points. Given that only the Vocabulary subtest of the HAWIE was included at Waves 10 and 11, raw scores had to be used for this variable. The mean scores indicate that participants' vocabulary slightly increased from age 18 to age 23. To test whether this change was significant and whether previous sex differences found for verbal IQ in the LOGIC sample would generalize to the vocabulary measure, we carried out a repeated-measure analysis of variance with *vocabulary*

TABLE 2.2

Mean IQs, Standard Deviations, and Ranges for the Various Psychometric Intelligence Tests Used in the LOGIC Study, and Mean Standard Deviations and Ranges for Number Conservation (Items Correctly Answered) and the Arlin Test Measures (% Correct)

Variable	M	SD	Minimum	Maximum
Verbal IQ				
Hannover-Wechsler Intelligence Scale for Preschool Children (HAWIVA; Wave 1)	106.62	13.14	70	137
HAWIVA (Wave 2)	107	11.06	768	130
Hamburg-Wechsler Intelligence Scale for Children (HAWIK; Wave 4)	100.52	10.47	78	130
HAWIK (Wave 6)	107.22	8.89	77	131
HAWIK (Wave 9)	108.97	12.9	77	148
HAWIK (Wave 10, raw data)	19.25	4.09	9	29
HAWIK (Wave 11, raw data)	21.7	4.51	8	31
Nonverbal IQ				
Columbia Mental Maturity Scale (CMMS; Wave 1)	108.82	11.94	74	139
CMMS (Wave 3)	107.92	12.55	79	150
CMMS (Wave 5)	107.96	12.94	70	144
Culture Fair Intelligence Test (CFT; Wave 7)	109.63	14.6	71	152
CFT (Wave 9)	114.34	13.97	78	149
CFT (Wave 10)	120.5	14.48	79	147
CFT (Wave 11, raw data)	39.68	4.73	18	46
Piagetian Tasks				
Number conservation (Wave 1)	3.23	2.21	0	12
Number conservation (Wave 2)	7.01	4.47	0	14
Arlin Test of Formal Reasoning (Arlin test; Wave 8)	39.99	14.63	8	83
Arlin test (Wave 9)	45.39	15.08	13	92
Arlin test (Wave 10)	61.39	16.56	24	96

as the dependent variable and *sex* as the independent variable. There was a significant sex effect, $F(1, 148) = 7.12$, $p < .01$, but no effect of measurement point, and no Sex by Measurement Point interaction. Male participants outperformed females on both occasions, a finding replicating previous results from the LOGIC study (e.g., Schneider & Stefanek, 2006) but certainly deviating from normative results, given that most IQ tests report comparable verbal IQ levels for males and females.

We were also unable to calculate IQ scores for the CFT measure used with the 23 year olds because no age norms are available. A comparison of the CFT mean raw scores obtained at Waves 10 and 11 indicates that mean scores significantly improved between the ages of 18 and 23 years, $F(1, 142) = 35.13$, $p < .01$. There was no sex effect and no significant interaction.

The means given for the number conservation task in Table 2.2 show that number invariance increased substantially from age 4 to age 6, $t(186) = 9.31$, $p < .01$, with standard deviations also increasing considerably during this time period. The situation was as clear for the Arlin test. As can be seen from Table 2.2, mean scores did not increase much from Wave 8 to Wave 9 (ages 11–12), whereas the gain in operational reasoning obtained between Waves 9 and 10 (that is, between the ages of 12 and 18) was substantial. This pattern of findings would be expected from a Piagetian point of view as the major transition from concrete to formal operations takes place during adolescence. An analysis of variance using sex as the independent variable and time as the dependent variable showed main effects of (a) sex, $F(1,171) = 12.43$, $p < .01$; and (b) time, $F(2, 342) = 200.06$, $p < .001$. The Sex by Time interaction was not significant, $F(2, 342) = 2.95$, $p < .06$. To summarize, there was clear improvement over time, males generally performed better on this test than females, and the difference between males and females showed a trend of increasing over the course of the study.

2.4.1   INTERCORRELATIONS AMONG VERBAL AND
NONVERBAL IQ COMPONENTS OVER TIME

Intercorrelations among the various verbal and nonverbal intelligence components are depicted in Table 2.3. Most intercorrelations were of moderate size and considerably lower than those reported in the literature. Although this might occur because we occasionally related subsets of psychometric tests (i.e., verbal components of the HAWIVA and HAWIK) with full scales (CMMS and CFT), the intercorrelations among full scales were of about the same moderate size. A more likely explanation for this discrepancy is that several of the longitudinal studies with young children (e.g., Bayley, 1949) used several measurement points per year and then aggregated these IQ scores across annual measurement points. This procedure increases reliability scores and may also overestimate true long-term stability.

The developmental pattern of correlations shows some evidence for the simplex pattern (that correlations closer in time are higher) reported in most previous studies, particularly when developmental changes were considered from the beginning onward. The pattern also supports the claim of higher correlations from the school years and beyond when compared to the preschool period. Although intercorrelations between verbal and nonverbal IQ tests tended to be

TABLE 2.3
Intercorrelations Among Verbal and Nonverbal Intelligence Components

Variable	1	2	3	4	5	6	7	8	9	10	11	12	13	14
1. HAWIVA 1	x	.52	.47	.46	.42	.26	.26	.45	.31	.20	.30	.27	.21	.23
2. HAWIVA 2		x	.51	.47	.49	.40	.34	.27	.37	.27	.35	.25	.27	.24
3. HAWIK 4			x	.81	.69	.51	.54	.40	.49	.43	.44	.35	.38	.35
4. HAWIK 6				x	.80	.60	.59	.39	.43	.43	.47	.45	.44	.42
5. HAWIK 9					x	.72	.66	.34	.43	.40	.54	.43	.46	.46
6. HAWIK 10						x	.70	.28	.30	.31	.42	.29	.37	.39
7. HAWIK 11							x	.35	.34	.38	.47	.41	.40	.46
8. CMMS 1								x	.55	.41	.36	.38	.33	.36
9. CMMS 3									x	.53	.51	.52	.51	.45
10. CMMS 5										x	.53	.46	.52	.43
11. CFT 7											x	.68	.69	.63
12. CFT 9												x	.69	.61
13. CFT 10													x	.74
14. CFT 11														x

lower than those obtained for verbal tests alone or for nonverbal tests alone, this difference was not substantial. From grade 1 onward, the stability of individual differences was rather high.

Overall, the correlational analyses yielded developmental trends similar to those found in classic longitudinal studies. The patterns found for tests of verbal and nonverbal intelligence were roughly comparable, and IQ test performance assessed in preschool was significantly related to IQ performance in the later school years, regardless of the type of test (i.e., verbal versus nonverbal). In contrast to previous studies, however, the average size of intercorrelations was generally lower for the LOGIC data.

2.4.2 INTERRELATIONS AMONG PSYCHOMETRIC INTELLIGENCE TESTS AND OPERATIONAL REASONING: DEVELOPMENTAL PATTERNS

Intercorrelations among measures of psychometric intelligence and the logical thinking tasks were computed separately for preschool and school periods. The data obtained for the preschool period are depicted in Table 2.4. As can be seen from this table, most intercorrelations were of low to moderate size, ranging between 0 (verbal intelligence and number conservation) and .24 (nonverbal intelligence and number conservation measured at the ages of 5 and 6). Overall, these correlations were considerably lower than those obtained among the various psychometric tests during the preschool period.

The pattern or relations found for psychometric variables and indicators of formal operational reasoning assessed during the school years and beyond are different, as shown in Table 2.5. Most of the correlations ranged between .45 and .60, indicating interrelations of moderate to high size. It is worth noting that diachronous and synchronous correlations did not differ much. Overall, the intercorrelations found among measures of formal operation (the Arlin test) and verbal and nonverbal intelligence ranged between .37 and .59, and are comparable to those found between measures of verbal and nonverbal intelligence obtained for

---

TABLE 2.4

Intercorrelations Among Measures of Psychometric Intelligence and Cognitive Developmental Tasks Observed in the Preschool Years

Scale	Number Conservation	
	NC1	NC3
HAWIVA1	−.03	.17
HAVIWA2	.10	.24
CMMS1	.09	.03
CMMS3	.12	.24

Note: The number immediately following a variable indicates a wave number.

TABLE 2.5

Intercorrelations Among Measures of Psychometric Intelligence and Piagetian Tasks Observed for the School Years and Beyond

Scale	Formal Operations		
	ATFR 8	ATFR 9	ATFR 10
HAWIK 4	.47	.43	.39
HAWIK 6	.45	.52	.46
HAWIK 9	.47	.59	.55
HAWIK 10	.28	.38	.50
HAWIK 11	.40	.40	.49
CMMS 5	.37	.40	.44
CFT 7	.54	.55	.55
CFT 9	.44	.47	.50
CFT 10	.53	.53	.61
CFT 11	.36	.51	.51

Note: The number immediately following a variable indicates a wave number.

the same age range (see Table 2.3). This finding indicates that the type of assessment of intellectual skills did not seem to make a big difference after participants had entered school. Overall, interrelations among psychometric measures of intelligence and task-oriented assessments of operational thinking were substantial and reliable over the school years and beyond.

2.4.3 TEST–RETEST STABILITIES OF THE PSYCHOMETRIC INTELLIGENCE TESTS AND THE OPERATIONAL REASONING TASKS

One important issue treated in most longitudinal studies on the development of intelligence concerns stability over time. In the present analyses, we roughly distinguish between *short-term stabilities* of individual differences, which we arbitrarily define as stabilities for time intervals up to 5 years, and *long-term stabilities* for time intervals of more than 5 years. Table 2.6 gives these stabilities as a function of intelligence component (i.e., verbal, nonverbal, and operational reasoning).

As can be seen from Table 2.6, short-term stabilities for the verbal and nonverbal intelligence components were moderate to high from the beginning. From the ages of 4 to 8, short-term stabilities were moderate, varying between .50 and .55, regardless of the intelligence component under study. From age 8 and older, short-term stabilities for the verbal intelligence component ranged between .70 and .81 and were higher than those found for the nonverbal intelligence component (range: .53–.74).

In agreement with our expectations, long-term stabilities were lower for all intelligence components. However, from age 7 and older, long-term stabilities were reasonably high, with test–retest correlations over 15 years exceeding .4 for nonverbal intelligence and .5 for verbal intelligence. Test–retest stabilities were .7 and higher for the comparisons between 18 and 23 years, indicating that the rank order of participants on tests of verbal and nonverbal intelligence did not change much after adolescence.

Table 2.6 also shows that the findings for the operational-level variables were somewhat different. The test–retest correlations found for the Piagetian number conservation task between the ages of 4 and 6 were nonsignificant. Although most children improved their performance between these two measurement points,

---

TABLE 2.6

Short-Term Stabilities and Long-Term Stabilities as a Function of Intelligence Component (verbal intelligence, nonverbal intelligence, and operational reasoning)

Verbal Intelligence

Stabilities for Shorter Time Intervals

Age	4–5	5–7	7–9	9–12	12–18	
Stability	.521	.507	.808	.796	.726	

Stabilities for Longer Time Intervals

Age	4–23	5–23	7–23	9–23	12–23	18–23
Stability	.257	.341	.537	.588	.664	.697

Nonverbal Intelligence

Stabilities for Shorter Time Intervals

Age	4–6	6–8	8–10	10–12	12–18	
Stability	.553	.530	.526	.654	.686	

Stabilities for Longer Time Intervals

Age	4–23	6–23	8–23	10–23	12–23	18–23
Stability	.356	.447	.432	.633	.615	.744

Operational Reasoning

Stabilities for Shorter Time Intervals

Age	4–6	6–11	11–12
Stability	.017	.351	.523

Stabilities for Longer Time Intervals

Age	6–12	6–18	11–18
Stability	.326	.418	.634

they obviously did so at a different pace. From age 6 onward, however, short-term stabilities were reliable. Although the test–retest correlation between the ages of 6 and 11 was only moderate (.35), this finding still seems impressive given that different tests were used on each occasion. Unexpectedly, the long-term stability of test scores between ages 6 and 18 was even higher, approaching a correlation coefficient of .42. This finding indicates that performance on the Arlin test at age 18 was more similar to performance on the number conservation task at age 6 than performance on the Arlin test at the age of 11. It is also interesting in this regard that the (1 year) short-term stability assessed for the Arlin test between the ages of 11 and 12 ($r = .52$) was lower than the (6 year) long-term stability assessed between the ages of 12 and 18 ($r = .63$). These results are not surprising from a Piagetian perspective, which would predict large and stable shifts between different cognitive levels, but variable changes within those levels as the components of the next level are acquired.

Overall, the findings obtained for the psychometric and nonpsychometric components of intellectual ability demonstrate that interindividual stabilities in intraindividual change were substantial from the beginning of elementary school. Substantial test–retest correlations were obtained even during the preschool period for psychometric tests of intelligence. Test–retest correlations were not uniformly high for the operational reasoning measures even though test–retest correlations obtained for a much shorter time interval (6 weeks) in an independent pilot study were substantial, indicating that this concept could be reliably assessed. The test–retest stabilities across operational "boundaries" (e.g., preoperational-operational or operational-formal operational levels) support the idea of describing intellectual growth in terms of different levels of thinking.

2.4.4 INTRAINDIVIDUAL CHANGES IN INTELLIGENCE OVER TIME: THE IMPACT OF INDIVIDUAL DIFFERENCE VARIABLES

From a methodological point of view, properly assessing intraindividual change over time is a challenging task. When we started this longitudinal study, innovative methodological approaches known as *individual growth modeling* had just entered the literature (e.g., Rogosa, Brandt, & Zimowski, 1982). During the last 2 decades, the situation has improved substantially, with statistical packages devoted to *hierarchical linear modeling* (HLM; Raudenbush & Bryk, 2002) available in large multipurpose statistical packages. However, application of these sophisticated methods still lags behind. In a review of more than 50 longitudinal studies published in the American Psychological Association journals in 1999, fewer than five used individual growth modeling, even though most studies attempted to analyze individual change (Singer & Willett, 2001). Apparently, one cause for this situation is that the application of more sophisticated longitudinal methods requires substantial statistical knowledge, which still is not sufficiently covered in most popular applied statistics books.

To address the methodological challenges related to assessing intraindividual change in intelligence, we used a multilevel model of change (mixed models with multiple imputations) described in more detail by Singer and Willett (2003). In a first step, we analyzed the causes for missing data, which did not follow a systematic pattern. Overall, 176 cases with complete data sets in the predictor variables (age group, sex, and socioeconomic status [SES]) could be included in our statistical analyses (please note that the mixed modeling procedure can compensate for missing data in the dependent variables but not in the predictor variables). A comparison of the subsamples with complete versus incomplete data in the dependent variables did not show any significant differences, a finding replicated after missing values had been imputed. To improve the interpretation of results, we recentered the predictors following a procedure described by Singer and Willett (2003, p. 113). Rather than entering time as a predictor in its raw form, we subtracted a constant from each observed value. As a consequence, we obtained a time scale based on the estimated initial age of the participants (3 years and 4 months), which no longer was dependent on the cadence of "variably spaced measurement occasions" (see Singer & Willett, 2003, pp. 139ff). Due to the recentering procedure, the effect parameters found for our predictors on the person level could be interpreted as robust estimates for participants who score normally on all other predictors.

Based on this multilevel model of change, we were able to estimate intraindividual developmental functions for all participants and all dependent measures included in the study, and also to assess the impact of our predictor measures on initial status (i.e., individual differences observed at the very beginning of our study) as well as on intraindividual growth in the various intelligence components over time. We chose to include chronological age group (young versus old) as a separate predictor variable in addition to sex and SES because we had repeatedly found effects of age group on our dependent variables—even at later measurement points—despite the fact that the mean age difference between the two subsamples was not more than 8 months. Ratings of the social prestige of fathers' occupation (high, medium, or low) and mothers' educational level were included as indicators of SES.

2.4.4.1 Development of Verbal Intelligence

To assess developmental change in verbal IQ, raw scores from the HAWIK (Waves 4, 6, and 9) were included in the analyses. Given that these data were already included in our previous report (Schneider et al., 1999), where we used hierarchical linear modeling (Raudenbush & Bryk, 2002), we did not expect different findings based on multilevel change modeling. Figure 2.1 shows the mean estimated growth curve averaging individual trajectories.

Figure 2.1 suggests an almost linear increase over time. However, this function should be interpreted with caution because the time intervals between measurement points were not equidistant (16 months for the time interval between T1 and T2 and 36 months for the time interval between T2 and T3). In fact, findings from the multilevel modeling procedure confirmed the HLM analyses presented by Schneider et al. (1999) that a nonlinear model of growth fitted the data best,

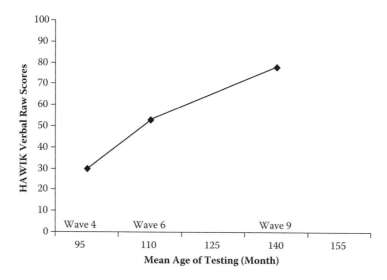

FIGURE 2.1   Changes in Hamburg-Wechsler Intelligence Scale for Children (HAWIK) verbal raw score estimates for Waves 4, 6, and 9 (i.e., age 7, 9, and 12).

suggesting a negatively accelerated growth curve. Figure 2.1 indicates that the sample showed a slight deceleration in the increases in their estimated scores over the age period between 9 and 12 years. Although the verbal IQ data for Waves 10 and 11 could not be used for growth modeling given that only vocabulary was assessed, the data indicate that this component of verbal intelligence did not increase significantly between the ages of 18 and 23 (see the analyses reported above).

2.4.4.2   Development of Nonverbal Intelligence

Given that the same test of nonverbal intelligence (CFT) was used in Waves 7, 9, 10, and 11, that is, at the ages of 10, 12, 18, and 23 years, it was possible to estimate the developmental function for the time period between childhood and young adulthood. The mean growth curve is depicted in Figure 2.2, and the results of the mixed models analysis are given in Table 2.7.

The findings in Table 2.7 show that the fit for the unconditional means model (Model A), which does not consider time-related changes in the dependent measures, is worse than that obtained for the remaining growth curve Models B and C. Overall, the best fit results for Model C. In this model, there is a significant effect of age group on initial status (children in the older subsample performed better initially), and significant linear as well as quadratic trends in the growth curve estimates. Neither sex nor SES contributed to initial status or individual differences in the growth curves. Overall, the quadratic trend was rather small when compared with the linear component. However, a closer look at Figure 2.2

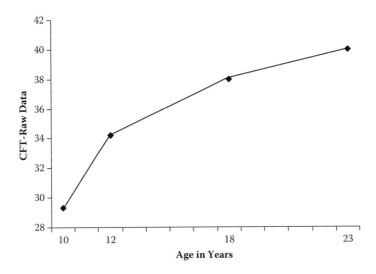

FIGURE 2.2   Changes in Culture Fair Intelligence Test (CFT) nonverbal raw scores between the ages of 10, 12, 18, and 23 years.

TABLE 2.7
Results of the Mixed Models Analysis for Nonverbal Intelligence

Fixed Effects		Model A	Model B	Model C
Initial status	Intercept	34.56 (0.35)	29.43 (0.39)	27.89 (0.51)
	Age			3.09 (0.70)
Rate of change	Time		1.14 (0.09)	1.16 (0.09)
	Time^2		–0.05 (0.01)	–0.05 (0.01)
	Time^3		0.01 (0.00)	0.00 (0.00)
	Age * Time			–0.05 (0.02)
Goodness-of-fit	Deviance	4268.36	3674.50	3654.81
		ICC: 0.63	rInt.time: –0.03	

reveals that the slope of the growth functions flattens at the later measurement points, indicating the influence of a nonlinear trend. Interestingly, there was a significant Age Group by Time interaction, showing that the difference between the two age groups diminished as a function of time, even though it was still reliable at the very end of the study.

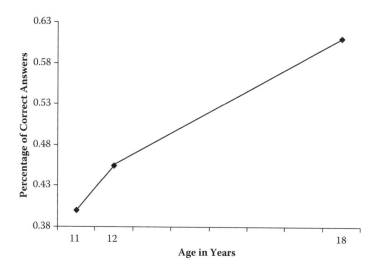

FIGURE 2.3   Changes in Arlin Test scores between the ages of 11, 12, and 18 years.

TABLE 2.8
Results of the Mixed Models Analysis for Formal Reasoning (Arlin Test)

Fixed Effects

		Model A	Model B	Model C
Initial status	Intercept	0.485 (0.010)	0.409 (0.010)	0.385 (0.020)
	Gender			−0.039 (0.020)
	Socioeconomic status			0.037 (0.019)
	Age			0.046 (0.018)
Rate of change	Time		0.012 (0.001)	0.013 (0.001)
	Gender * Time			−0.003 (0.001)
Goodness-of-fit	Deviance	−367	−635	−660
		ICC: 0.66	rInt.time: 0.21	

2.4.4.3   Development of Operational Reasoning Abilities

Raw scores on the Arlin test of formal reasoning obtained for Waves 8, 9, and 10 (ages 11, 12, and 18) were used for the multilevel change analysis. The resulting growth curve estimates are given in Figure 2.3, whereas the findings of the mixed model analysis are depicted in Table 2.8.

As can be seen from Figure 2.3, there was a linear trend in the growth curve data. Again, the fit for the unconditional means model (Model A) was worse than that for the growth curve Models B and C (see Table 2.8). The best-fitting Model C not only confirmed the linear trend in the data but also indicated that all of the three predictor variables accounted for the variance in initial status of the operational reasoning measure. There was no main effect of these variables on individual differences in the slope of the growth function. However, the Sex by Time interaction was reliable, indicating that initial differences in favor of males increased over time.

2.5 CONCLUSIONS

In this chapter, we explored interindividual differences in intraindividual changes in different components of intelligence and operational reasoning from the preschool period to early adulthood. We addressed the developmental relation between changes in psychometric intelligence performance and Piagetian-type cognitive ability measures in detail. What did we learn from our analyses? We discuss the outcomes separately for the issues of (a) changes in correlational patterns over time, (b) the relation between early and later IQ assessments, (c) the relation between psychometric intelligence and other cognitive ability measures over time, and (d) patterns of interindividual differences in intraindividual change.

2.5.1 INDIVIDUAL DIFFERENCES IN IQ AND CHANGES IN CORRELATIONAL PATTERNS OVER TIME

Our findings indicate that there were moderate relationships between verbal and nonverbal IQ components from preschool age onward, which did not change substantially after children entered school. Test–retest correlations during the preschool period for repeated assessments based on the same instruments typically were of moderate size and not significantly higher than correlations between measures of verbal and nonverbal intelligence. This pattern changed after grade 1, when test–retest correlations obtained for the verbal (HAWIK) IQ component were considerably higher than those found between verbal and nonverbal IQ scores. Although the results were not similarly clear for the nonverbal IQ component, our findings are compatible with the view that intraindividual changes in verbal and nonverbal components of intelligence follow different patterns. However, whereas stability of individual differences within each component (verbal versus nonverbal) increased as a function of time, cross-domain comparisons did not indicate any reliable increase in intercorrelations over time. Overall, these findings essentially replicate results from classic longitudinal studies on intelligence development. The only difference concerns the size of the correlations over time, which was higher in previous studies and probably attributable to aggregation procedures.

2.5.2   THE RELATION OF EARLY PERFORMANCE ON MENTAL
ABILITY TESTS AND LATER IQ ASSESSMENTS

Our findings deviate from those obtained in the classic American longitudinal studies. We found more instability in young children's performance during the preschool years, particularly for verbal IQ and Piagetian-type tasks. Although early performance on nonverbal IQ tests predicted later performance better than performance on the two other intelligence components, our preschool measures generally did not explain as much variance in IQ assessments during the school years and beyond as reported for most classic longitudinal studies. As noted above, we suspect that the test aggregation procedure used in these studies led to an overestimation of the stability of early IQ.

On the other hand, our data do agree with those from the classic studies in showing long-term stabilities in verbal and nonverbal IQ for the time period between the elementary school years and early adulthood. For instance, verbal IQ differences assessed at the age of 7 predicted IQ differences in early adulthood, explaining about 28% of the variance in adult IQ. Verbal IQ at age 9 accounted for almost 35% of the variance in the criterion variable. This finding seems impressive given that the time lag between the two measurement points was 14 years.

Overall, then, our findings are in accord with those of previous large-scale longitudinal studies, which all showed substantial individual stability in psychometric IQ measures over time. The new aspect found in the LOGIC study was that individual stability in Piagetian-type measures such as the Arlin test of formal reasoning was similarly high over time from the advanced elementary school years onward, indicating that most participants progressed to higher levels of performance at about the same pace.

2.5.3   RELATIONS BETWEEN COGNITIVE DEVELOPMENTAL AND
PSYCHOMETRIC MEASURES OF CHILDREN'S INTELLECTUAL COMPETENCIES

Assessments for the preschool and school periods led to different patterns of results. There were almost no reliable correlations between psychometric measures of intelligence and operational reasoning tasks during the preschool years. As noted by Bjorklund (1999) in his comments on our first report on the LOGIC intelligence data, this pattern suggests that different cognitive abilities underlie the "intelligences" assessed by psychometric and Piagetian-type reasoning tests during the preschool years. The literature contains inconsistent information on this issue. Our findings are not in accord with those of Kuhn (1976), who reported substantial correlations (.69) between a battery of Piagetian tasks and psychometric intelligence in a sample of 5- and 6-year-old children. Perhaps the use of a more complete battery of Piagetian-type tasks would have yielded higher coefficients in our study as well. Due to organizational constraints, however, this was simply impossible to accomplish.

When data for the school period and beyond were analyzed, a different correlational pattern was found, with cross-age correlations between psychometric and operational reasoning tasks being almost as high as the cross-age correlations for the psychometric intelligence tests. Given the high overlap in correlations, it seems unlikely that cognitive developmental measures and psychometric IQ measures used with 7- to 12-year-old children tap qualitatively different intellectual abilities. This finding is consistent with findings of other researchers such as Humphreys et al. (1985) or Keating (1975; see also Anderson, 1992; Carroll, Kohlberg, & DeVries, 1984), although not in agreement with the data reported by Kuhn (1976), who found a nonsignificant correlation of .22 between mental age derived from the WISC and a battery of formal operations obtained for a sample of schoolchildren. Given this inconsistency in findings, we still need to be cautious with our interpretations. Further research is needed that investigates this relationship more closely, ideally providing further validation for our conclusions on this issue.

2.5.4   PATTERNS OF INTERINDIVIDUAL DIFFERENCES IN INTRAINDIVIDUAL CHANGE

Our multilevel change analyses yielded several interesting results. There was a nonlinear trend in the trajectory of verbal IQ, with estimated scores increasing between the ages of 7 and 12. At the same time, there was a nonlinear decrease in raw score gains. Although only one subcomponent of verbal IQ (vocabulary) was assessed at the ages of 18 and 23, our analyses of change scores for these two measurement points did not indicate reliable increases in verbal intelligence from adolescence onward. Although we are tempted to interpret this as a first sign of the eventual leveling off at asymptote, further research including older adolescents and young adults and including a more comprehensive set of verbal intelligence components is necessary to validate this claim.

Nonlinear growth curves over time also fit the nonverbal IQ data best. Although the slope of the growth function also flattened as a function of time, the findings differ from those obtained for verbal IQ in that the increase in nonverbal IQ from age 18 to age 23 was significant. Last, when we looked at the development of operational reasoning abilities, the Arlin test data were compatible with a linear growth curve model, indicating substantial improvement between the ages of 12 and 18. Unfortunately, nothing can be said about developmental trends beyond this age because the Arlin test was not given to the 23 year olds due to time restrictions.

Overall, the multilevel change analyses revealed that the impact of individual difference variables such as sex, SES, and age group was substantial at the very beginning of the LOGIC study at age 4, but generally did not influence differences in the growth curve patterns. Although there were exceptions to this rule, such as the impact of age group on the growth of nonverbal IQ, this finding suggests that important individual differences in intellectual functioning are established before children enter preschool. Of course, given the constraints on the LOGIC data, a more comprehensive longitudinal approach focusing on early childhood (preferably starting with newborns) is necessary to support this claim.

REFERENCES

Anderson, M. (1992). *Intelligence and development: A cognitive theory.* Oxford: Blackwell.

Arlin, P. K. (1984). *Arlin Test of Formal Reasoning (ATFR): Test manual for middle school, high school, and adult levels.* New York: Slossen Publications.

Bayley, N. (1949). Consistency and variability in the growth of intelligence from birth to eighteen years. *Journal of Genetic Psychology, 75,* 165–196.

Bayley, N. (1955). On the growth of intelligence. *American Psychologist, 10,* 805–818.

Bayley, N. (1970). Development of mental abilities. In P. H. Mussen (Ed.), *Carmichael's manual of child psychology* (3rd ed., pp. 1163–1209). New York: Wiley.

Berg, C. A. (1992). Perspectives for viewing intellectual development throughout the life course. In R. J. Sternberg & C. A. Berg (Eds.), *Intellectual development* (pp. 1–15). Cambridge: Cambridge University Press.

Bidell, T. R., & Fischer, K. W. (1992). Beyond the stage debate: Action, structure, and variability in Piagetian theory and research. In R. J. Sternberg & C. A. Berg (Eds.), *Intellectual development* (pp. 37–52). Cambridge: Cambridge University Press.

Bjorklund, D. F. (1999). Comment: What individual differences can teach us about developmental function, and vice versa. In F. E. Weinert & W. Schneider (Eds.), *Individual development from 3 to 12: Findings from the Munich Longitudinal Study* (pp. 29–37). New York: Cambridge University Press.

Bjorklund, D. F. (2005). *Children's thinking: Cognitive development and individual differences* (4th ed.). Belmont, CA: Wadsworth.

Bloom, B. S. (1964). *Stability and change in human characteristics.* New York: Wiley.

Brainerd, C. J. (1978). The stage question in cognitive-developmental theory. *Behavioral and Brain Sciences, 1,* 173–182.

Burgemeister, B., Blum, L., & Lorge, J. (1972). *Columbia Mental Maturity Scale.* New York: Harcourt Brace Jovanovich.

Carroll, J. B., Kohlberg, L., & DeVries, R. (1984). Psychometric and Piagetian intelligences: Toward resolution of controversy. *Intelligence, 8,* 67–91.

Case, R. (1992). Neo-Piagetian theories of child development. In R. J. Sternberg & C. A. Berg (Eds.), *Intellectual development* (pp. 161–196). Cambridge: Cambridge University Press.

Case, R. (1998). The development of conceptual structures. In D. Kuhn & R. S. Siegler (Vol. Eds.), *Handbook of child development. Vol. 2: Cognition, perception, and language* (5th ed., pp. 745–800). New York: Wiley.

Demetriou, A. (Ed.). (1988). *The neo-Piagetian theories of cognitive development: Toward an integration.* Amsterdam: North Holland.

Demetriou, A., & Kazi, S. (2001). *Unity and modularity in the mind and the self.* London: Routledge.

Eggert, D. (1978). *Hannover-Wechsler-Intelligenztest für das Vorschulalter* [German version of the Hannover-Wechsler Intelligence Scale for Preschool Children]. Bern, Switzerland: Huber.

Fischer, K. W. (1987). Relations between brain and cognitive development. *Child Development, 57,* 623–632.

Fischer, K. W., & Bidell, T. (1998). Dynamic development of psychological structures in action and thought. In R. M. Lerner (Vol. Ed.), *Handbook of child development. Vol. 1: Theoretical models of human development* (5th ed., pp. 467–561). New York: Wiley.

Gardner, M. K., & Clark, E. (1992). The psychometric perspective on intellectual development in childhood and adolescence. In R. J. Sternberg & C. A. Berg (Eds.), *Intellectual development* (pp. 16–43). Cambridge: Cambridge University Press.

Goodenough, F. L. (1946). The measurement of mental growth in childhood. In L. Carmichael (Ed.), *Manual of child psychology* (pp. 450–475). New York: Wiley.

Hilden, A. J. (1949). A longitudinal study of intellectual development. *Journal of Psychology, 28,* 187–214.

Hindley, C. B., & Owen, C. F. (1978). The extent of individual changes in I.Q. for ages between 6 months and 17 years in a British longitudinal sample. *Journal of Child Psychology and Psychiatry, 19,* 329–350.

Honzik, M. P., MacFarlane, J. W., & Allen, L. (1948). The stability of mental test performance between two and eighteen years. *Journal of Experimental Education, 17,* 309–324.

Humphreys, L. G. (1980). Me thinks they do protest too much. *Intelligence, 4,* 179–183.

Humphreys, L. G., Rich, S. A., & Davey, T. C. (1985). A Piagetian test of general intelligence. *Developmental Psychology, 21,* 872–877.

Hunt, E. (1980). Intelligence as an information-processing concept. *British Journal of Psychology, 71,* 449–474.

Kail, R., & Pellegrino, J. W. (1985). *Human intelligence: Perspectives and prospects.* New York: Freeman.

Keating, D. P. (1975). Precocious cognitive development at the level of formal operations. *Child Development, 46,* 276–280.

Kingma, J. (1984). Traditional intelligence, Piagetian tasks, and initial arithmetic in kindergarten and primary school grade one. *Journal of Genetic Psychology, 145,* 49–60.

Kuhn, D. (1976). Relations of two Piagetian stage transitions to IQ. *Developmental Psychology, 12,* 157–162.

McCall, R. B. (1981). Nature-nurture and the two realms of development: A proposed integration with respect to mental development. *Child Development, 54,* 408–415.

McCall, R. B., Hogarty, P. S., & Hurlburt, N. (1972). Transitions in infant sensimotor development and the prediction of childhood IQ. *American Psychologist, 27,* 728–748.

Moffitt, T. E., Caspi, A., Harkness, A., & Silva, P. A. (1993). The natural history of change in intellectual performance: Who changes? How much? Is it meaningful? *Journal of Child Psychology and Psychiatry, 34,* 455–506.

Piaget, J. (1952). Autobiography. In E. G. Boring (Ed.), *A history of psychology in autobiography* (Vol. 4, pp. 237–256). Worcester, MA: Clark University Press.

Raudenbush, S., & Bryk, A. (2002). *Hierarchical linear models: Applications and data analysis methods* (2nd ed.). Newbury Park, CA: Sage.

Rogosa, D. R., Brandt, D., & Zimowski, M. (1982). A growth curve approach to the measurement of change. *Psychological Bulletin, 90,* 726–748.

Schaie, K. W. (1994). The course of adult intellectual development. *American Psychologist, 49,* 304–313.

Schneider, W. (1989). Problems of longitudinal studies with young children: Conceptual and methodological issues. In M. Brambring, F. Lösel, & H. Skowronek (Eds.), *Children at risk: Assessment and longitudinal research* (pp. 313–335). New York: de Gruyter.

Schneider, W., Perner, J., Bullock, M., Stefanek, J., & Ziegler, A. (1999). Development of intelligence and thinking. In F. E. Weinert & W. Schneider (Eds.), *Individual development from 3 to 12: Findings from the Munich Longitudinal Study* (pp. 9–28). New York: Cambridge University Press.

Schneider, W., & Stefanek, J. (2006). Entwicklung der Rechtschreibleistung vom frühen Schul-bis zum frühen Erwachsenenalter [Spelling development from elementary school age to young adulthood]. *Zeitschrift für Pädagogische Psychologie, 21,* 77–82.

Siegler, R. S. (1994). Cognitive variability: A key to understanding cognitive development. *Current Directions in Psychological Science, 3,* 1–5.

Siegler, R. S., & Richards, D. D. (1982). The development of intelligence. In R. J. Sternberg (Ed.), *Handbook of human intelligence* (pp. 897–971). Cambridge: Cambridge University Press.

Singer, J. D., & Willett, J. B. (2001, April). Improving the quality of longitudinal research. Paper presented at the annual meeting of the American Educational Research Association, Seattle, WA.

Singer, J. D., & Willett, J. B. (2003). *Applied longitudinal data analysis: Modeling change and event occurrence.* New York: Oxford University Press.

Sontag, L. W., Baker, C. T., & Nelson, V. L. (1958). Mental growth and personality development: A longitudinal study. *Monographs of the Society for Research in Child Development, 23*(Serial No. 68).

Sternberg, R. J., & Detterman, D. K. (Eds.). (1986). *What is intelligence? Contemporary viewpoints on its nature and definition.* Norwood, NJ: Ablex.

Sternberg, R. J., & Powell, J. S. (1983). The development of intelligence. In J. H. Flavell & E. M. Markman (Vol. Eds.), *Handbook of child psychology. Vol. 3: Cognitive development* (4th ed., pp. 341–419). New York: Wiley.

Tewes, U. (Ed.). (1983). *Hamburg-Wechsler-Intelligenztest für Kinder, Revision (HAWIK-R)* [German version of the revised WISC]. Bern, Switzerland: Huber.

Weiss, R. (1976). *Grundintelligenztest CFT20* [Basic intelligence test CFT20]. Braunschweig, Germany: Westermann.

Yule, W., Gold, R. D., & Busch, C. (1982). Long-term predictive validity of the WPPSI: An 11-year follow-up study. *Personality and Individual Differences, 3,* 65–71.

3 Developmental Changes and Individual Stability of Motor Abilities from the Preschool Period to Young Adulthood

Jutta Ahnert, Wolfgang Schneider, and Klaus Bös

3.1 INTRODUCTION: GENERAL PROBLEMS WITH THE PREDICTION OF MOTOR SKILL DEVELOPMENT

There is a generally held belief that children who show better motor performance in early childhood than the majority of their peers continue to be athletically adept in youth and adulthood. Evidence is scarce, however, for the existence of a broad, stable motor ability, especially over longer time frames (cf. Ahnert, 2005; Ahnert, Bös, & Schneider, 2003; Malina, 2001; Matton et al., 2006; Schott, Bös, & Mechling, 1997).

Questions about the stability of motor abilities are important across a number of areas, including the fields of talent selection and development, the early identification of clumsy and motor-impaired children, and the application of properly timed preventive measures for teens. Related questions concerning the lability of motor abilities underlie issues such as the age at which developmental impairments and motor deficits can still be compensated for and the age beyond which improvement is doubtful. These questions have become especially salient with an increased prevalence of children and teens with motor deficits and health problems as a result of physical inactivity and obesity (Armstrong & van Mechelen, 2000; Bös, 2003; Raczek, 2002; Tomkinson, Olds, & Gulbin, 2003; Tomkinson, Olds, Kang, & Kim, 2007; Wang & Lobstein, 2006; Wedderkopp, Froberg, Hansen, & Andersen, 2004).

The relation between age and motor ability level can be affected by several factors, including the rate of motor development and specific learning experiences (Malina, 1996, 2001). A variety of internal and environmentally contingent factors (moderators) can lead to varying degrees of inter- and intraindividual instability in individual development speed and level. Internal factors include physical factors, such as body physique, and cognitive, motivational, and emotional factors, including intelligence, motivation to achieve, and anxiety (see overviews by Ahnert, 2005; Haywood & Getchell, 2005; Kohl & Hobbs, 1998; Trost, Saunders, & Ward, 2002; Wu, Pender, & Noureddine, 2003). External conditions, such as socialization through physical activity in the family or in school, through peer groups, and in athletic clubs, can also affect motor development (Baur, 1989; Haywood & Getchell, 2005; Kohl & Hobbs, 1998). The complexity of the developmental processes involved makes long-term prognoses of general motor abilities a difficult undertaking.

3.2   SUMMARY OF RESEARCH FINDINGS CONCERNING MOTOR DEVELOPMENT FROM CHILDHOOD TO ADULTHOOD

Tracing the course of motor development requires longitudinal analyses. Of the several longitudinal studies of motor development, only a few are of sufficient length (i.e., covering a time span of over 10 years) to capture the transition from childhood to adulthood (for an overview of relevant longitudinal studies, see Ahnert, 2005). Among these, the Wisconsin Growth Study (Rarick & Smoll, 1967), the Leuven Growth Study (Beunen et al., 1974, 1988; Ostyn, Simons, Beunen, Renson, & Van Gerven, 1980), the Amsterdam Growth Study (Kemper, 1985, 1995, 2004), and the Longitudinal Study on the Predictability of Motor Competencies (Mechling, Schott, & Bös, 1998; Multerer, 1991; Schott, 2000) proved to be particularly informative, including a wide range of motor abilities such as sprinting, aerobic endurance, and gross and coordination skills. From these studies, a number of basic conclusions can be drawn.

3.2.1   TYPICAL DEVELOPMENTAL PATTERNS

The majority of motor abilities investigated in longitudinal studies showed a typical overall developmental pattern. They developed very quickly from early childhood until adolescence, reached their maximum in the late teens or early adulthood, maintained a short period of stability, and then began to decline, generally in an individual's thirties or forties. There were, however, many variations in the rate of increase or decline, as well as the timing and span of optimal performance during the life span in specific motor tasks (Bös, 1994). For example, maximum performance peaked during the teen years for activities such as sprinting, obstacle course and agility tests (Crasselt, Forchel, & Stemmler, 1985), aerobic endurance (Cooper tests; Kemper & van Mechelen, 1995), and flexibility (e.g., "Sit-and-Reach"; van Mechelen & Kemper, 1995). In contrast, peak performance was generally attained in early adulthood for the majority of strength measures (e.g., "Jump and Reach"; see Crasselt et al., 1985; van Mechelen & Kemper, 1995) and balance exercises (e.g., "Standing on One Leg"; see Schott, 2000).

Accelerated development in motor skills from age 11 to 18 years seems primarily due to biological changes in physical maturity (e.g., height, weight, and muscle mass) that begin during this time (Bös, 1994). Sex differences in developmental patterns in those tasks that generally favor males begin in early adolescence (12–13 years), especially in endurance and functional strength tasks. Whereas males show strong improvement in endurance and especially functional strength tasks until their late teens (18–19 years), females have already reached their optimal functioning in their midteens (14–15 years) (see Crasselt et al., 1985; van Mechelen & Kemper, 1995; Schott, 2000).

3.2. STABILITY OVER TIME

The available longitudinal studies suggest that different motor abilities and skills (e.g., gross or fine motor abilities, strength, speed, endurance, coordination, and flexibility) differ in their stability over time (Beunen et al., 1981, 1988; Kemper, 1985, 1995, 2004; Malina, 2001; Rarick & Smoll, 1967; Schott et al., 1997). Thus, any comparison across studies must include *type of motor test* as a variable in addition to age, achievement level, and measurement time interval to adequately asses stability. Overall, motor abilities throughout childhood, youth, and early adulthood exhibit moderate stability in the range of .30–.70 (see overview by Ahnert, 2005). More specifically, strength and flexibility levels are more stable, with relatively high coefficients in the range of .50–.70 (Beunen et al., 1997; Kemper, 1995, 2004; Lefevre et al., 2000; Maia et al., 1998, 2001; Rarick & Smoll, 1967; Schott et al., 1997) over longer time frames. Similarly, speed shows moderate stability through childhood and youth (.38 to .55; see Beunen et al., 1981, 1988; van Mechelen & Kemper, 1995; Schott et al.). Cardiorespiratory endurance shows a lower range of stability (.20–.44; see Beunen et al., 1997; Lefevre et al.; Maia et al., 1998, 2001; Schott et al., 1997), which can be explained by the malleability of endurance by training, as well the effects of large interindividual differences in physical activity. Overall, there are little data on the stability of motor coordination. Schott et al. reported that stability varied across task type (speed versus accuracy trade-off) and the task demands of gross and fine motor skills. In general, stability coefficients increase after puberty.

These general conclusions must be qualified by noting that there is inconsistency in stability coefficients across studies due to the design, variable selection, and assessment strategies used in different studies. A number of specific problems can be summarized as follows:

- The majority of longitudinal studies began when children were in elementary school and did not extend beyond middle school.
- In many of the early longitudinal studies, overall motor abilities were assessed with tasks that tapped only a limited range of motor abilities, or with tasks for which no psychometric properties were presented.
- Sample sizes in early longitudinal studies were often too small for researchers to be able to make generalizable statements.

- Many studies on competitive sports and talent selection did not seem suited to offer clear conclusions about developmental stages in average people. Variables predicting competitive sports performance in elite athletes may differ from those predicting sports performance in average populations. In addition, there is likely to be smaller variance within predictors for elite athletes, which would decrease the likelihood of detecting predictive relationships from correlational data (Wendland, 1986).
- Only a few studies incorporated environmental or behavioral variables from other domains (e.g., differences in upbringing or athletic involvement) in their interpretation of motor development processes.

3.3 GOALS OF MOTOR SKILL ASSESSMENT IN THE LOGIC STUDY

In the Munich Longitudinal Study on the Ontogenesis of Individual Competencies (the LOGIC study), an attempt was made to overcome some of the specific problems listed above. We started the assessment of motor skill development when children were about 4 years of age, and continued the measurement of motor skills on a regular basis until the children were about 12 years old. A comprehensive follow-up assessment was provided at the last measurement point at the age of 23 years. Thus, data on motor development were collected at the ages of 4, 5, 6, 8, 10, 12, and 23 years, providing a time frame of almost 20 years. Although the focus was on fine motor skill development, we added a few measures that tapped gross motor skills (see below). The sample size was 205 at the beginning of the LOGIC study, dropped to 184 when the children were 12 years old, and was 152 at the last assessment at age 23. Given that the LOGIC study focused on various aspects of cognitive and social development as well as personality development, it was also possible to link motor development to other relevant behavioral domains such as intelligence and (athletic) self-concept.

3.3.1 MAJOR MOTOR DEVELOPMENT ISSUES ANALYZED IN THE LOGIC STUDY

We used the LOGIC data to extend our understanding of motor development (see Ahnert et al., 2003). We explored a number of expectations and hypotheses concerning motor skill development in more detail.

3.3.1.1 Relationship Between Intellectual and Motor Development

From the very beginning, we were interested in the time course of the relationship between early intellectual and early motor development. Although our theoretical knowledge concerning this relationship and its course over the preschool and kindergarten periods as well as the elementary school years was rather scarce, there was reason to assume that young children's coordination skills and intellectual abilities may be related. For instance, according to Ackerman's (1988) model of motor learning, there should be a reliable positive relationship between (fine) motor skills and intellectual abilities in the preschool period, which should decrease over time as soon as the motor skill level increases. Whereas a rapid decrease in the relationship was assumed for rather easy (consistent) motor tasks that should be perfectly mastered within short periods of time, a much slower decrease in the relationship was expected for complex motor tasks where the transition from conscious, effortful action to automatized action takes considerably more time. Overall, we expected substantial correlations between performance on motor tasks and on intelligence tests at the beginning of the LOGIC study, which should decrease over time and disappear during the course of the elementary school years.

3.3.1.2 Rate of Development and Sex Differences

Based on the available literature, we expected to find rapid progress of motor performance from the preschool period until the end of elementary school, with speed of development varying as a function of the amount of practice devoted to specific motor abilities and their complexity. We also anticipated that changes in motor skills would occur from early adolescence to early adulthood, but that they would be different for the two sexes. Because girls generally reach their performance maximum at 14 or 15 years of age (Bös, 1994) and athletic activity declines sooner for women during their teens and young adulthood, we expected that female motor performance from puberty until the age of 23 would hardly grow. In the case of male participants, on the other hand, we anticipated a performance increase in endurance exercises and motor tasks requiring physical strength, due to higher androgen secretion levels and the accompanying growth spurt (i.e., the growth of muscle mass) during puberty (Bös, 1994; Crasselt et al., 1985; Kemper, 1995). This difference in motor skill changes over time should also be reflected in sex-specific changes concerning the athletic self-concept and their relations to motor performance.

3.3.1.3 Stability Over Time

We also expected that test–retest stability coefficients would vary as a function of the time of assessment and the type of motor skill under study. During the preschool and kindergarten years, the development of children's motor abilities should be very dynamic due to the varying speed of physical maturation, yielding only low to moderate individual stability coefficients. Based on longitudinal findings for the elementary school period (see Bös, 1994), we anticipated that stability over time would increase during the elementary school years. However, in late childhood and during adolescence, considerable body changes (height, weight, muscle mass, and proportions) and a modified physical activity level may exert a significant influence on motor and also coordination abilities, causing temporary instability in the data. Overall, however, we expected to find relatively stable test–retest correlations among the various motor tasks from the early school years onward.

3.3.2 PROBLEMS RELATED TO THE ASSESSMENT OF MOTOR ABILITY IN THE LOGIC STUDY

Longitudinal studies that observe developmental progress over a long time period pose test sampling issues because making assessments age appropriate means that different tests may be applied at different ages. In addition, the standard profile of any test must be adjusted to the performance norm for each age group. In the area of motor skill development, there are no standardized test procedures that can be applied from preschool through early adulthood.

Thus, different test instruments were used for preschool children (ages 4 to 6 years) and for elementary school children (ages 6 to 12 years) and young adults. Using different instruments represents a challenge to the attempt to compare results, especially when the instruments claim to test the same motor or psychological constructs (see Schneider, 1989, 1993).

Table 3.1 gives an overview of the motor tests and measurement time points in the LOGIC study. The Motor Test for 4–6 Year Olds (MOT 4–6; Zimmer & Volkamer, 1984) was used to assess motor skill development during the preschool and kindergarten period. For elementary school children, adolescents, and young adults (assessments at 8, 10, 12, and 23 years), the Körperkoordinationstest für Kinder (KTK, or Body Coordination Test for Children; Kiphard & Schilling, 2000) and related measures such as a Balance task, a Reaction Time test, and a Standing Long Jump measure were used. Because of organizational constraints, motor skills were not assessed at the measurement point between ages 12 and 23 (Wave 10, when participants were about 18 years of age). Given the lack of a measurement point between 12 and 23 years, the specific type of growth curve reflecting changes in motor skills during this time period (i.e., linear versus nonlinear) could not be assessed.

3.3.3 TEST INSTRUMENTS USED DURING THE PRESCHOOL AND KINDERGARTEN PERIOD (AGES 4, 5, AND 6)

During the first three waves of the LOGIC study, the psychometric test of motor abilities (MOT 4–6; Zimmer & Volkamer, 1984) was used to assess such motor skills as sense of balance, agility, movement accuracy, and coordination. The MOT 4–6 is designed to assess typical movement requirements of preschool children and to capture as many of the different aspects of children's motor activity as possible. It measures basic motor skills and provides a test–retest reliability over 4 weeks of $r = .85$ (Bös, 2001).

The MOT consists of 18 items that can be organized into the following abilities profile:

- Strength and speed (two exercises, e.g., skipping rope)
- Speed of movement (two exercises, e.g., tapping)
- Reaction time (one exercise, e.g., grasping a stick)

TABLE 3.1
Overview of Measurement Time Points

Wave and Age	1, 4 Years	2, 5 Years	3, 6 Years	5, 8 Years	6, 9 Years	7, 10 Years	8, 11 Years	9, 12 Years	10, 18 Years	11, 23 Years
Motor Test	MOT[a]	MOT[a]	MOT[a]	KTK[b]		KTK[b]		KTK[b]		KTK[b]
Standing Long Jump	X	X	X	X		X		X		X

[a] MOT: Motor Test for 4- to 6-year-old children (MOT 4–6).
Source: Zimmer and Volkamer (1984).
[b] *KTK:* Körperkoordinationstest für Kinder.
Source: Kiphard and Schilling (2000).

- Coordination in timed task (one exercise, e.g., a shuttle run while storing balls)
- Coordination in precision tasks (12 exercises, e.g., throwing a ball at a target, and balancing)

Because no meaningful multifactorial structure has been found for this test in multivariate analyses (cf. Bös, 2001), we used a sum score representing children's *general coordination skill* and derived a standardized *motor quotient* (MQ) similarly constructed as IQ scores and standardized *T* values in our analyses. An analysis of internal consistency revealed that reliability scores found for the LOGIC sample (Cronbach's alpha = .70) were sufficient and roughly comparable to those found for Zimmer and Volkamer's (1984) standardization sample (alpha = .74).

3.3.4   Test Instruments Used During Childhood, Adolescence, and Young Adulthood (Ages 8, 10, 12, and 23)

Because the MOT is normed only until age 6, other tests of motor ability were used for the elementary school period and beyond. These were the Körperkoordinationstest für Kinder and the Standing Long Jump given at ages 8, 10, 12, and 23, and a Bicycle Ergometry test at the last measurement point at age 23 to assess aerobic fitness.

3.3.4.1   Körperkoordinationstest für Kinder (KTK)

The standardized KTK (or, as mentioned above, Body Coordination Test for Children; see Kiphard & Schilling, 2000) includes important features of body coordination skills and whole-body control and also assesses endurance, strength, and speed (see Bös, 2001; Kiphard, 1972). According to its authors, this test instrument is recommended for children between the ages of 5 and 14. The KTK consists of four subtests tapping various body coordination skills.

The first subtest, *walking backward on a balance beam*, consists of walking backward on each of three balance beams that are 6 cm, 4.5 cm, and 3 cm wide. After a practice trial, participants are instructed to walk slowly backward on the 6 cm balance beam, trying to avoid touching the ground. There are nine trials, three for each balance beam. The dependent measure is the number of error-free steps backward, summed across trials. The maximum number of points for each trial was 8, yielding a maximum score of 72.

The second subtest, the *monopedal high jump*, requires participants to jump over rubber cushions on one foot. The experimenter instructs participants to start jumping forward on one foot about 1.50 m away from a cushion barrier, then jump over the cushion and continue jumping for two more steps, always using the same foot. Participants are told that changing to the other foot during the exercise would count as an error. The initial height of the barrier is 15 cm (three cushions). After each successful trial, one cushion (= 5 cm) is added until a maximum height of 60 cm is reached. Three trials are possible for a given height. Three, two, or one points are given for successful performance on the first, second, or third trial, respectively. If the height is not mastered after the third trial, the test is continued only when participants have received at least five points for the last two preceding successful trials. Participants always begin jumping with the right foot; then the test is repeated with the left foot. A maximum of 39 points could be scored per foot, yielding a maximum score of 78. For the young adults the maximal height of the barrier was increased to 120cm.

The third subtest, *number of jumps to the left and right*, consists of jumping to the left and right over a dividing line as quickly as possible during a total time of 15 seconds, taking off from and landing on both feet simultaneously. There are two trials. The total number of jumps is the dependent variable.

The fourth test is *lateral movement*. This task requires participants to move small wooden blocks in a sequence from left to right, continually placing both feet on the block just moved to the right, like stepping stones. Participants are told that the most important variable is performance speed, and that the task is to move the block as fast as possible for a period of 20 seconds. There are two trials. The dependent variable is the number of moves summed across the two trials.

Whereas the first two subtests (walking backward and monopedal high jump) require coordination only, both coordination and timing are important for the last two tasks (i.e., number of jumps to the left and right and lateral movement). Test norms are available until the age of 15.

3.3.4.2 Standing Long Jump Test

The *standing long jump* measured leg strength and speed. In this task, participants were required to jump as far as possible from a starting line marked on the floor. Participants stood with their toes on the line, feet comfortably apart, and then had to bend their knees and take their arms backward. In jumping, participants simultaneously extended their knees and swung their arms forward. No restrictions were placed on arm or leg movements. Three trials were given. The distance in centimeters obtained for the best trial was used as the dependent variable.

3.3.4.3 Bicycle Ergometry Test

The Bicycle Ergometry test was presented in the last wave, when participants were age 23, to measure bodily performance abilities, particularly aerobic fitness (cf. Mellerowicz, 1975; Stemper, Dammer, & Noll, 1999). The ergometer used was a freely programmable bicycle ergometer that works independently of speed and revolutions per minute. Testing was conducted according to the recommendations given by Stemper et al. The workload (physical burden or strain required to pedal) was increased incrementally in 2-minute time periods. The level of the imposed physical strain (number of watts) was based on a participant's body weight. Each starting load corresponded to the participant's weight, and increases in the wattage were made to be half the participant's weight per time interval. The test was discontinued when the heart rate reached 180 beats per minute (bpm), or when other criteria mandated stopping the test earlier. These other criteria were a failure to reach the recommended revolutions per minute (rpm) level (indicating muscular exhaustion), or a manifestation of health problems (such as cardiovascular problems or dizziness). Each participant's pulse was recorded during the periods of physical strain. Heart rate (bpm) was measured before the beginning of the test, during the last 10 seconds of each 2-minute interval of physical strain, and 1 minute after the end of the task. Additionally, to determine a common measure of physical working capacity, performance in watts for the set heart rate of 170 bpm was recorded (the variable was called *PWC 170*). Because almost 40% of the women and 30% of the men ended the test before reaching 170 bpm due to physical exhaustion (*too hard to pedal*), the amount of physical strain (in watts) at a pulse of 170 (variable *PWC 170*) was extrapolated from the existing record of test values (pulse and watt recordings up to that point), through the use of regression equations.

Standardized comparisons were computed on the basis of relative performance capacity as determined by *PWC 170* and the individual's body weight (watts/kg) to produce a measure of watts/kg. This measure can be compared with corresponding norms and values according to sex and age.

3.3.5 Additional Measures Considered for Subsequent Analysis

Given that the interrelationship between motor development and IQ was of special interest, measures of verbal and nonverbal intelligence already described elsewhere (see chapter 2, this volume, by Schneider, Stefanek, & Niklas) were included in the statistical analysis. Furthermore, the subtest Sports Competence included in the Pictorial Scale of Perceived Competence (Harter & Pike, 1981) and in the Self-Perception Profile (Harter, 1985) was used to analyze the relationship between participants' athletic self-concept and their motor performance.

3.4 MAJOR RESULTS

In the following, we first summarize findings obtained for the early preschool and kindergarten assessment period, focusing on the relationship between motor and intellectual ability over time. Next, the development of motor skills over time will be described in more detail. A final section addresses individual stability of motor skills over time.

3.4.1 Relationships Between Motor Skill and Intellectual Abilities

Overall, the inspection of diachronous correlations between the MOT 4–6 sum scores and verbal and nonverbal intelligence measures revealed that our expectations concerning the change in relationships over the preschool period were only partially confirmed. That is, although the intercorrelations between the MOT 4–6 sum scores and measures of verbal intelligence (the Hannover-Wechsler Intelligence Scale for Preschool Children, or HAWIVA) decreased over time (from $r = .29$ at age 4 to $r = .17$ at age 6), the relationship between the MOT 4–6 sum scores and nonverbal IQ (assessed via the Columbia Mental Maturity Scale, or CMMS) was rather low and stable over the preschool and kindergarten period ($r = .19$ and .16 at ages 4 and 6, respectively). Contrary to expectations, the relationship between motor skill (represented by the KTK sum score) and the CMMS assessed at age 8 was considerably higher ($r = .34$), whereas the relationship between the KTK sum score and verbal IQ (the Wechsler Intelligence Scale for Children, or WISC) was generally low during the elementary school years, yielding correlation coefficients of .19, .17, and .17 for the ages of 8, 10, and 12, respectively.

In a more sophisticated analysis of this interrelationship, Schneider (1993) specified a latent variable structural equation model that combined indicators of verbal and nonverbal intelligence into an intelligence construct and two subscales of the MOT 4–6 representing pure motor coordination skills as well as coordination skills, including an endurance component to build up a motor skill construct. The resulting causal model based on EQS (Bentler, 1985) is shown in Figure 3.1. For the sake of clarity, only the interrelations among latent variables are included in the path diagram. As can be seen from Figure 3.1, the effects of intelligence at Wave 1 (age 4) on subsequent motor skills assessed at Wave 2 (age 5) almost doubled the corresponding effect of earlier motor skills on subsequent intelligence. This finding indicates a predominance of intelligence over motor skills for the preschool years. No reliable reciprocal causal effects were found for the later phase of data collection (i.e., the time interval between Waves 2 and 3), indicating rather independent development of intellectual and motor abilities. The model estimates seem compatible with our developmental trend hypothesis in that the correlations between the IQ and motor skill constructs dropped significantly over time (from .64 at Wave 1 to .25 at Wave 3). Please note that the correlations calculated for the latent constructs were considerably higher than those obtained

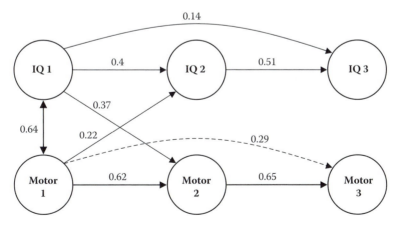

FIGURE 3.1 EQS structural equation model based on a distribution-free estimation procedure that fits the data well.

for the manifest variables. An inspection of test–retest correlations reveals that stabilities over time obtained for the two constructs were moderately high, with those obtained for the motor skill construct tending to be even higher than those found for the IQ construct.

3.4.2 Development of Motor Abilities

3.4.2.1 Preschool and Kindergarten Period (ages 4–6)

In accord with our expectations, motor performance overall increased between 4 and 6 years of age (see Figure 3.2). There was a main effect of Time, ($F(2, 238) = 200.25$, $p < .001$), indicating a rather fast progression of motor coordination skills within a time period of about 3 years. Moreover, we found a main effect of Sex, $F(1, 119) = 4.10$, $p < .05$. Girls outperformed boys on the MOT 4–6 sum score at all measurement points. A closer look at the individual subtest scores revealed that the sex difference found for the MOT 4–6 sum scores was primarily due to girls' superior performance in those exercises requiring coordination under time pressure (i.e., balancing) and in fine motor tasks like collecting matches. In comparison, boys showed superior performance at all time points in the exercise involving throwing a ball at a target.

3.4.2.2 School Period and Beyond (ages 8–12 and 23)

Developmental progress in the KTK is shown in Figure 3.3, separately for male and female participants. There was a significant main effect of Age, $F(3, 354) = 432.27$, $p < .001$, which was qualified by a reliable Age by Sex interaction, $F(2, 254) = 25.66$, $p < .001$. As can be seen from Figure 3.3, motor skills generally

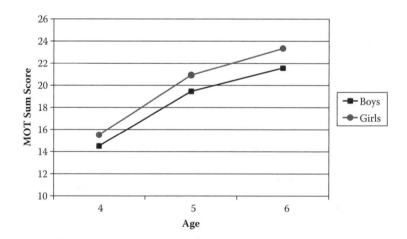

FIGURE 3.2 Performance development in the motor test for 4–6 year olds (MOT 4–6) in preschool-aged girls and boys.

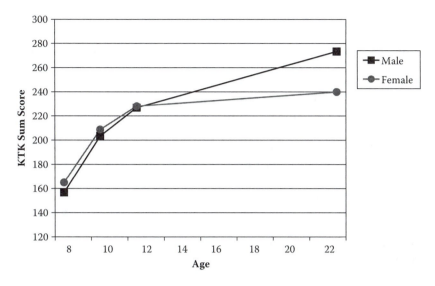

FIGURE 3.3   Performance development in the Körperkoordinationstest für Kinder (KTK) in males and females aged 8 to 23 years.

increased from ages 8 to 12, with no reliable sex differences. The interaction effect found in our data was mainly due to sex differences observed between Waves 9 and 11, that is, from age 12 to age 23. Males improved their motor performance by 48 points in the KTK sum score during this time interval, thus showing significantly better motor skills at 23 years than at 12 years ($t(67) = 10.7, p < .001$). Although females' improvement over the same time interval was also significant, $t(61) = 2.6, p < 01$, they only gained nine points in the KTK sum score from elementary school until young adulthood. Whereas hardly any performance differences were found between males and females in elementary school, there was a clear advantage in favor of males at age 23, $t(136) = 4.7, p < .001$.

3.4.2.3   Developmental Progress Identified in the Subtests of the KTK and the Standing Long Jump Measure

A closer look at performance changes in the various KTK subtests showed that during the course of elementary school, motor skills increased in both boys and girls, regardless of the subtest under study. From age 12 to 23, males increased their performance in those tasks requiring endurance and strength, such as Jumping Back and Forth, ($t(74) = 10.3, p < .001$); One-Footed Jumping, ($t(73) = 26.3, p < .001$); and Standing Long Jump, ($t(73) = 23.6, p < .001$). In comparison, females showed performance improvements in only some of the subtests requiring endurance and strength, for instance, in Jumping Back and Forth ($t(61) = 10.3, p < .001$) and the Standing Long Jump ($t(63) = 5.05$,

$p < .001$). However, they showed a performance decline in One-Footed Jumping ($t(62) = -2.5, p < .015$).

In less strength-oriented subtests such as Backward Balancing and Lateral Movement, males and females did not improve their performance over time, showing equal or in some cases even worse performance at age 23 than at the age of 12 years. In particular, general performance decreases resulted for Backward Balancing, $t(140) = -4.7, p < .001$. Figures 3.4, 3.5, 3.6, and 3.7 depict motor skill performance development in the three subtests of the KTK (Backward Balancing, One-Footed Jumping, and Jumping Back and Forth) and in the task Standing Long Jump, separately for each age. A closer inspection of the individual performance characteristics in the subtests of the KTK (see Figures 3.4, 3.5, 3.6, and 3.7) shows that the overall differences in favor of males at 23 years of age are mainly due to the males' clear advantage in the One-Footed Jumping exercise. In the remaining KTK subtests, only small sex differences were found.

Findings for the Standing Long Jump measure were roughly comparable to those of the One-Footed Jumping task. There were main effects of time and sex, and also a significant Sex by Time interaction, $F(3, 125) = 123.85, p < .01$. Whereas males and females significantly improved performance during the elementary school years, only males gained substantially from age 12 to age 23 (for details, see Ahnert, 2005).

3.4.2.4   The Impact of Athletic Self-Concept, Sports Activity, and Weight on Motor Skill Development

Interestingly, improvements in motor skills over the elementary school years were not accompanied by similar increases in athletic self-concept (cf. Ahnert & Schneider, 2006). On the contrary, self-perceptions of athletic competencies

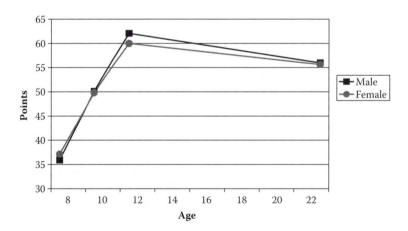

FIGURE 3.4   Performance development in backward balancing in males and females aged 8 to 23 years.

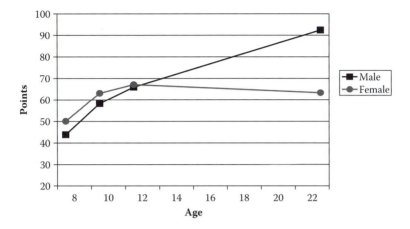

FIGURE 3.5 Performance development in one-footed jumping in males and females aged 8 to 23 years.

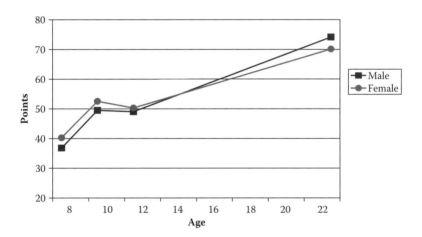

FIGURE 3.6 Performance development in jumping back and forth in males and females aged 8 to 23 years.

significantly decreased over time. Whereas girls reported more competence than boys at age 8, the picture reversed from age 9 onward. These findings parallel those reported for other self-concept components in the literature (cf. Schrader & Helmke, chap. 7, this volume). At the beginning of school, boys and girls tend to overestimate their athletic potential. The decreases found over the following years seem to indicate that self-concepts of athletic competence become increasingly realistic.

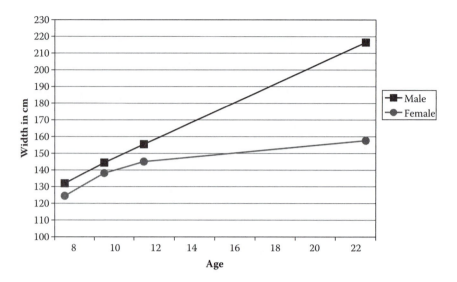

FIGURE 3.7 Performance development in standing long jump in males and females aged 8 to 23 years.

Additional analyses focused on the impact of (retrospective) sports activity reports on motor skills and fitness shown at the age of 23. Participants were classified as *very active* (5 or more hours of sports activities per week), *moderately active* (2–5 hours), and *not active* (less than 2 hours) based on their self-reports. Although self-reported activity was positively related to overall KTK performance at the age of 23, findings differed as a function of sex (see Figure 3.8, upper half). There were reliable main effects of sex and activity group, qualified by a significant Sex by Activity Group interaction. As can be seen from Figure 3.8, there were clear KTK performance differences between very active, moderately active, and inactive males. However, although very active females performed as well as very active males and clearly outperformed the two remaining female groups, the latter did not differ from each other. Whereas in males the self-report measure was related to performance differences in all three activity groups, only the very active females performed clearly better than moderately active and inactive females, with the two latter subgroups not differing from each other.

Interestingly, a similar pattern was found for the Bicycle Ergometry test (see Figure 3.8). As described above, we used the physical working capacity for a set heart rate of 170 beats per minute (*PWC 170*) as the criterion measure. Overall, the *PWC 170* means for males and females (3.14 and 2.65, respectively) corresponded well with values reported for young adults in representative samples (3.0 and 2.5 for males and females, respectively; see Ahnert, 2005). As can be seen from Figure 3.8, very active males performed better than their moderately active counterparts, who in turn outperformed inactive males. This pattern was not replicated for females. Here, the very active participants showed very good fitness

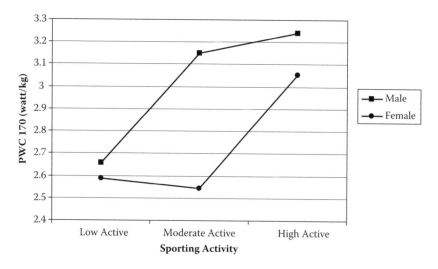

FIGURE 3.8   Performance on the Bicycle Ergonametry Test (BET) by 23-year-old partici-pants, as a function of sporting activity.

(almost comparable to that of very active males) and clearly outperformed the two remaining activity groups, who did not differ from each other.

Performance was compared across three weight groups, based on the Body Mass Index (BMI). Participants with a BMI of 25 or more were considered to be overweight, those with a BMI of 18.5 or less were classified as underweight, and participants with a BMI between 18.5 and 25 were considered to be in the normal weight range.

Comparisons of performance on the KTK for the three BMI groups at the ages of 10 and 23 as a function of sex showed that overweight participants performed worst, regardless of sex and time of assessment (see Figure 3.9). The pattern of body weight findings differed for males and females in that underweight females tended to perform better than those of normal weight, whereas the opposite was true for males, regardless of measurement point.

Similar results were found for the ergometric fitness test given at the age of 23. Again, there were significant effects of sex and BMI group, indicating that males outperformed females and that overweight participants performed worse than the two other BMI groups. Whereas underweight females tended to per-form best, males with normal weight showed superior *PWC 170* scores. However, posthoc analyses indicated that the differences between underweight and normal groups shown in Figure 3.9 were not reliable, regardless of sex.

3.4.3   STABILITY OF MOTOR ABILITIES

Table 3.2 gives an overview of the correlations among participants' performances on the MOT 4–6 at preschool age and their performance on the KTK at elemen-tary school age (8–12 years) and in young adulthood (23 years), separately for

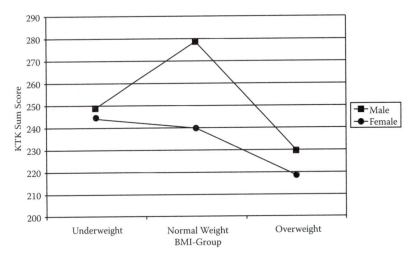

FIGURE 3.9   Performance on the Körperkoordinationstest für Kinder (KTK) by 23-year-old participants as a function of Body Mass Index.

males and females. Because an age difference of a few months turned out to affect motor abilities in preschool-aged children, it is possible that the correlation between two or more motor abilities assessed at the preschool and kindergarten age is due to this third variable, given that these variables are all correlated with *age in months*. A few months' age difference has, on the other hand, no influence on the performance level of children in elementary school. Therefore, correlations among preschool motor skill measures were calculated after partialing out the influence of the variable *age in months* (see Table 3.2).

Assessing stability over time was straightforward for the ages 8 to 23 because the same KTK and Long Jump tasks were used at these ages. Predicting performance from preschool performance tasks required comparisons across different tasks. However, we believe that this approach could be justified because the MOT 4–6 includes a large number of motor tasks (14 to 18 in total) that primarily enlist a child's coordination abilities (see Bös, 2001) and correlates moderately high to high with the KTK sum score at the ages of 5 to 6 years (mean validity coefficient $r = .68$; see Bös, 2001).

3.4.3.1   Short-Term Stability

As can be seen from Table 3.2, 2 year stability coefficients were significant from preschool age onward, ranging between .31 and .84. Stabilities were lower in preschool than in elementary school, and were higher for boys than girls throughout the preschool and kindergarten period. For boys, preschool correlations averaged .62, whereas the corresponding average correlation obtained for girls was about .42. Later on, substantially higher short-term stabilities were observed for the KTK, averaging .80 and .75 for males and females, respectively. With the excep-

TABLE 3.2

Correlation Coefficients and Stability Coefficients *r* Between the MOT 4–6 and the KTK in Range of Age from 4 to 23 Years[a]

Motor Test and Age	MOT, 4 Years	MOT, 5 Years	MOT, 6 Years	KTK, 8 Years	KTK, 10 Years	KTK, 12 Years	KTK, 23 Years
MOT, 4 years		.31**	.47**	.51**	.331*	.40**	.30*
MOT, 5 years	.58**		.44***	.49**	.37**	.44**	.54**
MOT, 6 years	.69**	.58**		.65**	.34**	.54**	.46**
KTK, 8 years	.54**	.62**	.67**		.745**	.72**	.52**
KTK, 10 years	.52**	.53**	.58**	.80**		.80**	.61**
KTK, 12 years	.51**	.48**	.50**	.76**	.84**		.57**
KTK, 23 years	.37**	.34**	.42**	.59**	.63*	.60**	

Note: In preschoolers, the stability of the MOT 4–6 was adjusted for age in months.

[a] Values for male participants are subdiagonal; values for female participants are above the diagonal.

* $p < 0.05$. ** $p < 0.01$.

tion of the early test–retest stabilities found for girls, these findings generally indicate moderately high to high stability in motor skills over time.

3.4.3.2   Long-Term Stability

Long-term stability (as indicated by correlations of MOT and KTK measures assessed during the preschool and school years with KTK performance at the age of 23) was likewise highly significant for all age ranges (see Table 3.2). Motor skills assessed as early as during the preschool period showed moderate to moderately high correlations ranging between .30 and .54 with KTK performance up to 20 years later. From elementary school onward, stability coefficients relating KTK performance in elementary school with that observed at the age of 23 ranged from .52 to .63 for both males and females, thus indicating moderately high to high long-term stability.

For the Standing Long Jump, an average stability coefficient in the range from .46 to .61 was observed (see Table 3.3) in both males and females from elementary school until early adulthood, that is, for a time period up to 15 years.

3.4.4   RELATIONS BETWEEN ATHLETIC SELF-CONCEPT AND MOTOR SKILL DEVELOPMENT DURING THE SCHOOL YEARS

We used structural equation modeling to explore the relationship between athletic self-concept and motor skill development over time (for details, see Ahnert & Schneider, 2006). Given that previous causal models exploring the relationship between academic self-concept and academic performance had favored a skill development model assuming that skills influence self-concept and not vice versa (e.g., Helmke & van Aken, 1995), a skill development model was also assumed to hold in the case of motor performance data. Findings from a LISREL model specified for motor skill and athletic self-concept data assessed at ages 8, 10, and 12 basically confirmed our prediction (see Figure 3.10). As can be seen from the causal model (which fit the data reasonably well), motor skills and athletic self-concept were moderately intercorrelated at age 8 ($r = .49$). There was a clear causal predominance of skill over self-concept, particularly at the early stages of elementary school. That is, whereas motor skill at age 8 significantly influenced athletic self-concept at age 10, the reverse was not true. Although athletic self-concept at age 10 predicted motor skills assessed at age 12, the impact of motor skills at age 10 on athletic self-concept assessed 2 years later was considerably stronger. Overall, these findings seem to confirm the skill development model, even though evidence for reciprocal causal relations was found between ages 10 and 12.

3.5   DISCUSSION

One of the main issues we tackled in the LOGIC study concerned the interrelationships between motor skill development and intellectual development over the

TABLE 3.3
Stability Coefficients of the Standing Long Jump from Elementary School Until Young Adulthood[a]

Motor Test and Age	Standing Long Jump, 8 Years	Standing Long Jump, 10 Years	Standing Long Jump, 12 Years	Standing Long Jump, 23 Years
Standing Long Jump, 8 Years		.671**	.57**	.464**
Standing Long Jump, 10 Years	.62**		.77**	.61**
Standing Long Jump, 12 Years	.735**	.678**		.490**
Standing Long Jump, 23 Years	.60**	.52**	.58**	

[a] Values for male participants are subdiagonal; values for female participants are above the diagonal.
p < 0.05. ** p < 0.01.

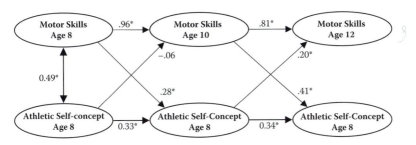

FIGURE 3.10 Relations between athletic self-concept and motor skill development during the school years.

course of childhood and beyond. Mainly based on Ackerman's (1988) theoretical approach, we expected that interrelations between the two concepts would be rather close in early childhood and continuously decrease as a function of time. Overall, this expectation was only partially confirmed by the data. Decreases over time were found for the relation between verbal IQ and motor skills, but not for nonverbal IQ. More elaborated analyses based on structural equation modeling and taking advantage of all relevant information in the data suggested a predominance of intelligence over motor skills in the preschool period. From that point in time onward, no reliable interrelations between the two constructs were found, indicating rather independent trajectories for the motor and IQ domains.

A second major question addressed in this chapter concerned the development of motor skills from early childhood to early adulthood. Our findings indicate that the basic developmental pattern was similar for boys and girls during the preschool and early elementary school period, but that different patterns for the two sexes were obtained from adolescence onward. During early childhood, girls tended to perform better than boys. In comparison, only a few sex differences were found during the elementary school years, regardless of the motor task under consideration. From early adolescence onward, however, the dominance of the male participants increasingly emerged, especially in strength-oriented exercises. Although the gap between the sexes seemed to widen after age 12, we could not prove this assertion based on our data. It is unfortunate in this respect that we were not able to measure motor skills at the age of 18, due to organizational constraints. Thus, it remains unclear when exactly the sex differences first occur, and how exactly the growth curves found for males and females differ (e.g., linear or nonlinear trends). However, our findings are in accord with other longitudinal data covering this age period (e.g., Malina, 2001). The enormous growth in performance found for males seems at least partially due to hormone-dependent increases in muscle mass during the course of puberty. Aside from this, after puberty, men show a clearly better trainability in strength-dependent motor functions (Haywood & Getchell, 2005). Thus, we confirmed previous findings showing that young adult males exceed females above all in leg strength exercises such as the Standing Long Jump and One-Footed Jumping. When physical strength is less important, for example in the Backward Balancing, Jumping Back and Forth, and Lateral Movement tasks, young male adults still on average perform somewhat better. However, their performance advantage in relation to women was not reliable.

We can only speculate about the origins of sex differences found after early adolescence. Although they may be in part biologically determined, it is likely that they are also determined by social factors (Gregson & Colley, 1986; Haywood & Getchell, 2005; Higginson, 1985). For example, gender stereotypes may dictate differences in preference for sports and physical activity. Although the athletic activity of boys and girls does not differ much in early and midchildhood (Brettschneider & Bräutigam, 1990; Brettschneider & Naul, 2004), the situation changes from early adolescence onward. Girls try out for substantially fewer sports and are less likely to be members of sport teams or clubs than boys (see Armstrong & Welsman, 2006; Brettschneider & Naul, 2004; van Mechelen, Twisk, Post, Snel, & Kemper, 2000), a finding also confirmed for the LOGIC sample (see Ahnert, 2005). Sex differences in athletic participation can also indicate different motor skill development in boys and girls. Unfortunately, this hypothesis could not be tested with the LOGIC data, because athletic activity and sports activity socialization (e.g., types of sports practiced) were not measured prospectively.

Although there is no doubt that motor skill development progresses rapidly from early childhood to early adolescence, the growth curve representing developmental changes between the ages of 12 and 23 still is not determined. According to Bös (1994), peak performance is reached in youth for speed and endurance, coordination under time pressure, and flexibility, whereas the best results are first achieved in early adulthood for the majority of strength measures and balance (coordination in precision tasks). However, in these content areas, it also appears that peak performance for those who are not specifically trained as athletes occurs at an earlier point in time as a result of increasing inactivity. Thus, there is reason to believe that peak performance in the majority of exercises in the KTK and in the Standing Long Jump task depending on sex and task occurs as early as in the mid- or late teens. Our analyses concerning the impact of sports activity level and weight seem to confirm the hypothesis that body characteristics as well as activity level substantially influence motor skill development, regardless of sex. If this hypothesis is correct, our motor skill assessments at age 23 most likely portray a stagnation period or decrease in performance. Given that our longitudinal data are not suited to prove this hypothesis, it should be tested in future studies.

The performance decreases found for the time between late childhood and early adulthood were restricted to specific tasks. The clearly worse balancing ability found in adults could be due to a scarcity of balance-related exercise in the level of movement involved in everyday activities. For problems associated with lateral movement, biomechanically unfavorable body proportions in men and women (i.e., longer arms and legs) may also be partly responsible. In this context, one may ask whether the KTK should be used with young adults. Given that we did not observe ceiling effects in the adult sample, our decision to stay with the KTK seems justified after the fact. Certainly, applying the same test—if also only normed for children and youth—to young adults seems reasonable and offers the best possibility for portraying the development of motor ability over decades with the most precision. Nonetheless, we recommend a test of the validity of the KTK for young adults for future studies, perhaps by combining this measure with a parallel test already demonstrated to assess coordination skill in adulthood.

The last major issue dealt with in the present analysis concerned the individual stability of motor skill development over time. Overall, our results seem in accord with previous findings in that rapid progress is observed between the ages of 4 and 12, followed by a period of slow progression (cf. Bös, 1994). Does this mean that most participants proceeded at about the same pace? What evidence is offered for the long-term stability of individual differences in development? As expected, the stability coefficients varied as a function of age and task type. In general, lower stabilities were found for the preschool and kindergarten periods. Overall, the hypothesis that long-term stability of motor performance is already moderate between preschool and early adulthood (.30 to .54) and reaches moderately high values (.50 to .65) between elementary school and adulthood was confirmed. This finding seems impressive given that different motor tests were used during the different time periods. Apparently, individual differences in intraindividual changes are more pronounced in early childhood, as compared to subsequent phases. The increase in individual stability found for the elementary school years and beyond cannot be explained by differences in test intervals, especially because test–retest intervals were shorter in the preschool period than later on. Thus, higher stabilities found for the later assessment periods indicate that most participants proceeded at about the same pace as far as their motor skill development was concerned.

In particular, the moderate to high long-term stability of motor skills from elementary school until early adulthood (up to .65) observed for the coordination ability (KTK) and for strength of leg muscles (Standing Long Jump) confirms the findings from previous longitudinal studies (see the overviews by Ahnert, 2005; Bös, 1994). Altogether, however, stability for coordination and strength falls below stability found for other physical attributes, such as body size or weight, where stability ranges between .60 and .80 over the same time period (Ahnert, 2005). The relatively high stability of motor abilities already observable in elementary school indicates the strong influence of biological factors in motor development, probably comparable to that found for the development of IQ (see Schneider, Stefanek, & Niklas, chap. 2, this volume).

The remaining instability in motor abilities observed in early adulthood can be at least partly accounted for by growing physical changes during puberty (e.g., weight gain and changes in body proportions). Major changes in life circumstances that take place at the end of childhood and in early adolescence may also play a role. These changes (e.g., graduation and moving away from home) include variations in athletic participation, which have an undeniable influence on motor skill development. The relatively high stability of motor abilities from grade school to adulthood clearly shows, however, that integral foundations of motor skill development are already laid in early childhood, determining further motor development until adulthood.

REFERENCES

Ackerman, P. L. (1988). Determinants of individual differences during skill acquisition: Cognitive abilities and information processing. *Journal of Experimental Psychology: General, 117*, 288–318.

Ahnert, J. (2005). *Motorische Entwicklung vom Vorschul- bis ins frühe Erwachsenenalter—Einflussfaktoren und Prognostizierbarkeit* [Motor development from the preschool period until early adulthood: Moderating factors and predictability]. Unpublished doctoral dissertation, University of Würzburg. Retrieved January 10, 2008, from http://opus.bibliothek.uni-wuerzburg.de/volltexte/2006/1634/pdf/diss-ahnert-internet.pdf

Ahnert, J., Bös, K., & Schneider, W. (2003). Motorische und kognitive Entwicklung im Vorschul- und Schulalter: Befunde der Münchner Längsschnittstudie LOGIK [Motor development and cognitive development during the preschool and elementary school periods: Findings from the Munich Longitudinal Study LOGIK]. *Zeitschrift für Entwicklungspsychologie und Pädagogische Psychologie, 35*, 185–199.

Ahnert, J., & Schneider, W. (2006). Selbstkonzept und motorische Leistungen im Grundschulalter—Ein dynamisches Wechselspiel? [Self-concept and motor performance in elementary school: Indications of a dynamic interaction?]. In I. Hosenfeld & F-W. Schrader (Eds.), *Schulische Leistung—Grundlagen, Bedingungen, Perspektiven* (pp. 145–168). Münster, Germany: Waxmann.

Armstrong, N., & van Mechelen, W. (2000). *Paediatric exercise science and medicine*. Oxford: Oxford University Press.

Armstrong, N., & Welsman, J. R. (2006). The physical activity patterns of European youth with reference to methods of assessment. *Sports Medicine, 36*, 1067–1086.

Baur, J. (1989). *Körper- und Bewegungskarrieren* [Body and movement careers]. Schorndorf, Germany: Hofmann.

Bentler, P. M. (1985). *Theory and implementation of EQS: A structural equations program*. Los Angeles: BMDP Statistical Software.

Beunen, G., de Beul, G., Ostyn, M., Renson, R., Simons, J., & Van Gerven, D. (1981). Die Konstanz motorischer Leistungen bei 12- bis 17-jährigen Jungen [The consistency of motor achievements in 12–17-year-old youth]. In K. Willimczik & M. Grosser (Eds.), *Die motorische Entwicklung im Kindes- und Jugendalter* (pp. 278–284). Schorndorf, Germany: Hofmann.

Beunen, G., Malina, R. M., Van't Hof, M. A., Simons, J., Ostyn, M., Renson, R., et al. (1988). *Adolescent growth and motor performance: A longitudinal study of Belgian boys.* Champaign, IL: Human Kinetics.

Beunen, G., Ostyn, M., Renson, R., Simons, J., Swalus, P., & Van Gerven, D. (1974). Skeletal maturation and physical fitness of 12 to 15 year old boys. *Acta Paediatrica Belgium, 28*(Suppl.), 221–232.

Beunen, G., Ostyn, M., Simons, J., Renson, R., Claessens, A. L., Vanden Eynde, B., et al. (1997). Development and tracking in fitness components: Leuven Longitudinal Study on Lifestyle, Fitness and Health. *International Journal of Sports and Medicine, 18*, 171–178.

Bös, K. (1994). Differentielle Aspekte der Entwicklung motorischer Fähigkeiten [Differential aspects of the development of motor skills]. In J. Baur, K. Bös, & R. Singer (Eds.). *Motorische Entwicklung—Ein Handbuch* (pp. 238–256). Schorndorf, Germany: Hofmann.

Bös, K. (2001). *Handbuch motorischer Tests* [The handbook of motor tests] (2nd ed.). Göttingen, Germany: Hogrefe.

Bös, K. (2003). Motorische Leistungsfähigkeit von Kindern und Jugendlichen [Motor skills achievements in children and adolescents]. In W. Schmidt, I. Hartmann-Tews, & W-D. Brettschneider (Eds.), *Erster Deutscher Kinder- und Jugendsportbericht* (pp. 85–107). Schorndorf, Germany: Hofmann.

Brettschneider, W., & Bräutigam, M. (1990). *Sport in der Alltagswelt von Jugendlichen—Forschungsbericht* [Sports in adolescents' everyday life: A research report] (Materialien zum Sport in Nord-Rhein-Westfalen, 27). Frechen, Germany: Kultusministerium des Landes Nord-Rhein-Westfalen.

Brettschneider, W-D., & Naul, R. (2004). *Study on young people's lifestyles and sedentariness and the role of sport in the context of education and as a means of restoring the balance: Final report.* Retrieved January 11, 2007, from http://europa.eu.int/comm/sport/documents/lotpaderborn.pdf

Crasselt, W., Forchel, I., & Stemmler, R. (1985). *Zur körperlichen Entwicklung der Schuljugend in der Deutschen Demokratischen Republik* [Body development of school youth in the German Democratic Republic]. Leipzig, Germany: Ambrosius Barth.

Gregson, J. F., & Colley, A. (1986). Concomitants of sport participation in male and female adolescents. *International Journal of Sport Psychology, 17*, 10–22.

Harter, S. (1985). *Manual for the Self-Perception Profile for Children.* Denver, CO: University of Denver.

Harter, S., & Pike, R. (1981). *Manual for the Pictorial Scale of Perceived Competence and Social Acceptance for Children.* Denver, CO: University of Denver.

Haywood, K., & Getchell, N. (2005). *Life span motor development* (4th ed.). Champaign, IL: Human Kinetics.

Helmke, A., & van Aken, M. (1995). The causal ordering of academic achievement and self-concept of ability during elementary school: A longitudinal study. *Journal of Educational Psychology, 87*, 624–637.

Higginson, D. C. (1985). The influence of socializing agents in the female sport-participation process. *Adolescence, 20*, 73–82.

Kemper, H. C. G. (1985). *Growth, health and fitness of teenagers: Longitudinal research, international perspective* (Medicine and Sport Science Series, 20). Basel, Switzerland: Karger.

Kemper, H. C. G. (2004). Amsterdam Growth and Health Longitudinal Study: A 23-year follow-up from teenager to adult about lifestyle and health. In J. Borms, M. Hebbelinck, & A. P. Hills (Eds.), *Medicine and sport science* (Vol. 47). Basel, Switzerland: Karger.

Kemper, H. C. G. (Ed.). (1995). *The Amsterdam Growth Study: A longitudinal analysis of health, fitness and lifestyle* (HK Sport Science Monograph Series, 6). Champaign, IL: Human Kinetics.

Kemper, H. C. G., & van Mechelen, W. (1995). Physical fitness and the relationship to physical activity. In H. C. G. Kemper (Ed.), *The Amsterdam Growth Study: A longitudinal analysis of health, fitness and lifestyle* (HK Sport Science Monograph Series, 6, pp. 135–158). Champaign, IL: Human Kinetics.

Kiphard, E. J. (1972). *Bewegungsdiagnostik bei Kindern* [Movements tests for children]. Gütersloh, Germany: Flöttmann.

Kiphard, E. J., & Schilling, F. (2000). *Körperkoordinationstest für Kinder—KTK* [Body coordination test for children] (2nd ed.). Weinheim, Germany: Beltz.

Kohl, H. W., & Hobbs, K. E. (1998). Development of physical activity behaviors among children and adolescents. *Pediatrics, 101*(3, Suppl.), 549–554.

Lefevre, J., Philippaerts, R. M., Delvaux, K., Thomis, M., Vanreusel, B., Eynde, B. V., et al. (2000). Daily physical activity and physical fitness from adolescence to adulthood: A longitudinal study. *American Journal of Human Biology, 12*, 487–497.

Maia, J. A. R., Lefevre, J., Beunen, G., Claessens, A., Vanden Eynde, B., Vanreusel, B., et al. (1998). Stability in physical fitness: A study on Belgian males followed longitudinally from 12 to 30 years. *Medicine & Science in Sports & Exercise, 30*(Suppl. 305), 765–771.

Maia, J. A., Lefevre, J., Claessens, A., Renson, R., Vanreusel, B., & Beunen, G. (2001). Tracking of physical fitness during adolescence: A panel study in boys. *Medicine & Science in Sports & Exercise, 33*, 765–771.

Malina R. M. (1996). Tracking of physical activity and fitness across the lifespan. *Research Quarterly for Exercise and Sport, 67*, 48–57.

Malina, R. M. (2001). Physical activity and fitness: Pathways from childhood to adulthood. *American Journal of Human Biology, 13*, 162–172.

Matton, L., Thomis, M., Wijndaele, K., Duvigneaud, N., Beunen, G., Claessens, A. L., et al. (2006). Tracking of physical fitness and physical activity from youth to adulthood in females. *Medicine & Science in Sports & Exercise, 38*, 1114–1120.

Mechling, H., Schott, N., & Bös, K. (1998). Prognostizierbarkeit von sportlichen Leistungen [Predictability of sport achievement]. In D. Teipel, R. Kemper, & D. Heinemann (Eds.), *Sportpsychologische Diagnostik, Prognostik, Intervention* (pp. 185–192). Köln: bps-Verlag.

Mellerowicz, H. (1975). *Ergometrie* [Ergonometrics]. München, Germany: Urban & Schwarzenberg.

Multerer, A. (1991). *Die Prognostizierbarkeit von sportmotorischen Leistungen und sportlicher Aktivität* [The predictability of motor sports achievement and sport activity]. Unpublished doctoral dissertation, University of Frankfurt.

Ostyn, M., Simons, J., Beunen, G., Renson, R., & van Gerven, D. (Eds.). (1980). *Somatic and motor development of Belgian secondary schoolboys: Norms and standards.* Leuven, Belgium: Leuven University Press.

Raczek, J. (2002). Entwicklungsveränderungen der motorischen Leistungsfähigkeit der Schuljugend in drei Jahrzehnten (1965–1995) Tendenzen, Ursachen und Konsequenzen. [Developmental changes in motor achievement skills in school youth over three decades: Trends, causes and consequences]. *Sportwissenschaft, 32*, 201–216.

Rarick, G. L., & Smoll, F. L. (1967). Stability of growth in strength and motor performance from childhood to adolescence. *Human Biology, 39*, 295–306.

Schneider, W. (1989). Problems of longitudinal studies with children: Practical, conceptual, and methodological issues. In M. Brambring, F. Lösel, & H. Skowronek (Eds.), *Children at risk: Assessment, longitudinal research and intervention* (pp. 313–335). New York: De Gruyter.

Schneider, W. (1993). The longitudinal study of motor development: Methodological issues. In A. Kalverboer, B. Hopkins, & R. Geuze (Eds.), *Motor development in early and later childhood: Longitudinal approaches* (pp. 317–342). Cambridge, MA: Cambridge University Press.

Schott, N. (2000). *Prognostizierbarkeit und Stabilität von sportlichen Leistungen über einen Zeitraum von 20 Jahren: eine Nachuntersuchung bei 28jährigen Erwachsenen* [Predictability and stability of sport achievement in a 20 year period: A follow-up study with 28-year-old adults]. Unpublished doctoral dissertation, Technical University Karlsruhe. Retrieved January 10, 2008, from: http://digbib.ubka. uni-karlsruhe.de/volltexte/2292000

Schott, N., Bös, K., & Mechling, H. (1997). Diagnose und Prognostizierbarkeit der motorischen Leistungsfähigkeit bei Jugendlichen und jungen Erwachsenen [Measurement and predictability of motor achievement in youth and young adults]. In D. Schmidtbleicher, K. Bös, & A. Müller (Eds.), *Sport im Lebenslauf.* Hamburg: Czwalina.

Stemper, T., Dammer, M., & Noll, G. (1999). *Lehrbuch lizenzierter Fitness-Trainer DSSV* [Textbook for fitness training licensure]. Hamburg: SSV-Verlag.

Tomkinson, G. R., Olds, T. S., & Gulbin, J. (2003). Secular trends in physical performance of Australian children: Evidence from the talent search program. *Journal of Sports and Medical Physical Fitness, 43*, 90–98.

Tomkinson, G. R., Olds, T. S., Kang, S. J., & Kim, D. Y. (2007). Secular trends in the aerobic fitness test performance and Body Mass Index of Korean children and adolescents (1968–2000). *International Journal of Sports Medicine, 28*, 314–320.

Trost, S. G., Saunders, R., & Ward, D. S. (2002). Determinants of physical activity in middle school children. *American Journal of Health Behavior, 26*, 95–102.

Van Mechelen, W., & Kemper, H. C. G. (1995). Body growth, body composition and physical fitness. In H. C. G. Kemper (Ed.), *The Amsterdam Growth Study: A longitudinal analysis of health, fitness and lifestyle* (HK Sport Science Monograph Series, 6, pp. 52–85). Champaign, IL: Human Kinetics.

Van Mechelen, W., Twisk, J. W. R., Post, G. B., Snel, J., & Kemper, H. C. G. (2000). Physical activity of young people: The Amsterdam Longitudinal Growth and Health Study. *Medicine & Science in Sports & Exercise, 32*, 1610–1616.

Wang, Y., & Lobstein, T. (2006). Worldwide trends in childhood overweight and obesity. *International Journal of Pediatric Obesity, 1*, 11–25.

Wedderkopp, N., Froberg, K., Hansen, H. S., & Andersen, L. B. (2004). Secular trends in physical fitness and obesity in Danish 9-year-old girls and boys: Odense School Child Study and Danish substudy of the European Youth Heart Study. *Scandinavian Journal of Medicine & Science in Sports, 14*, 150–155.

Wendland, U. (1986). *Individuelle Leistungsprognosen im Spitzensport* [Prediction of individual achievement in top athletes]. Schorndorf, Germany: Hofmann.

Wu, T-S., Pender, N., & Noureddine, S. (2003). Gender differences in the psychosocial and cognitive correlates of physical activity among Taiwanese adolescents: A structural equation modeling approach. *International Journal of Behavioral Medicine*, *10*, 93–105.

Zimmer, R., & Volkamer, M. (1984). *Motoriktest für 4–6jährige* [Motor test for 4 to 6 year olds]. Weinheim, Germany: Beltz.

4 Verbal Memory Development from Early Childhood to Early Adulthood

Wolfgang Schneider, Monika Knopf, and Beate Sodian

4.1 INTRODUCTION

Although scientific research on memory development shares the same long tradition as the scientific study of psychology (i.e., about 130 years), the majority of studies have been conducted within the past 4 decades, stimulated by a shift away from behaviorist theories toward information-processing theories (Schneider & Pressley, 1997). Among these are thousands of empirical studies that have investigated the development of children's and adolescents' ability to store and retrieve information from memory (for reviews, see Cowan, in press; Kail, 1990; Schneider & Bjorklund, 1998, 2003; Schneider & Pressley, 1997).

In the following, we first briefly summarize the state of the art concerning the development of verbal memory when we started the Munich Longitudinal Study on the Ontogenesis of Individual Competencies (the LOGIC study) in the mid-1980s. Next, we describe the instruments used to measure different aspects of verbal memory such as short-term memory capacity, strategic memory, and memory for text used during the different stages of the study. Finally, we present longitudinal findings that describe the developmental course within each of the various components of verbal memory and that explore interrelationships among these components from early childhood to young adulthood.

4.2 VERBAL MEMORY DEVELOPMENT BETWEEN 5 AND 15

Although young children's memory development was explored in some early studies, the vast majority of studies on memory development conducted in the 1960s, 1970s, and early 1980s were carried out with schoolchildren, mainly dealing with explicit (that is, conscious) remembering of facts and events. There was almost no research on memory in infants and very young children at that time, a situation that changed dramatically over the years to follow. The memory skill investigated in schoolchildren was also labeled *declarative memory* and distinguished from *procedural memory*, which refers to unconscious memory for skills. It was repeatedly found that particularly clear improvements in declarative memory were observed in the age range between 6 and 12 years, which roughly corresponds to the elementary school period in most countries. Different sources of memory development were identified to explain these rapid increases over time. There was general agreement among memory researchers that changes in *basic capacities, memory strategies, metacognitive knowledge*, and *domain knowledge* all contribute to developmental changes in memory performance. There was also broad agreement that some of these sources of development contribute more than others, and that some play an important role in certain periods of childhood but not in others.

4.2.1 THE ROLE OF BASIC CAPACITIES

One of the most controversial issues about children's information processing explored at that time was whether the amount of information children can actively process at one time changes with age. The concept of memory capacity usually refers to the amount of information that can be held in the short-term store (STS) and has been typically assessed via *memory span tasks* or measures of *working memory*. Whereas memory span tasks require children to immediately recall a given number of items in the correct order, working memory tasks are more complex in that they not only require the exact reproduction of items but also are embedded in an additional task because children must transform information held in the STS. The maximum number of items a person can correctly recall in those tasks defines his or her memory capacity.

In general, children's performance on working memory tasks and memory span tasks shows the same age-related increase, although the absolute performance level is somewhat lower in working memory tasks. Several cross-sectional studies showed that development is related to significant increases in information-processing speed, which are most obvious in early ages, with the rate of changes slowing thereafter (Kail, 1991).

Although there is little doubt that performance on memory span and working memory tasks improves with age, the implications for whether memory capacity changes with age were not so obvious. It remained unclear whether the total capacity store factually increases with age or whether changes in information-processing speed, strategies, and knowledge allow more material to be stored within the same overall capacity.

4.2.2 EFFECTS OF MEMORY STRATEGIES

Memory strategies are defined as mental or behavioral activities that achieve cognitive purposes and are effort consuming, potentially conscious, and controllable (Flavell, 1985; Pressley, Forrest-Pressley, Elliott-Faust, & Miller, 1985). Since the early 1970s, numerous studies have investigated the role of strategies in memory development. Strategies can be executed either at the time of learning (encoding) or later on when information is accessed in long-term memory (retrieval). The *encoding strategies* explored in the majority of studies include *rehearsal*, which involves the repetition of target information; *organization*, which involves the combination of different items in categories; and *elaboration*, which involves the association of two or more items through the generation of relations connecting these items. *Retrieval strategies* refer to strategic efforts at the time of testing, when the task is to access stored information and bring it back into consciousness.

Typically, these strategies are not observed in children younger than 5 or 6 years. I might say here that the lack of strategic behaviors was given different explanations depending on age. In very young children, the lack of strategic behavior was said to be due to a *mediational deficiency* because even when told to use strategies, young children showed no evidence that strategy use would help to improve or "mediate" their memory performance. In older children, in contrast, the lack of strategic behavior was said to be due to a *production deficiency* because it was shown that when these children were told to use strategies and did so, strategy use improved performance.

More recently, the construct of a *utilization deficiency* has been proposed to account for the finding that strategies initially often fail to improve young children's memory performance (Flavell, Miller, & Miller, 1993; Schneider & Bjorklund, 1998). The explanation for this discrepancy favored by most researchers is that executing new strategies may consume too much of young children's memory capacity.

In the 1980s, the view adopted by most researchers was that age-related improvements in the frequency of use and quality of children's strategies play a major role in memory development between the preschool years and adolescence. However, there already was increasing realization that the use of encoding and retrieval strategies largely depends on children's strategic as well as nonstrategic knowledge. There was broad consensus that the narrow focus on developmental changes in strategy use should be replaced by an approach that takes into account the effects of various forms of knowledge on strategy execution.

4.2.2.1   The Role of Metacognitive Knowledge (Metamemory)

One knowledge component that had been systematically explored since the early 1970s is children's knowledge about memory. The term *metamemory* was introduced to refer to a person's potentially verbalizable knowledge about memory storage and retrieval (Flavell & Wellman, 1977; Schneider, 1985). Two broad categories of metacognitive knowledge were distinguished in the literature. *Declarative metacognitive knowledge* refers to what children factually know about their memory. This type of knowledge is explicit and verbalizable and includes knowledge about the importance of person variables (e.g., age or IQ), task characteristics such as task difficulty, or strategies for resulting memory performances. In contrast, *procedural metacognitive knowledge* is mostly implicit (subconscious) and relates to children's self-monitoring and self-regulation activities while dealing with a memory problem.

Early empirical research exploring the development of declarative metamemory revealed that children's knowledge of facts about memory increases considerably over the primary grade years, but is still incomplete by the end of childhood and in early adolescence (Cavanaugh & Perlmutter, 1982; Schneider, 1985). Other studies showed that increases in knowledge about strategies are paralleled by the acquisition of strategies, and that metamemory–memory behavior relationships tend to be moderately strong (see Schneider & Weinert, 1989). Thus, what children know about their memory obviously influences how they try to remember. Nonetheless, although older grade school children seemed to know much about strategies, there was also evidence that many adolescents (including college students) had little or no knowledge of some important and powerful memory strategies.

4.2.2.2 The Impact of Domain Knowledge

In most domains, older children know more than younger ones, and differences in knowledge are closely linked to performance differences. How can we explain this phenomenon? First, one effect that rich domain knowledge has on memory is to increase the speed of processing for domain-specific information. Second, rich domain knowledge enables more competent strategy use. Finally, rich domain knowledge can have nonstrategic effects, that is, diminish the need for strategy activation.

Evidence for the latter phenomenon comes from studies using the *expert–novice paradigm*. These studies compared experts and novices in a given domain (e.g., baseball, chess, or soccer) on a memory task related to that domain. It could be demonstrated that rich domain knowledge enabled a child expert to perform much like an adult expert and better than an adult novice—thus showing a disappearance and sometimes reversal of usual developmental trends. Experts and novices differed not only with regard to quantity of knowledge but also regarding the quality of knowledge, that is, in the way their knowledge is represented in the mind. Moreover, several studies also confirmed the assumption that rich domain knowledge can compensate for low overall aptitude on domain-related memory tasks, as no differences were found between high- and low-aptitude experts on various recall and comprehension measures (Bjorklund & Schneider, 1996).

In the early 1980s, striking effects of domain knowledge on performance in memory tasks had been provided in a few developmental studies. For instance, the memory of chess experts and novices was compared in a classic study by Chi (1978). Her twist was that knowledge was negatively correlated with age. That is, children were the experts, and adults were the novices. When both groups were tested on a task that required the memorization of chess positions, the young experts outperformed the adult novices. Similar findings were obtained in other studies based on baseball and soccer expertise (see Recht & Leslie, 1988; Schneider, Körkel, & Weinert, 1989).

Taken together, these findings indicate that domain knowledge increases greatly with age and is clearly related to how much and what children remember. Undoubtedly, domain knowledge also contributes to the development of other competencies that have been proposed as sources of memory development, namely, basic capacities, memory strategies, and metacognitive knowledge.

4.3   THE STUDY OF VERBAL MEMORY IN THE LOGIC STUDY

Given that most studies on memory development conducted in the 1960s and 1970s were based on a cross-sectional design, we knew a lot about developmental *differences* among various age groups but almost nothing about developmental *changes* within individuals over time. One of the major goals of the LOGIC study was to learn more about interindividual differences in intraindividual memory changes over time. In our view, theories and models of memory development proposed in the late 1970s and early 1980s were idealistic in nature, supporting a tendency to overestimate the universality, intraindividual homogeneity, and interindividual consistency of developmental changes in verbal memory (see Schneider & Weinert, 1989). As a consequence, memory development was viewed as a regular, rule-bound sequence of changes in cognitive competencies and related memory skills. Deviations from this ideal sequence were either treated as error variance or interpreted as individual acceleration or retardation, compared to a prototypical developmental sequence.

Although we would not go so far as to say that all of the problems caused by cross-sectional research on memory development can be solved by focusing on a longitudinal approach, several advantages related to the longitudinal study design seemed obvious:

1. Within-subject assessments of memory performance changes allow for analyses of the type of developmental function (linear versus nonlinear) operating in a given sample. For instance, we cannot tell from cross-sectional findings whether information on developmental trends based on group mean information is also valid on the individual level. Improvements on the group mean level could be due to some children making enormous progress, whereas others remain the same or even decline. Individual developmental curves in children's memory performance could be much less continuous than the cross-sectional database suggests. One way to examine this issue is to calculate a "lability" score that measures the amount of across-age variability shown in an individual's relative standing within the reference group (longitudinal sample). For instance, Kunzinger (1985) calculated lability scores to examine interindividual differences in intraindividual change during the acquisition of rehearsal strategies in elementary school children (from age 7 to age 9), and found rather high stability over time.

2. Longitudinal studies that not only focus on one memory measure but also combine a variety of memory indicators provide opportunities to go

beyond the typical narrow analysis of change patterns in a specific memory aspect. They can provide information about interactional patterns in the development of different memory paradigms, allowing us to assess the homogeneity versus heterogeneity of individual memory development (see Wohlwill, 1973). The issue of domain-specific versus global memory development has been an issue since Ebbinghaus (1885) first proposed that we must question the existence of a unitary memory system. In the field of verbal memory development, cross-sectional research devoted to the issue of intraindividual consistency in performance across several memory tasks yielded inconsistent findings (see Cavanaugh & Borkowski, 1980; Kail, 1979; Weinert, Schneider, & Knopf, 1988).

To investigate the course of verbal memory development longitudinally in the LOGIC study, we decided to include indicators of memory capacity, strategic memory, and memory for text from the very beginning. A specific effort was made to include measures related to these constructs that could be used over a longer time span and thus were suited to explore developmental changes. Although this was possible in most cases, some of the measures had to be modified due to ceiling effects in later stages of the study.

4.3.1 ASSESSMENT OF MEMORY PERFORMANCE IN THE LOGIC STUDY

The complete set of memory variables used in the course of the study is depicted in Table 4.1.

TABLE 4.1
Memory Tasks Included in the LOGIC Study, as a Function of Wave (measurement print)

	Word Span	Sentence Span	Sort–Recall	Text Recall
Wave 1	X		X	X
Wave 2				X
Wave 3	X	X	X	X
Wave 4		X		X
Wave 5	X	X	X	X
Wave 6				X
Wave 7		X	X	X
Wave 8	X			
Wave 9			X	X
Wave 10		X	X	X
Wave 11		X	X	X

4.3.1.1 Verbal Memory Capacity

To assess children's *memory span for words*, a paradigm developed by Case, Kurland, and Goldberg (1982) was adopted. In this task, 10 different word sets with three to seven items were used. Children were instructed to first listen to the entire tape-recorded set and to reproduce it immediately. The major difference between our procedure and that used by Case et al. was that operational efficiency (i.e., reaction time) and memory span were not measured independently in our study. Beginning with the smallest set of three words, children were given two trials for each set size. They were instructed to listen to the entire set and then to repeat the words they heard. Whenever an item set could be correctly reproduced, the next set including $n + 1$ items was presented. This procedure continued until the children could no longer recall all of the items. Two different dependent measures were calculated. The first word span measure was identical to that used by Case et al. Participants were given credit for correctly recalling a set of items as long as they could remember all of the words, regardless of order (i.e., unconstrained word span). According to Case and colleagues, this measure ensures that developmental differences in span are not confounded with differences in encoding and preserving information about order. A second measure was the serial word span (words had to be recalled in the correct order), which enabled us to explore differences in these two span measures as a function of age.

Efficient phonetic coding in working memory seems important for various memory purposes, and it may play a particularly crucial role for beginning readers because it frees the maximum amount of cognitive resources for the difficult task of blending sounds together to form words (see Wagner & Torgesen, 1987). The use of memory span tasks with items such as letters, numbers, words, or sentences to tap efficient processing of information is based on the theoretical assumption that working memory has storage and processing functions that compete for a shared, limited capacity (see Baddeley, 1986; Case et al., 1982).

4.3.1.1.1 Sentence Span
The main reason to include a sentence span (listening span) memory measure was to explore the impact of working memory on the development of reading and spelling. Thus, we adopted the Daneman and Blennerhassett (1984) listening span measure and first used it in Wave 3, when children were in their last kindergarten year. The test was repeated in Waves 5 and 7 (ages 8 and 10), and in Waves 10 and 11 (ages 18 and 23) when the participants were no longer children. Including the listening span test in later assessments enabled us to explore the impact of individual differences in working memory on memory performance in other tasks.

In our version of the listening span task, participants first listened to a set of sentences read to them by the experimenter, and then recalled each sentence verbatim. The test was constructed with 75 sentences that were three to seven words in length. Each sentence ended in a different word. There were 25 sets of sentences in all, including five sets of one, two, three, four, and five sentences. The prerecorded sentences in each set were presented to the participants as a playback from tape. For sets containing more than one sentence, the sentences were read in quick succession. At the end of each set, a tone was emitted that was a cue to recall, verbatim, each sentence in the set. Participants began with the five 1-sentence sets, and were then presented with sets containing increasingly more sentences. Testing terminated when the participants failed all five sentences of a set at a particular level. Subjects were encouraged to repeat the sentences in the order presented, but if they could not recall the order, they were to say back as many sentences as possible in any order.

Participants were given credit for correctly recalling a set as long as they repeated each sentence verbatim, regardless of the order in which they repeated the sentences. In accord with the criterion used by Daneman and Blennerhassett (1984), the level at which a participant was correct on at least three out of five sets was taken as a measure of his or her listening span. In addition, the total number of correct sentences and the total number of words reproduced in the correct order were used as dependent variables.

4.3.1.1.2 Strategic Memory

We decided to use a semantic organization task to assess the development of sorting and clustering strategies. In the preschool and kindergarten period (i.e., in Waves 1 and 3, when children were 4 and 6 years old), the item lists used for the sort–recall task consisted of 16 toys (four each of animals, furniture, vehicles, and household items). Later on, 24 picture cards (six each of the tools, animals, fruit, and vehicles categories) were used for the 8-, 10-, 12-, and 18-year-olds. Items were presented in a random order, and participants were instructed to try to remember as many items as possible and to do whatever they thought was useful for remembering the items. After a study period of 2 minutes, a photograph was taken showing the final arrangement of the items, which were then hidden. Children were then asked to recall as many of the names of the toys (the pictures) as possible. The particular version of the sort–recall task used in Wave 11 with the 23-year-olds was first employed in Wave 10 and will be referred to as the *difficult version* in the following. Whereas the item materials used in Waves 5 to 10 were easy in the sense that interitem associations were rather high and items were taken from familiar categories (see above), the items (24 pictures of familiar objects) used in the difficult version came from less familiar categories. Also, interitem associations were comparably low. The more difficult version was added in Wave 10 because there were indications that the easy materials yielded ceiling effects in the sample of adolescents.

The sort–recall task was followed by a short metamemory interview in which the children were presented with photographs that showed three different arrangements of the items used in the sort–recall task: a random order, an ordering by conceptual category, and an ordering by color (in Waves 1 and 3) or by alphabet (from Wave 5 onward). Participants were asked to rank these arrangements in terms of their usefulness (see Sodian & Schneider, 1999). In addition to this task-specific metamemory interview, we assessed children's general metamemory with an interview procedure modeled after Kreutzer, Leonard, and Flavell (1975).

Results concerning metamemory were described in some detail by Sodian and Schneider (1999), and will not be discussed in this chapter.

4.3.1.1.3   Memory for Text

Four narratives were constructed to assess children's memory for text. The number of stories presented to the children in different measurement waves varied between one and three. Each text was presented twice, and then children were asked to retell each story as accurately as possible. The criterion variable calculated for each of the stories was the number of text propositions correctly recalled. The time schedule of the text memory tasks across the LOGIC study is given in Figure 4.1.

Three of the four texts were similar to story materials already used in other studies that assessed the impact of scripted knowledge on children's text recall (see Fivush & Stackman, 1986; Hudson & Nelson, 1983). These three stories were labeled "Birthday Party," "Playing in the Afternoon," and "Removal," and focused on familiar event sequences in their canonical or usual order. These three texts were also similar regarding the number of propositions (72–74), the number of sentences (15), and the number of events included in the stories (see Knopf, 1999). The fourth narrative ("Mauerburg") described events that happened to a boy when walking through a fictitious German town (Mauerburg), where he was

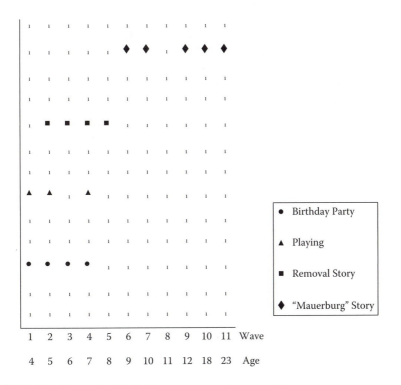

FIGURE 4.1   Time schedule for the assessment of text recall.

doing errands for his grandmother. Although the Mauerburg story consisted of familiar events, there was no predictable order in these events. Moreover, this text was considerably longer than the three others, comprising a total of 362 propositions and 31 sentences. The Mauerburg story was included from Wave 6 onward, when children were about 9 years old. As can be seen from Figure 4.1, the text materials were presented repeatedly in different combinations between Waves 1 and 5. After that, only the more difficult Mauerburg story was presented in Waves 6, 7, 9, 10, and 11. We thus have measures for text memory for every measurement point except Wave 8.

4.3.1.1.4 Standardized Memory Test
To assess general verbal learning and memory skills, a standardized test of verbal learning and memory was given in Waves 10 and 11 (the Lern- und Gedächtnistest, or LGT [in English, the Learning and Memory Test]; Bäumler, 1974). This test was developed to assess verbal and nonverbal ("figural") memory in adolescents and adults, and consists of six subscales: a list-learning task (Items), a paired associate learning task (Turkish Vocabulary), another paired associate learning task that combines names and telephone numbers (Telephone Numbers), a test assessing nonverbal memory for a route through a city depicted on a map (City Map), a task assessing memory for text (Library Construction), and a figural learning task that assesses memory for artificial logos (Logo). In Waves 10 and 11, the part of the test assessing verbal learning and memory was used that consists of the three verbal learning tasks (i.e., Turkish Vocabulary, Telephone Numbers, and Library Construction). These three subscales were moderately intercorrelated in the standardization sample (1,250 adolescents and adults), with r's ranging between .45 and .55. The subscales turned out to be sufficiently reliable, with test–retest correlations assessed after 2 weeks ranging from .72 (Telephone Numbers) to .85 (Library Construction).

4.4 MAJOR FINDINGS ON THE DEVELOPMENT OF VERBAL MEMORY

In the following, we first describe developmental changes in measures of verbal memory capacity (i.e., the word span and sentence span tasks), and then focus on the development of semantic categorization strategies in the sort–recall task. Information on developmental changes in the various text recall measures is given next, followed by a description of changes in verbal test scores in the LGT from adolescence to early adulthood. In a final step of analysis, interrelationships in intraindividual changes among the various verbal memory measures are explored, and the LGT verbal memory measure is regressed on measures of verbal memory capacity, strategic memory, as well as text recall assessed in early and middle childhood.

4.4.1   CHANGES IN VERBAL MEMORY CAPACITY

4.4.1.1   Word Span Development

Two measures were calculated to assess word span changes. *Unconstrained word span* measures developmental differences in span that are not confounded with differences in encoding and preserving information about order, and *serial word span* assesses the maximum number of items a person can remember in the correct order of presentation.

Preliminary analyses revealed that there were no sex differences in word span. Thus, data were aggregated across this variable. Given that we were interested in effects of chronological age on verbal memory development, we divided the sample into two groups according to the median of the age distribution. The mean age difference between the younger and the older age groups was about 4 months. In preliminary analysis, this variable was found to show significant effects for all of the memory measures under study. Accordingly, age group was used in our analyses as a separate factor.

Similar to Case et al. (1982), mean scores for the unconstrained word span were significantly higher than those obtained for the serial span, regardless of measurement point (see Table 4.2, all p's $< .05$). As can be seen from Table 4.2, the mean differences between unconstrained and serial word spans were particularly pronounced for the early measurement points (i.e., Waves 1 and 2, when children were 4 and 5 years old, respectively), and decreased with increasing age. Overall, our longitudinal findings corresponded well with those reported by Case and colleagues. There was a substantial increase in serial word span from age 4 to age 6, but only moderate increases during the elementary school period and beyond. Correlations between unconstrained and serial word spans varied between .52 for the 4 year olds and .80 for the 10 year olds, indicating increasing correspondence between the two span measures over time. An analysis of variance carried out for the unconstrained word span measure using Age Group as the independent factor and Measurement Point as the dependent factor yielded

---

TABLE 4.2

Development of Serial and Unconstrained Word Span, as a Function of Age Group (standard deviations in parentheses)

	Unconstrained Word Span		Serial Word Span	
	Younger Group	Older Group	Younger Group	Older Group
Wave 1	2.99 (0.95)	3.38 (0.70)	1.93 (1.39)	2.71 (1.34)
Wave 2	3.69 (0.77)	3.96 (0.81)	3.35 (1.00)	3.59 (0.94)
Wave 3	4.31 (0.75)	4.61 (0.85)	4.02 (0.83)	4.28 (0.91)
Wave 4	5.16 (0.91)	5.40 (0.88)	4.60 (0.89)	4.95 (0.80)

a significant effect of Age Group, $F(1, 128) = 16.56$, $p < .01$, and Measurement Point, $F(3, 127) = 256.22$, $p < .001$. There was no significant interaction. Overall, unconstrained word span increased over time, and the older children in the sample outperformed the younger group, regardless of measurement point. This pattern of findings was basically replicated for the serial word span measure.

4.4.1.2　Sentence Span Development

Preliminary analyses revealed that there were no sex differences, so findings were aggregated across this variable. Sentence span sum scores varied between 2 and 56 (i.e., number of sentences correctly reproduced across trials). A repeated measures analysis of variance using Age Group as the independent factor and Measurement Points as the dependent factor revealed significant main effects of Age Group, $F(1, 135) = 5.56$, $p < .05$, and Measurement Point, $F(5, 675) = 519.45$, $p < .001$. There was no Age Group by Measurement Point interaction. Subsequent posthoc tests revealed that sentence span did not improve between Waves 1 and 2, but increased significantly between adjacent measurement points until adolescence (i.e., Wave 10). There was no significant difference in sentence span between Waves 10 and 11 (ages 18 and 23), indicating that a peak in verbal memory capacity was reached by late adolescence. As can be seen from Figure 4.2, particularly pronounced increases in sentence span were observed from the ages of 7 to 8 and the ages of 12 to 18. The number of sentences per item set correctly remembered was about one during the preschool years and was doubled until the end of the elementary school years.

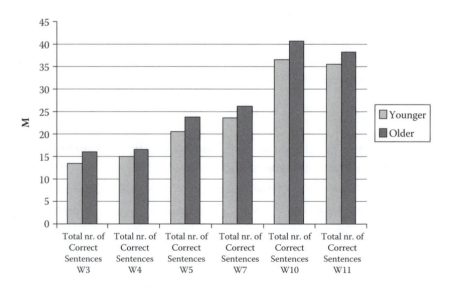

FIGURE 4.2　Development of sentence span, as a function of age group.

One unexpected finding concerns the durable effect of age group. Although we anticipated an effect of this variable for the early measurement points, we did not expect persistent effects of age group. To assess the effect of background variables such as *intelligence (IQ)* and *socioeconomic status (SES)* on this outcome, additional analyses of covariance were carried out that used *IQ* and *SES* as covariates. When *IQ* was used as a covariate, effects of age group were largely reduced but still remained significant. Accordingly, the two age subgroups also differed regarding their average IQ, with the younger age group showing lower IQ score than the older group. There was no significant effect of SES.

An interesting difference between the word and sentence span measures concerned individual stability over time. Test–retest correlations obtained for the word span measure were low to moderate, ranging between .15 (for ages 4–6) and .48 (for ages 8–11). In comparison, test–retest correlations obtained for the sentence span measure were considerably higher from age 6 onward, ranging between .57 (for ages 6–18) and .75 (between ages 8–10). Obviously, there was some intraindividual instability in word span changes over time, whereas initial individual differences in sentence span remained stable during the course of our study.

4.4.1.3 Strategy Development

As reported in earlier publications on the LOGIC study (e.g., Sodian & Schneider, 1999), one of the primary goals regarding the analysis of strategic memory development was to replicate previous cross-sectional findings on developmental trends in sorting, clustering, and recall performance, and to explore the interrelationships among these components over time. A second major goal was to explore whether conclusions drawn based on group means from cross-sectional and longitudinal studies are valid on the individual level. Given that changes on the group level could be due to some children making considerable progress, whereas others remain the same or even decline, it seemed important to analyze the course of intraindividual changes in strategy use over time.

In a first step, *group means* for recall performance were calculated, as a function of measurement point (see Figure 4.3). Please note that only 16 toys were presented during the first two measurement points (when children were 4 and 5 years old, respectively), whereas 24 pictures were presented for the 8–18 year olds, and a more difficult list of 24 pictures was presented at the last measurement point, Wave 11 (23-year-olds). Thus, only the findings for the age span 8–18 years are directly comparable. A repeated measures analysis of variance using Age Group as the independent factor and memory performance at each measurement point from 8 through 18 years revealed significant effects of Age Group, $F(1, 169) = 11.21$, $p < .001$, and Measurement Point, $F(3, 507) = 136.29$, $p < .001$. Linear, quadratic, and cubic trends were all significant, $F(1, 169) = 328.48$, 15.85, and 15.43, respectively, with all p's $< .001$, indicating the presence of nonlinear developmental trends in the data. Overall, children in the older age group remembered more than those in the younger group, and memory performance increased

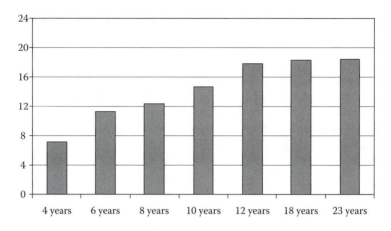

FIGURE 4.3   Free recall in the sort–recall task, as a function of time.

steadily over time until the age of 12. Although memory performance also tended to increase between ages 12 and 18, the difference was not significant. Obviously, mean memory performance in a strategic memory task such as sort–recall does not increase reliably after participants reach early adolescence. There was no significant Age Group × Measurement Point interaction, indicating that the memory advantage of the older group remained stable over time.

Group means were also calculated for sorting during study and clustering during recall, and are given in Figure 4.4. The mean ratio of repetition (RR) scores for sorting during study suggest a rather continuous increase from age 8 to age 12, with no further improvement observed from age 12 onward, which seems mainly due to ceiling effects. Given that a more difficult item list was used with the 23 year olds, the decrease in sorting from age 18 to age 23 does not come as a surprise. A repeated measures analysis of variance using Age Group as the independent factor and Measurement Point (spanning the period between 8 and 18 years) as the dependent factor yielded a significant main effect of Measurement Point, $F(3, 501) = 45.45, p < .001$. There was no effect of Age Group and no interaction. The respective analysis of variance carried out for the clustering scores showed a similar pattern of results, even though the absolute level of group means was below that obtained for the sorting scores. Overall, these data seem to indicate that most participants improved their memory strategies and recall performance as a function of time, at least until the age of 12.

A second major step of analysis concerned the *stability of individual differences*. If the majority of children roughly followed the developmental paths that the group data suggest, then one would expect high group stabilities over time. That is, the rank orders of participants concerning their strategic behavior and memory performance should remain relatively constant, with those showing an advantage at an early measurement point also keeping this advantage over

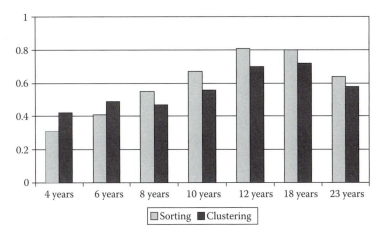

FIGURE 4.4   Sorting during encoding and clustering during recall in the sort–recall task (ratio of repetition [RR] scores), as a function of age.

time. This is not what we found. As can be seen from Table 4.3, individual stability of recall performance was moderate, ranging between .29 and .36, whereas the stabilities for both sorting at encoding and clustering during recall tended to be low and mostly nonsignificant (scores ranging between .07 and .29). These findings cannot be attributed to measurement error because short-term stabilities assessed within intervals of 2–3 weeks were high even for the preschoolers (see the last column of Table 4.3). It appears, then, that individual children considerably changed their relative position in the sample between adjacent measurement points. Accordingly, the model of gradual improvement that fits the group data pretty well does not adequately describe strategy acquisition in most children.

A closer inspection of intraindividual change scores concerning the sorting strategy confirmed this hypothesis. Interestingly, about 80% of the children "jumped" from chance level to near perfection, another 8% were almost perfect from the start, and 8% showed a pattern of gradual increase as suggested by the group data. Almost 4% of the participants did not acquire the sorting strategy during the course of the longitudinal study. Figure 4.5 further shows that there was considerable variation in the age at which children first used the strategy. Thus, some of the instability in strategic behavior over time can be explained by individual variation in the time of strategy discovery. Participants went from chance levels to near perfection, but they did so at different points in time. Finally, it seems important to note that not everybody who acquired the strategy also kept it further on. In fact, a large percentage of children showing the sorting strategy at an early age subsequently lost it, and then rediscovered the strategy at a later point in time. The later the strategy was first discovered, the higher the probability that it was kept throughout the study.

TABLE 4.3

Short-Term[a] and Long-Term Individual Stabilities for the Recall, Sorting, and Clustering Measures

A. Short-Term Stabilities

| | Age | | | | | |
	4–6	6–8	8–10	10–12	12–18	Short Term
Recall	.36	.29	.39	.38	.36	.68
Sorting	.17	.12	.07	.16	.06	.85
Clustering	.12	.16	.12	.29	.17	.64

B. Long-Term Stabilities

| | Age | | | | |
	4–8	8–12	6–12	4–12	4–18
Recall	.30	.36	.30	.16	.14
Sorting	.08	.16	–.09	.06	.07
Clustering	.08	.17	.004	.22	.10

[a.] Short-term stabilities for a 6-week interval are given in the last column of the upper part of the table.

In sum, our analyses of individual change patterns showed that the large majority of participants deviated considerably from the developmental pattern suggested by the group data. Participants showed "leaps" and U-shaped curves, and they did so at different points in time. This finding also explains the low stabilities described above: It was impossible to predict the relative position of individual children at any measurement point from their ranking at a previous measurement point.

When the findings of low individual stabilities in sorting and clustering over time were first reported (Sodian & Schneider, 1999), one response was to highlight the problem of long delays between adjacent measurement points (about 2 years). Theoretically, it could well be that the "rapid" transition from nonstrategic to strategic behavior observed within 2 years could reflect a steady, more continuous change (see Ornstein, 1999). To test for this possibility, we carried out another short-term longitudinal study, the Würzburg Longitudinal Memory Study, in Würzburg, Germany, that used the same instruments but measured performance over shorter test–retest intervals (i.e., 6 months). The findings of this more recent longitudinal study (Schneider, Hünnerkopf, & Kron-Sperl, in press) are contrasted with those of the LOGIC study in Figure 4.5.

Given that the age range for the Munich Longitudinal Study was considerably larger (4–12 years) than that of the Würzburg study (6–10 years) and that the Würzburg materials included a more difficult item list, it is not surprising that there were fewer nonstrategists and more "jumpers" in the Munich Longi-

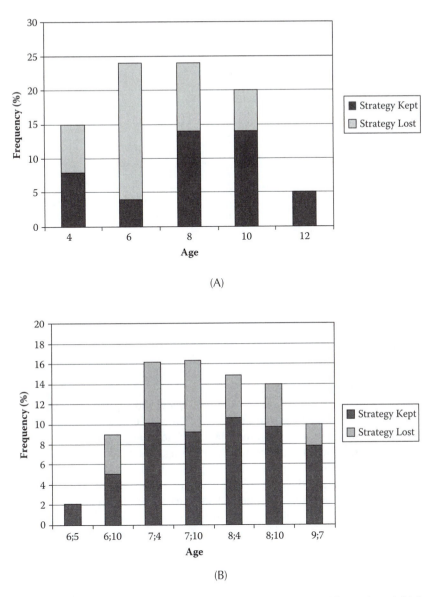

FIGURE 4.5   Patterns of Strategy acquisition found in (a) the LOGIC sample and (b) the Würzburg Longitudinal Study.

tudinal Study than in the Würzburg sample. The findings for the two samples, compared in Figure 4.6, show more "jumpers" in the LOGIC sample than in the Würzburg study, and more gradual increasers in the Würzburg study. However, a closer analysis of the Würzburg data reveals that the number of children who jumped from chance to perfect sorting from one measurement point to the next

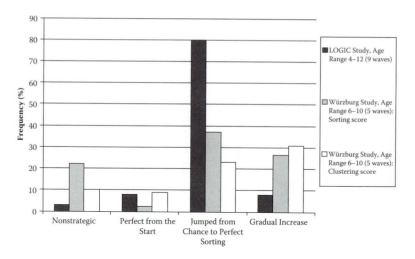

FIGURE 4.6 Individual patterns of strategy acquisition.

was greater than the number of children who gradually acquired the strategy. A similar pattern arose when clustering scores were used to define strategic behavior, even though the proportion of nonstrategic children and "jumpers" was lower compared to that found for the sorting data.

Another comparison addressed the frequency with which children maintained or lost the strategy as a function of age. Most of the LOGIC children who acquired the sorting strategy in kindergarten subsequently lost it again, whereas the majority of children who first used the sorting strategy during the course of the elementary school years kept it in subsequent waves. Although Würzburg children who first used the strategy in elementary school also tended to retain it, particularly in the age range between 7 and 9 years, those few children from the Würzburg sample who picked up the sorting strategy during kindergarten did not lose it again at later measurement points. Overall, significantly more children kept than lost the strategy.

In both samples, a comparison of *strategy discoverers* and *nonstrategists* showed that strategy acquisition was in fact accompanied by significantly increased recall performance for most of the strategy discoverers. Thus, the findings of the Munich Longitudinal Study by and large generalized to those obtained in the Würzburg Longitudinal Study, even though the instability in strategy acquisition patterns observed in the Munich Longitudinal Study was less pronounced. A comparison of the two studies does confirm the importance of time lag size between adjacent measurement points.

4.4.1.4   Text Recall

In the following, we analyze developmental trends in memory for text information as a function of story type, and we explore interrelations in age-related increases in recall obtained for the four stories. A detailed account of findings for the age period of 4–12 years can be found in Knopf (1999). Figure 4.7 presents some of these data. As can be seen from the upper part of Figure 4.7, the number of propositions recalled for the three stories presented in the earlier stages of the LOGIC study increased with age. Preliminary analyses revealed that there were no sex differences. Consequently, data were aggregated across this variable. Repeated measures analyses of variance using Age Group as the independent factor yielded significant effects of Age Group and Measurement Point, regardless of story type. That is, memory performance was generally better for the older subgroup, and overall performance increased significantly as a function of time. There was no significant interaction. Posthoc tests revealed that with one exception, all memory improvements between adjacent measurement points were statistically significant, regardless of the story under study. The only exception was the "Removal" story, where the difference in recall performance in Waves 3 and 4 was not statistically reliable. Overall, 4 year olds recalled about 20% of the information included in the "Birthday Party" and "Playing in the Afternoon" texts; and 8-year-olds recalled about 50% of the text information, reflecting substantial improvement in text recall from the preschool to the early elementary school years.

In Wave 6, the considerably longer Mauerburg story ($N = 362$ propositions and 31 sentences) was first presented to the 9-year-old participants. This story was also given in Waves 7, 9, 10, and 11. As can be seen from the lower part of Figure 4.7, recall of the Mauerburg text propositions increased remarkably between Waves 6 and 9, but remained stable after that. A repeated measures analysis of variance on the Mauerburg propositional units using Age Group as the independent factor yielded main effects of Age Group, $F(1, 127) = 8.99$, $p < .01$, and Measurement Point, $F(4, 508) = 92.54$, $p < .001$. Both the linear and quadratic trends for Measurement Point turned out to be significant, $F(1, 127) = 146.33$ and 49.75, respectively, with both p's $< .001$. There was no significant interaction. Subsequent post-tests revealed that participants in the older group outperformed those in the younger group on all measurement points, and that improvements observed between Waves 6 and 7 and between Waves 7 and 9 were statistically reliable. From Wave 9 onward, there was no significant increase in text recall. It appears, then, that memory for text reached its peak by early adolescence. Given that less than one third of the text propositions were correctly remembered at Wave 9 or subsequent measurement points, these findings could not be attributed to possible ceiling effects in the data.

In contrast to the findings reported for the sort–recall task, *interindividual differences in text recall* were rather stable over time. As already noted by Knopf (1999), autocorrelations obtained for the same measures between adjacent measurement points were moderate to high, varying between .45 and .56 for the three texts given in the early phase of the LOGIC study (i.e., "Birthday Party," "Playing

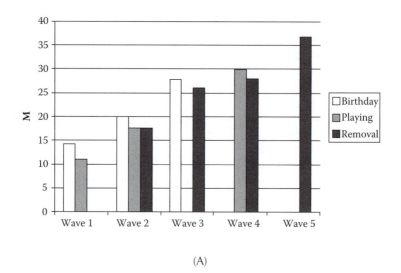

(A)

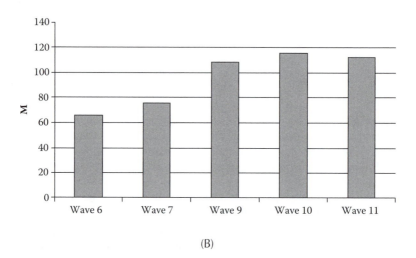

(B)

FIGURE 4.7   Development of text recall (number of propositions). *Note*: a = Stories presented in the early phase of the study (B = "birthday party," P = "playing in the afternoon," and R = "removal story"). b = development of text recall for the "Mauerburg" story (*n* of propositions).

in the Afternoon," and "Removal"). Test–retest correlations for the Mauerburg story were even more impressive, ranging from .55 for the 6-year period between Waves 9 and 10 to .65 for the 2-year interval between Waves 7 and 9, and .66 for the 5-year interval between Waves 10 and 11. These results make it clear that individual differences in the various text recall measures were already stable from an early point in time onward, and became even more stable with age. The ability to learn, store, and recall text information seems to develop rather early in childhood and to progress at a similar pace.

There were also substantial synchronous and diachronous intercorrelations among the various text recall measures, with coefficients ranging between .26 ("Birthday Party" at age 4 with the Mauerburg text at the age of 23) and .65 (the "Birthday Party" and "Removal" stories at the age of 5). Interestingly, the synchronous and diachronous correlations found for these two stories between ages 4 and 8 tended to be higher than their autocorrelations during the same age period. Moreover, text recall was generally substantially intercorrelated with verbal IQ, with coefficients varying between .36 and .54.

4.4.1.5   Standardized Memory Test

As noted above, a standardized verbal learning and memory test (the LGT) consisting of three components (Vocabulary, Telephone Numbers, and Library Instructions) was presented in Waves 10 and 11. Raw scores were calculated for each of the subscales and combined to form a total score. The total raw scores were converted to standardized scores (T scores). Preliminary analyses revealed that there were no sex differences, regardless of measurement point. This variable was not included in the analyses reported below.

A repeated measures analysis of variance on the LGT total test scores using Age Group as an independent variable revealed effects of Age Group, $F(1, 125) = 6.24$, $p < .05$, and Measurement Point, $F(1, 125) = 86.02$, $p < .001$. Overall, the older age group performed better than the younger group, and test performance increased significantly from age 18 to age 23. The latter finding was unexpected given that the results for the other memory measures reported earlier in this chapter all indicated peak performance in early or late adolescence. There was no interaction effect.

In a next step, repeated measures analyses of variance were carried out on the three verbal subtests of the LGT, using Age Group as the independent factor. Significant effects of Measurement Point were found for all subtests (Vocabulary: $F(1, 145) = 29.20$; Telephone Numbers: $F(1, 145) = 13.40$; and Library Construction: $F(1, 145) = 70.28$, with all p's < .01). There were also significant effects of Age Group for the Telephone Numbers and Library Construction subtests, $F(1, 145) = 4.26$ and 7.73, respectively, with all p's < .05. However, there was no effect of Age Group on Vocabulary, and no significant interaction. Table 4.4 gives the means and standard deviations in raw scores for the three verbal subtests, as a function of Age Group.

One of the reasons to include the standardized verbal memory measure(LGT) in our study was to use it as a criterion measure, reflecting verbal memory ability in adolescence and early adulthood. Given that LGT total scores obtained for Waves 10 and 11 were highly correlated ($r = .66$), only the LGT score obtained in Wave 11 was used as a criterion variable in subsequent regression analyses. In a first stepwise multiple regression analysis, IQ, age group, sentence span, recall

TABLE 4.4
Raw Scores for the Three Verbal Subtests of the Learning and Memory Test (LGT) as a Function of Measurement Wave

	Wave	Mean	SD	Minimum	Maximum
Turkish Vocabulary					
Total sample (N = 167)	10	9.87	3.36	3	20
Total sample (N = 148)	11	11.76	3.83	3	20
Telephone Numbers					
Total sample (N = 174)	10	6.37	2.93	0	13
Total sample (N = 150)	11	7.31	3.23	0	13
Library Construction					
Total sample (N = 174)	10	8.53	4.33	0	21
Total sample (N = 150)	11	12.29	3.62	0	22

in the sort–recall task, and text recall (the "Removal" story) assessed in the last year of kindergarten were used as predictors. Both IQ and age group turned out to be significant predictors of performance in the LGT test, explaining about 13% of the variance in the criterion variable. Surprisingly, no further impact of text recall and working memory was found. A second regression analysis tested the assumption that using similar predictors assessed in late childhood would explain more variance in the standardized verbal memory test given about 10 years later. Again, IQ, age group, sentence span, recall in the sort–recall task, and text recall (the "Mauerburg" story) served as predictor variables. Much to our surprise, only the verbal IQ measure and text recall contributed to the prediction of performance in the LGT test, explaining about 15% of the variance in the criterion variable. To explore whether the same predictor variables assessed in late adolescence would explain a more substantial amount of variance in LGT performance in young adulthood, a further regression analysis included IQ, age group, sentence span, recall in the sort–recall task, and text recall ("Mauerburg") assessed at Wave 10 as predictor variables. Verbal IQ and free recall in the sort–recall task turned out to be reliable predictors, accounting for about 25% of the variance in the criterion variable. This pattern did not change much when a set of Wave 11 predictors was used to predict performance on the LGT. Again, verbal IQ and free recall in the free recall task explained most of the variance, followed by the sentence span measure. In total, about 33% of the variance in the LGT criterion measure was accounted for by these three predictors.

4.4.1.6   Interrelations Among Working Memory, Strategic Memory, and Text Recall

One issue that has not been addressed in previous research on memory development is whether interrelations among various components of verbal memory assessed at a particular point in time will change with age. So far, most studies on intraindividual consistency in memory performance are cross-sectional, comparing memory performance in kindergarteners and elementary school children (e.g., Cavanaugh & Borkowski, 1980; Kail, 1979; Knopf, Körkel, Schneider, & Weinert, 1988; Kurtz-Costes, Schneider, & Rupp, 1995). Overall, the outcomes of these studies were similar in that intertask correlations obtained for various verbal memory tasks were rather low and nonsignificant in most cases. Although some studies reported greater consistency in performance across tasks for older children (e.g., Cavanaugh & Borkowski, 1980; Knopf et al., 1988), others did not show such a pattern of age-related increase (Kail, 1979; Kurtz-Costes, et al., 1995). A first longitudinal assessment using data from the LOGIC study (Schneider & Weinert, 1995) also did not support the view of verbal memory as a unitary function.

In the following, we update the data analysis carried out by Schneider and Weinert (1995), including relevant data from late childhood to early adulthood. We correlated memory performance on the sentence span, free recall (sort–recall), and text recall tasks obtained in Waves 3 (end of kindergarten), 7 (grade 3), and 11 (young adulthood). An aggregate score for text recall based on the three stories was calculated for Wave 3. Table 4.5 shows the intercorrelations among these three verbal memory measures, as a function of measurement point. As a main result, it was found that working memory, strategic memory, and text recall

---

TABLE 4.5

Intercorrelations Among Measures of Working Memory, Strategic Memory (Sort–Recall), and Text Recall as a Function of Time

	Free Recall	Text Recall
Sentence Span		
Wave 3	.222**	.303**
Wave 7	.290**	.383**
Wave 11	.124	.327**
Free Recall		
Wave 3	1	.331**
Wave 7		.258**
Wave 11		.374**

** p = .01.

were only moderately associated throughout the course of the longitudinal study. Correlations between the sentence span and sort–recall measures were lowest, compared to correlations between working memory and text recall or between sort–recall and text recall. Remarkably, none of these correlations increased significantly over time. Accordingly, one major conclusion drawn from these findings is that the overlap in variance among measures tapping various aspects of verbal memory is rather modest, regardless of time of measurement. Although there has been plenty of evidence in the literature showing that memory is not a unitary function, the fact that verbal memory is not a unitary function either was less well-known.

4.5 CONCLUSIONS

Although some assumptions regarding memory development from childhood to young adulthood predominant in the early 1980s when the LOGIC study started have been revised over the past decades, most issues relevant at that time are still important today. For instance, we still want to know more about the "normal" course of verbal memory development and are interested in issues of stability in memory functions over time.

In our view, one of the major outcomes of the LOGIC study is that the developmental function regarding different memory components such as working memory, strategic memory, and text recall may reach its peak by middle to late adolescence. Whereas earlier analyses including the age range between 4 and 12 years suggested more or less continuous, linear change patterns over time (see Weinert, Bullock, & Schneider, 1999), this view cannot be maintained based on the data collected during adolescence and young adulthood. Accordingly, the developmental functions found for the three verbal memory components under consideration in this chapter are similar in that they suggest nonlinear trends, even though the local maxima may vary as a function of the component under study.

A second interesting finding concerns interindividual stability in intraindividual change over time. In the few longitudinal studies on memory development already available at the beginning of the LOGIC study, stabilities characterizing individuals' relative standing in their reference group across longer time intervals were similar to average group stabilities over time (e.g., Kunzinger, 1985). This conclusion was supported for the developmental trends found for the sentence span and text recall measures used in the LOGIC study. This finding indicates that for these memory variables, most participants increase performance at about the same pace, with the implication that interindividual differences found in initial phases of assessment persist over time. However, such stability was not similarly true for the word span measure, and was completely different for strategic memory in the sort–recall task. In the strategic memory task, we found that group stabilities were low from the beginning. Thus, the pattern of steady increases over time indicated by the group mean development (and suggested from cross-sectional studies) was in fact misleading: The majority of children "jumped" from nonstrategic to strategic between two adjacent measurement points, and only a minority showed a pattern of gradual increase as suggested by the group data or cross-sectional studies. The pattern of linear increase in the group data occurred because the rapid change in individuals from nonstrategic to strategic occurs at different points in time. Although subsequent longitudinal studies such as the Würzburg Memory Study revealed that the number of "jumpers" may have been overestimated given the large time lag between the two adjacent measurement points in the LOGIC study (about 2 years), using a much shorter time lag in the Würzburg study did not change the pattern of findings fundamentally. Thus, it appears that interindividual stability in intraindividual change varies across verbal memory domains.

This could explain another unexpected finding: Although we did not have very clear-cut expectations about developmental changes in interrelationships among the three verbal memory components (either increasing or decreasing over time), we expected them to be rather closely related from the beginning. This turned out to be an incorrect assumption: Intercorrelations among the three verbal memory components were of only moderate size at the start of the LOGIC study and did not change much over the course of the project. In fact, the size of correlations among the three verbal memory components was comparable to that found for their correlation with verbal IQ. Although it was already clear from the literature that memory cannot be considered as a unitary function, the insight that it may be more appropriate to talk about several distinct verbal memory abilities instead of assuming a single verbal memory factor was a new finding and somewhat surprising to us. The fact that performance on the standardized verbal memory test (LGT) assessed in young adulthood was not well predicted by the verbal memory measures confirms this conclusion.

Analyses of the impact of differences in relative chronological age on memory performance yielded unexpected results that cannot be found in cross-sectional studies. Originally, we had believed that a mean age difference of a few (3–4) months in the sample might affect memory performance, especially in young childhood, given that each additional month of life experience seems to count for increased cognitive performance during the preschool years. We did not expect, however, that the two age groups selected by a median split procedure would also show different levels of memory performance in later periods of the study. A closer look at the data revealed that this finding may be due to a sampling problem. The younger children in the LOGIC sample had lower IQs than the older children, with mean IQ differences varying between 5 and 10 points across measurement points. These IQ differences were found from the very beginning onward and did not disappear in later phases of the study. Using IQ as a covariate did substantially reduce the impact of the age factor on memory performance. This finding also shows that deficits in cognitive functioning in general and memory abilities in particular first identified during preschool seem to persist until young adulthood. In accord with this observation, the subsample of children in the younger age group ($N = 29$) who started elementary school one year later than the rest of the sample had lower IQs from the very beginning onward and never caught up with the older participants regarding IQ and memory performance. In sum, we believe that the LOGIC study provides many interesting insights about memory changes from young childhood to early adulthood. Although recent research on memory development (still mostly cross-sectional in nature) has addressed issues not included in the LOGIC study such as infant memory, memory in toddlers, and children's testimony (see Bauer, 2006; Bruck & Ceci, 1999), and also further elaborated on many of the concepts included in our study such as working memory and strategic memory (see contributions to Cowan, in press; Schneider & Bjorklund, 2003), there is little doubt that findings from the LOGIC study gave us new insight into the developmental course of verbal memory functions and the important role of interindividual differences in intraindividual memory changes (not available from cross-sectional research). Needless to say, the study also leaves several open questions and unsolved problems. Fortunately, more longitudinal research on memory development is on its way, which should further improve our understanding of how skilled remembering appears and develops from early childhood to adulthood.

REFERENCES

Baddeley, A. D. (1986). *Working memory.* New York: Oxford University Press.

Bauer, P. (2006). *Remembering the times of our lives: Memory in infancy and beyond.* Mahwah, NJ: Erlbaum.

Bäumler, G. (1974). *Lern- und Gedächtnistest LGT-3* [Learning and Memory Test LGT-3]. Göttingen, Germany: Hogrefe.

Bjorklund, D. F., & Schneider, W. (1996). The interaction of knowledge, aptitudes, and strategies in children's memory performance. In H. W. Reese (Ed.), *Advances in child development and behaviour* (Vol. 25, pp. 59–89). San Diego, CA: Academic Press.

Bruck, M., & Ceci, S. J. (1999). The suggestibility of children's memory. *Annual Reviews of Psychology, 50,* 419–439.

Case, R., Kurland, D. M., & Goldberg, J. (1982). Operational efficiency and the growth of short-term memory span. *Journal of Experimental Child Psychology, 33,* 386–404.

Cavanaugh, J. C., & Borkowski, J. G. (1980). Searching for metamemory-memory connections: A developmental study. *Developmental Psychology, 16,* 441–453.

Cavanaugh, J. C., & Perlmutter, M. (1982). Metamemory: A critical examination. *Child Development, 53,* 11–28.

Chi, M. T. H. (1978). Knowledge structures and memory development. In R. S. Siegler (Ed.), *Children's thinking: What develops?* (pp. 73–96). Hillsdale, NJ: Erlbaum.

Cowan, N. (In press). *The development of memory in childhood* (2nd ed.). Hove, UK: Psychology Press.

Daneman, M., & Blennerhassett, A. (1984). How to assess the listening comprehension skills of prereaders. *Journal of Educational Psychology, 76,* 1372–1381.

Ebbinghaus, H. (1885). *Über das Gedächtnis* [About memory]. Leipzig, Germany: Duncker.

Fivush, R., & Stackman, E. (1986). The acquisition and development of scripts. In K. Nelson (Ed.), *Event knowledge: Structure and function in development* (pp. 71–96). Hillsdale, NJ: Erlbaum.

Flavell, J. H. (1985). *Cognitive development* (2nd ed.). Englewood Cliffs, NJ: Prentice Hall.

Flavell, J. H., Miller, P. H., & Miller, S. (1993). *Cognitive development* (3rd ed.). Englewood Cliffs, NJ: Prentice Hall.

Flavell, J. H., & Wellman, H. M. (1977). Metamemory. In R. V. Kail & J. W. Hagen (Eds.), *Perspectives on the development of memory and cognition* (pp. 3–33). Hillsdale, NJ: Erlbaum.

Hudson, J. A., & Nelson, K. (1983). Effects of script structure on children's story recall. *Developmental Psychology, 19*, 625–635.

Kail, R. V. (1979). Use of strategies and individual differences in children's memory. *Developmental Psychology, 15*, 251–255.

Kail, R. V. (1990). *The development of memory in children* (3rd ed.). New York: Freeman.

Kail, R. V. (1991). Processing time declines exponentially during childhood and adolescence. *Developmental Psychology, 27*, 259–266.

Knopf, M. (1999). Development of memory for texts. In F. E. Weinert & W. Schneider (Eds.), *Individual development from 3 to 12: Findings from the Munich Longitudinal Study* (pp. 106–122). Cambridge: Cambridge University Press.

Knopf, M., Körkel, J., Schneider, W., & Weinert, F. E. (1988). Human memory as a faculty versus human memory as a set of specific abilities: Evidence from a life-span approach. In F. E. Weinert & M. Perlmutter (Eds.), *Memory development: Universal changes and individual differences* (pp. 331–352). Hillsdale, NJ: Erlbaum.

Kreutzer, M. A., Leonard, S. C., & Flavell, J. H. (1975). An interview study of children's knowledge about memory. *Monographs of the society for research in child development, 40*(1, Serial No. 159), 1–60.

Kunzinger, E. L. (1985). A short-term longitudinal study of memorial development during early grade school. *Developmental Psychology, 21*, 642–646.

Kurtz-Costes, B., Schneider, W., & Rupp, S. (1995). Is there evidence for intraindividual consistency in performance across memory tasks? New evidence on an old question. In F. W. Weinert & W. Schneider (Eds.), *Memory performance and competencies: Issues in growth and development* (pp. 245–262). Mahwah, NJ: Erlbaum.

Ornstein, P. A. (1999). Comments: Toward an understanding of the development of memory. In F. E. Weinert & W. Schneider (Eds.), *Individual development from 3 to 12: Findings from the Munich Longitudinal Study* (pp. 94–105). Cambridge: Cambridge University Press.

Pressley, M., Forrest-Pressley, D. L., Elliott-Faust, D. J., & Miller, G. E. (1985). Children's use of cognitive strategies, how to teach strategies, and what to do if they can't be taught. In M. Pressley & C. J. Brainerd (Eds.), *Cognitive learning and memory in children* (pp. 1–47). New York: Springer.

Recht, D. R., & Leslie, L. (1988). Effect of prior knowledge on good and poor reader's memory of text. *Journal of Educational Psychology, 80*, 16–20.

Schneider, W. (1985). Developmental trends in the metamemory-memory behavior relationship: An integrative review. In D. L. Forrest-Pressley, G. E. MacKinnon, & T. G. Waller (Eds.), *Metacognition, cognition, and human performance* (Vol. 1, pp. 57–109). Orlando, FL: Academic Press.

Schneider, W., & Bjorklund, D. F. (1998). Memory. In D. Kuhn & R. S. Siegler (Vol. Eds.), *Handbook of child psychology. Vol. 2: Cognition, perception, and language* (5th ed., pp. 467–521). New York: Wiley.

Schneider, W., & Bjorklund, D. F. (2003). Memory and knowledge development. In J. Valsiner & K. J. Connolly (Eds.), *Handbook of developmental psychology* (pp. 370–395). London: Sage.

Schneider, W., Hünnerkopf, M., & Kron-Sperl, V. (In press). The development of young children's memory strategies: Evidence from the Würzburg Longitudinal Memory Study. *European Journal of Developmental Psychology.*

Schneider, W., Körkel, J., & Weinert, F. E. (1989). Domain-specific knowledge and memory performance: A comparison of high- and low-aptitude children. *Journal of Educational Psychology, 81,* 306–312.

Schneider, W., & Pressley, M. (1997). *Memory development between 2 and 20.* Hillsdale, NJ: Erlbaum.

Schneider, W., & Weinert, F. E. (1989). Universal trends and individual differences in memory development. In A. de Ribaupierre (Ed.), *Transition mechanisms in child development: The longitudinal perspective* (pp. 68–106). Cambridge: Cambridge University Press.

Schneider, W., & Weinert, F. E. (1995). Memory development during early and middle childhood: Findings from the Munich Longitudinal Study (LOGIC). In F. E. Weinert & W. Schneider (Eds.), *Memory performance and competencies: Issues in growth and development* (pp. 263–279). Mahwah, NJ: Erlbaum.

Sodian, B., & Schneider, W. (1999). Memory strategy development: Gradual increase, sudden insight or roller coaster? In F. E. Weinert & W. Schneider (Eds.), *Individual development from 3 to 12: Findings from the Munich Longitudinal Study* (pp. 61–77). Cambridge: Cambridge University Press.

Wagner, R., & Torgesen, J. (1987). The nature of phonological processing and its causal role in the acquisition of reading skills. *Psychological Bulletin, 101,* 192–212.

Weinert, F. E., Bullock, M., & Schneider, W. (1999). Universal, differential, and individual aspects of child development from 3 to 12: What can we learn from a comprehensive longitudinal study? In F. E. Weinert & W. Schneider (Eds.), *Individual development from 3 to 12: Findings from the Munich Longitudinal Study* (pp. 324–350). Cambridge: Cambridge University Press.

Weinert, F. E., Schneider, W., & Knopf, M. (1988). Individual differences in memory development across the life-span. In P. B. Baltes, D. L. Featherman, & R. M. Lerner (Eds.), *Life-span development and behavior* (Vol. 9, pp. 39–85). Hillsdale, NJ: Erlbaum.

Wohlwill, J. (1973). *The study of behavioural development.* New York: Academic Press.

5 Moral Motivation from Childhood to Early Adulthood*

Gertrud Nunner-Winkler

5.1 INTRODUCTION

In the following, I will address the development of one aspect of moral development, the development of moral motivation. *Moral motivation* refers to the concerns and motives underlying moral actions (e.g., reasons for "why" one should follow moral rules). Data from the Munich Longitudinal Study on the Ontogenesis of Individual Competencies (the LOGIC study) allow tracing the development of moral motivation from childhood to early adulthood. In this chapter I will first specify the research questions, and then summarize the measurement procedures used in early childhood at ages 4, 6, and 8 and findings on children's understanding of moral rules and on the types of concerns motivating conformity that have been published (Nunner-Winkler, 1998, 1999). Next, I will describe the measurement procedures used in adolescence and early adulthood at ages 18 and 23 and will present longitudinal analyses that concern the distribution of strength of moral motivation and the stability of interindividual differences. I will conclude with an exploration of the factors affecting differences in stability.

5.2 RESEARCH QUESTIONS

Over the past 30 years, research on morality has primarily focused on moral reasoning following Kohlberg's (1981, 1984) original assumption of a cognitive-affective parallelism. Kohlberg claimed that in moral development there is a structural equivalence between the reasons justifying norm validity (cognitive aspect) and the concerns motivating conformity (affective aspect). To illustrate: At the preconventional level of moral development (i.e., up to age 10–11), children believe norms are valid because they are set by authorities and backed by

---

* In the present text children's ages are one year above the ages I had reported in previous publications, e.g. childhood testing ages are now given as 5, 7, and 9 years and before where given as 4, 6, and 8 years. In fact, at the time of testing for moral understanding, the children were between 4–5, 6–7 etc. In LOGIC, the various measurement points of each wave, at which the different variables were assessed, were distributed over the year whereas in the present publication the mappings of ages and waves were harmonized across variables.

sanctions and are followed to avoid punishment or win rewards. At the conventional level (characteristic of most people), norms are believed to be valid because they are in fact predominant and are followed to win social acceptance or avoid pangs of conscience. Only at the postconventional level (attained by just a few people) are norms believed to be derived from universal moral principles (e.g., justice, equality, and dignity of the person) and followed from insight.

Theoretical analyses (Blasi, 1980, 1983; Rest, 1986, 1999) and more recent empirical work (Colby & Damon, 1992; Nunner-Winkler, 1998; Thoma, 1986; Walker, 1999; Walker, de Vries, & Trevethan, 1987), however, suggest that moral reasoning (i.e., reflections on the question "What is right?") and moral motivation (i.e., reflections on the question "Why do what is right?") are partially independent dimensions of morality. In consequence, researchers today have explicitly addressed the "relative neglect of moral character and virtues" in Kohlberg's model (Walker & Pitts, 1998, p. 403) and considered the study of moral motivation an "important complement and extension" of work on moral reasoning (Pratt, Hunsberger, Pancer, & Alisat, 2003, p. 582). The present research focuses on this dimension.

In the course of the LOGIC study, we explored the development of *moral motivation* from childhood until early adulthood. We addressed several issues: (a) the types of motives underlying norm conformity, (b) the strength of moral motivation, (c) the stability of moral motivation across the age span in the study, and (d) factors explaining differences in strength of moral motivation.

5.2.1 TYPES OF MOTIVES UNDERLYING NORM CONFORMITY

People have been hypothesized to follow norms for different reasons or causes. They may be guided by personal interests or by concerns about the welfare of others. They may be disposed to follow norms because of a well-developed and deeply ingrained habitual need disposition for conformity (Parsons, 1964) or because they internalized social rules during the course of the oedipal crisis and feel rigidly controlled by a severe superego (Freud, 1933/1974). They may act from a desire to maintain their personal integrity or from respect for moral rules (Kant, 1785/1962).

Of course, not all of these concerns qualify as moral. For example, exclusively self-serving interests that focus on personal benefits or costs are excluded from the class of moral motives in the lay understanding of morality (Strawson, 1962). In the following we define a motive as moral only if an individual's judgment is based on an understanding of the obligatory character of the moral "ought" and if the concern motivating the imperative behavior is intrinsically oriented to this understanding. Thus, moral motivation is conceptualized as agents' willingness, even at personal cost, to do what they—to the best of their knowledge—judge to be right. This definition is in line with Kohlberg's cognitive emphasis and also agrees with everyday moral understanding. "Concern about doing the right thing" was given the highest prototypical rating as a descriptor for a moral person (Walker & Pitts, 1998).

The existence of a truly moral motivation is debated. Some theorists characterize humans as motivated exclusively or at least primarily by egotistic or self-directed interests, defined in material, social, or internal terms. Thus, people are motivated to follow norms to avoid punishment or gain rewards (behaviorism), to avoid social disdain (Luhmann, 1990) or win a good reputation (rational choice theories), to avoid suffering from a guilty conscience (psychoanalytic approaches), or to obtain an "inner warm glow feeling" (Andreoni, 1990). However much as the different models of behaviorism, systems theory, rational choice theories, or psychoanalytic approaches differ in some respects, they concur in the basic assumption that human action is guided by individual cost–benefit calculations. Other theories allow for intrinsic value orientations and assume the existence of intrinsic interest in knowledge and truth and in aesthetic, religious, or moral values. Some theories, such as Kohlberg's, organize these different concerns in a hierarchical order to explain why people are motivated to conform. According to Kohlberg, at the postconventional level of moral development an earlier preconventional preoccupation with material gratification and an earlier conventional focus on social and internal sanctions recede and are replaced by a commitment to universal moral principles.

Empirically, there is evidence that both self-serving and intrinsically moral motives underlie dutiful behavior. Thus, fear of detection keeps some people from committing specific offenses (e.g., tax evasion, stealing free rides on public transport, and shoplifting; Hermann, 2003). However, other actions, such as unselfishly helping others or even putting one's life in danger for others, especially visible during times of social unrest, war, or persecution, provide examples of action based on empathic concerns or moral persuasion (Eisenberg, 1986; Monroe, Barton, & Klingemann, 1990; Oliner & Oliner, 1988). Little is known, however, about the relative weight that instrumental considerations or commitment to values has in explaining adherence to norms in unselected samples.

5.2.2 Strength of Moral Motivation

People differ in the importance they attribute to the moral domain. At one end of a continuum, some individuals, called *moral exemplars*, will do what they perceive to be right even if high personal costs are involved (Colby & Damon, 1992). At the other end of the continuum, others (e.g., persons with superego pathologies; Fonagy et al., 1997) seem to lack a moral sense. Little is known, however, about the range of people in between, that is, whether people differ in the extent to which they are willing to follow moral rules, especially when doing so entails personal costs, or, if they do differ, how much they differ.

5.2.3 Stability of Moral Motivation

It is as yet unclear whether to characterize moral motivation as a more or less stable personality trait or as a variable feature. We do know that a seemingly complete lack of concern for others seems to be a stable characteristic, because some children display harmful behavior early in life and remain chronically aggressive through adolescence (Tremblay, 2000, 2003). In addition, some offenders with clear superego deficits repeatedly commit violent crimes (Bittner, 1994; Fonagy, 2004; Marneros, 2002; Rauchfleisch, 1992). It also appears that moral exemplars show high moral commitment throughout their lives. However, the strength of moral motivation might be more intraindividually variable among individuals in the intermediate range.

Also, it is unclear whether the issues that underlie motivation remain the same or change across the life cycle. Theorists such as Kohlberg (1981, 1984) assumed developmental changes from instrumental (prudential) concerns to concerns about social acceptance and then to motivation based on universal moral principles. Thoma and Rest (1999) proposed a more cyclical model in which the content of moral concerns changes as a correlate of the process of restructuring moral reasoning: Instrumental considerations tend to increase as individuals make the transition to a higher stage and to decrease as they reach consolidation in that stage. A longitudinal analysis can address stability issues as they concern the strength of moral motivation and the underlying basis for moral motivation.

5.2.4 CAUSAL FACTORS

There are different explanations for people's willingness to follow moral expectations. Explanations range from genetic predisposition (e.g., to account for altruistic behavior favoring relatives), to early experience (e.g., secure attachment patterns; Bowlby, 1987), to socialization practices that rely on argumentative reasoning rather than on physical punishment (Hoffmann & Salzstein, 1967) and use a correct mix of warmth and control (Baumrind, 1971; Kochanska, Aksan, Knaack, & Rhines, 2004; Kochanska, Aksan, & Koenig, 1995; for an overview, see Gibbs, 2003). Opportunities for role-taking experiences and demands for accepting responsibility (e.g., in just communities) are assumed to promote moral development and thus the growth of intrinsic moral motivation (Higgins, 1991; Higgins, Power, & Kohlberg, 1984). Norm consistency between the family and school, sport clubs and church associations, and the workplace and the community (Damon, 1997), as well as higher social economic status, are seen to protect against deviant and criminal behaviors. Gender is assumed to be of importance, with women taken to be more considerate, helpful, and cooperative (Gilligan, 1982; Gilligan & Wiggins, 1987).

5.3 THE DEVELOPMENT OF MORAL UNDERSTANDING BETWEEN 5 AND 9

The starting point for the data to be presented is a controversy in the description of children's moral understanding. As noted above, Kohlberg (1984) assumed that children until about 10 to 11 years believe that moral rules are valid because they are set by authorities and backed by sanctions and are obeyed because people seek to avoid punishment or win rewards. Turiel (1983; Nucci & Turiel, 1993), however, found that from early on, children clearly differentiate between moral rules (to which they ascribe an unalterable, universal, and intrinsic validity) and conventional rules (that are set by authorities or are socially agreed upon). Further, research on altruism has shown that even young children unselfishly help others and share with them (Eisenberg, 1986, Eisenberg & Mussen, 1989, Eisenberg & Strayer, 1987, Hoffman, 2000; for a review see Gibbs, 2003). These seemingly contradictory characterizations might result from differences in measurement procedures. Kohlberg assessed moral understanding by requesting action recommendations in moral dilemmas, whereas Turiel explored children's understanding of norms, and altruism researchers observed children's spontaneous behavior. A distinction between moral understanding and moral motivation may help clarify these seemingly inconsistent findings. Before children have well-developed moral motivation, it is possible that although they do understand the intrinsic nature of moral norms in line with Turiel's findings, they nonetheless provide pragmatic answers to Kohlberg's question "What should the protagonist do?" and recommend doing what best serves the protagonist's needs. Analogously, in line with findings on altruism, although children might be quite willing to help and share, this may occur only when they feel like doing so. For clarifying these issues, one needs to disentangle the measurement of moral knowledge and moral motivation and assess moral motivation in situations where spontaneous desires collide with moral norms. The measures of moral motivation in the LOGIC study were developed with these goals in mind.

5.3.1 MEASURES

5.3.1.1 Measure of Moral Motivation

At ages 5, 7, and 9 (Waves 2, 4, and 6), children were presented four moral conflicts in which a (same-sex) protagonist was tempted to transgress a moral rule to satisfy a personal desire. The stories were structurally identical across measurement points. Across stories, there were two negative duties (e.g., not to steal and not to profit from an injustice) and two positive duties (e.g., to share and to help). Only superficial adaptations of content were made to increase age appropriateness (e.g., helping related to making cookies at age 5, and to solving math problems at age 9). For each story, children's moral knowledge of the rules in question was assessed by asking about obligation (e.g., "May one take the sweets, or may one not?" "Does one have to share an unfairly awarded prize with the wronged child?" "Does one have to share one's own drink with a thirsty child?" and "Does one have to help another child in a competitive task?") and asking why each obligation held or did not hold. The story went on to show that the protagonist gave in to the temptation (i.e., stole, or did not share or help). Children's moral motivation was assessed by asking them to say how the wrongdoer felt and to justify this emotion ascription. In one of the stories, another character did not give in to the temptation, but helped. Strength of moral motivation was operationalized by the number of moral emotion attributions. A child's attribution was classified as *moral* if the emotions were morally appropriate (i.e., if he or she stated that the protagonist felt bad after the rule transgression or good after rule conformity, and justified these on moral terms).

The basis for operationalizing moral motivation by emotion attributions to hypothetical wrongdoers is a cognitivist understanding of emotions according to which emotions reflect cognitive judgments concerning the subjective importance attributed to given facts (Montada, 1993; Solomon, 1976). In the stories, two facts were simultaneously true of the protagonist: He or she transgressed a norm, and he or she fulfilled a personal desire. By attributing an emotion, children effectively indicate which of these two facts they deem more important (given that younger children tend to attribute to others the same emotions they expect to feel in a like situation; see Barden, Zelko, Duncan, & Masters, 1980).

5.3.1.2   Measure of Moral Behavior

At age 8 (Wave 5), we conducted two interventions to measure moral behavior. Children were tempted to cheat in a guessing game to win an attractive prize and to ruthlessly push through their own interests in a distribution task (see details in Asendorpf & Nunner-Winkler, 1992).

5.3.1.3   Measure of Prima Facie Validity

At age 11 (Wave 8), children's understanding of justifiable exceptions to moral rules was explored. They were questioned about keeping a promise (to cooperate in cleaning up the day after the party) when either a personal desire (e.g., to go swimming instead) or another norm (helping a lost child find the way home) collided with the promise.

5.3.2   RESULTS AND DISCUSSION

The main findings from these earlier measures of moral motivation will briefly be summarized (for details, see Nunner-Winkler, 1998, 1999).

5.3.2.1   Knowledge of Moral Rules

Children know moral rules from early on: 98% of the 5 year olds indicated that stealing is wrong, and 85–90% of the 7 year olds judged that one ought to share or help in the story situations.

5.3.2.2   Understanding the Validity of Moral Rules

Across all stories and measurement points, less than 12% of the participants justified the validity of their choices by referring to positive or negative consequences to the protagonist (e.g., punishment or praise by authorities, acceptance or rejection by peers, or expectations of concrete reciprocity). Consequences to the victim were only mentioned in the drink-sharing story (e.g., "He should share—otherwise, [the victim] will die from thirst"). Children mostly provided deontic judgments, that is, they referred to the fact that a valid norm exists or gave negative evaluations of the wrongdoer or the wrong committed. It is noteworthy that despite superficial similarities, children clearly differentiated between the two sharing stories in their norm justifications. In the "prize story" (sharing an unfairly gained prize), sharing was seen to be required regardless of any consequences either to the protagonist or to the victim because profiting by injustice was judged as intrinsically wrong. In the "drink story" (sharing with a thirsty child), however, sharing was called for because the victim was needy. These findings show that children understand the intrinsic validity of moral rules. This concurs with Turiel's findings and clearly contradicts Kohlberg's description of preconventional children's instrumentalist rule understanding.

5.3.2.3 Prima Facie Validity of Moral Norms

By 10 to 11 years, children judged that breaking a promise for self-serving needs was not legitimate. Nevertheless, they noted that exceptions even to strict negative duties might be justifiable in the service of impartially minimizing harm. As one child put it, "It is worse if the lost child and his parents are in fear than if the other kids have to do a little more cleaning work. If they were in my place, they would decide the same way." Thus, in contrast to Kant's (1797/1959) "ethics of intentions," which may have reflected an earlier moral basis, contemporary children adhered to an "ethics of responsibility" (Weber, 1956), which may reflect sociohistorical differences.

5.3.2.4 Emotion Attributions to Hypothetical Wrongdoers

Despite a quite adequate cognitive moral understanding, most 5 year olds (e.g., 80% in the theft story) and 7 year olds (between 60 and 75% across all stories) expected the wrongdoer to feel good because he or she satisfied his or her own desires. This is a robust finding (Nunner-Winkler & Sodian, 1988) that has been widely replicated and that has been labeled the "happy victimizer" (Arsenio & Kramer, 1992; Arsenio & Lover, 1995; Murgatroyd & Robinson, 1993, 1997; for a review, see Arsenio, Gold, & Adams, 2006).

There are, however, large differences across studies concerning the extent and interpretation of children's amoral emotion attributions. These inconsistencies may be related to differences in measurement procedures. To illustrate with one exemplary study, Keller, Lourenco, Malti, and Saalbach (2003) found that fewer amoral emotions are given when the self rather than a hypothetical protagonist fills the role of the wrongdoer. They concluded from this finding that children's amoral emotion ascriptions to hypothetical wrongdoers need not indicate lack of moral motivation, as is claimed in the present study. Rather, they argued that children tend to take a descriptive psychological stance when attributing an emotion to a hypothetical wrongdoer, even though they are quite able to take a moral stance when their own transgressions are involved. This interpretation, however, does not consider that with the attainment of self-reflexive role-taking abilities (i.e., from age 6 onward; Selman & Byrne, 1974), children might guide their emotion attributions to the self by social desirability concerns. Also, stories differ in how much the moral demands contradict personal desires. Fewer amoral emotions will be attributed when following the norm is compatible with fulfilling one's own needs or spontaneous desires. For example, in one of their stories, Keller et al. presented a protagonist who broke a promise to play table tennis with another child to watch TV. Many children expected the protagonist to feel bad. This might be an example of moral motivation, but it might also be an example of self-serving reasons if children perceived playing table tennis as an intrinsically enjoyable activity that offers an opportunity for gaining the friendship of another child. In other words, projecting their own preferences on the hypothetical scene might lead children to expect the protagonist to regret his or her decision not for moral but for self-serving reasons.

The motivational interpretation of emotion ascriptions argued for in the present study is strengthened by the results from the two interventions: Children who had consistently expected a protagonist to feel bad after transgressing (e.g., showed moral motivation) were significantly more likely to resist a real-life temptation to cheat to win an attractive prize or to gain their own interests in a distribution task (Asendorpf & Nunner-Winkler, 1992). Also, meanwhile, there are studies showing that amoral emotion ascriptions and aggressiveness in peer interactions are correlated and that conflict initiators do in fact openly display happy emotions (Arsenio et al., 2006; Gasser & Alaskar, 2005). Altogether, these findings support the validity of the moral motivation measurement.

5.3.2.5 Types of Concerns Motivating Norm Conformity

Children's understanding of moral motivation can be reconstructed from the justifications provided for negative emotion ascriptions to the wrongdoer. We analyzed the following dimensions of moral motivation: intrinsic quality, formal stance, and second-order desire. The following describes each dimension and summarizes children's understanding.

- Moral motivation is *intrinsic*: People follow norms not in view of personal costs and benefits but because they deem it right to do so. Most LOGIC study participants understood moral motivation as intrinsic. Across all stories and measurement points, most children who expected the protagonist to feel bad explained that what he or she did was wrong, he or she should have helped or shared, or he or she proved to be bad, mean, or unfair. Mention of consequences (positive or negative) ensuing to the wrongdoer never exceeded 18% of the participants.
- Moral motivation is *formal*: Determining what is right requires moral reasoning depending on context-specific cognitive judgments. In the LOGIC study, this aspect was reflected by responses to the sharing stories: Between 80% (age 5) and 96% (age 9) of the justifications given

for the demand of sharing referred to justice concerns in the prize story. In contrast, in the drink story most justifications, especially those of the younger children, referred to altruistic concerns (70% at age 5, and 40% at age 9). However, these differences in rule justifications were not reflected in the reasons given for negative emotion attributions to the wrongdoer. In both stories, most justifications referred to the fact that a wrong had been done (drink story: between 82% at age 5 and 62% at age 9; prize story: between 73% at age 5 and 78% at age 9) rather than to justice or to care concerns. In other words, judgments reflecting moral motivation were not contextualized but reflected a formal readiness to do what one judges to be "right" under the given circumstances. Thus, moral motivation was tied to moral reasoning.

- Moral motivation is a *second-order desire*: Moral motivation requires taking a stance toward one's spontaneous (first-order) desires (Frankfurt, 1988) and acting only upon those desires that agree with moral norms. To illustrate: In the "helper" story, children were asked to attribute an emotion to both the helper and the nonhelper. Among the 6 year olds, some children (19%) gave a moral attribution pattern (the helper feels good for having helped, and the nonhelper feels bad for not having helped), and others (26%) gave an amoral pattern (the helper feels bad for having made so few cookies, and the nonhelper feels good for having made many cookies). Most children (32%), however, produced a kind of "ideal world" pattern, in which they expected both protagonists to feel good—the helper because he or she followed the norm and helped, and the nonhelper because he or she fulfilled a personal desire to do well on the task. In other words: Everyone was expected to feel good upon following his or her spontaneous inclinations. Now undoubtedly, acting upon altruistic inclinations is good; however, it does not necessarily indicate moral motivation. Moral motivation is warranted only when a person does what is right, even when doing so goes counter to his or her spontaneous (first-order) desires.

To summarize: Our results suggested that moral development is a two-step process. In a first, universal process, children acquire an adequate understanding of the intrinsic, albeit only prima facie, validity of moral rules. In a second, later process, children begin to build moral motivation. This second process is not universal. Children differ in how rapidly and how successfully they complete this second acquisition process. However, it is important to note that those who do begin to reflect moral concerns understand moral motivation to be intrinsic. Thus, contrary to Kohlberg, even children grasp the deontological nature of morality. Moral development, then, may mainly concern sociocognitive development, allowing for increasingly more adequate rule applications to complex situations.

TOURO COLLEGE LIBRARY

5.4   THE MEASUREMENT OF MORAL
MOTIVATION AT AGES 18 AND 23

5.4.1   Moral Motivation Stories

At ages 18 and 23, the strength of moral motivation was assessed by a rating procedure based on participants' hypothetical action decisions and their emotional
reactions (Nunner-Winkler, Meyer-Nikele, & Wohlrab, 2007). We presented participants with three moral conflicts in which personal desires collided with well-
known moral norms, and one moral dilemma in which two moral norms were in
conflict. Participants were asked (a) to specify what they themselves (or a same-
sex protagonist) would do in the situation, (b) to justify their choice, (c) to ascribe
an emotion that they (or a protagonist) would feel as an agent of a transgression or
as the victim of another's transgression, and (d) to justify the attribution of these
emotions. The stories are described in Table 5.1.

Three criteria were followed in the construction of the stories: (a) We chose
conflicts with structures believed to be familiar to adolescents, (b) the situations
involved clear moral issues, and (c) the stories allowed for an easy justification
of the immoral action decisions (with one exception: story 2, the moral dilemma
with two conflicting moral norms) by reference to standard practices (e.g., in stories 1 and 3, maximizing personal profit is common in the market or in professional life) or to pragmatic problems preventing the moral action (e.g., in story 4,
the old woman has already disappeared).

5.4.2   Scoring of Moral Motivation

In scoring the protocols for moral motivation, we first discussed theoretically
derived criteria using examples from 20 interview protocols. Then, two independent coders rated the strength of moral motivation on a 5-point Moral Motivation
Scale (MoMo Rating Scale). Interrater reliability was adequate ($r = .80$), with
disagreements settled by discussion.

The Moral Motivation Scale was constructed from (a) participants' justifications of action decisions or emotion ascriptions, (b) asymmetry in responses to
protagonist and victim, (c) "qualifications" to their moral judgments or emotion
attributions, and (d) a search for a moral compromise in the dilemma story.

5.4.2.1   Justifications

Justifications of action decisions or emotion ascriptions were scored as reflecting
moral or *pragmatic* concerns. Concerns were considered moral if they referred to
moral principles or rules, such as justice, fairness, or honesty, or to harm done to
third parties. Examples are as follows: (story 3) decides not to lie: "Because it is
unfair to the colleague who actually deserved the promotion"; and (story 1) waits
and feels bad: "Because I agreed to such a bad bargain, but I'd still wait because
I promised to do so." Concerns were considered pragmatic if they expressed an

TABLE 5.1
Stories and Test Questions for the MoMo Rating Scale

Story 1: Moped Sale

You offer your moped for sale. You want to sell it for € 500. A young man is interested. He bargains with you, and you agree on € 400. Then he says, "Sorry, I don't have the money on me, I'll quickly run home to fetch it. I'll be back in half an hour." You say, "Agreed, I'll wait for you." Shortly after he is gone, another customer shows up who is willing to pay the full price.Test questions: Action decision and justification: "What would you do? Why?" Emotion ascription and justification to self as agent: "How would you feel? Why?" Emotion ascription and justification to self as victim: "Imagine you were the first customer. When you return with the money, the seller tells you that he already sold the moped to another customer who paid the full price. How would you feel? Why?" Final exploration: "Can you understand the seller? In what respect?"

Story 2: Allowing the Blaming of an Innocent

Your friend has sprayed the walls in the newly decorated youth center. Another innocent adolescent is accused of this and threatened to be excluded from the center.

Story 3: Lying for a Career

X is offered a promotion in reward for a brilliant idea, which, however, unknown to X's boss, was produced by X's colleague.

Story 4: Keeping a Lost Good

You have found a purse with € 200 in it that was lost by a poor-looking elderly woman.

---

exclusive interest in gaining personal profit or in avoiding sanctions or if they ignored any harm done to others. Examples are as follows: (story 3) lies: "For he'll greatly profit from that"; and (story 4) keeps the money and feels good: "Because I found so much money."

5.4.2.2 Argumentative Asymmetries

Argumentative asymmetries between the protagonist and victim were scored when participants responded differently to the story depending on whether they reflected on the perspective of the agent or the victim. An example would be an expression of delight in the profit gained by an immoral action decision followed by indignation at unfair treatment in the role of the victim. Such a response was taken to indicate that participants knew the rule was obligatory, yet would transgress it for self-serving interests. That is, they violate the core moral principle of impartiality and make a purely strategic use of their moral knowledge. For example, (story 1) breaks the promise: "If somebody pays more, I would sell it to him. That's normal market behavior. Anybody would do that." ("How would you feel?") "Great; after all, that's a lot of money." ("If you were the first customer, how would you feel?") "I'd be absolutely furious. After all, he promised to wait for me."

5.4.2.3   Qualifications to Moral Judgments or Emotion Attributions

Quite often, participants qualified their responses. Reinforcing a moral action decision or intensifying a negative emotion ascription after wrongdoing was taken to indicate high moral motivation, whereas weakening a moral action decision or mitigating a negative emotion attribution after transgression was taken to indicate low moral motivation. For example: (story 4) on keeping a lost good: "I would never do such a thing" versus "I don't think I'd keep it; I'd give it back—probably"; and (story 4) emotion ascription: "I'd feel absolutely bad" versus "I'd feel somewhat bad, I guess."

5.4.2.4   Search for a Moral Compromise

Attempts in the moral dilemma story (story 2) to follow both the particularistic duty of loyalty to one's friend and the universalistic duty to avoid injustice were taken to indicate high moral motivation. For example, "I'd talk my friend into confessing." Giving priority to the particularistic obligation was scored as indicating low moral motivation only if the harm done to the innocent was totally ignored (e.g., in the victim's role, the participant cannot understand that the friend will protect the innocent): "Well, I know my friends wouldn't let me on. If ever one did, he'd not be my friend anymore."

The Moral Motivation Scale (MoMo Rating Scale) was constructed by a weighting process across ratings for the individual stories. The Moral Motivation Scale ranges from 1 to 5, with 1 indicating a higher level of moral motivation. Higher ratings on the Moral Motivation Scale (1, 2) were given if participants chose a moral action decision and justified it exclusively (1) or almost exclusively (2) on moral terms across stories 1–3 and expected to feel very bad (1) or bad (2) for moral concerns after having violated the moral obligation in story 4. Lower ratings (4, 5) were given if participants justified their action decisions and emotion attributions almost exclusively (4) or exclusively (5) on pragmatic terms, that is, by an interest in avoiding negative consequences to self or in securing personal benefits. The middle value (3) was based on a more hermeneutic weighting of the frequency and/or gravity of ignoring moral concerns, and thus reflects a set of different patterns of responses, including argumentation in which moral and pragmatic concerns were evenly balanced; choice of the moral action in most stories in a hesitating manner, often backed by pragmatic interests; clear mitigation of negative emotion attributions after wrongdoing; or large inconsistency in moral emotion attributions across stories.

The variability in responses that were assigned the middle-range rating was to be expected. In moral conflicts, action choices depend on the relative strength of moral motivation as compared to the desire for the good sacrificed by the moral decision. Different individuals will assess the conflicts presented in the stories differently and will differ in their valuation of nonmoral goods or in the costs implied by a moral action choice. Thus, they will be differentially tempted by the same moral conflict. To illustrate: The intensity of the conflict experienced in story 3 (age 23: lying for a career) clearly differed. Some participants considered the promotion to be a highly important personal goal; others were afraid of being unable to fulfill the expectations tied to higher positions. Even if they were morally indifferent, participants who were afraid of the higher position might use moral arguments (e.g., one ought not to lie) to back a decision that might (also) be motivated by their personal fear of failure. Thus, ratings at the two extremes of the Moral Motivation Scale were easier to assess. Indeed, for several analyses the 5-point Moral Motivation Scale was collapsed to a classification of high (values 1 and 2), middle (value 3), and low (values 4 and 5) moral motivation.

5.4.3   VALIDATING MEASURES

Two measures were used to assess the validity of the MoMo Rating Scale.

5.4.3.1   Moral Concerns Test

Participants were given a rating task for moral concerns. They were asked to imagine they had kept a purse containing a considerable sum of money that had been lost by a very poor-looking old woman. They then had to state how much they would feel each of a list of possible emotional reactions to this transgression. At age 18, the Moral Concerns Test consisted of a list of 36 items that participants had to equally distribute in a Q-sort procedure on a 6-point scale ranging from 1 ("I would feel exactly that way") to 6 ("I wouldn't feel that way at all"). At age 23 the list was condensed to 6 items, which participants had to rate on the same 6-point scale. The items used in both measurements reflected (a) fear of internal sanctions (e.g., "I'd be conscience stricken"), (b) moral commitment (e.g., "I find this so wrong that I can hardly imagine doing something like that"), and (c) openly amoral reactions (e.g., "I suppose it would not matter that much to me"). Items used at age 18 but not age 23 reflected fear of religious and social sanctions and a deeply ingrained need disposition for conformity. These reactions were of interest in the context of an intergenerational comparison concerning sociohistoric changes in the structure of moral motivation (Nunner-Winkler, 2004, 2008).

5.4.3.2   Self-Report of Real-Life Behavior (age 23)

Participants were presented a list of minor delinquent acts and asked to mark how often they had committed each within the last 12 months. The list included riding on public transport without paying, lying, breaking a promise, stealing things worth less than 10 euros, stealing things worth more than 10 euros, bullying others, and driving under the influence of alcohol. A Rule Transgressions Index was constructed from points assigned to each transgression based on the frequency or gravity of the transgression (e.g., riding on public transport without paying: *never* 0, *rarely/sometimes* 1, and *quite often/frequently* 2; theft: *nothing* 0, *value less than 10 euros* 1, and *more than 10 euros* 2; and so on).

5.4.4 RESULTS OF THE VALIDATING PROCEDURES

5.4.4.1 Moral Concerns Test

The types of concerns motivating norm conformity (Q-sort age 18; rating age 23) and classification of the strength of moral motivation as low, middle, and high were cross-classified. At age 23, participants high in moral motivation, especially compared with participants low in moral motivation, tended to more strongly reject amoral reactions (e.g., "At first I'd feel a bit bad, but I'd soon forget about it" means MoMo high 1.40, MoMo low 3.43, $p < .00$) and affirm moral reactions if these were expressed in nonconventional terms that are less susceptible to social desirability concerns (e.g., "I find this so wrong that I can hardly imagine doing something like that" means MoMo high 1.40, MoMo low 3.46, $p < .00$). The same was true at age 18.

The agreement found between participants' own preferences of moral or amoral concerns and raters' assessment of the strength of moral motivation supports the validity of the moral motivation ratings.

5.4.4.2 Self-Report of Real-Life Behavior

The percentages of the 23-year-old participants who admitted to committing a delinquent action at least once within the last 12 months were as follows: lying, 88%; breaking a promise, 76%; not paying for public transportation, 58%; driving under the influence of alcohol, 42%; bullying others, 24%; stealing something with a value of less than 10 euros, 7%; and stealing something with a value above 10 euros, 3%. Index values ranged between 0 and 10, with a mean of 3.68 and a standard deviation of 1.92.

There was a significant, albeit not very high, correlation between the Rule Transgressions Index and the 5-point MoMo Rating Scale ($r_p = .30, p < .001$). The higher the moral motivation, the fewer delinquent acts are reported.

Table 5.2 presents the Rule Transgressions Index means of subjects' high, middle, and low in moral motivation. Again, there was a significant relation between the strength of moral motivation and the frequency of delinquent behaviors. As can be seen, the participants low in moral motivation showed an espe-

---

TABLE 5.2
"Rule Transgressions" and Moral Motivation

Moral Motivation	Index "Rule Transgression" Mean (std)	N
High	3.36 (1.86)	72
Middle	3.42 (1.56)	53
Low	5.00 (2.16)	28

NOVA: F(2, 150) = 6.20, $p = .00$.

cially high rate of rule transgressions. The findings support the validity of the MoMo Rating Scale at age 23.

5.5 CROSS-SECTIONAL AND LONGITUDINAL ANALYSES

5.5.1 SAMPLE

Cross-sectional analyses were conducted with all subjects who participated at the respective measurement points. Longitudinal analyses were conducted with participants who participated in all the relevant measurements (see Table 5.3).

5.5.2 DEVELOPMENT OF MORAL MOTIVATION: POPULATION MEANS

Participants were classified as showing high, middle, or low moral motivation at each measurement point. At ages 5, 7, and 9, participants were classified as *high*, *middle*, or *low* if they had ascribed 3 or 4 (high), 2 (middle), or 0 or 1 (low) moral emotion(s) to the protagonist. At ages 18 and 23, they were classified as *high*, *middle*, or *low* according to their ratings in the MoMo Scale of 1 or 2 (high), 3 (middle), or 4 or 5 (low), as described above.

Figure 5.1 presents the frequencies of low, middle, or high moral motivation strength at ages 5, 7, 9, 18, and 23. Figure 5.1 shows that there is a clear increase in the strength of moral motivation with age and that the percentage of participants

---

TABLE 5.3
Number of Participants in Waves 2, 4, 6, 10, and 11

Age	5	7	9	18	23
Boys	110	105	96	92	80
Girls	103	98	89	80	73
Total	213	203	185	172	153

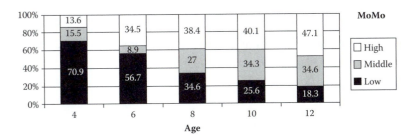

FIGURE 5.1   Percentage of participants at ages 5, 7, 9, 18, and 23 with high, middle, and low motivation.

low in moral motivation decreases most clearly. Nevertheless, at age 23 almost 20% of the participants (still) were indifferent to moral concerns.

5.5.3 INDIVIDUAL STABILITY IN STRENGTH OF MORAL MOTIVATION

Consistency at the individual level was measured by test–retest correlations or stability coefficients in moral motivation across the span of the LOGIC study. Stability coefficients indicate the uniformity or diversity of individual developmental trajectories. High positive coefficients imply that those who were relatively high in moral motivation at younger ages remain relatively high throughout the time span measured and that those who were relatively low at younger ages keep lower values throughout development. Low correlation coefficients imply that individuals change their relative positions in the group and/or display inconsistent developmental tracks.

Table 5.4 shows the stability coefficients across the five measurement points. As can be seen, there was a moderately high consistency between ages 5 and 7 (.36), followed by a slight drop between ages 7 and 9 (.12). There is a remarkable drop, in fact a reversal, between ages 9 and 18 (–.21). Between ages 18 and 23, consistency again rises to a moderately high level (.36). Stability coefficients do not allow researchers to disentangle the relative frequency of downward versus upward development among unstable participants or the absolute level of stable participants.

Table 5.5 gives the percentage of participants who remained stable at the high, medium, or low level of moral motivation or showed an increase or decrease in strength of moral motivation between adjacent measurement points. As can be seen, quite a few participants experienced a decrease in strength of moral motivation: 10% between ages 5 and 7, 22% between ages 7 and 9, 29% between 9 and 18, and 20% between 18 and 23. Table 5.5 also shows that the two higher stability coefficients found between ages 5 and 7 and ages 18 and 23 (.36) reflect quite different phenomena. Between 5 and 7, stability was due largely to the high percentage of participants with low values at both measurement points (i.e., to the fact that many children had not yet begun to develop moral motivation). Between

---

TABLE 5.4
Correlations Between Strength of Moral Motivation across Measurement Points

Wave		4	6	10	11
	Age	7	9	18	23
2	5	.36 (.00)	.06 (.45)	.00 (1.00)	.02 (.83)
4	7		.12 (.10)	–.11 (.14)	.05 (.54)
6	9			–.21 (.01)	–.15 (.07)
10	18				.36 (.00)

TABLE 5.5
Percentage of Participants with Stable High, Middle, and Low Values, and Increases and Decreases, in Strength of Moral Motivation Between Ages

Ages	++ High	00 Middle	-- Low	Stable	Increase	Decrease
5–7	9.0	2.0	47.5	58.9	31.5	10.0
7–9	15.9	3.3	23.5	42.7	35.0	22.4
9–18	17.9	8.0	11.1	37.0	34.0	29.0
18–23	24.3	12.2	9.5	46.0	33.8	20.3

ages 18 and 23, in contrast, there were more participants who remained stable at the high level. At all measurement points, more participants showed an increase than a decrease in relative position, which reflects the average increase in population means. Nevertheless, there was considerable intraindividual variability, with more than half of the participants switching relative positions.

The diversity of developmental trajectories and the extent of individual variability become even more obvious if long-term stabilities are analyzed. Table 5.6 depicts the percentage of participants who remain stable at high or low values of moral motivation across longer time spans. As can be seen, moral motivation at age 5 is not predictive of moral motivation at age 23—only 3% remain stable. The predictive power increases as children grow older and measurement points are closer: 7% remain stable from age 7 onward, 16% from age 9, and 34% from age 18.

Roberts and DelVecchio (2000) presented a meta-analysis of 152 studies in which more than 3,000 rank-order coefficients of personality variables (the "big five") were calculated from more than 50,000 participants across 124 samples. They reported a moderately high level of consistency across the life course, yet at the same time considerable change until late adulthood. There was little consistency in the earliest years (.35). There were steplike increases during the pre-

TABLE 5.6
Percentage of Participants With Stable High or Low Moral Motivation Across Ages 9–23

Ages	High	Low
5, 7, 9, 18, and 23	.7	2.1
7, 9, 18, and 23	4.3	2.8
9, 18, and 23	11.3	5.0
18 and 23	24.3	9.5

school years (.52) and between the college years and young adulthood (.57). A peak was reached only after 50 years (.75), which, however, was still well below unity. Their results thus fall somewhere between the two polar conceptualizations of personality—an assumption of stable traits that are essentially fixed in adulthood (Costa & McCrae, 1997) or an assumption of only states that are mostly situationally determined (Mischel, Shoda, & Mendoza-Denton, 2002).

The present findings on the growth of moral motivation agree with these results inasmuch as considerable changes are found across the age range studied. Yet, the consistency coefficients between childhood (ages 5, 7, and 9) and young adulthood (ages 18 and 23) are lower than those reported in the literature, and there the negative relation between ages 12 and 18 suggests that there is considerable interindividual variability in the rate of change in moral motivation.

Methodological reasons might account for both discrepancies. For one, the measurements of moral motivation were taken at inconsistent time intervals. The interval was 2 years between the three childhood measures, a 9-year pause, and then 5 years between the two young adult measures. Long time intervals might account for low stabilities. In addition, there were changes in the measurements between childhood and adulthood. The differences between these two procedures might also contribute to a lack of consistency. Although consistent over the course of the study, we used open-ended interviews to collect responses that may have lowered possible consistency. Floor and ceiling effects may have also served to decrease the correlations over time.

In addition to methodological reasons, there may be substantive reasons that limit the ability to detect consistency across time. First, moral motivation may not be similar to the more typical "big five" personality traits. *Strength of moral motivation* refers to the relative importance attributed to moral versus nonmoral values or personal interests. Value orientations may be more liable to change in response to changing life circumstances and social context factors than personality traits. This might be especially true given the more formal structure of present-day moral motivation: The early formation of a conformity disposition or the rigid internalization of strict rules that were more characteristic for former generations (Nunner-Winkler, 2004, 2008) may be less amenable to revisions. We found that moral motivation stability was especially low during adolescence. This is the time of identity development in societies that grant young people a moratorium (Erikson, 1950). Due to their hypothetical thinking ability (Inhelder & Piaget, 1958), adolescents are able to consciously take a stance toward beliefs and moral persuasions built up during childhood, and in the course of an intense adolescence crisis experience they may also revise affective commitments entered previously (Döbert & Nunner-Winkler, 1975).

5.5.4 Demographic Correlates of the Strength and Stability of Moral Motivation

The cross-sectional findings showed a considerable average increase in the strength of moral motivation with age. Data from the LOGIC study allowed us to explore two possible determinants of strength of moral motivation: socioeconomic status and sex.

5.5.4.1 Socioeconomic Status: Occupational Role

In Germany, students are separated into educational tracks after grade 4. Students in the lower educational track usually begin a trade apprenticeship at around 15–16 years of age, whereas students in the higher track (Gymnasium) remain in the educational system until at least ages 19–20. If direct confrontation with pragmatic issues (e.g., concrete job expectations leading to issues of self-assertion, power, and success) is important in affecting moral motivation and leads to the reevaluation of moral as compared to other values, the moral motivation decrease between ages 9 and 18 should be especially pronounced among lower educational track students.

As can be seen from Figure 5.2, higher track students were slightly higher in strength of moral motivation across all measurement points, even before tracking began. This difference, however, was significant only at age 5. In other words, the development of moral motivation showed the same rate and pattern for higher and lower track students. Thus, educational track does not explain the lack of a correlation between the ages of 9 and 18 observed in the sample as a whole.

5.5.4.2 Sex

The claim of sex differences in moral areas is frequently made (Freud, 1925/1972; Gilligan, 1982; Gilligan & Wiggins, 1987; for an overview of philosophical positions, see Pieper, 1993). Females are characterized as guided mostly by care concerns, and males by justice concerns. There are various explanations for this presumed difference. Evolutionary biology explanations refer to differences in reproduction strategies: Only those women who bestow great care upon their few offspring can pass on their genes. Psychoanalytic theories argue for early differences in self-structure: All newborns first identify with their caregiver (mostly the mother) and draw "early moral wisdom" from this identification. Little girls

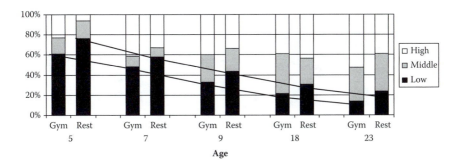

FIGURE 5.2 Moral motivation and educational track.

remain in this primary identification and develop a *relational self.* Little boys, in contrast, distance themselves during the oedipal crisis to become a "true man" and develop an *autonomous self,* forfeiting the "early moral wisdom" (Gilligan & Wiggins, 1987) that girls retain. Sociological explanations focus on the effects of the division of labor: Women (still) mainly fill family roles, that is, "diffuse" roles that entail an obligation to care for all the needs of all other family members; and men fill occupational roles, that is, "specific" roles that strictly limit rights and duties.

Figure 5.3 presents the relationship between strength of moral motivation and sex across all measurement points. As can be seen, sex differences are first apparent at age 9 (Wave 6), when girls show higher moral motivation than boys, and increase at age 18 (Wave 10).

The finding that sex differences begin to appear only at the end of childhood fits neither an evolutionary nor a psychoanalytic explanation. We further explored the sociological interpretation by exploring the impact of gender stereotypes and gender identification on moral motivation. To the extent that there are morally relevant differences in gender role expectations, they might have a bearing on commitments to moral value orientations, especially during adolescence, the time of identity formation.

5.5.4.3   Gender Role Stereotypes

At age 23, we assessed gender role stereotypes and self-identification of gender roles. Participants were given a list of traits and asked to rate how typical these were for a "true woman" and a "true man," and how desirable for an "ideal partner" and for their own "ideal self." The "true man" and "true woman" ratings showed contrasting profiles (correlation −.59, $p < .05$; see Figure 5.4).

As can be seen, men are regarded as more assertive, unwilling to admit to weaknesses, and shrewd (the German specification was "always want to out-

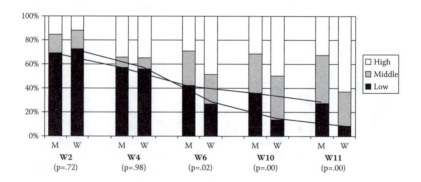

FIGURE 5.3   Moral motivation and gender.

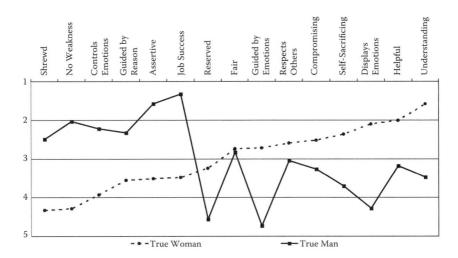

FIGURE 5.4   Gender stereotypes.

smart others"), and women as more helpful, willing to compromise, and willing to set aside their own needs. In other words, the male stereotype contains more traits that are aversive to morality, and the female stereotype contains traits that are conducive to morality; for although assertiveness may at times be warranted, efforts at outsmarting others and a tendency to deny one's own faults do not agree with the moral principles of fairness and truthfulness. And although helpfulness and readiness to agree to a compromise and set aside one's own needs may not always be morally adequate, on average they will contribute to alleviating harm and striking a fair balance between conflicting perspectives and interests.

The description of the "ideal partner" more strongly resembled the female stereotype (.89) than the male stereotype (–.26). Male and female self-ideals were rather similar (.91) and more resembled the female stereotype (female "ideal self"/"true woman": .73; "male ideal self"/"true woman": .48), although both sexes expressed a slightly higher preference for traits typical for their own sex (female "ideal self"/"true woman": .73; male "ideal self"/"true man": .31) (see Figure 5.5).

These findings show that the female gender stereotype much more than the male gender stereotype contains traits that both men and women deem desirable for an ideal partner and for themselves. This may be taken as further support for interpreting differences in gender stereotypes in moral terms. People tend to give the highest ratings to moral qualities over and above nonmoral traits, personal interests, or concerns when asked what makes a good partner (Noelle-Neumann & Köcher, 1997, p. 143) or what they consider most important about their own person (Nunner-Winkler, 2002).

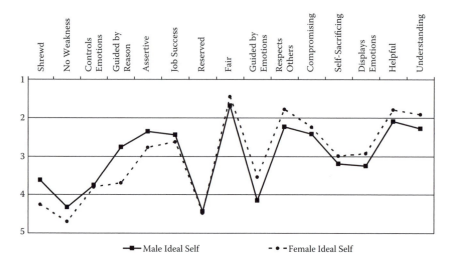

                    — ■ — Male Ideal Self   - ● - Female Ideal Self

FIGURE 5.5   Male and female "ideal self."

5.5.4.4   Gender Identification

Gender stereotypes express collectively shared expectations. People, however, differ in the personal importance they attribute to these expectations. Participants' gender identification was measured as a profile similarity between the "ideal self" and "true man" for male participants and between the "ideal self" and "true woman" for female participants. We hypothesized that a strong desire to closely conform to gender expectations that either emphasize or devalue moral traits might have an impact on the strength of moral motivation. Figure 5.6 shows the percentage of participants with above- or below-average gender identification displaying high, middle, and low moral motivation.

As can be seen, there is no difference in the strength of moral motivation among male and female participants with low gender identification. However, among highly gender-identified participants, there were significantly more males with low moral motivation and fewer males with high moral motivation.

5.5.4.5   Stability

Sex predicts stability of moral motivation between ages 9 and 18 ($p < .05$) and ages 18 and 23 ($p < .001$). Gender identification (measured at age 23) predicts boys' strength of moral motivation between 18 and 23 ($p < .001$), with highly gender-identified boys overrepresented among participants experiencing a decrease in strength of moral motivation between 18 and 23.

The adverse effect of gender identification on males' strength of moral motivation replicates results of a study with 200 14–15-year-old participants, balanced for sex, educational track, and upbringing in the "new" (e.g., the former East

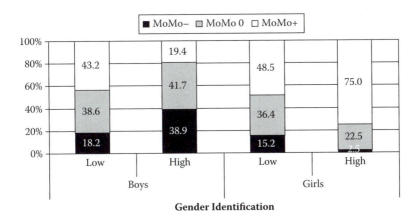

FIGURE 5.6   Gender identification and strength of moral motivation.

Germany) and the "old" (e.g., the former West Germany) German states (Nunner-Winkler et al., 2007). Gender stereotypes were explored by an open-ended question ("Do you think men and women differ by nature? In what respect?"), and only descriptions rated as morally conducive or aversive by two independent raters were taken into account. For assessing gender identification, we asked participants to rate on a 5-point scale how different a person they would be were they of the other sex. Male stereotypes were predominantly morally aversive (e.g., "They'd sell their grandmother for their career," "Show macho behavior," "Go overboard"), and female stereotypes were largely morally conducive (e.g., "They think about consequences," and they are "reliable," "considerate," and "helpful"). There was a significant correlation ($p > .05$) between gender identification and moral motivation: The higher the boys' gender identification, the higher the percentage with low moral motivation.

In contrast to the LOGIC findings, gender identification in girls had no effect on moral motivation. The reason might be that participants of the lower educational track and of the "new" German states held clearly more critical female stereotypes than participants from the "old" states and from the higher educational track. Given that LOGIC participants were from the "old" German states (e.g., the former West Germany) only and many more attended the higher educational track, they presumably held more positive female stereotypes.

In both studies, among highly gender-identified participants, males showed considerably lower moral motivation than females. This corresponds to the fact that male stereotypes contained more morally aversive traits, and female stereotypes (especially in the "old" West German states and in the higher educational tracks) more favorable traits. This difference might reflect the traditional division of labor between the sexes (still more highly approved of in the "old" states and in the higher strata; Statistisches Bundesamt, 2006, p. 516). Compared to the "female" task of family care, the occupational achievements expected of men require decidedly more assertiveness, maybe even ruthlessness. This interpretation is given some support by the significant gender difference found in story 3 (lying for a career), with women more often refusing to lie (women 76% versus men 54%, χ^2 (2, N = 150) = 9.91, p < .01) and men more often justifying lying for their career interests by claiming egotism to be normal behavior, especially in business life (e.g., "Everybody looks out for himself first," and "In business, one needs elbows").

5.6 CONCLUSIONS

Over the course of development, there is a clear increase in the average strength of moral motivation. The percentage of participants with low moral motivation decreased from 70% at age 5 to 18% at age 23, and the percentage of participants with high moral motivation increased from 14% at age 5 to 47% at age 23. On the individual level, however, there was little overall stability. In other words, individuals followed divergent developmental trajectories, and more than a quarter of the participants showed decreases in moral motivation between adjacent measurement points. Taken together these findings, along with findings from the literature, suggest that moral motivation is a facet of moral reasoning that is not fixed from early attachment patterns or socialization styles, but that is affected by interactions with peers (Krappmann, 1993), by experiences in school (Higgins, 1991) and in the community (Damon, 1997), and by public discourse, for example on sex differences and gender roles. Future research is needed to analyze the stability of moral commitment during later phases in the life cycle.

ACKNOWLEDGMENTS

I wish to thank Beate Sodian for her participation in the development of the childhood moral motivation measure, Tina Hascher for coordinating the data collection during childhood assessments, Doris Wohlrab for cooperation in the final assessment, and Marion Meyer-Nikele for statistical analyses throughout the entire study. I also want to thank Merry Bullock for her careful reading of the first draft and helpful suggestions.

A brief presentation of some of the core findings of the longitudinal analysis has appeared in *Journal of Moral Education*, *36*(4), 2007, 399–414.

REFERENCES

Andreoni, J. (1990). Impure altruism and donations to public goods: A theory of warm-glow giving. *Economic Journal*, 100, 464–477.
Arsenio, W. F., Gold, J., & Adams, E. (2006). Children's conceptions and displays of moral emotions. In M. Killen & J. Smetana (Eds.), *Handbook of moral development* (pp. 581–609). Mahwah, NJ: Erlbaum.
Arsenio, W., & Kramer, R. (1992). Victimizers and their victims. *Child Development, 63*, 915–927.

Arsenio, W., & Lover, A. (1995). Children's conceptions of sociomoral affect: Happy victimizers, mixed emotions, and other expectancies. In M. Killen & D. Hart (Eds.), *Morality in everyday life* (pp. 87–128). New York: Cambridge University Press.

Asendorpf, J. B., & Nunner-Winkler, G. (1992). Children's moral motive strength and temperamental inhibition reduce their immoral tendencies in real moral conflicts. *Child Development, 63*, 1223–1235.

Barden, R. C., Zelko, F. A., Duncan, S. W., & Masters, J. C. (1980). Children's consensual knowledge about the experiential determinants of emotion. *Journal of Personality and Social Psychology, 39*, 968–976.

Baumrind, D. (1971). Current patterns of parental authority. *Developmental Psychology Monograph, 4*(Pt. 2), 1–103.

Bittner, G. (1994). *Problemkinder. Zur Psychoanalyse kindlicher und jugendlicher Verhaltensauffälligkeiten* [Problem children: Psychoanalysis of childhood and adolescent behavior problems]. Göttingen, Germany: Vandenhoeck & Ruprecht.

Blasi, A. (1980). Bridging moral cognition and moral action: A critical review of the literature. *American Psychological Association, 88*, 1–45.

Blasi, A. (1983). Bridging moral cognition and moral action: A theoretical perspective. *Development Review, 3*, 178–210.

Bowlby, J. (1987). *Attachment and loss.* Harmondsworth, UK: Penguin.

Colby, A., & Damon, W. (1992). *Some do care: Contemporary lives of moral commitment.* New York: Free Press.

Costa, P. T., Jr., & McCrae, R. R. (1997). Longitudinal stability of adult personality. In R. Hogan, J. A. Johnson, & S. R. Briggs (Eds.), *Handbook of personality psychology* (pp. 825–847). San Diego, CA: Academic Press.

Damon, W. (1997). *The Youth Charter: How communities can work together to raise standards for all our children.* New York: Free Press.

Döbert, R., & Nunner-Winkler, G. (1975). *Adoleszenzkrise und Identitätsbildung* [Adolescent crises and identity formation]. Frankfurt am Main: edition suhrkamp.

Eisenberg, N. (1986). *Altruistic emotion, cognition, and behavior.* Hillsdale, NJ: Erlbaum.

Eisenberg, N. and P. Mussen, Eds. (1989). *The roots of prosocial behavior in children.* Cambridge: Cambridge University Press.

Eisenberg, N. and J. Strayer, Eds. (1987). *Empathy and its development.* Cambridge: Cambridge Universtiy Press.

Erikson, E. H. (1950). Growth and crises of the "healthy personality." In M. J. E. Senn (Ed.), *Symposium on the Healthy Personality. Suppl. II: Problems of infancy and childhood, transactions of 4th conference* (pp. 91–146). New York: Josiah Macy, Jr. Foundation.

Fonagy, P. (2004). Personality disorder and violence: A psychoanalytic-attachment theory perspective. In O. Kernberg & H-P. Hartmann (Eds.), *Narzißtische Persönlichkeitsstörungen.* Stuttgart, Germany: Schattauer.

Fonagy, P., Target, M., Steele, M., Steele, H., Leigh, T., Levinson, A., et al. (1997). Morality, disruptive behavior, borderline personality disorder, crime, and their relationship to security of attachment. In L. Atkinson & K. J. Zucker (Eds.), *Attachment and psychopathology* (pp. 233–274). New York: Guilford Press.

Frankfurt, H. G. (1988). *The importance of what we care about: Philosophical essays.* Cambridge: Cambridge University Press.

Freud, S. (1972). *Einige psychischen Folgen des anatomischen Geschlechtsunterschieds* [Some psychological consequences of the anatomical distinction between the sexes]. Gesammelte Werke, Band 14: Werke aus den Jahren 1925–1931. Frankfurt am Main: Fischer. (Originally published in 1925)

Freud, S. (1974). Neue Folge der Vorlesungen zur Einführung in die Psychoanalyse [New introductory lectures on psychoanalysis]. In S. Freud (Ed.), *Studienausgabe* (Vol. 1, pp. 447–608). Frankfurt am Main: Fischer. (Originally published in 1933)

Gasser, L., & Alaskar, F. D. (2005, June). *Implications of moral emotion attributions for children's social behavior and relationships.* Paper presented at the meeting of the Jean Piaget Society, Vancouver, Canada.

Gibbs, J. C. (2003). *Moral development and reality: Beyond the theories of Kohlberg and Hoffman.* Thousand Oaks, CA: Sage.

Gilligan, C. (1982). *In a different voice: Psychological theory and women's development.* Cambridge, MA: Harvard University Press.

Gilligan, C., & Wiggins, G. (1987). The origins of morality in early childhood relationships. In J. Kagan & S. Lamb (Eds.), *The emergence of morality in young children* (pp. 277–305). Chicago: University of Chicago Press.

Hermann, D. (2003). *Werte und Kriminalität* [Values and criminality]. Wiesbaden, Germany: Westdeutscher Verlag.

Higgins, A. (1991). The just community approach to moral education: Evolution of the idea and recent findings. In W. M. Kurtines & J. L. Gewirtz (Eds.), *Handbook of moral behavior and development. Vol. 3*: Application (pp. 111–141). Hillsdale, NJ: Erlbaum.

Higgins, A., Power, C., & Kohlberg, L. (1984). The relationship of moral atmosphere to judgments of responsibility. In W. M. Kurtines & J. L. Gewirtz (Eds.), *Morality, moral behavior, and moral development* (pp. 74–106). New York: John Wiley.

Hoffman, M. L. (2000). *Empathy and moral development: Implications for Caring and Justice,* New York, Cambridge University Press.

Hoffmann, M. L., & Salzstein, H. D. (1967). Parent discipline and the child's moral development. *Journal of Personality and Social Psychology, 5,* 45–57.

Inhelder, B., & Piaget, J. (1958). *The growth of logical thinking from childhood to adolescence.* London: Routledge & Kegan Paul.

Kant, I. (1962). *Grundlegung zur Metaphysik der Sitten* [Foundations of the metaphysics of morals]. Hamburg: Felix Meiner Verlag. (Originally published in 1785)

Kant, I. (1959). Über ein vermeintliches Recht, aus Menschenliebe zu lügen [On a supposed right to lie from altruistic motives]. In K. Vorländer (Ed.), *Immanuel Kant: Kleinere Schriften zur Geschichtsphilosophie Ethik und Politik* (pp. 199–206). Hamburg: Felix Meiner Verlag. (Originally published in 1797)

Keller, M., Lourenco, O., Malti, T., & Saalbach, H. (2003). The multifaceted phenomenon of "happy victimizers": A cross-cultural comparison of moral emotions. *British Journal of Developmental Psychology, 21,* 1–18.

Kochanska, G., Aksan, N., Knaack, A., & Rhines, H. M. (2004). Maternal parenting and children's conscience: Early security as moderator. *Child Development, 75*(4), 1229–1242.

Kochanska, G., Aksan, N., & Koenig, A. L. (1995). A longitudinal study of the roots of preschoolers' conscience: Committed compliance and emerging internalization. *Child Development, 66,* 1752–1769.

Kohlberg, L. (1981). *Essays on moral development: Vol. 1. The philosophy of moral development. Moral stages and the idea of justice.* San Francisco: Harper & Row.

Kohlberg, L. (1984). *Essays on moral development: Vol. 2. The psychology of moral development. The nature and validity of moral stages.* San Francisco: Harper & Row.

Krappmann, L. (1993). Self threat in the peer world: Observations of twelve-year-old children in natural settings. In G. Noam & T. Wren (Eds.), *The moral self.* Cambridge, MA: MIT Press.

Luhmann, N. (1990). *Paradigm lost: Über die ethische Reflexion von Moral* [Paradise lost: An ethical reflection on morality]. Frankfurt am Main: Suhrkamp.

Marneros, A. (2002). *Hitlers Urenkel. Rechtsradikale Gewalttäter—Erfahrungen eines wahldeutschen Gerichtsgutachters* [Hitler's great grandson, right-wing perpetrators of violence: Experiences of a forensics expert German by choice]. Bern: Scherz.

Mischel, W., Shoda, Y., & Mendoza-Denton, R. (2002). Situation-behavior profiles as a locus of consistency in personality. *Current Directions in Psychological Science, 11,* 50–54.

Monroe, K., Barton, M. C., & Klingemann, U. (1990). Altruism and the theory of rational action: Rescuers of Jews in Nazi Europe. *Ethics, 101,* 103–122.

Montada, L. (1993). Understanding oughts by assessing moral reasoning or moral emotions. In G. Noam & T. E. Wren (Eds.), *The moral self* (pp. 292–309). Cambridge, MA: MIT Press.

Murgatroyd, S. J., & Robinson, E. (1993). Children's judgements of emotion following moral transgression. *International Journal of Behavioral Development, 16,* 93–111.

Murgatroyd, S. J., & Robinson, E. J. (1997). Children's and adults' attributions of emotion to a wrongdoer: The influence of the onlooker's reaction. *Cognition and emotion, 3,* 83–101.

Noelle-Neumann, E., & Köcher, R. (Eds). (1997). *Allensbacher Jahrbuch der Demoskopie 1993–1997* [Allensbach yearbook of public opinion research 1993–1997] (Vol. 10). Munich: K. G. Saur.

Nucci, L. P., & Turiel, E. (1993). God's word, religious rules, and their relation to Christian and Jewish children's concepts of morality. *Child Development, 64,* 1475–1491.

Nunner-Winkler, G. (1998). The development of moral understanding and moral motivation. *International Journal of Educational Research, 27,* 587–603.

Nunner-Winkler, G. (1999). Development of moral understanding and moral motivation. In F. E. Weinert & W. Schneider (Eds.), *Individual development from 3 to 12: Findings from the Munich Longitudinal Study* (pp. 253–290). New York: Cambridge University Press.

Nunner-Winkler, G. (2002). Identität und Moral [Identity and morality]. In J. Straub & J. Renn (Eds.), *Transitorische Identität. Der Prozesscharakter des modernen Selbst* (pp. 56–84). Frankfurt am Main: Campus.

Nunner-Winkler, G. (2004). Sociohistoric changes in the structure of moral motivation. In D. K. Lapsley & D. Narvaez (Eds.), *Moral development, self, and identity* (pp. 299–333). Mahwah, NJ: Erlbaum.

Nunner-Winkler, G. (2008). From Super-Ego and Conformist Habitus to Ego-Sytonic Moral Motivation. Sociohistoric Changes in Moral Motivation. In Malti, T., Gummerum, M., Keller, M., *Moral Emotions and Moral Cognitions, Special Issue of the European Journal of Developmental Science.*

Nunner-Winkler, G., Meyer-Nikele, M., & Wohlrab, D. (2007). Gender differences in moral motivation. *Merrill Palmer Quarterly, 53*(1), 26–52.

Nunner-Winkler, G., & Sodian, B. (1988). Children's understanding of moral emotions. *Child Development, 59,* 1323–1338.

Oliner, S. P., & Oliner, P. M. (1988). *The altruistic personality: Rescuers of Jews in Nazi Europe*. New York: Free Press.

Parsons, T. (1964). *The social system*. London: Free Press of Glencoe.

Pieper, A. (1993). *Aufstand des stillgelegten Geschlechts. Einführung in die feministische Ethik* [Rise of the silenced sex: Introduction to feminist ethics]. Freiburg, Germany: Herder.

Pratt, M. W., Hunsberger, B., Pancer, S. M., & Alisat, S. (2003). A longitudinal analysis of personal values socialization: Correlates of a moral self-ideal in late adolescence. *Social Development, 12*(4), 563–585.

Rauchfleisch, U. (1992). *Allgegenwart von Gewalt* [Ubiquity of power]. Göttingen, Germany: Vandenhoeck und Ruprecht.

Rest, J. R. (1986). *Moral development: Advances in research and theory*. New York: Praeger.

Rest, J. R. (1999). Die Rolle des moralischen Urteilens im moralischen Handeln [The role of moral judgments in moral behavior]. In D. Garz, F. Oser, & W. Althof (Eds.), *Moralisches Urteil und Handeln* (pp. 82–116). Frankfurt am Main: Suhrkamp.

Roberts, B. W., & DelVecchio, W. F. (2000). The rank-order consistency of personality traits from childhood to old age: A quantitative review of longitudinal studies. *Psychological Bulletin, 126*(1), 3–25.

Selman, R. L., & Byrne, D. F. (1974). A structural-development analysis of levels of role-taking in middle childhood. *Child Development, 45*, 803–806.

Solomon, R. C. (1976). *The passions*. Garden City, NY: Anchor Press.

Statistisches Bundesamt. (2006). *Datenreport 2006* [Data report 2006] (Schriftenreihe Band 544). Bonn, Germany: Bundeszentrale für politische Bildung.

Strawson, P. F. (1962). Freedom and resentment. *Proceedings of the British Academy, 48*, 187–211.

Thoma, S. J. (1986). Estimating gender differences in the comprehension and preference of moral issues. *Developmental Review, 6*, 165–180.

Thoma, S. J., & Rest, J. R. (1999). The relationship between moral decision making and patterns of consolidation and transition in moral judgment development. *Developmental Psychology, 35*(2), 323–334.

Tremblay, R. (2000). The development of aggressive behavior during childhood: What have we learned in the past century? *International Journal of Behavioral Development, 24*, 129–141.

Tremblay, R. (2003). Why socialization fails: The case of chronic physical aggression. In B. B. Lahey, T. Moffitt, & A. Caspi (Eds.), *Causes of conduct disorder and juvenile delinquency* (pp. 182–224). New York: Guilford Press.

Turiel, E. (1983). *The development of social knowledge: Morality and convention*. Cambridge: Cambridge University Press.

Walker, L. J. (1999). Die Rolle des Urteils im Wirken der Moral [The role of judgment in moral functioning]. In D. Garz, F. Oser, & W. Althof (Eds.), *Moralisches Urteil und Handeln* (pp. 137–167). Frankfurt am Main: Suhrkamp.

Walker, L. J., de Vries, B., & Trevethan, S. D. (1987). Moral stages and moral orientations in real-life and hypothetical dilemmas. *Child Development, 58*, 842–858.

Walker, L. J., & Pitts, R. C. (1998). Naturalistic conceptions of moral maturity. *Developmental Psychology, 34*, 403–419.

Weber, M. (1956). Der Beruf zur Politik [The profession of politics]. In M. Weber (Ed.), *Soziologie, Weltgeschichtliche Analysen. Politik* (pp. 167–185). Stuttgart, Germany: Kröner.

6 Personality Trajectories from Early Childhood Through Emerging Adulthood

*Jens B. Asendorpf, Jaap J. A. Denissen,
and Marcel A. G. van Aken*

6.1 INTRODUCTION

This chapter concerns personality trajectories from early childhood into emerging adulthood. It uses the notion of empirically based personality types, a relatively new approach to studying personality that originates in the seminal work of Jack Block in his book *Lives Through Time* (1971). Block's theoretical approach predicts three personality types (Resilients, Overcontrollers, and Undercontrollers) that indeed seem to exist in childhood and adolescence, in various countries (see Caspi & Shiner, 2006). The Munich Longitudinal Study on the Ontogenesis of Individual Competencies (the LOGIC study) sample was one of the samples in which these types were found (Asendorpf & van Aken, 1999), and this chapter takes the three types as a departing point for studying the individual trajectories of two personality characteristics, shyness and aggression.

6.2 WHAT DO WE KNOW ABOUT PERSONALITY DEVELOPMENT BETWEEN 3 AND 23?

One of the most frequently posed questions in developmental research is the extent to which it is possible to predict developmental outcomes later in life from data that were gathered in early childhood. One of the domains in which this question has been phrased is the domain of personality: Is it possible to predict personality in adulthood from differences observed at a very early age in childhood in temperament or personality?

In their meta-analysis on the stability of individual differences in personality traits, Roberts and DelVecchio (2000) concluded that although this stability is moderate (approximately .45 over an average prediction interval of 7 years), it is lower in the younger age ranges, making it difficult to predict from early childhood to adulthood. Among the several longitudinal studies that have attempted such a prediction are demonstrations not only that personality in early and middle childhood is predictive of similar personality traits but also that it predicts important adjustment outcomes in early adulthood, in several domains (e.g., Caspi, 2000; Friedman et al., 1995; Huesmann, Eron, Lefkowitz, & Walder, 1984). Without being exhaustive, these studies include the Berkeley Guidance Study on children born in 1928 (data reanalyzed by Caspi, Elder, & Bem, 1987, 1988); the Dunedin Longitudinal Study on a representative New Zealand birth cohort (Caspi & Silva, 1995); the Fels Longitudinal Study (Kagan & Moss, 1962); Kerr, Lambert, and Bem's (1996) reanalysis of the data of a Swedish cohort; Block and Block's (1980) study on ego resiliency and ego control in the San Francisco Bay area; and the Jyväskylä Longitudinal Study of Personality and Social Development (Pulkkinen, 2006). Although these studies differed somewhat in the age of the children at the start, all of them demonstrate clear trajectories of personality traits from early or middle childhood into adulthood, and clear predictions from early personality to later functioning in several domains.

The two trajectories that are studied in this chapter, shyness and aggression, can be regarded as examples of externalizing and internalizing tendencies (Achenbach & Edelbrock, 1981), a dimensional distinction that is sometimes made by clinicians and researchers in child psychopathology. Although it is clear that shyness and internalizing problems cannot be fully equated (see Asendorpf, Denissen, & van Aken, 2008), nor can aggression and externalizing problems (Bongers, Koot, van der Ende, & Verhulst, 2003), the two trajectories of shyness and aggression discussed in this chapter are meant to be taken as illustrative of trajectories of internalizing and externalizing problem behaviors. At present, research on developmental trajectories of problem behaviors over such a long time is lacking. Rather, personality in early childhood is more typically related to personality in late adolescence or adulthood, ignoring the developmental period linking the two.

Thus, much of the available evidence on the prediction of later outcomes by earlier personality is based on bivariate correlations between two time points. Although this does demonstrate the importance of early personality, it does not show the shape of a developmental trajectory, with possibly periods of change versus more stable periods. The LOGIC data, however, with frequent measurements over the course of development, enable us to estimate developmental trajectories empirically.

Another asset of the LOGIC data is the detailed character of the measurements, at all ages, including the last one, spanning the developmental period between 18 and 23 years of age. This period has been labeled "emerging adulthood" (Arnett, 2000) and treated as a distinct period of the life course, not just a period of rapid changes. It has been stated that the demographic shifts of the past half century in Western cultures (such as a higher age at the time of marriage, first childbirth, and entering the labor force) have considerably changed the period of the late teens and the early twenties. One new characteristic of this period is that it has increasingly become a period of frequent change and exploration, instead of commitments.

As social investment theory (Roberts, Wood, & Smith, 2005) prdicts, personality development might go hand in hand with taking up adult roles during this period. To capture this, we will consider outcomes such as work, education, and relationships as well as describe the developmental trajectories of shyness and aggression from early childhood to young adulthood. We assume that although the processes of work, education, and relationships are partly the result of a developmental trajectory, failure or success in these outcomes (that is, in taking up these adult roles) might mediate such a trajectory.

6.3 THE STUDY OF PERSONALITY IN THE LOGIC STUDY

In 1983, when the LOGIC team began to discuss how personality should be studied, it was clear that such a long-term project would require (a) a broad measure of personality that would cover a wide array of young children's individual characteristics, and (b) a few focal constructs that could be studied in detail with assessments that entailed multiple judgment perspectives and behavioral observations.

Franz E. Weinert, the *spiritus rector* of the LOGIC study, was not only an eminent scientist and politician of science but also an extremely successful mentor for the young, eager researchers in the LOGIC group. His mentoring was guided by the principle that you must first discover what *really* interests your student (*not* what the mentor is most interested in and *not* what is currently in the mainstream). Rather than maximizing the short-lived impact factor of research by following the crowd, this strategy encourages young researchers to express their own ideas in research that may eventually create a new mainstream and make them leaders of new crowds—the kind of foresight typical for Franz E. Weinert. This is a risky strategy that requires a tough preselection of students, but then increases the likelihood for a spin-off in terms of new lines of research and creative solutions to long-standing problems. Consequently, Weinert restricted himself to suggestions for the broad measure of personality but left the decision for the focal personality constructs to his postdoc, Jens B. Asendorpf.

Regarding the broad measure, it is important to note that when the LOGIC discussions began in 1983, variable-centered research on the "Big Five" factors of personality differences (John & Srivastava, 1999; the five factors are extraversion, neuroticism, conscientiousness, agreeableness, and intellect or culture) that currently dominates personality research in both adults and children (e.g., De Fruyt et al., 2006; Kohnstamm, Halverson, Mervielde, & Havill, 1998) did not yet exist. A measure based on the Big Five was not an option. Instead, the person-centered approach to childhood personality by Block and Block (1980) was chosen, including the broad Q-sort measure of early childhood personality, the California Child Q-Set (CCQ). In this measure, a large number of personality-descriptive items, each printed on a card, is sorted by a judge into numerous piles that represent the saliency of the trait for the judged child, from *extremely uncharacteristic* to *extremely characteristic*. The full 100-item CCQ was too long for our purposes of obtaining Q-sort descriptions for multiple children by the same preschool teacher.

We thus used a short 54-item version of the CCQ by Schiller (1978), translated into German using a translation and back-translation procedure (Göttert & Asendorpf, 1989).

For the specific constructs, Asendorpf decided to focus on internalizing tendencies such as shyness, low self-esteem, loneliness, and social anxiety because at that time externalizing tendencies such as aggressiveness, impulsivity, and hyperactivity dominated the literature, and because Asendorpf had already developed a broader concept of shy-inhibited tendencies, based on concurrent research on shyness in adults (Asendorpf, 1987, 1989), which included inhibition based on temperament and inhibition based on experiences of being neglected or rejected by others. Somewhat later, Asendorpf became aware of the related research of Jerome Kagan and colleagues on behavioral inhibition to the unfamiliar (Kagan, Reznick, Clarke, Snidman, & Garcia-Coll, 1984). However, the research on shyness and inhibition in the LOGIC study developed somewhat independently from the research by the Kagan group.

The LOGIC study also benefited from collaboration with researchers outside the LOGIC group. In response to a letter that Asendorpf sent to numerous researchers well-known for their developmental studies of shyness and related constructs, Kenneth Rubin responded enthusiastically. In this letter, researchers were invited to collaborate with the LOGIC study. Rubin's sophisticated view on different facets of social withdrawal (see Rubin, 1982, 1985) and his theoretical model of the development of internalizing difficulties (e.g., Rubin, LeMare, & Lollis, 1990) that he presented in 1985 during a one-month visit to the Max Planck Institute for Psychological Research strongly influenced Asendorpf's further research. Asendorpf and Rubin closely collaborated for many years thereafter (e.g., Rubin & Asendorpf, 1993).

Asendorpf's strong focus on the development of shyness and inhibition led to numerous publications on this topic (Asendorpf, 1990, 1991, 1993, 1994; Asendorpf & van Aken, 1994). The last one was coauthored with Marcel van Aken, who spent 3 postdoc years at the Max Planck Institute from 1990 to 1993 and became Asendorpf's closest collaborator in the LOGIC study. In his dissertation, conducted independently of the LOGIC study at the University of Nijmegen, van Aken had investigated the stability and cross-judge consistency of Q-sort descriptions of children's personality (van Aken & van Lieshout, 1991), and fueled Asendorpf's interest in social-relationship correlates of personality (Asendorpf & van Aken, 2003a; van Aken & Asendorpf, 1997) as well as in person-centered approaches to personality (Asendorpf & van Aken, 1991, 1999, 2003b)—with a spin-off for personality research in adults (Asendorpf, 2003; Asendorpf, Borkenau, Ostendorf, & van Aken, 2001; Asendorpf, Caspi, & Hofstee, 2002; Asendorpf & Wilpers, 1998; Neyer & Asendorpf, 2001).

Asendorpf and van Aken were joined by Jaap Denissen for the analyses of the last LOGIC assessment. Denissen also studied psychology at the University of Nijmegen, the Netherlands, and did most of the person-focused analyses (Asendorpf & Denissen, 2006; Denissen, Asendorpf, & van Aken, 2008) on which the present chapter is based when he was a fellow at the International Max Planck

Research School LIFE and of the Department of Psychology at Humboldt University, Berlin.

The present chapter focuses on the person-centered personality research in the LOGIC study. Each individual is described by a broad array of personality characteristics, represented by a Q-sort profile. Table 6.1 presents three examples for such personality profiles of young children. The first one describes a "resilient child" characterized as self-confident and cognitively competent, able to cope with stress, and not moody. The second one depicts an "overcontrolled" child described as agreeable, not aggressive, and not self-confident. The third one describes an "undercontrolled" child described as energetic, restless, antisocial, uninhibited, and inattentive.

The terms *resilient, overcontrolled,* and *undercontrolled* refer to the conceptual framework developed by Block and Block (1980). These authors assumed that young children's personality varies in a two-dimensional space with the dimensions ego resiliency and ego control. *Ego resiliency* refers to the tendency to respond flexibly rather than rigidly to changing situational demands, particularly stressful situations. *Ego control* refers to the tendency to contain versus

TABLE 6.1
Personality Profiles for Three Prototypical Children at Ages 4–6

Ego-Resilient Child	Overcontrolled Child	Undercontrolled Child
CCQ Item (number)	CCQ Item (number)	CCQ Item (number)
Attentive, able to concentrate (66)	Gets along well with other children (4)	Vital, energetic, lively (28)
Competent, skillful (89)	Considerate of others (2)	Restless and fidgety (34)
Self-reliant, confident (88)	Helpful and cooperative (6)	Pushes and stretches limits (13)
Becomes strongly involved (74)	Obedient and compliant (62)	Expresses negative feelings directly (18)
Curious and exploring (40)	Uses and responds to reason (25)	Transfers blame to others (11)
Persistent in activities (41)	Neat and orderly (59)	Stubborn (90)
Inhibited and constricted (35)	Seeks to be independent (83)	Attentive, able to concentrate (66)
Rapid shifts in mood (54)	Self-reliant, confident (88)	Fearful and anxious (23)
Immature behavior under stress (12)	Pushes and stretches limits (13)	Gives in in conflict (44)
Disorganized under stress (46)	Self-assertive (82)	High standards for self (47)
Sulky or whiny (94)	Teases other children (80)	Inhibited and constricted (35)
Cries easily (33)	Aggressive (85)	Ruminates and worries (24)

Note: Shown are the six highest-ranking and six lowest-ranking CCQ items in the empirically derived prototypic profiles for ego-resilient, overcontrolled, and undercontrolled children. Abbreviated item descriptions. Item numbers refer to the original 100-item CCQ by Block and Block.

Source: Asendorpf and van Aken (1999, Table 2); Block and Block (1980).

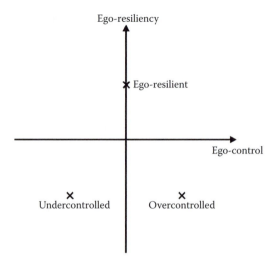

FIGURE 6.1   Theoretically expected position of prototypical ego-resilient, overcontrolled, and undercontrolled children according to Block and Block (1980).

express emotional and motivational impulses (overcontrol versus undercontrol). Block and Block assumed that both extremely high and low ego control are related to low ego resiliency. Therefore, three types of children can be distinguished (see Figure 6.1): ego resilients (high scores in ego resiliency, intermediate scores in ego control), overcontrollers (high in ego control, low in ego resiliency) and undercontrollers (low in ego control, low in ego resiliency).

In fact, Table 6.1 describes these three personality types in terms of their empirically derived prototypic Q-sort profile (only the six highest-scoring and six lowest-scoring items of all 54 items are listed). These prototypic profiles were derived as follows. First, each child of the LOGIC sample was described by the child's teacher on the German CCQ in every year in preschool and kindergarten. For the 151 children who were judged in this way three times, the CCQ scores were averaged across the three assessments to increase the reliability of the Q-sort profiles. Second, these individual Q-sort profiles were factor analyzed by Q-factor analysis (also called *inverse factor analysis* because the roles of persons and variables in ordinary factor analysis are reversed). The resulting Q-factors represented prototypic personality patterns that fitted the expected prototypes of resilient, overcontrolled, and undercontrolled children quite well (see Asendorpf & van Aken, 1999, for the Q-factor loadings of the items).

Following a procedure proposed by Robins, John, Caspi, Moffitt, and Stouthamer-Loeber (1996), 141 children were subsequently classified into personality types by assigning them to the most similar prototypic profile (10 of the original sample of 151 could not be clearly classified; see Asendorpf & van Aken, 1999, for details). Of the 141 children, 49% were classified as resilient, 21% as overcontrollers, and 31% as undercontrollers. As one might expect, boys were overrepresented among the undercontrollers, and therefore underrepresented among the resilients; in contrast, boys and girls were equally represented among the overcontrollers. The following analyses refer to these three groups of children identified at ages 4–6 years.

6.4 CONCURRENT CORRELATES OF EARLY CHILDHOOD PERSONALITY

The three personality types in early childhood can be described in the LOGIC study by their concurrent correlates in terms of social competence, shyness-inhibition, aggressiveness, and cognitive achievement (see Table 6.2). Compared to the well-adjusted ego resilients, the overcontrollers are expected to be more shy-inhibited, whereas the undercontrollers are expected to be more aggressive and lower in cognitive achievement. These expected differences between the three types were evaluated by using the ego resilients as a reference group and contrasting this group with the overcontrollers and the undercontrollers.

Table 6.2
Concurrent Correlates of the Three Personality Types in Early Childhood

Correlates	Ego Resilients (n = 69)		Overcontrollers (n = 29)		Undercontrollers (n = 43)	
	M	SD	M	SD	M	SD
Teacher judgment: socially competent[a]	.53	.16	.27*	.22	.07*	0.25
Teacher judgment: shy-inhibited[a]	.04	.16	.37*	.12	−.27*	0.14
Teacher judgment: aggressive[a]	−.41	.18	−.45	.19	.22*	0.18
Parental judgment: shy-inhibited (1–7)[a]	3.27	1.03	4.16*	1.02	2.94	0.82
Parental judgment: aggressive (1–7)[a]	2.66	0.66	2.66	0.86	3.16*	0.81
Latency to first request from peer (minutes)	6.32	6.25	10.92*	5.63	4.12	5.47
Observed aggressiveness with peers (%)	1.79	3.05	1.16	2.03	6.20*	6.09
IQ[a]	103.4	9.18	98.7*	9.90	95.0*	12.21
Late schooling[b]	0.11	0.31	0.12	0.33	0.32*	0.47

* Indicates significant ($p < .05$) difference from resilient group.
[a.] Average across ages 4, 5, and 6.
[b.] Percentage not yet attending elementary school in expected school year.

The first three correlates of Table 6.2 refer to *individual* correlations between a child's Q-sort and a prototypic Q-sort for a socially competent, shy-inhibited, or aggressive child that were independently obtained from other German preschool teachers. These correlations describe how similar the Q-sort profile of a particular child was to one of the prototypic profiles. The three similarity coefficients that were obtained for each child at ages 4, 5, and 6 years were averaged. These average similarity coefficients characterize the stable personality of the LOGIC children in early childhood from the perspective of their teachers.

The data for social competence indicate that ego resilients were described by the teachers as significantly higher in social competence than both the over- and the undercontrollers because the Q-sort profiles of the ego-resilient children resembled more strongly the prototypic profile of a socially competent child (mean correlation of .53 with a standard deviation of .16) than the Q-sort profiles of the overcontrollers (mean correlation of .27) and the undercontrollers (mean correlation of .07). Similarly, the next two rows in Table 6.2 indicate that the teachers judged the overcontrollers as having a personality more typical for a shy-inhibited child (.37) than the ego resilients (.04), whereas they judged the undercontrolled children as being not typical for a shy-inhibited child (–.27). Furthermore, they judged the undercontrollers as resembling more the prototype of an aggressive child (.22) than both the ego resilients (–.41) and the overcontrollers (–.45). It should be noted that these relationships were so strong because they were based on the same teacher judgments of multiple children.

To cross-validate these results, we collected independently obtained personality judgments by the children's parents (nearly always the mother). Table 6.2 indicates that indeed the overcontrollers were judged as particularly shy inhibited (a mean rating of 4.16 on a scale ranging from 1 to 5), and the undercontrollers as particularly high in aggressiveness (3.16). This latter score was somewhat underestimated by the fact that the parental judgments for aggressiveness did not correlate with the teacher judgments or with behavioral observations in the preschools at age 4, but did correlate with both measures of aggressiveness at ages 5 and 6. It seems that children's aggressiveness was highly context specific at age 4 such that their aggressiveness outside of the preschool (observed by the parents) was not related to their aggressiveness in the preschool (observed by the teachers and our observers), and this inconsistency suppressed the aggressiveness scores of the undercontrollers (defined by teacher judgments) at age 4 and therefore also the average for ages 4–6. Except for this particular problem for age 4, the parental judgments were consistent with the personality types defined by the teacher judgments.

Further evidence for the validity of the personality types comes from observational data (see Table 6.2). According to Kagan and associates' concept of behavioral inhibition toward the unfamiliar (Kagan et al., 1984), shy-inhibited children are expected to have problems with contact with strangers, particularly unfamiliar peers. To test this hypothesis, the LOGIC children were invited at age 4 to play for 10–15 minutes with an unfamiliar, same-sex peer from the LOGIC sample in the Max Planck Institute. Analyses of the videotaped behavior showed that, as expected, the overcontrolled children needed much more time until they requested something from their playmate (e.g., asking a question); see Table 6.2 (and Asendorpf, 1990, for more details). Aggressive behavior was rarely observed in these dyadic play sessions; it occurred more often in preschool. Table 6.2 indicates that, as expected, the undercontrollers were more often observed to react aggressively by trained observers who were sent to their preschools and observed each child on at least 5 different days for a total of approximately 100 minutes during free-play periods in class (see Asendorpf, 1990, for more details).

Table 6.2 indicates that, as expected, undercontrollers had lower IQ scores (average of two nonverbal and two verbal IQ tests conducted between ages 4 and 6) and made the transition to elementary school later than the ego resilients (see Asendorpf & van Aken, 1999, for details of the IQ assessments). Somewhat surprisingly, the overcontrollers also had a somewhat lower IQ than the ego resilients (4 points less on average; see Table 6.2). For a proper interpretation of these results, it is important to note that IQ is tested interactively in young children (they cannot read instructions) such that test achievement is due not only to cognitive competence but also to temperamental factors such as inhibition to strangers (relevant for the overcontrollers) and distractibility (relevant for the undercontrollers). Therefore, the slightly lower IQ of the overcontrollers and part of the low test achievement of the undercontrollers can be attributed to these temperamental factors.

Similarly, the late schooling of the undercontrollers seems to be attributable not only to their lower cognitive competence but also to their temperament. When the IQ differences between the undercontrollers and the ego resilients were statistically controlled by analysis of covariance, the undercontrollers still made the transition to elementary school marginally later ($p < .15$). Although this seems to be a very weak effect, controlling for IQ is actually a form of overcorrection because the achievement in the IQ tests is affected by temperament as well. The bottom line is that there is no clear evidence that overcontrollers are lower in cognitive competence than ego resilients. There is, however, evidence that undercontrollers are already underachievers at the transition to elementary school (they achieve less than one might expect on the basis of their cognitive competence).

Together, these results strongly support the validity of the three personality types in early childhood. Their concurrent correlates in terms of key variables of internalizing and externalizing tendencies (shyness-inhibition and aggressiveness) and in terms of their social and cognitive competence draw a consistent picture of differences between the types. Although the types were only empirically derived (Q-factor analysis of Q-sort descriptions, followed by assignment of each child to the most similar Q-factor), they are consistent with expectations based on Block and Block (1980), and begin to tell a coherent story about important personality differences in early childhood. How does this story continue as we follow the LOGIC children over childhood, adolescence, and the first years of adulthood?

6.5 TRAJECTORIES INTO ADULTHOOD

By the time of the last assessment at age 23, 27% of the 141 children initially classified dropped from the study. As noted earlier, initial attrition was primarily because the child and family had moved away from the greater Munich area. However, after age 12, attrition was increasingly due to the LOGIC participants themselves. Therefore, it was important to check the data for systematic attrition effects by comparing the 38 dropouts with the 103 longitudinal participants. In line with other studies showing a higher dropout rate for more problematic participants (e.g., clinical groups versus controls, or low IQ versus high IQ), only 33% of the dropouts were ego resilient, whereas a majority of the longitudinal participants were ego resilient (55%)—a significant difference. Thus, ego resilience contributed to the participants' cooperation in the LOGIC study. Consequently, differences between the overcontrollers and the ego resilients and differences between the undercontrollers and the ego resilients were somewhat attenuated by the selective dropout. Fortunately, the proportions of over- and undercontrollers among the non-ego-resilient participants remained constant; they were not affected by selective attrition. In other words, *if* characteristics were found that distinguished the two non-ego-resilient groups from the ego-resilient group in the assessments after early childhood, they could be trusted, and there was no bias in the LOGIC study in the ease of finding characteristics of overcontrollers or undercontrollers.

Because dropout occurred for different participants at different times, and because sometimes data could not be assessed for just one point in time or one assessment procedure, there was a complex pattern of missing data over the course of the LOGIC study. Reducing the data to those participants who had nonmissing data in all assessments would have extremely reduced the sample of participants, and would have introduced additional problems with selective attrition. One solution to this problem is to analyze individual developmental trajectories based on available points in time, which means that the trajectory basis may differ between participants. This approach was introduced into the LOGIC study early on by Asendorpf, who demonstrated that more intelligent and more socially competent children became less shy over the first 6 years of the LOGIC study than less intelligent or less socially competent children (Asendorpf, 1994).

The specific measure used to analyze individual developmental trajectories was hierarchical linear modeling (HLM; Bryk & Raudenbush, 1992; Raudenbush & Bryk, 2002). This methodological approach was also used to assess long-term developmental change (Asendorpf & van Aken, 1999; Denissen et al., 2008). Each participant's repeated assessments are regressed at level 1 of the hierarchical model on age or (if nonlinear change is studied) on particular functions of age such as age squared (U-shaped or inverted U-shaped trajectories), or functions describing exponential change. Thereby, each participant's development is described by at least two parameters: level (average over all repeated assessments) and change (the slope of a straight line describing linear change and/or other parameters describing nonlinear change). This can be accomplished separately for each participant, followed at level 2 of the analysis by an analysis of interindividual differences in these parameters (e.g., correlating the slope of changes in shyness with the initial level of IQ; Asendorpf, 1994). HLM offers even more powerful opportunities such as simultaneous Bayesian estimates of both level and change that weight each individual's parameter by its intraindividually determined reliability (see Raudenbush & Bryk, 2002).

The following analyses of the developmental trajectories of the three personality types are based on such Bayesian estimates of change (see Denissen et al., 2008, for details). Similar to the analysis of concurrent correlates of the different personality types (see Table 6.2), they contrast ego resilients with overcontrollers and undercontrollers. Instead of contrasting them in terms of correlates assessed at the same age, these longitudinal analyses contrast them in terms of the level and linear and quadratic change in individual trajectories. Denissen et al. applied this approach to the developmental change in parental judgments of shyness and aggressiveness that were obtained over the course of the LOGIC study, from ages 4 through 23. One particular advantage of these analyses is that the definition of the three personality types was based on data sources (teacher Q-sort judgments) that were completely independent in terms of judges and methods from the dependent variables (parental questionnaires). This removes the possibility that relations between the personality types and developmental change could be due to shared methods.

6.5.1 Shyness

Figure 6.2 shows the average developmental trajectories of the three personality types for parental judgments of shyness. The figure suggests an overall decrease in these judgments. An HLM model including quadratic trends did not show any significant quadratic effects. Therefore, a linear model was chosen that contrasted overcontrollers with ego resilients, undercontrollers with ego resilients, and males with females, and that estimated overall effects for (male) ego resilients (no sex effects were found such that the overall effects also apply to females). The logic behind this approach is that the ego resilients are something like a control group representing "normal" development, and that the development of the over- and undercontrollers is then described as a deviation from this normal pattern.

Ego resilients' overall level of shyness between ages 4 and 23 was estimated as 2.77 on the scale ranging from 1 to 7, thus clearly below the mean 4 of the rating scale. Note that this estimate is not simply the average of all available data for the (male) ego resilients because the individual trajectories were weighted by their reliability. Shyness was estimated to significantly decrease over time by 0.087 points per year in this group. Thus, over the 19-year period, the (male) ego resilients were judged as 1.65 points less shy at age 23 than they were at age 4.

We then looked at deviations of the two non-ego-resilient groups from the ego-resilient group pattern. Figure 6.2 suggests that the overcontrollers were constantly judged as more shy than the ego resilients, whereas the undercontrollers started off with the lowest shyness scores but ended up with as high

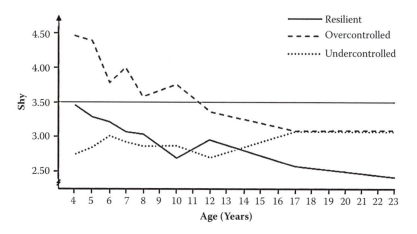

FIGURE 6.2   Developmental trajectories of ego-resilient, overcontrolled, and undercontrolled children for parent-judged shyness. Reprinted from Denissen, Asendorpf, and van Aken (2008, Figure 1).

shyness scores as the overcontrollers. The overcontrollers were judged as 0.55 points more shy overall than the ego resilients (a significant difference), and were not significantly different from the ego resilients in terms of their slope in shyness. In contrast, the undercontrollers were judged equally shy as the ego resilients overall, but their shyness decreased less strongly than the shyness of the ego resilients (the difference was 0.060 points per year, for a total of 1.14 points between ages 4 and 23). In other words, whereas the ego resilients' shyness decreased by 1.65 points, the undercontrollers' shyness decreased only (1.65 – 1.14 =) 0.51 points on the 7-point parental shyness scale. All in all, the expected overall higher shyness of overcontrollers was confirmed, but in addition an unexpected shift of the initially below-average shyness levels of the undercontrollers to above-average shyness levels was found.

Additional analyses of the participants' *self-judgments* of shyness that were obtained at ages 12, 17,[1] and 23 did not show any effects of early personality on level or change in the self-concept for shyness. Also, the concurrent correlations between the self-judgments and parent judgments of shyness were rather low (below .32 for all ages). It seems that the later self-concept of shyness is independent from early personality and follows its own developmental trajectory from late childhood into adulthood.

Analyses of the relationship between self- and parent judgments of shyness and the quality of the LOGIC participants' social relationships with their peers and parents suggest that the self-concept of shyness is related to the quality of peer relationships in adolescence and emerging adulthood. The perceived support from peers and parents was reported by the LOGIC participants at ages 12, 17, and 23. Table 6.3 presents the concurrent correlations between the two measures

Table 6.3
Concurrent Relationships Between Shyness and Perceived Support from Peers and Parents

| | | Perceived Support from | |
Shyness	Age	Peers	Parents
Self-judgment	12 years	−.09	−.02
Parental judgment	12 years	−.21*	−.05
Self-judgment	17 years	−.35***	−.12
Parental judgment	17 years	−.09	.07
Self-judgment	23 years	−.30***	−.11
Parental judgment	23 years	−.21*	−.01

Note: N varies between 115 and 182.
* p < .05. *** p < .001.

of shyness with perceived support. Perceived support from the parents was unrelated to both measures of shyness, but perceived support from peers was related to these measures, particularly to the self-report of shyness at ages 17 and 23 (see Table 6.3).

The most likely interpretation of these results is that during adolescence, the self-concept of shyness becomes linked with negative experiences with peers such as perceptions of lack of support or even peer rejection. To the extent that parents observe the quality of peer relationships (which might be particularly difficult for them during adolescence), their shyness judgment is also influenced by these perceptions.

This context may help explain the increase in undercontrollers' shyness between the ages of 12 and 23 (see Figure 6.2). This increase was found for only parental judgments of shyness, not self-judgments. Indeed, perceived support from peers was unrelated to the early personality types, both in terms of overall level across the 11 year period between ages 12 and 23 and in terms of change (there was a significant increase over this period shared by all three types). In particular, undercontrollers' perceptions of support did not increase less than ego resilients' perceptions of support. This suggests that the perceived increase in parental judgments of shyness might be due to increasing problems in undercontrollers' relationships with their *parents*. Indeed, the undercontrollers and the ego resilients perceived the same amount of conflict with their parents at age 12, but the undercontrollers tended to perceive more conflict at ages 17 and 23. In contrast, the overcontrollers perceived the same amount of conflict as the ego resilients at all three ages. The bottom line is that the increases in parents' perceptions of the undercontrollers' shyness between ages 12 and 23 may be based on issues in the parent–child relationship.

6.5.2 Aggressiveness

As can be seen in Figure 6.3, there is only a small initial difference in aggressiveness between the personality types at age 4. As discussed above, the lack of a larger difference may be attributed to problems with the parental judgments as a measure of aggressiveness at this early age (see Section 6.4, above, on concurrent correlates of the types). Later, undercontrollers were judged as consistently more aggressive than the ego resilients, and overcontrollers were perceived as increasingly more aggressive, starting off with low scores at age 6, reaching resilients' level of aggressiveness at around age 12, and increasing further, particularly between the ages of 17 and 23 (accelerated increase).

This pattern was confirmed by the HLM analyses. A model including linear and quadratic trends as well as sex indicated that male undercontrollers, but not male overcontrollers, were judged by their parents as significantly more aggressive than male ego resilients (an average of 0.80 points higher on the 7-point aggressiveness scale). Also, females were judged as significantly less aggressive than males (their scores were an average of 0.26 lower). Thus, the effect of undercontrol on aggressiveness was three times as large as the effect of sex.

The analyses of linear and quadratic trends indicated a significant mean decrease in parental judgments of aggressiveness for male ego resilients. The corresponding decrease rate was .067 points per year on the 7-point scale. Thus, over the 19 year period, ego-resilient male participants were judged as 1.27 points less aggressive at age 23 than at age 4. There was a significant additional influence of sex on this linear change such that females decreased 0.028 points per year *less* than boys. An additional significant positive mean quadratic trend indicated that this overall decrease was particularly strong in the beginning but less strong or even reversed into an increase toward the end. Indeed, Fig-

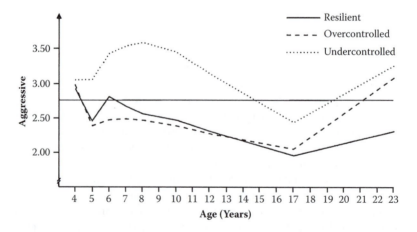

FIGURE 6.3 Developmental trajectories of ego-resilient, overcontrolled, and undercontrolled children for parent-judged aggressiveness. Reprinted from Denissen, Asendorpf, and van Aken (2008, Figure 1).

ure 6.3 indicates an increase rather than a decrease of the aggressiveness scores between ages 17 and 23.

There were also differences across personality type. There was a significant difference for the male overcontrollers for both the linear and the quadratic trend in aggressiveness. The male overcontrollers' aggressiveness scores decreased 0.03 points per year *less* than the aggressiveness scores of the male ego resilients, amounting to a total of 0.57 points over the 19 year period. In addition, male overcontrollers' aggressiveness scores showed an even stronger positive quadratic trend than those of the male ego-resilient participants. Inspection of Figure 6.3 reveals that this was mainly due to a particularly strong increase between ages 17 and 23; this increase was shared to some extent by the undercontrollers.

Analyses of the participants' *self-judgments* of aggressiveness that were obtained at ages 12, 17 and 23 showed only an effect of undercontrol on the level of aggressiveness; as expected, the undercontrollers reported significantly higher aggressiveness than the ego resilients. The concurrent correlations between self- and parent judgments of aggressiveness were low to intermediate (between .26 and .40).

Similar to the results for undercontrollers' shyness, the stronger increase of overcontrollers' and undercontrollers' aggressiveness was not supported by the self-judgments of the LOGIC participants. Although the self-judgments also showed a significant increase of aggressiveness between ages 17 and 23, this increase was very similar for all three personality types. Thus, the specific increase for over- and undercontrollers was due to specifics of the parental perceptions of aggressiveness. Conflict in the parent–child relationship can be excluded because neither the overcontrollers nor the undercontrollers reported more change between ages 17 and 23 than the ego resilients. Instead, as we will see in the next section, the increase in parents' perceptions of aggressiveness was due to a delayed adoption of adult roles by the nonresilient participants.

6.6 OUTCOMES OF EARLY PERSONALITY IN EMERGING ADULTHOOD

Important developmental outcomes of the early personality types after the 18th birthday (that marks in Germany the transition into adult roles and obligations) were studied retrospectively by a Life History Interview conducted at the last assessment (age 23). In this interview (see Denissen et al., 2008, for details), major life history data between the 18th birthday and the time of the interview (at age 23) were reconstructed on a monthly basis. In this section, we discuss five such outcomes: leaving the parental home, establishing romantic relationships, continuing education, integration into the labor force, and delinquency.

6.6.1 LEAVING THE PARENTAL HOME

There were no significant differences between the early personality types in the age of leaving the parental home for the first time (some participants moved back for some time after leaving). Indeed, according to Arnett (2000), leaving home and returning home as a transitional phase of living are irregular developmental patterns in emerging adulthood, and therefore difficult to predict. Separate analyses for males and females indicated that male ego resilients left home one year earlier than non-ego-resilient males, whereas no such effect was found for females (Denissen et al., 2008). However, this sex difference should be considered with caution because the Sex by Type interaction was only marginally significant.

6.6.2 ROMANTIC RELATIONSHIPS

Analyses of the time until the participants established a stable romantic relationship again showed no significant overall differences between the personality types, but there was a strong sex effect (males needed 1.1 years more time than females, a difference of nearly 1 standard deviation). A marginal Sex by Type interaction was due to the fact that overcontrolled males needed significantly more time to establish a romantic relationship than ego-resilient males, whereas no such difference was found for females. This sex difference is consistent with traditional gender roles, where males are expected to show more initiative than females (which, in turn, may be more difficult for overcontrolled males).

6.6.3 EDUCATION

A strong effect of early personality type on the level of education (highest achieved educational degree) was due to the fact that undercontrollers reached a significantly lower educational level than the other participants (the overcontrollers did not significantly differ from the ego resilients). This effect of early undercontrol applied to both males and females. Of the undercontrollers, only 28% finished high school (0% of the five female undercontrollers, and 35% of the 20 male undercontrollers), whereas 63% of the remaining participants finished high school. Because the undercontrollers had a lower IQ in early childhood (see Table 6.2), we statistically controlled the educational data for early IQ by analysis of covariance. After this control, the undercontrollers still showed a significantly lower educational level and a significantly lower percentage of finishing high school. Thus, the undercontrollers were educational underachievers who failed to reach the educational level expected by their IQ.

Because underachievement has been regularly found to be linked with the socioeconomic status of the family of origin (as operationalized by the occupational prestige of the parents), because undercontrollers were found to be significantly lower in socioeconomic status than the remaining participants, and because socioeconomic status correlated significantly with educational level ($r = .37$), we also statistically controlled for socioeconomic status when analyzing the influence of undercontrol on educational level. After this control, and even after controlling for both early IQ and socioeconomic status, the undercontrollers continued to show a significantly lower educational level and a significantly lower percentage of finishing high school. Thus, early undercontrol led to educational underachievement even when socioeconomic status was controlled.

6.6.4 WORK

We analyzed three different variables that indicate important steps toward integration into the labor force: latency to the first part-time job, latency to the first full-time job, and percentage of time in a full-time job (all variables were computed for the interval from the 18th birthday to the day of the Life History Interview). Educational level significantly correlated with both latencies, but in different directions (with latency to part-time work, –.42; with latency to full-time work, .25). This correlational pattern is very likely due to the fact that it is difficult to combine higher education, particularly at university, with a full-time job, although it can be combined with a part-time job (most students in Germany work part-time). Because of this close relation between education and part-time versus full-time work, it is important to control educational level in analyses of work.

The early personality types did not show significant differences in either latency to full-time work or the percentage of time spent in full-time work. However, when educational level was statistically controlled, the undercontrollers spent significantly less time after their 18th birthday in full-time work (12%) than the other two types (resilients, 25%; overcontrollers, 21%). Interestingly, latency to the first full-time job was not significantly related to early personality when educational level was controlled. Thus, undercontrollers were not only educational underachievers but also occupational underachievers. They engaged less in full-time work than was expected by their educational level, and this was due to interruptions of jobs rather than a late start of those jobs.

The ego resilients started a part-time job one year earlier than the other two personality types ($p < .005$). When educational level was controlled, only a marginally significant difference remained ($p < .09$). Thus, the effect of early ego resiliency on engagement in a part-time job was largely mediated by the higher educational level of the ego resilients. The remaining effect reflects the fact that ego resilients start to adopt adult work roles earlier than the other two personality types (see Denissen et al., 2008). The reason for not adopting these roles may be different for these other two types, however. The undercontrollers may show a lack of interest in work and may not be willing to fulfill work requirements such as reliable engagement, whereas the overcontrollers may have problems in securing a job.

Whatever the reasons for not engaging in a part-time job, latency to a part-time job was an important mediator of the somewhat surprising and as yet unexplained increase in parent-judged aggressiveness between ages 17 and 23 (see Figure 6.3). This increase was predicted by *not* being ego resilient in early childhood, and this predictive relation was fully mediated by latency to part-time work because this latency (a) was predicted by being not ego resilient in early childhood, and (b) predicted increasing parent-judged aggressiveness (see Figure 6.4).

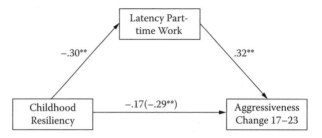

FIGURE 6.4   Mediation of the effect of early ego resiliency on the change in parent-judged aggressiveness between ages 17 and 23 by latency to first part-time work. Reprinted from Denissen, Asendorpf, and van Aken (2008, Figure 2).

Interestingly, educational level, although related to latency to part-time work and early ego resiliency, did *not* mediate ego resiliency's effect on increased aggressiveness judgments (a significant path remained). Therefore, in line with Denissen et al. (2008), it seems that engaging in part-time work prevents aggressiveness in young adults who have not fully adopted adult roles and responsibilities, at least as far as parental judgments are concerned.

6.6.5 Delinquency

A last analysis concerned the self-reported number of criminal charges because of delinquency after the 18th birthday, standardized in terms of charges within 5 years. As expected on the basis of the findings by Caspi, Moffitt, Newman, and Silva (1996), undercontrollers reported more such charges (.10 charges on average) than the other two types (.01 charges in both cases). Thus, they reported nine times more charges than the other LOGIC participants. This effect of early undercontrol on later delinquency was only partially mediated by socioeconomic status. Undercontrollers were significantly lower in socioeconomic status than the other participants, and socioeconomic status correlated −.24 (*p* < .01) with delinquency, but after controlling for socioeconomic status, early undercontrol continued to significantly predict later delinquency (the corrected rate was still 9%).

In line with the self-selection of the longitudinal LOGIC sample for higher ego resiliency, the rate of charges reported even by the undercontrolllers was low; only 28% of them reported any charges (as compared to 5% of the ego resilients and the overcontrollers). Most charges related to drug trafficking, traffic violations, and physical assault. In the two most delinquent cases, one participant was incarcerated for dealing in drugs; another was ordered to undergo therapy after five different charges had been laid for theft and drug usage. Both were classified as undercontrollers in early childhood.

6.7 DISCUSSION

Our analyses of the long-term effects of early personality relied on a person-centered approach where broad personality patterns were empirically classified into a few personality types. Alternatively, the LOGIC data can be analyzed from a variable-centered perspective with regard to specific personality dimensions such as shyness or inhibition, aggressiveness, social competence, or the Big Five factors of personality; see Asendorpf and van Aken (2003b), Asendorpf and Denissen (2006), and Asendorpf et al. (2008) for such analyses. Because differences between the three personality types are systematically related to these personality dimensions (e.g., overcontrollers differ from ego resilients primarily in terms of higher shyness-inhibition, undercontrollers differ from ego resilients primarily in terms of higher aggressiveness, and ego resilients differ from the other two types primarily in terms of higher social competence), presenting both approaches would be largely redundant. We chose the person-centered approach here mainly because (a) the results can be presented in terms of group differences, which are easier to grasp for most readers than correlational findings; (b) because the results can be directly compared with the results of the Dunedin Longitudinal Study (Caspi & Silva, 1995); and (c) because the person-centered perspective is one characteristic that sets the LOGIC study apart from most other longitudinal studies of personality development.

The empirical classification of the early personality patterns identified three personality types—ego resilients, overcontrollers, and undercontrollers—that were strikingly similar in terms of their concurrent correlates to those introduced by Block and Block (1980), and to three of the five personality types in 3 year olds that were identified by Caspi and Silva (1995) in the Dunedin Longitudinal Study (well-adjusted, inhibited, and undercontrolled children).

The analyses of the personality trajectories of the LOGIC types in terms of parental judgments of shyness and aggressiveness (key indicators of internalizing and externalizing tendencies, respectively) showed an impressive stability of the differences between the types from early childhood into young adulthood (see Figures 6.2 and 6.3). Contrary to many longitudinal studies where the predictive validity of initial personality differences decreases with increasing prediction interval, the predictive power of the early identified LOGIC types remained surprisingly constant over the 19-year period (see also Asendorpf & Denissen, 2006). It should be noted that the systematic dropout of ego resilients over the course of the LOGIC study should diminish differences between the ego-resilient group and the over- and undercontrollers, but, as Figures 6.2 and 6.3 show, this was not the case.

Although this constancy of the validity of the types may be partly attributed to an unrealistic continuity of parents' perceptions of their child's personality—once formed, these parental perceptions may become highly resistant to change—the successful predictions of numerous important life outcomes from the LOGIC types such as education level, integration into the labor force, and delinquency attest to their real predictive power over the long run.

The key to this successful prediction very likely was that the predictors were based on judgments by preschool teachers who knew the children very well, and that the predictors were based on highly aggregated data—aggregated over many Q-sort items, over many children of the same personality type, and over three yearly assessments. The aggregation over time reduced the impact of fluctuating situational variables that often affect personality assessments.

Turning now to the specifics of the long-term trajectories, we discuss them here in terms of characteristics that distinguish overcontrollers, or undercontrollers, from the "control group" of the ego resilients. The ego-resilient group can indeed be considered a control group because it was the largest one, comprising half of the sample.

6.7.1 OVERCONTROLLERS

Initially, the overcontrollers were characterized by shy-inhibited behavior as judged by both teachers and parents, and supported by observations of play with an unfamiliar peer. A slightly lower IQ in early childhood can be attributed to shyness in the interactive testing situations. In line with this interpretation are the facts that later IQ tests in adolescence and emerging adulthood no longer showed significant IQ differences between overcontrollers and ego resilients, and that the overcontrollers achieved the same educational level as the ego resilients by age 23.

Shy-inhibited behavior continued to characterize the overcontrollers over the entire course of the LOGIC study, at least as far as parental perceptions were concerned. Interestingly, overcontrollers' self-perceptions of shyness were not different from ego resilients' self-perceptions. Analyses of perceived support from parents and peers revealed that the self-concept of shyness, more than the parental perception of shyness, was associated with perceived lack of support from peers (but not from parents). The specificity of this relation rules out the interpretation that the association between self-perceived shyness and self-perceived lack of peer support was simply due to a generalized negative bias in perception. Instead, it seems that problems with peers that are not predictable from early personality influenced the emerging self-concept of being a shy person. Similar to the influence of peer relationships on internal working models of attachment (Furman, Simon, Shaffer, & Bouchey, 2002), peer relationships shape the self-concept of shyness in important ways.

Male overcontrollers (but not female overcontrollers) needed more time to engage in a stable romantic relationship. This finding is consistent with earlier studies demonstrating that shy men but not women marry later than their more outgoing counterparts, both in the United States and in Sweden (Caspi et al., 1988; Kerr et al., 1996). This delay can be attributed to the fact that, according to the traditional gender roles, males are expected to play the active part in dating and heterosexual relationships.

Finally, overcontrollers shared the undercontrollers' tendency to engage later in a part-time job—thus, a tendency shared by both nonresilient types. In the case of the overcontrollers, this tendency was not so much explained by a lower educational level. Instead, similar to the male overcontrollers' problems with securing a date, overcontrollers of both sexes seem to have problems with securing a part-time job. When educational level was controlled, they began such a job 10 months later than the ego resilients. Mortimer and Staff (2004) showed that part-time work in adolescence is associated with resilience and psychological well-being in early adulthood, in part because it prepares young people for stressful occupations in adulthood. Also, part-time work may offer an early opportunity to test out different occupational identities and gain (partial) financial independence, which are both essential features of emerging adulthood (Arnett, 2000).

In the LOGIC study, the delayed adoption of an important adult role led to problems with the parents, who, in turn, judged the overcontrollers at age 23 as being as aggressive as the parents of undercontrollers judged the undercontrollers to be. In other words, working at least part-time prevented an increase in parental perceptions of aggressiveness. This finding offers some interesting suggestions regarding the prevention of violence in young adults and adolescents. For example, O'Donnell and colleagues (1999) described a violence prevention program for adolescents including a component requiring students to provide services in local health care agencies. In a controlled, large-scale evaluation study, they found that when provided with sufficient intensity, this intervention was successful in reducing students' level of violence. This is consistent with Roberts and colleagues' (Roberts et al., 2005) notion that assuming responsibility in taking up social roles is associated with personality maturation. The current study also suggests that the effects of work interventions may differ according to participants' personality makeup. Knowledge about the moderating role of personality on the effects of (part-time) work on aggressiveness could be used to identify individuals who are especially vulnerable to the deleterious effects of forced exclusion from the labor market.

6.7.2 UNDERCONTROLLERS

Initially, the undercontrollers were characterized by aggressive behavior as judged by their teachers and by observers in the preschool and kindergarten; their parents also shared this view from age 5 onward. A somewhat lower IQ in early childhood may be partly attributed to distractibility in the interactive testing situations.

Aggressive behavior continued to characterize the undercontrollers over the entire course of the LOGIC study, measured by parental perceptions and later by self-perceptions. Interestingly, parents perceived the undercontrollers as becoming increasingly shy, starting with scores below those of the ego resilients and ending with scores as high as those of the overcontrollers. Parents' increasing shyness judgments after age 12 were paralleled by increasing perceptions by the undercontrollers that their relationships with their parents were conflict laden. Perhaps these parent–child conflicts led to frequent withdrawal on the side of the undercontrolled children, which, in turn, was perceived by their parents as shyness.

At age 23, the undercontrollers reached a much lower educational level than the other participants. For example, not a single female undercontroller finished high school, and only a clear minority of the male undercontrollers did so, whereas the majority of the overcontrollers and ego resilients finished high school. More detailed analyses showed that the undercontrollers were educational underachievers (Mandel, 1997; McCall, Evahn, & Kratzer, 1992) who failed to reach the educational level expected by their IQ. Controls for socioeconomic status did not substantially change this conclusion. Thus, distractibility and difficulties in concentration that characterize undercontrollers showed long-lasting effects on their educational achievement.

Lower educational achievement, in turn, was the main reason why the undercontrollers engaged in part-time work later than the ego resilients, and the delayed adoption of this adult role led to an increased parental perception of aggressiveness, as noted above in the section on overcontrollers.

The undercontrollers also turned into occupational underachievers who did not become as fully engaged in full-time work as one would expect from their educational level. Interestingly, this effect was found only for the percentage of time in full-time employment, not for latency to the first full-time job. The discrepancy suggests that the undercontrollers had problems with following a continuous career after they had entered the job market. This result corresponds well with the more erratic work pattern found in the Berkeley Guidance Study (Caspi et al., 1987), an effect already found early on in the participants' working lives.

Undercontrollers were more at risk for the most serious outcome of early undercontrol, delinquency in adulthood. The undercontrollers were nine times more likely to have criminal charges after their 18th birthday than the other two personality types, and the two most delinquent participants of the sample were classified as undercontrollers at ages 4–6. The predictive validity of early undercontrol for later delinquency did not change substantially when we controlled for socioeconomic status. These impressive figures should be considered with caution because (a) the delinquency rate was low overall, which might be attributed in part to the higher dropout rates for undercontrolled children in the LOGIC study; and (b) only a minority of the undercontrollers reported criminal charges. These rates are also lower than rates in most other longitudinal studies (e.g. Caspi et al., 1996; Huesmann et al., 1984). This may be because the LOGIC sample consisted of children growing up in Bavaria, a prosperous part of Germany that provided a relatively benign social-cultural environment. It is interesting that childhood undercontrol was a risk factor for delinquency even in this benign environment, where the overall delinquency rate is among the lowest in Germany (Bundesministerium des Inneren, 2005).

One reason for the successful prediction of delinquency from early childhood in the relatively small LOGIC sample study may be that delinquency was restricted to charges after the 18th birthday, which is a watershed in the German legal system. Delinquency after 18 is considered as much more serious, and the response is much harsher. This distinction between adolescent and adult delinquency maps onto the distinction between adolescence-limited and life course–persistent antisocial behavior (Moffitt, 1993). Our measure captured predominantly life course–persistent, serious antisocial behavior that is expected to be more predictable from early childhood aggressiveness than antisocial behavior during adolescence.

6.8 CONCLUSION

In the early days of developmental personality research, psychoanalysts as well as behaviorists strongly believed in the power of early experiences in the family. Later, when the first empirical data on the rather moderate stability of personality differences over long periods of time appeared, the pendulum swung to an emphasis on developmental plasticity and change, and critiques of what was seen as a widespread myth of the power of early childhood experiences (Clarke & Clarke, 1977; Kagan, 1984). Later, research on the temperamental underpinnings of personality, including its genetic and physiological basis, made the pendulum swing once again, with emphasis on the now firmer evidence for the rather stable but not immutable temperamental core of personality (Caspi, 2000; Kagan, Snidman, Arcus, & Reznick, 1994). The last decade has seen a more differentiated view, emphasizing both stability and change in personality across the entire life course (Fraley & Roberts, 2005; Roberts & DelVecchio, 2000), based on complex mechanisms of gene–environment transactions (Rutter, 2006).

The LOGIC study adds a small but significant piece to this large body of empirical evidence, emphasizing the surprising predictive power of early identified personality types even for a period in life, emerging adulthood, where individual trajectories seem to be particularly hard to predict.

NOTE

1. The average age given for Wave 10 (17 years old) deviates from that given in the other chapters (18) because only a subsample of the LOGIC group was used, in which the average age was 17.5 years.

REFERENCES

Achenbach, T. M., & Edelbrock, C. S. (1981). Behavioral problems and competencies reported by parents of normal and disturbed children aged four through sixteen. *Monographs of the Society for Research in Child Development, 46*(1, Serial No. 188), 1–82.

Arnett, J. J. (2000). Emerging adulthood: A theory of development from the late teens through the twenties. *American Psychologist, 55*, 469–480.

Asendorpf, J. B. (1987). Videotape reconstruction of emotions and cognitions related to shyness. *Journal of Personality and Social Psychology, 53*, 542–549.

Asendorpf, J. B. (1989). Shyness as a final common pathway for two different kinds of inhibition. *Journal of Personality and Social Psychology, 57*, 481–492.

Asendorpf, J. B. (1990). Development of inhibition during childhood: Evidence for situational specificity and a two-factor model. *Developmental Psychology, 26*, 721–730.

Asendorpf, J. B. (1991). Development of inhibited children's coping with unfamiliarity. *Child Development, 62,* 1460–1474.

Asendorpf, J. B. (1993). Abnormal shyness in children. *Journal of Child Psychology and Psychiatry & Allied Disciplines, 34,* 1069–1081.

Asendorpf, J. B. (1994). The malleability of behavioral inhibition: A study of individual developmental functions. *Developmental Psychology, 30,* 912–919.

Asendorpf, J. B. (2003). Head-to-head comparison of the predictive validity of personality types and dimensions. *European Journal of Personality, 17,* 327–346.

Asendorpf, J. B., Borkenau, P., Ostendorf, F., & van Aken, M. A. G. (2001). Carving personality description at its joints: Confirmation of three replicable personality prototypes for both children and adults. *European Journal of Personality, 15,* 169–198.

Asendorpf, J. B., Caspi, A., & Hofstee, W. B. K. (Eds.). (2002). The puzzle of personality types. *European Journal of Personality, 16,* S1–S5.

Asendorpf, J. B., & Denissen, J. J. A. (2006). Predictive validity of personality types versus personality dimensions from early childhood to adulthood: Implications for the distinction between core and surface traits. *Merrill-Palmer Quarterly, 52,* 486–513.

Asendorpf, J. B., Denissen, J. J. A., & van Aken, M. A. G. (2008). Inhibited and aggressive preschool children at 23 years of age: Personality and social transitions into adulthood. *Developmental Psychology, 44,* 997–1011.

Asendorpf, J. B., & van Aken, M. A. G. (1991). Correlates of the temporal consistency of personality patterns in childhood. *Journal of Personality, 59,* 689–703.

Asendorpf, J. B., & van Aken, M. A. G. (1994). Traits and relationship status. *Child Development, 65,* 1786–1798.

Asendorpf, J. B., & van Aken, M. A. G. (1999). Resilient, overcontrolled, and undercontrolled personality prototypes in childhood: Replicability, predictive power, and the trait-type issue. *Journal of Personality and Social Psychology, 77,* 815–832.

Asendorpf, J. B., & van Aken, M. A. G. (2003a). Personality-relationship transaction in adolescence: Core versus surface personality characteristics. *Journal of Personality, 71,* 629–666.

Asendorpf, J. B., & van Aken, M. A. G. (2003b). Validity of Big Five personality judgments in childhood: A 9-year longitudinal study. *European Journal of Personality, 17,* 1–17.

Asendorpf, J. B., & Wilpers, S. (1998). Personality effects on social relationships. *Journal of Personality and Social Psychology, 74,* 1531–1544.

Block, J. (1971). *Lives through time.* Berkeley, CA: Bancroft Books.

Block, J. H., & Block, J. (1980). The role of ego-control and ego-resiliency in the organization of behavior. In W. A. Collins (Ed.), *Minnesota Symposium on Child Psychology* (Vol. 13, pp. 39–101). Hillsdale, NJ: Erlbaum.

Bongers, I. L., Koot, H. M., van der Ende, J., & Verhulst, F. C. (2003). The normative development of child and adolescent problem behavior. *Journal of Abnormal Psychology, 112,* 179–192.

Bryk, A. S., & Raudenbush, S. W. (1992). *Hierarchical linear models.* Newbury Park, CA: Sage.

Bundesministerium des Inneren. (2005). *Polizeiliche Kriminalstatistik 2005* [German police crime statistics 2005]. Berlin: Bundesdruckerei.

Caspi, A. (2000). The child is father of the man: Personality continuities from childhood to adulthood. *Journal of Personality and Social Psychology, 78,* 158–172.

Caspi, A., Elder, G. H., & Bem, D. J. (1987). Moving against the world: Life-course patterns of explosive children. *Developmental Psychology, 23,* 308–313.

Caspi, A., Elder, G. H., & Bem, D. J. (1988). Moving away from the world: Life-course patterns of shy children. *Developmental Psychology, 24*, 824–831.

Caspi, A., Moffitt, T. E., Newman, D. L., & Silva, P. A. (1996). Behavioral observations at age 3 years predict adult psychiatric disorders. *Archives of General Psychiatry, 53*, 1033–1039.

Caspi, A., & Shiner, R. L. (2006). Personality development. In N. Eisenberg, W. Damon, & R. M. Lerner (Eds.), *Handbook of child psychology. Vol. 3: Social, emotional, and personality development* (6th ed., pp. 300–365). Hoboken, NJ: Wiley.

Caspi, A., & Silva, P. A. (1995). Temperamental qualities at age three predict personality traits in young adulthood: Longitudinal evidence from a birth cohort. *Child Development, 66*, 486–498.

Clarke, A. M., & Clarke, A. D. B. (Eds.). (1977). *Early experience: Myth and evidence.* New York: Free Press.

De Fruyt, F., Bartels, M., Van Leeuwen, K. G., De Clercq, B., Decuyper, M., & Mervielde, I. (2006). Five types of personality continuity in childhood and adolescence. *Journal of Personality and Social Psychology, 91*, 538–552.

Denissen, J. J. A., Asendorpf, J. B., & van Aken, M. A. G. (2008). Childhood personality predicts long-term trajectories of shyness and aggressiveness in the context of demographic transitions in emerging adulthood. *Journal of Personality, 76*, 67–99.

Fraley, C. R., & Roberts, B. W. (2005). Patterns of continuity: A dynamic model for conceptualizing the stability of individual differences in psychological constructs across the life course. *Psychological Review, 112*, 60–74.

Friedman, H. S., Tucker, J. S., Schwartz, J. E., Tomlinson-Keasey, C., Martin, L. R., Wingard, D. L., et al. (1995). Childhood conscientiousness and longevity: Health behaviors and cause of death. *Journal of Personality and Social Psychology, 68*, 696–703.

Furman, W., Simon, V. A., Shaffer, L., & Bouchey, H. A. (2002). Adolescents' working models and styles for relationships with parents, friends, and romantic partners. *Child Development, 73*, 241–255.

Göttert, R., & Asendorpf, J. B. (1989). Eine deutsche Version des California Child Q Sort, Kurzform [A German short version of the California Child Q-Set]. *Zeitschrift für Entwicklungspsychologie und Pädagogische Psychologie, 21*, 70–82.

Huesmann, L. R., Eron, L. D., Lefkowitz, M. M., & Walder, L. O. (1984). Stability of aggression over time and generations. *Developmental Psychology, 20*, 1120–1134.

John, O. P., & Srivastava, S. (1999). The Big Five trait taxonomy: History, measurement and theoretical perspectives. In L. A. Pervin & O. P. John (Eds.), *Handbook of personality: Theory and research* (pp. 102–138). New York: Guilford Press.

Kagan, J. (1984). *The nature of the child.* New York: Basic Books.

Kagan, J., & Moss, H. A. (1962). *Birth to maturity: A study of psychological development.* New York: Wiley.

Kagan, J., Reznick, J. S., Clarke, C., Snidman, N., & Garcia-Coll, C. (1984). Behavioral inhibition to the unfamiliar. *Child Development, 55*, 2212–2225.

Kagan, J., Snidman, N., Arcus, D., & Reznick, J. S. (1994). *Galen's prophecy: Temperament in human nature.* New York: Basic Books.

Kerr, M., Lambert, W. W., & Bem, D. J. (1996). Life course sequelae of childhood shyness in Sweden: Comparison with the United States. *Developmental Psychology, 32*, 1100–1105.

Kohnstamm, G. A., Halverson, C. F., Mervielde, I., & Havill, V. L. (Eds.). (1998). *Parental descriptions of child personality: Developmental antecedents of the Big Five?* Mahwah, NJ: Erlbaum.

Mandel, H. P. (1997). *Conduct disorder and underachievement: Risk factors, assessment, treatment, and prevention.* New York: Wiley.

McCall, R. B., Evahn, C., & Kratzer, L. (1992). *High school underachievers.* Newbury Park, CA: Sage.

Moffitt, T. E. (1993). Adolescence-limited and life-course-persistent antisocial behavior: A developmental taxonomy. *Psychological Review, 100,* 674–701.

Mortimer, J. T., & Staff, J. (2004). Early work as a source of developmental discontinuity during the transition to adulthood. *Development and Psychopathology, 16,* 1047–1070.

Neyer, F. J., & Asendorpf, J. B. (2001). Personality-relationship transaction in young adulthood. *Journal of Personality and Social Psychology, 81,* 1190–1204.

O'Donnell, L., Stueve, A., San Doval, A., Duran, R., Atnafou, R., Haber, D., et al. (1999). Violence prevention and young adolescents' participation in community youth service. *Journal of Adolescent Health, 24,* 28–37.

Pulkkinen, L. (2006). The Jyväskylä Longitudinal Study of Personality and Social Development (JYLS). In L. Pulkkinen, J. Kaprio, & R. J. Rose (Eds.), *Socioemotional development and health from adolescence to adulthood* (pp. 29–55). New York: Cambridge University Press.

Raudenbush, S. W., & Bryk, A. S. (2002). *Hierarchical linear models: Applications and data analysis methods* (2nd ed.). Newbury Park, CA: Sage.

Roberts, B. W., & DelVecchio, W. F. (2000). The rank-order consistency of personality traits from childhood to old age: A quantitative review of longitudinal studies. *Psychological Bulletin, 126,* 3–25.

Roberts, B. W., Wood, D., & Smith, J. L. (2005). Evaluating five factor theory and social investment perspectives on personality trait development. *Journal of Research in Personality, 39,* 166–184.

Robins, R. W., John, O. P., Caspi, A., Moffitt, T. E., & Stouthamer-Loeber, M. (1996). Resilient, overcontrolled, and undercontrolled boys: Three replicable personality types. *Journal of Personality and Social Psychology, 70,* 157–171.

Rubin, K. H. (1982). Non-social play in preschoolers: Necessarily evil? *Child Development, 53,* 651–657.

Rubin, K. H. (1985). Socially withdrawn children: An "at risk" population? In B. H. Schneider, K. H. Rubin, & J. E. Ledingham (Eds.), *Peer relationships and social skills in childhood* (pp. 125–139). New York: Springer.

Rubin, K. H., & Asendorpf, J. B. (Eds.). (1993). *Social withdrawal, inhibition, and shyness in childhood.* Hillsdale, NJ: Erlbaum.

Rubin, K. H., LeMare, L. J., & Lollis, S. (1990). Social withdrawal in childhood: Developmental pathways to peer rejection. In S. R. Asher & J. D. Coie (Eds.), *Peer rejection in childhood* (pp. 217–249). Cambridge: Cambridge University Press.

Rutter, M. (2006). *Genes and behavior: Nature-nurture interplay explained.* Malden, MA: Blackwell Publishing.

Schiller, J. (1978). *Child care arrangements and ego functioning: The effects of stability and entry age on young children.* Unpublished doctoral dissertation, University of California, Berkeley.

van Aken, M. A. G., & Asendorpf, J. B. (1997). Support by parents, classmates, friends and siblings in preadolescence: Covariation and compensation across relationships. *Journal of Social and Personal Relationships, 14,* 79–93.

van Aken, M. A. G., & van Lieshout, C. F. M. (1991). Children's competence and the agreement and stability of self- and child descriptions. *International Journal of Behavioural Development, 14,* 83–99.

7 Development of Self-Confidence from Adolescence to Early Adulthood

Friedrich-Wilhelm Schrader
and Andreas Helmke

7.1 INTRODUCTION

Self-concept and identity are personal characteristics that play an important role in adolescence and during the transition from adolescence to adulthood. According to Erikson's theoretical framework, an identity crisis is the major psychological issue of adolescence, and resolving this crisis is the main developmental task of this life period. In more current overviews of adolescence, the development of identity and self-concept is a prominent theme (Gullotta, Adams, & Markstrom, 2000; Steinberg, 1996). *Identity* refers to the individual's general sense of self comprising a coherent and integrated self-image that combines past and present states, gives direction to the future, and reflects a commitment to basic values (Fuhrer & Trautner, 2005; Gullotta et al., 2000; Wigfield, Byrnes, & Eccles, 2006). As proposed by Rosenberg (1979), the self-concept can be conceptualized as an attitude toward the own person, including a cognitive, an affective, and a behavioral component (Pinquart & Silbereisen, 2000). The *cognitive* component comprises knowledge about oneself (i.e., one's attributes), the *affective* component refers to the evaluation of these attributes, and the *behavioral* component refers to the action tendencies with respect to the own person. The latter aspect also can be denoted as the *conative* component that comprises mental processes or behaviors directed toward action.

This chapter focuses on the affective and conative aspects of the self that can be labeled as *self-confidence*. Self-esteem and self-efficacy are key constructs, and optimism and nondepressive self-view are included as further characteristics. *Self-esteem* refers to the affective component. Targets of evaluation can be single attributes as well as the person as a whole (global self-esteem, or general self-worth). Self-esteem often is conceptualized as hierarchical and multidimensional, with global self-esteem at the topmost level. Important subdomains are the academic, social, emotional, and physical domains. Each of these domains may be further subdivided into specific topics within these domains, such as specific tasks and behaviors in specific situations (Helmke, 1994; Marsh & Shavelson, 1985). *Self-efficacy* represents the behavioral component of the self and can be considered as a sense of trust in one's own capabilities, that is, an expectation to be able to act effectively and to cope with difficult problems by powerful action (Bandura, 1997). *Optimism* is a general orientation to see life in a favorable way, and is characterized by positive expectations concerning the own person as well as the environment. What we denote as *nondepressive self-view* is a low propensity to react with depressive symptoms. Depression includes symptoms such as negative affect, behavioral inhibition, and a reduced ability to deal with problems and decisions in an effective and confident manner. Whereas depression as a psychological disorder affects only a minority of people, a propensity to react with depressive symptoms can be used to characterize people in general. It is so strongly related to low self-esteem that both concepts often cannot be disentangled empirically (Harter, 1998).

Many scientists consider self-confidence as relevant for psychosocial adaptation, favorable social relations, life success, psychological health, and subjective well-being. Adolescents with high self-esteem are likely to be both happier and more effective human beings who try hard to find a positive place for themselves in important domains of life such as school, home, the workplace, and the community (Gecas, 1982; Gullotta et al., 2000). But other scientists deny a causal role to self-esteem for future adjustment and consider self-esteem merely as a consequence of other favorable outcomes (see Trzesniewski, Donnellan, & Robins, 2003; Trzesniewski et al., 2006).

Development of the self-concept is driven by cognitive and physical development and is influenced by socialization processes within major domains such as family, peers, and school (Filipp & Mayer, 2005; Harter, 1998, 2006). Cognitive development leads to an increasing ability to differentiate between one's attributes. As a consequence, evaluation also becomes more differentiated and domain specific (Helmke, 1994). In late childhood and adolescence, hypothetical and abstract thinking, as described by Piaget's theory and neo-Piagetian approaches, improves, resulting in an increasingly differentiated and integrated view of one's own person. Detecting inconsistencies among one's attributes often is an intermediary step that contributes to problems of identity, and overcoming inconsistencies by integrating them into higher order concepts is a way of solving problems of identity (Steinberg, 1996; Wigfield et al., 2006). Furthermore, physical changes during puberty direct adolescents' attention to their own person and influence the way they perceive themselves. An important factor is, among others, how young people are prepared for these changes and how they process them (Pinquart & Silbereisen, 2000; Wigfield et al., 2006). During this life period, normative life changes, particularly school transitions, occur that are associated with changes in young people's self-concept and self-esteem. When adolescents make these transitions, they have to cope with changes in the nature of the academic and social environment and related changes in their roles and responsibilities (Harter, 1998; Roeser, Peck, & Nasir, 2006). In adolescence, long-term decisions concerning future life including education, career, marriage, and commitments to other persons and organizations are required, and new social roles have to be established (Steinberg, 1996). Whereas family factors such as parental beliefs, expectations, and parenting styles remain important, in adolescence friendships and peers become more salient (Pinquart & Silbereisen; Wigfield et al., 2006).

Following Erikson and others, adolescence usually is considered as a time of self-exploration or even crisis. A popular assumption is that adolescence and early adulthood are periods of instability or "storm and stress" for which a decline in self-esteem as well as differential changes are expected. But empirical research does not support this view among nonclinical populations (e.g., Block & Robins, 1993; Hirsch & DuBois, 1991). For example, Fend (1997) reported that for several indicators of self-concept, no major reductions in mean level could be observed from grade 6 to grade 10, that is, *mean-level stability* was high. Block and Robins found no changes in mean level of self-esteem tested at the ages of 14, 18, and 23 years. Results concerning *rank-order stability* of global self-esteem (i.e., stability with respect to one's position in a group or population) are described in a meta-analysis by Trzesniewski et al. (2003). For adolescence and young adulthood, correlations are about .50 over time intervals from 1 to 6 years. Stabilities increase from childhood (6–11 years) to early adolescence (12–17 years), and late adolescence (18–21 years) to early adulthood (22–29 years), followed by a decrease in later periods of life (Trzesniewski et al., 2003; see also Fend, 2003; Steinberg & Morris, 2001). Thus, rank-order stability also fails to support the view that adolescence and early adulthood are periods of instability.

The results of the meta-analysis by Trzesniewski et al. (2003) suggest that self-esteem is a stable traitlike attribute. Occasionally, arguments for a statelike view of self-esteem are presented. Some authors have made a distinction between barometric and baseline self-esteem. Barometric self-esteem fluctuates from moment to moment, and baseline self-esteem is relatively stable over time (see Harter, 1998, 2006; Trzesniewski et al., 2003). Studies that demonstrate instability of self-esteem seem to focus on barometric self-esteem. But adolescents often vary in volatility of barometric self-esteem, and there may be different trajectories of self-esteem changes (see Steinberg, 1996; Trzesniewski et al., 2003). Hirsch and DuBois (1991) analyzed changes in self-esteem over four time periods between the end of the sixth grade and the end of the eighth grade by a cluster analytic approach. They found four clusters with different trajectories. One cluster had a steep decline in self-esteem. Only this group (21.1%) demonstrated the loss in self-esteem that often is attributed to the majority of adolescents. Predictors of differential changes were peer support and satisfaction with school. Galambos, Barker, and Krahn (2006) used a multilevel model to demonstrate individual differences in trajectories (slopes of self-esteem on time) in a sample ranging in age from 18 to 25 years. Sex was the only significant predictor: Self-esteem increased more rapidly among females so that the discrepancy between males and females in initial self-esteem decreased at the age of 25 years.

7.1.1 FACTORS THAT AFFECT THE DEVELOPMENT OF SELF-CONCEPT, SELF-ESTEEM, AND SELF-CONFIDENCE

In addition to earlier self-esteem, the determinants of self-esteem are relatively stable factors such as social class, sex, birth order, academic ability, parental approval, peer support, adjustment, and success in school (e.g., Bachman & O'Malley, 1977; Steinberg, 1996; Steinberg & Morris, 2001; Trzesniewski et al., 2006). In general, personal characteristics, family, peers, and school can be distinguished. In this section, in addition to earlier self-confidence, we focus on success in school, general competencies and dispositions, well-being as an indicator of adjustment, and peer support.

7.1.1.1 Success in School

Academic achievement is the most obvious criterion for success in school. Self-esteem is related to achievement, with a stronger relation for domain-specific self-concepts than for global esteem (Marsh & Yeung, 1997; Steinberg, 1996). School type (educational track) is another indicator of success because in Germany it is strongly related to level of achievement. Results from Fend (1997) show that school type accounts for 1 to 2% of the differences in self-concept. He also reported positive correlations between indicators of self-concept and grades (summary grades) that vary for school type, age, and sex. If extreme groups of high-achieving and low-achieving students are compared, substantial differences with respect to various aspects of self-concept as well as other personal characteristics such as well-being, test anxiety, and health problems are observed (Fend, 1997).

7.1.1.2 General Competencies and Dispositions

Beyond academic achievement, the acquisition of more general competencies and dispositions such as achievement orientation, a positive attitude toward learning, coping with various demands, overcoming test anxiety, volition, control of attention, learning strategies, and metacognition is crucial. These factors not only are prerequisites of school success but also can be seen as criteria for success and academic achievement. According to Fend (1997, 2003) a main task in late childhood and early adolescence is to form a coherent identity that integrates achievement and social experiences into the self-system. Conflicts between achievement and social integration may be a problem, especially for high-achieving students (Fend, 2003; Juvonen, 2006; Wigfield et al., 2006). According to Roeser and Lau (2002), *positive (versus negative) student identities* are associated with positive academic performance (versus academic failure), good relationships (versus difficulties) with classmates, positive (versus negative) emotions related to academic goals, high (versus poor) academic efficacy, positive (versus negative) conceptions of themselves as students, and a commitment to learning (versus diminishing aspirations for educational attainment) (Wigfield et al., 2006).

7.1.1.3   Well-Being and Critical Life Events

Psychological well-being is a broad concept dealing with psychological comfort, feeling good about oneself, and psychological states like happiness. It is related to self-confidence, a perceived ability to perform well, and self-efficacy (Gullotta et al., 2000). Life satisfaction is considered as a component of well-being and often is assessed with respect to particular domains of life (e.g., work, family, and school). Fend (1997), who considered high well-being as favorable and low well-being as a risk factor for adolescent development, used several indicators of life satisfaction: well-being at home, at school, and within the classroom; personal well-being; and well-being with respect to health. Global well-being (a summary score) was related to several components of the self-concept (Fend, 1997).

A further risk factor is *critical life events*, which are nonnormative disturbing events with which a person has to cope (Filipp & Ferring, 2002). One critical life event that seems to be especially important is parental divorce (Amato & Keith, 1991). Critical life events may reduce self-confidence, reduce personal well-being, and impede social adaptation. However, coping with these problems in a successful manner may stabilize and promote self-confidence.

7.1.1.4   Social Integration

Beyond family, peers are an important domain of socialization, especially for adolescents. Research has shown that approval by peers, social acceptance, and integration into a group of peers contribute to self-confidence (Fend, 2003). According to Harter (1998), approval from peers in the more public domains such as classrooms, organizations, and work settings is more strongly associated with self-esteem than is approval from close friends, who seem to function more as a secure psychological base than as a direct source of self-esteem.

What is the role of these factors during the transition from adolescence to early adulthood? Although research has demonstrated relations between these factors and self-confidence, a central question is whether and to what extent these factors contribute to self-confidence in early adulthood when self-confidence in adolescence and background characteristics are taken into account. The empirical evidence is scarce, because only a few longitudinal studies have covered the age range between adolescence and adulthood (Alsaker & Olweus, 1992; Trzesniewski et al., 2003). But most of them dealt with other questions, and none of them has explored the role of those factors used by us.

7.1.2   Research Questions

In this section, we explore several determinants of self-confidence in early adulthood. We focus on the transition from adolescence to early adulthood. We address the following questions:

- How are different indicators of self-confidence in early adulthood related? Is self-confidence a unitary construct? Or are there different distinguishable components?
- What factors in adolescence influence self-confidence in early adulthood? Based on prior research, we assume that background (e.g., socioeconomic status [SES], sex, and intelligence), earlier self-confidence, well-being, success in school, and peer influences are relevant.
- To what extent do these factors contribute to self-confidence in early adulthood when self-confidence in adolescence and background are taken into account?

7.1.2.1 Self-Confidence

We expect that optimism, self-esteem, self-efficacy, and nondepressive self-view are interrelated, and so can be seen as indicators of self-confidence. We assume that self-confidence is a moderately stable attribute, and that earlier self-confidence is one of the best predictors of adult self-confidence. We focus on rank-order stability, because indicators of self-confidence were not always assessed in a strictly comparative way and therefore comparisons of levels of self-confidence do not make sense.

7.1.2.2 Background Characteristics

Sex differences with respect to the self-concept and self-esteem are well established. Males have slightly higher self-esteem than females (Kling, Hyde, Showers, & Busswell, 1999). Also, differences in socioeconomic status are reported in the literature, with higher socioeconomic status related to higher self-esteem (Fend, 1997; Steinberg, 1996). Intelligence is an overall indicator of competence and is generally favorable for personal adaptation. Thus, we expect higher self-esteem for males than for females and for adolescents with higher socioeconomic status and higher intelligence levels.

7.1.2.3 Success in School

We assume that self-esteem is related to academic achievement and to more indirect success criteria such as aspirations, coping with test anxiety, volition, and control of attention.

7.1.2.4 Well-Being, Critical Life Events, and Social Integration

We distinguish personal well-being from well-being at school and at home so that the impact of major domains of socialization may be captured. Critical life events are factors that may reduce personal well-being and impede social adaptation. Although we consider cumulative effects (number of critical life events), we also focus on parents' divorce as one specific critical life event. Social integration into a group of peers should contribute to later self-confidence. We examine several indicators of social integration such as popularity among friends.

In summary, we assessed a broad set of variables in addressing differences in adult self-confidence. These included background variables, the earlier self-concept, cognitive factors such as achievement, emotional factors relating to well-being, motivational factors such as aspirations, anxiety, and social integration. We will first present descriptive data. Second, we will explore relations between self-confidence in early adulthood and factors in adolescence. Then we examine these factors in more detail. Finally, we present complex models for selected variables.

7.2 METHOD

7.2.1 SAMPLE

During adulthood (Wave 11), data were gathered for $N = 146$ persons ($N = 68$ females, $N = 78$ males). Unfortunately, the full sample was not available for all variables included in this chapter. In adolescence (Wave 10), several of the interview questions dealing with various aspects of schooling were put only to students, and participants who already had left school to start job training ($N = 23$) were not included. Thus, a sample of $N = 123$ (62 males and 61 females) is used in this chapter. The sample age range is from 21 to 23 years (21 years: $N = 2$; 22 years: $N = 76$; 23 years: $N = 40$). At the time of assessment, $N = 71$ were college students, $N = 26$ worked in a job, $N = 13$ trained for a job (apprenticeship), $N = 4$ were unemployed, and $N = 9$ reported some other kind of activity.

7.2.2 INSTRUMENTS AND MEASURES

In Wave 11, a comprehensive questionnaire was administered addressing basic sociodemographic issues and selected personal and social characteristics concerning psychosocial adaptation, education, and employment (for details and references, see Schrader, Helmke, & Heyne, 2006). In Wave 10, an interview and a student questionnaire were used (for details and references, see Helmke, 2000).

7.2.2.1 Measures of Adulthood (Wave 11)

The following variables were used:

- *Optimism* is a general positive orientation characterized by favorable expectations concerning the own person as well as the environment (example: "I always look at the bright side"; answer categories: *not true, likely not true, likely true,* and *exactly true*).
- *Self-esteem* is the affective evaluation of oneself as a person as well as of single personal attributes (example: "I am a valuable person"; same answer categories as above).

- *Self-efficacy* is the expectation that one has the potential to succeed and to overcome difficulties (example: "I always succeed in solving difficult problems when I try hard"; same answer categories as above).
- *Nondepressive self-view* was assessed by the reversed items of a depression questionnaire. For each item, three sentences expressing different degrees of depression were presented. Participants had to choose the one sentence that was most characteristic (example: "I rarely have felt bad," "I often have felt bad," or "I have felt bad all the time").
- *Critical life events:* The participants were asked for the occurrence of 14 critical life events (example: "My mother has died"), including a general nonspecified category (*other event*).

7.2.2.2   Measures for Adolescence (Wave 10) and General Background Characteristics

Four variables assessed in the student questionnaire were used for measuring self-confidence:

- *Future orientation/optimism*: An indicator based on two items was used (example: "I feel rather pessimistic about my future"; answer categories: *correct* or *not correct*).
- *Self-esteem*: A scale with four items was used (example: "I feel rather content about myself"; same answer categories as above).
- *Self-concept of ability*: A scale with nine items was used (example: "I can learn all I need for school rapidly without much effort"; same answer categories as above).
- *Nondepressive self-view*: The same scale as in Wave 11 was used.

The following motivational, cognitive, and background factors relating to school success and personal adjustment were measured:

- *Aspirations*: A scale with eight items from the student questionnaire was used (example: "Everybody should always do his best"; answer categories: *completely correct, somewhat correct, do not know, not correct,* and *not at all correct*).
- *Test anxiety*: A scale with 10 items taken from the interview was used (example: "How often does it occur that you are unable to concentrate on the problems during an examination?"; answer categories: *very often, often, sometimes, rarely,* and *never*).
- *Instructional attention*: A scale with six items from the student questionnaire was used (example: "It is difficult for me to pay attention during instruction"; answer categories: *correct* and *not correct*).
- *Volition*: A scale with 10 items taken from the interview was used (example: "How often does it occur that you postpone your homework?"; answer categories: *very often, often, sometimes, rarely,* and *never*; the

items tapping volitional deficits were reversed to get an indicator of volition).

- *School achievement*: In the interview, students were asked for their marks in three main topics (*mathematics, German language*, and *foreign language*) in their last report.
- *Learning strategies* were assessed with a 9-item scale from the student questionnaire (example: "When I prepare myself, I try to find appropriate examples"; answer categories: *completely correct, somewhat correct, do not know, not correct*, and *not at all correct*).
- *Intelligence*: Intelligence was measured at Wave 9 with the Hamburg-Wechsler Intelligence Scale for School Children (HAWIK). A verbal IQ was used, which is a composite of five subtests (vocabulary, general knowledge, general comprehension, numerical thinking, and commonalities; see Tewes, 1985).
- *Socioeconomic status (SES)*: This indicator was based on questions from a parent interview concerning parents' professional status and educational level (for details, see Schneider & Nunner-Winkler, 1989).

The following emotional and social factors were included:

- *Well-being at school*: A scale with three items was used. Two of the items were assessed in the student questionnaire, and one item in the interview (example: "How good do you feel at school?"; answer categories: *very good, rather good, average, not so good*, and *not at all good*).
- *Personal well-being*: The following item from the student questionnaire was used: "How content are you with yourself, on the whole?" (answer categories: *very content, rather content, average, not so content*, and *not at all content*).
- *Well-being at home*: The following item from the student questionnaire was used: "How well do you feel at home?" (answer categories: *very good, rather good, average, not so good*, and *not at all good*).
- *Well-being with respect to health*: In the interview, after several questions about health problems, the following question was put: "How well do you feel, on the whole, with respect to your health?" (answer categories: *very good, rather good, average, not so good*, and *not at all good*).
- *Social integration*: Four indicators were used: (a) *relation to students/ colleagues* ("How do you get along with other students at your school/ your colleagues?"; answer categories: *very good, good, average, not so good*, and *not at all*); (b) *popularity among students/colleagues* ("How popular are you in your class?"; answer categories: *very popular, rather popular, average, not very popular*, and *not at all popular*); (c) *esteem among students/colleagues* ("How many students in your class/colleagues like you very much?"; answer categories: *0, 1, 2, 3, 4–5, 6–10*, and *more than 10*); and (d) *friendship relations* ("How many students in

your class/colleagues would you call a special friend of yours?"; answer categories: *none of them, one, 2 to 3, 4 to 5,* and *more than 5*).

7.3 RESULTS

7.3.1 DESCRIPTIVE RESULTS

Table 7.1 gives an overview and descriptive statistics for the variables used in this chapter. Reliabilities for all scales were acceptable. The mean IQ of 111.74 shows that the sample was above average with respect to verbal intelligence. Indicators of self-confidence, on the average, ranged in the upper zone of the respective scales, as can be seen from their means and skewness scores. This was especially true for nondepressive self-view, which was based on a depression scale. When scales for test anxiety and volitional deficits are reversed, there is also a clear positive bias. So it is apparent that the sample is by no means a clinical sample with major psychopathological problems.

How representative is the actual sample with respect to those who took part at the beginning? The analyses reported in this chapter are based on those participants of Wave 11 who were students in Wave 10 ($N = 123$). All of them were already part of the Munich Longitudinal Study on the Ontogenesis of Individual Competencies (the LOGIC study) sample at Wave 2 ($N = 220$), which is the most complete sample and, therefore, was chosen as a reference. Data for the representativeness of this sample (participation, $N = 123$; nonparticipation, $N = 97$) are shown in Table 7.2.

Participants and nonparticipants in Wave 11 differed in intelligence scores when intelligence was measured in Wave 9. In Wave 9, however, intelligence test scores were available for only 63 persons of the nonparticipation group. There were no SES or sex differences. In the Wave 11 sample, 49.6% were female, 60.2% attended a high school in Wave 10, and 57.7% were reported to be university students. Thus, the sample is representative with respect to SES and sex but slightly biased with respect to intelligence.

In adulthood, four indicators of self-confidence were used. As Table 7.3 shows, these four indicators were highly correlated. That is, optimism with respect to life in general and one's own actions (self-efficacy), high self-esteem, and nondepressive self-view are strongly interrelated, and can be seen as different facets of self-confidence. For this reason, and because differential predictions are not intended in this chapter, a summary score was formed that proved to be reliable (Cronbach's $\alpha = .82$).

Does the mean level of self-confidence change from adolescence to early adulthood? This question can only be examined for nondepressive self-view, which was assessed in both waves by exactly the same items. A difference score was calculated from the original scores, which ranged between 0 and 1. The mean difference score was $M = .03$, $SD = .11$, $Min = -.42$, $Max = .50$, $t(120) = 2.92$, $p < .01$.

TABLE 7.1
Descriptive Statistics of All Variables Included in the Analyses of Self-Concept Development

	M	SD	Min	Max	Skewness	α
			Adulthood			
Self-Confidence						
Optimism	0.67	0.13	0.33	1.00	−0.19	.75
Self-esteem	0.75	0.16	0.27	1.00	−0.22	.77
Self-efficacy	0.64	0.13	0.20	0.97	−0.27	.85
Nondepressive self-view	0.83	0.10	0.34	1.00	−0.87	.84
			Adolescence			
Self-Confidence						
Future/optimism	0.84	0.32	0.00	1.00	−1.84	.74
Self-esteem	0.86	0.24	0.00	1.00	−1.69	.66
Nondepressive self-view	0.81	0.10	0.37	0.98	−1.19	.81
Self-concept of ability	0.72	0.28	0.00	1.00	−0.89	.83
Cognitive Factors						
Intelligence	111.74	12.31	77	148	0.31	.77*
Learning strategies	0.40	0.10	0.18	0.66	−0.20	.65
Academic achievement	3.82	0.78	2.00	6.00	0.36	—
Social-Emotional Factors						
Well-being at school	0.66	0.18	0.04	1.00	−0.88	.88
Personal well-being	0.71	0.20	0.00	1.00	−0.89	—
Well-being at home	0.85	0.20	0.25	1.00	−1.02	—
Well-being with respect to health	0.81	0.19	0.00	1.00	−1.24	—
Critical life events	1.28	1.02	1.00	4.00	0.46	—
Motivational Factors						
Aspirations	0.61	0.17	0.16	0.94	−0.28	.83
Test anxiety	0.32	0.14	0.08	0.83	1.00	.81
Control of attention	0.80	0.24	0.00	1.00	−1.29	.72
Volitional deficits	0.45	0.18	0.09	1.00	0.42	.88
Social integration	0.71	0.16	0.31	1.00	−0.22	.74

Note: Scales and items based on questionnaire and interview data were transformed into a range from 0 to 1.

Source: From Tewes (1985).

TABLE 7.2
Representativeness of the Sample of Young Adults

	Participation in Wave 11		Nonparticipation in Wave 11		
	M	SD	M	SD	Difference
SES	84.3	31.6	76.9	32.2	ns
Intelligence (HAWIK Nonverbal IQ, Wave 2)	105.4	14.3	104.9	15.0	ns
Intelligence (HAWIK Verbal IQ, Wave 2)	108.7	10.0	104.8	12.0	*
Intelligence (Columbia Mental Maturity Scale, Wave 9)	116.7	14.1	109.8	12.7	**
Intelligence (HAWIK Verbal IQ, Wave 9)	111.7	12.3	103.4	12.3	***
Sex (% proportion female participants)	49.6%		45.4%		ns

Note: * p < .05; ** p < .01; *** p < .001.

TABLE 7.3
Intercorrelations of Self-Confidence (Early Adulthood)

	2	3	4
1. Optimism	.63***	.54***	.48***
2. Self-esteem		.66***	.50***
3. Self-efficacy			.46***
4. Nondepressive self-view			

Note: *** p < .001.

That is, on the average, there was a small but significant increase in nondepressive self-view (effect size of $d = .30$, which is small to medium). In other words, there was no decline, and even a weak trend toward increased self-confidence.

Mean change, of course, can mask individual changes. Therefore, we additionally report individual change scores (scores > 0: increase; scores < 0: decrease). Figure 7.1 shows that although changes were small for most participants, there was considerable change for a few.

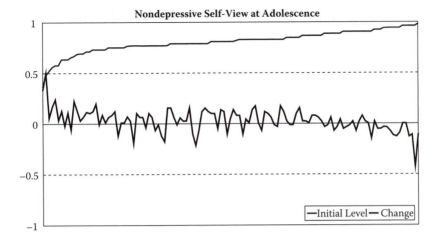

FIGURE 7.1   Initial level of nondepressive self-review, ordered from smallest to largest scores, and changes from adolescence to early adulthood.

7.3.2   SELF-CONFIDENCE IN EARLY ADULTHOOD: ROLE OF DETERMINANTS IN ADOLESCENCE

Results concerning sex, status as a university student, and school type were as follows: Males' self-confidence was higher than females' self-confidence, $M = 0.74$ ($SD = 0.09$) for males, $M = 0.70$ ($SD = 0.12$) for females, $F(1,121) = 4.40, p < .05$. University students had a higher degree of self-confidence than participants not attending a university, $M = 0.74$ ($SD = 0.12$) for university students, $M = 0.70$ ($SD = 0.09$) for other, $F(1,121) = 6.38, p < .05$. In contrast, adolescent self-confidence was not related to type of school (gymnasium, other), $M = 0.72$ for both groups ($SD = 10$ for gymnasium, $SD = 0.12$ for other). So the higher self-confidence of university students seems to emerge in youth.

Before the role of background variables and personal characteristics assessed in adolescence for self-confidence in early adulthood is explored, the intercorrelations among these variables are presented.

First, indicators of self-confidence in adolescence were substantially interrelated (correlations ranged from $r = .33$ to $r = .55, p < .001$). That is, the pattern of self-confidence that was shown in Table 7.3 for early adulthood does already exist in adolescence. Self-confidence is related to well-being (correlations ranging from $r = .19, p < .05$, to $r = .55, p < .001$) and most of the motivational variables (correlations between $r = .17, ns$, and $r = -.53, p < 0.001$), but only to some of the background and school-related variables (school type, achievement, and learning strategies). Although optimism, self-esteem, and nondepressive self-view are significantly related to frequency of experienced critical life incidents (correlations from $r = .22$, $p < .05$, to $r = .24$, $p < .01$), self-concept of ability is not. Among all self-confidence variables, only nondepressive self-view is related to social integration, $r = .25$, $p < .01$.

Second, all three background variables were significantly interrelated: (a) intelligence with SES ($r = .28$, $p < .01$), (b) SES with sex ($r = -.29$, $p < .01$), and (c) intelligence with sex ($r = -.36$, $p < .001$). The correlations with sex indicate that the SES level was higher for boys as was, surprisingly, verbal intelligence. The sex difference in verbal intelligence (males: $M = 116.2$; females: $M = 107.3$) corresponds to the analogous difference (males: $M = 112.8$; females: $M = 104.7$) reported by Schneider and Weinert (1995) for the Wave 9 sample. There are only few significant correlations with other variables. As can be expected, intelligence is significantly related to school type, $r = .49$, $p < .001$, and achievement, $r = .29$, $p < .01$.

Third, school type and academic achievement were not correlated. This is plausible because academic achievement was assessed by school grades, and grades are usually assigned within each school type, and not with regard to the absolute achievement level.

Finally, all indicators of well-being were moderately interrelated (correlations from $r = .13$, *ns*, to $r = .43$, $p < .001$), but with one exception (well-being with respect to health, $r = -.30$, $p < .001$) not related to the frequency of critical life events. All motivational characteristics (aspirations, test anxiety, attention, and volitional deficits) were significantly interrelated.

In Table 7.4, correlations of these variables with self-confidence in early adulthood as the dependent variable are presented. Following a procedure used by Block and Robins (1993), correlations with residualized self-esteem (i.e., semipartial correlations) are reported as well. Semipartial correlations indicate relations with change. However, relating the determinants to change may underestimate their effects on self-confidence, because they can be expected to have an impact not only on later self-confidence but also already on the initial level of self-confidence. Thus, simple correlations may be more appropriate to capture the summary effect that a determinant has. The correlation between level of self-confidence in adulthood and change is $r = .89$, $p < .001$. In addition, we calculated a multiple regression for each factor to get an estimate of the variance explained by this factor. Standardized regression coefficients (β) demonstrate the specific contribution a predictor has after partialing out the other predictors and, thus, represent specific effects of each determinant controlled for other determinants within the same set of variables.

As Table 7.4 shows, most variables were significantly related to self-confidence in early adulthood, and the relations are in the expected direction. Factors assessed in adolescence contributing to high self-confidence in early adulthood are favorable degrees of earlier self-confidence, well-being, motivation, intelligence, achievement, and social integration. Relations with earlier self-confidence, well-being, and attention were especially strong. Background variables and cognitive factors were modest predictors. As was shown in Table 7.4, some of these characteristics, especially well-being and motivation, were strongly

TABLE 7.4

Predicting Self-Confidence and Self-Confidence Change (Semipartial Correlation) in Early Adulthood by Means of Personal Characteristics in Adolescence

Personal Characteristics in Adolescence	r	$r_{semipart.}$	β	R^2
Self-confidence				.24***
Future/optimism	.30***	—	.09	
Self-esteem	.39***	—	.18(*)	
Nondepressive self-view	.45***	—	.29**	
Self-concept of ability	.30***	—	.06	
Background				.06 (*)
Sex (1 male, 2 female)	−.19*	−.09	−.17(*)	
Intelligence	.18*	.07	.15	
SES	−.04	.02	−.13	
Cognitive factors				.08*
School type	.00	.01	−.02	
Academic achievement	.23**	.08	.23*	
Learning strategies	.15	.12	.14	
Social-emotional factors				.24***
Well-being at school	.36***	.16	.17(*)	
Personal well-being	.35***	.12	.20*	
Well-being at home	.35***	.23**	.21*	
Well-being (health)	.24**	.01	.05	
Critical life events	−.18*	−.09	−.13	
Motivational factors				.17***
Aspirations	.26**	.17	.04	
Test anxiety	−.25**	−.04	.12	
Attention (school)	.41***	.25**	.29**	
Volitional deficits	−.26**	−.07	.06	
Social integration	.25**	.24**	.25*	.25**

Note: r: correlation with self-confidence in adulthood; $r_{semipart.}$: correlation with residualized self-confidence in adulthood (residuum of adulthood self-confidence when predicted by self-confidence in adolescence); β: standardized regression coefficients.
(*) p < .10; * p < .05; ** p < .01; *** p < .001.

related to self-confidence in adolescence. Taking the intercorrelations into account, only a few characteristics were significant predictors of self-confidence in adulthood.

To get a more complete picture, the relations between self-confidence and personal characteristics in adolescence are illustrated in Figure 7.2 by comparing

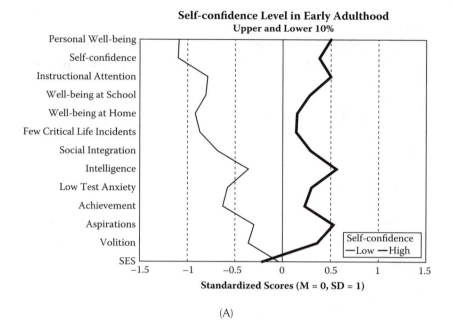

(A)

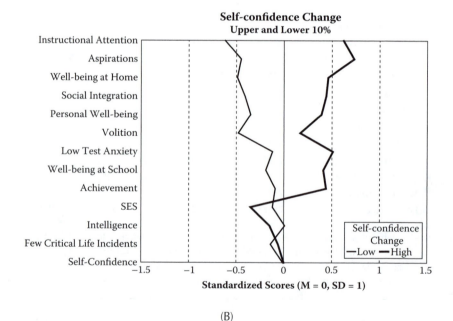

(B)

FIGURE 7.2   Profile of personal characteristics in adolescence for young adults high and low (A) in self-confidence and (B) change in self-confidence ($N = 12$ in both extreme groups) .

TABLE 7.5
Frequencies of Critical Life Events

Number of Critical Life Events	Frequency	%
0	31	25.2%
1	45	36.6%
2	31	25.2%
3	14	11.4%
4	2	1.6%

the results for extreme groups differing with respect to *level* of and *change* in self-confidence. As the attributes are listed according to the degree of difference in both parts of Figure 7.2, one can see that characteristics relevant for *level* do not exactly correspond to characteristics relevant for *change* of self-confidence.

Critical life events (e.g., Filipp & Ferring, 2002) are of special interest because they are environmental factors that may have an impact on self-confidence. Table 7.5 shows the frequencies of critical life events. About 25% of the participants reported no critical life event at all. Only two participants reported four critical life events.

As was shown in Table 7.4, the number of critical life events predicted self-confidence in early adulthood significantly, $r = -.18, p < .05$. But when self-confidence in adolescence was partialed out, the relation between the number of critical life events and self-confidence in early adulthood was no longer significant. That is, the experience of critical life events did not lead to a decline in self-confidence. The relation between self-confidence in adolescence and number of critical life events, $r = -.25, p < .01$, was even stronger than the relation between self-confidence in adulthood and number of critical life events. This is plausible because critical life events are believed to have a greater impact when persons are younger (for a more elaborated view, see Filipp & Ferring, 2002).

Twelve participants (9.8%) reported parents' divorce as a critical life event. Parents' divorce and self-confidence in early adulthood were significantly related, $r = -.32, p < .001$. This correlation remained significant even after self-confidence in adolescence was controlled, $r = -.24, p < .01$. That is, parents' divorce had a negative impact on change in self-confidence between adolescence and early adulthood.

As critical life events may lead to depressive reactions, the analyses were repeated for nondepressive self-view. The correlation between the number of experienced critical life events and nondepressive self-view was $r = -.30, p < .001$, in adulthood, and $r = -.22, p < .05$, in adolescence. When nondepressive self-view in adolescence was controlled, the partial correlation between number of critical life events and self-confidence in adulthood was $r = -.23, p < .05$. Exactly the same partial correlation resulted between parents' divorce and nondepressive self-view. Here, the simple correlations with nondepressive self-view were $r = -.28$, $p < .01$, in adulthood, and $r = -.22$, $p < .05$, in adolescence. That is, the negative impact of parents' divorce was confirmed for nondepressive self-view, too.

The analyses reported thus far demonstrate that background variables, earlier self-confidence, and cognitive, emotional, motivational, and social factors account for differences in adult self-confidence. A further question is the degree to which these factors contribute to adult self-confidence when background factors and former self-confidence are taken into account. We performed a series of regression analyses to answer this question.

As Table 7.6 demonstrates, none of the other factors contributed significantly to adult self-confidence when background variables and earlier self-confidence were taken into account. However, this does not mean that these factors are irrelevant: As they are correlated with earlier self-confidence, the effects of these variables are confounded with the effect of self-confidence. That is, a regression analysis yields a rather conservative estimation of the role of factors beyond background and earlier self-confidence. To elaborate this view, a series of commonality analyses were carried out between self-confidence and each other factor.

The results in Table 7.7 show that a large part of the variance cannot be separated for well-being. That is, well-being and self-confidence are confounded. To a lesser degree, this is also true for motivation. For cognitive factors and integration, the greatest portion of variance is specific to self-confidence, and only small portions of variance are specific to the other factor.

7.3.3   SELF-CONFIDENCE IN EARLY ADULTHOOD: COMPLEX MODELS

Thus far, we have used statistical tools such as multiple regression, commonality analysis, and partial correlation to describe the data. In the analyses that will be reported now, we take the complexity of causal relationships between variables measured at different points of time into account by using path analyses and

---

TABLE 7.6
Variance Explained by Various Sets of Explanatory Factors

Source	Partial R^2	R^2
Entry characteristics (EC)	—	.06(*)
EC and self-confidence	.19***	.25***
EC and self and cognitive factors	.02	.27***
EC and self and emotional factors	.05	.30***
EC and self and motivational factors	.05	.30***
EC and self and social integration	.02	.27***

Note: (*) p < .10; *** p < .001.

TABLE 7.7
Commonality Analyses: Self-Confidence and Second Factor

Second Factor	R^2 Total	R^2 Self- Confidence	R^2 Second Factor	Uniqueness Self- Confidence	Uniqueness Second Factor	Commonality
Cognitive factors	.26	.24	.08	.18 (70.6%)	.01 (5.5%)	.06 (23.9%)
Motivation	.27	.24	.17	.11 (38.8%)	.03 (10.7%)	.14 (50.4%)
Well-being	.29	.24	.24	.05 (16.2%)	.04 (15.2%)	.20 (68.4%)
Integration	.28	.24	.08	.20 (72.3%)	.04 (13.9%)	.04 (13.8%)

structural equation techniques (using the program Mplus; see Muthén & Muthén, 2007).

In a first series of analyses, we examined the role of cognitive factors, motivation, well-being, and social integration with simple models for each impact factor separately. Intelligence and sex were always included as predictors, whereas the impact factor was systematically changed. The structure of these models is depicted in Figure 7.3, and the results are shown in Table 7.8.

As Table 7.8 shows, each of these factors had a significant effect on self-confidence in adulthood. Only the model for motivation did not fit the data. Intelligence and sex had no direct impact on self-confidence in adulthood. Both variables were related in plausible ways to achievement, well-being, and self-confidence measured in adolescence, but not to social integration. Girls show lower self-confidence but higher achievement in adolescence.

To address which of these factors should be analyzed simultaneously, we considered their intercorrelations. Table 7.9 presents the intercorrelations of these

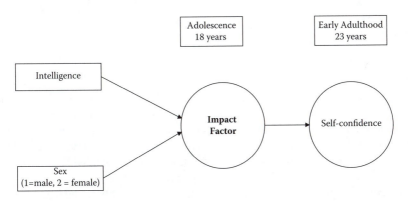

FIGURE 7.3 Basic model for the impact of factors measured in adolescence on self-confidence in adulthood, controlling for sex and intelligence.

TABLE 7.8
Results for Different Path Models Predicting Self-Confidence in Adulthood by Factors Assessed in Adolescence

Model	χ^2	df	CFI	TLI	RMSEA	Variable	β	R^2
1	56.19**	33	.933	.911	.076	Self-confidence	.59***	.35
						Intelligence	.25*	
						Sex	−.21*	
2	39.15*	25	.950	.930	.068	Academic	.26*	.07
						achievement	.46***	
						Intelligence	.31**	
						Sex		
3	37.40 ns	25	.953	.934	.063	Well-being	.64***	.41
						Intelligence	.19*ns	
						Sex		
4	42.30 ns	33	.970	.960	.048	Social	.26*	.07
						integration	ns	
						Intelligence	ns	
						Sex		
5	79.94***	33	.864	.818	.108	Motivation	No fit	—

Note: * p < .05; ** p < .01; *** p < .001.

TABLE 7.9
Intercorrelations Among Latent Factors in Adolescence

	(2)	(3)	(4)	(5)
1. Self-confidence	.41*	.74***	.93***	.26*
2. Academic achievement		.35*	.42**	−.20
3. Motivation			.70***	.07
4. Well-being				.43**
5. Social integration				

Note: * p < .05; ** p < .01; *** p < .001.

factors measured as latent variables. The correlation between self-confidence and well-being was so strong that these factors could not be separated empirically.

As noted above, the model using motivation as a predictor of self-confidence did not fit the data. Well-being could not be separated from self-confidence. Thus, only achievement, social integration, and self-confidence remained as viable factors for further modeling. In Figure 7.4, we present a model using achievement and social integration in adolescence as predictions of self-confidence in early adulthood.

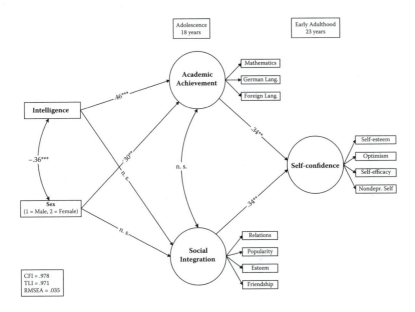

FIGURE 7.4   Model predicting self-confidence in adulthood by academic achievement and social integration in adolescence, controlling background variables.

Figure 7.4 demonstrates that academic achievement and social integration have a substantial effect on self-confidence in early adulthood even when they are analyzed simultaneously. The path coefficient for each factor was exactly the same. Academic achievement and social integration were not significantly interrelated. Academic achievement depended on intelligence and, to a lesser extent, on sex. More intelligent as well as female participants showed higher achievement. How does this pattern change when self-confidence in adolescence is included as an additional predictor variable?

Figure 7.5 confirms the result of the regression analyses reported above: Academic achievement and social integration in adolescence did not have a significant effect on adult self-confidence when self-confidence in adolescence was additionally included in the model. In this case, only adolescent self-confidence contributed significantly to adult self-confidence. That is, adolescents with high or low self-confidence can be expected to have high or low self-confidence in early adulthood. Self-confidence in adolescence was related to achievement and, to a lesser degree, social integration. But neither of these factors played a role for adult self-confidence any longer. The relations between academic achievement and self-confidence with background are in accord with what could be expected. Intelligence had a strong positive impact on academic achievement and a somewhat weaker impact on self-confidence. Female participants showed higher academic achievement but lower self-confidence. Social integration was not significantly related to background.

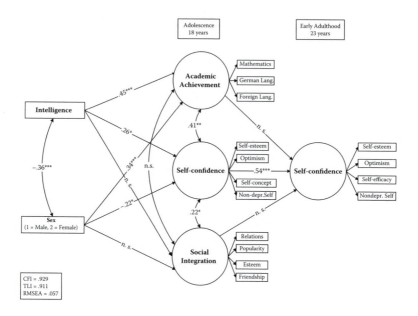

FIGURE 7.5   Model predicting self-confidence in adulthood by self-confidence, academic achievement, and social integration in adolescence, controlling background variables.

7.4   DISCUSSION

In this chapter, changes in self-confidence during the transition from adolescence (age 18) to early adulthood (age 23) were explored. The results can be summarized as follows:

1. Self-confidence is only a moderately stable attribute. That is, adolescents with high or low self-confidence in adolescence also tend to have high or low self-confidence in adulthood. However, the relation is not very strong. That is, many adolescents will experience an increase or a decline in self-confidence. Furthermore, a small but significant increase in the mean level of nondepressive self-view was observed.
2. Self-confidence in adulthood is predicted by a number of characteristics measured in adolescence. However, when self-confidence in adolescence is controlled, the effects of the other variables do not remain significant.
3. There is no effect of the number of critical life events on adult self-confidence when earlier self-confidence is controlled. However, the effect of specific critical incidents, such as parents' divorce, on adult self-confidence is significant even when self-confidence in adolescence is controlled. The number of critical life events as well as parents' divorce have a significant impact on nondepressive self-view.

Some limitations of these data should be mentioned. Assessments took place at age 18 and age 23, but not during the intervening time interval. This means that changes in self-confidence could be predicted only from variables such as social integration assessed at the same time as earlier self-confidence. We expect that changes in self-confidence could be better predicted if potential impact factors had been measured in the intervening time period between ages 18 and 23.

There were also measurement limitations. Apart from nondepressive self-view, indicators of self-confidence were not assessed by identical scales in each wave so that mean-level change could not be analyzed. Academic achievement was assessed by marks (i.e., teacher judgments that are not completely based on objective criteria) comparable among different classrooms. Although teachers' marks are somewhat problematic as achievement indicators, they are probably more important for self-confidence than results of standardized tests that are administered by an external institution.

Our result that the transition from adolescence to early adulthood is accompanied by a small increase in self-confidence is in line with other research (e.g., Block & Robins, 1993; Hirsch & DuBois, 1991). However, our conclusion is based on only one scale that was identical across measurement points. According to Harter (2006), the increase in self-esteem from adolescence to early adulthood may have the following reasons: The higher personal autonomy may provide more opportunities for selecting domains in which one is competent as well as groups that will give approval, and increased role-taking ability will support the individual to behave adequately and elicit favorable reactions from others.

As the meta-analysis by Trzesniewski et al. (2003) has shown, self-esteem is stable with respect to relative position in a sample. Their conclusion is that self-esteem is as stable as personality traits during much of the life span. According to Harter (2006), the question if self-esteem is more traitlike or more statelike is still controversial. In her own research, there was evidence that some individuals behaved in a traitlike fashion and others in a statelike fashion. Harter (2006) argued that "trait and state attributions lie in individuals, not in the construct themselves" (p. 554). We found that although self-confidence was moderately stable from age 18 to age 23, there was sufficient variance in later self-confidence not accounted for by earlier self-confidence so that other factors could have an impact.

Sex differences were compatible with other research. Males had higher self-confidence than females, but sex did not predict change in self-confidence. Galambos et al. (2006) found that the discrepancy in self-concept for males and females decreased as adolescents grew older.

Factors related to success in school (e.g., achievement and motivation) were significant predictors of self-confidence. That is, the ability to cope with the demands of school seemed to foster self-confidence. Well-being is a quite heterogeneous construct, including personal well-being and well-being at home and at school. However, all these aspects are interrelated and can be seen as indicators of personal adjustment. As our data show, personal adjustment predicts later self-confidence. Critical life events have a negative effect on self-confidence when nondepressive self-view is taken as a criterion or when parents' divorce is considered. Social integration also has a clear effect on self-esteem.

Although variables such as motivation, well-being, and social integration were significant predictors of later self-confidence, we could not demonstrate that these factors had a significant impact when earlier self-confidence was controlled. We are aware of only a few studies that could demonstrate significant effects of other variables on self-esteem when earlier self-esteem was taken into account, but none of them used the same constructs as we did. For example, Elliot (1996) explored the impact of work, family, and welfare receipt on young women's self-esteem. Self-esteem was moderately stable over a period of 7 years. The author found that marriage tended to improve self-esteem, whereas motherhood and welfare receipt depressed it. Block and Robins (1993) showed that various personality characteristics judged by experts correlated with residual change in self-concept. Bachman and O'Malley (1977) used a path model to show that self-esteem assessed in high school (10th grade) predicts self-esteem 8 years later ($\beta = .426$). Only one other predictor, occupational status, was significant when earlier self-esteem was controlled. The effect ($\beta = .113$) was small but significant because a large sample was used. The data may be somewhat limited because occupational status was measured at the same time as the criterion self-esteem.

In a study by Roberts and Bengtson (1996), the effect of parent–child affection on self-esteem was not significant. The authors concluded that "these results elaborate more clearly the role of stability in self-esteem as one psychological pathway on which past relational experiences are carried forward from adolescence to adulthood" (Roberts & Bengtson, p. 104). A somewhat different argument is that the impact of factors such as academic achievement, motivation, and social integration on the development of self-confidence in early adulthood has already been exhausted in adolescence. According to Roberts and Bengtson, stability in self-esteem may be "a conduit" through which earlier influences of other factors "are carried forward into adulthood" (p. 102). This conclusion is confirmed by the results of our study. Earlier self-confidence seems to be most important for later self-confidence.

Harter (2006) suggested a more elaborated interpretation: Instead of looking for global factors such as social integration as potential determinants of change in self-esteem, it may be more fruitful to look at changes in these factors and the way these factors are perceived and processed by individuals. For example, changes in the importance that academic achievement has for the individual might lead to changes in self-esteem and self-confidence. In line with these arguments, explanations for change in self-confidence may be more complex and idiosyncratic.

Two questions, at least, should be addressed in subsequent studies:

1. What are the processes and mechanisms that contribute to stability and change in self-confidence? For this sake, a closer look at processes operating during the period in which change takes place, including interactions with peers and groups as well as perceptions and evaluations, seems to be promising. As no data were gathered for the time period between age 18 and age 23, we cannot explore this question in the LOGIC study.
2. What are factors that contribute to self-confidence in adolescence? The LOGIC study offers a rich data basis to explore factors in childhood. Data on precursors to adolescent self-confidence may also be helpful to answer the practical question of what can be done to foster self-confidence in childhood and adolescence. As the last assessment in the LOGIC study took place in early adulthood, no data are available to examine the long-term consequences of self-confidence. Does self-confidence play a causal role for adjustment, or is it just an epiphenomenon, as suggested by some researchers?

In this chapter, we focused on the transition from adolescence to early adulthood using the last two waves of the LOGIC study, and we used a global construct of self-confidence that was based on four variables measuring different aspects of the self. This, of course, is only a first step. Next steps will be to include earlier waves to examine the role of factors measured in childhood as potential predictors of self-confidence in early adulthood, and to look at the different aspects of the self in much more detail.

REFERENCES

Alsaker, F. E., & Olweus, D. (1992). Stability of global self-evaluations on early adolescence: A cohort longitudinal study. *Journal of Research on Adolescence, 2,* 123–145.

Amato, P. R., & Keith, B. (1991). Parental divorce and adult well-being. *Journal of Marriage and the Family, 53,* 43–58.

Bachman, J. G., & O'Malley, P. M. (1977). Self-esteem in young men: A longitudinal analysis of the impact of educational and occupational attainment. *Journal of Personality and Social Psychology, 35,* 365–380.

Bandura, A. (1997). *Self-efficacy: The exercise of control.* San Francisco: Freeman.

Block, J., & Robins, R. W. (1993). A longitudinal study of consistency and change in self-esteem from early adolescence to early adulthood. *Child Development, 64,* 909–923.

Elliot, M. (1996). Impact of work, family, and welfare receipt on women's self-esteem in young adulthood. *Social Psychology Quarterly, 59,* 80–95.

Fend, H. (1997). *Der Umgang mit Schule in der Adoleszenz* [Coping with school in adolescence]. Bern: Huber.

Fend, H. (2003). *Entwicklungspsychologie des Jugendalters* [Development in adolescence] (3rd ed.). Opladen, Germany: Leske + Budrich.

Filipp, S. H., & Ferring, D. (2002). Die Transformation des Selbst in der Auseinandersetzung mit kritischen Lebensereignissen [The transformation of the self as a consequence of coping with critical life events]. In G. Jüttemann & H. Thomae (Eds.), *Persönlichkeit und Entwicklung* (pp. 191–228). Weinheim, Germany: Beltz.

Filipp, S-H., & Mayer, A-K. (2005). Selbstkonzept-Entwicklung [The development of the self-concept]. In J. B. Asendorpf (Ed.), *Soziale, emotionale und Persönlichkeitsentwicklung* (Enzyklopädie der Psychologie, Serie V: Entwicklungspsychologie, Vol. 2; pp. 259–334). Göttingen, Germany: Hogrefe.

Fuhrer, U., & Trautner, H. M. (2005). Entwicklung von Identität [The development of identity]. In J. B. Asendorpf (Ed.), *Soziale, emotionale und Persönlichkeitsentwicklung* (Enzyklopädie der Psychologie, Serie V: Entwicklungspsychologie, Vol. 2; pp. 335–424). Göttingen, Germany: Hogrefe.

Galambos, N. L., Barker, E. T., & Krahn, H. J. (2006). Depression, self-esteem, and anger in emerging adulthood: Seven-year trajectories. *Developmental Psychology, 42*, 350–365.

Gecas, V. (1982). The self-concept. *Annual Review of Sociology, 8*, 1–33.

Gullotta, T. P., Adams, G. R., & Markstrom, C. A. (2000). *The adolescent experience* (4th ed.). San Diego, CA: Academic Press.

Harter, S. (1998). The development of self-representations. In W. Damon & N. Eisenberg (Eds.), *Handbook of child psychology. Vol. 3: Social, emotional, and personality development* (5th ed., pp. 553–617). New York: Wiley.

Harter, S. (2006). The self. In N. Eisenberg (Ed.), *Handbook of child psychology. Vol. 3: Social, emotional, and personality development* (6th ed., pp. 1003–1067). Hoboken, NJ: Wiley.

Helmke, A. (1994). Development of the self-concept. In F. E. Weinert (Ed.), *International encyclopedia of education* (2nd ed., pp. 5390–5394). Oxford: Pergamon Press.

Helmke, A. (2000). Achievement-related motives, self-evaluations, and school experiences. In F. E. Weinert & W. Schneider (Eds.), *The Munich Longitudinal Study on the Genesis of Individual Competencies (LOGIC). Report No. 13: Assessment procedures and results of Wave 10* (pp. 41–52). Munich: Max Planck Institute for Psychological Research.

Hirsch, B. J., & DuBois, D. L. (1991). Self-esteem in early adolescence: The identification and prediction of contrasting longitudinal trajectories. *Journal of Youth and Adolescence, 20*, 53–72.

Juvonen, J. (2006). Sense of belonging, social bonds, and school functioning. In P. A. Alexander & P. H. Winne (Eds.), *Handbook of educational psychology* (2nd ed., pp. 655–674). Mahwah, NJ: Erlbaum.

Kling, K. C., Hyde, J. S., Showers, C. J., & Busswell, B. N. (1999). Gender differences in self-esteem: A meta-analysis. *Psychological Bulletin, 125*, 470–500.

Marsh, H. W., & Shavelson, R. J. (1985). The self-concept: Its multifaceted, hierarchical structure. *Educational Psychologist, 20*, 107–125.

Marsh, H. W., & Yeung, A. S. (1997). Causal effects of academic self-concept on academic achievement: Structural equation models of longitudinal data. *Journal of Educational Psychology, 89*, 41–54.

Muthén, L. K., & Muthén, B. O. (2007). *Mplus user's guide* (4th ed.). Los Angeles, CA: Muthén & Muthén.

Pinquart, M., & Silbereisen, R. K. (2000). Das Selbst im Jugendalter [The self in adolescence]. In W. Greve (Ed.), *Psychologie des Selbst* (pp. 75–95). Weinheim, Germany: Beltz/PVU.

Roberts, R. E., & Bengtson, V. L. (1996). Affective ties to parents in early adulthood and self-esteem across 20 years. *Social Psychology Quarterly, 59,* 96–106.

Roeser, R. W., & Lau, S. (2002). On academic identity formation in middle school settings during early adolescence. In T. M. Brinthaupt & R. P. Lipka (Eds.), *Understanding early adolescent self and identity: Applications and interventions* (pp. 91–131). Albany: State University of New York Press.

Roeser, R. W., Peck, S. C., & Nasir, N. S. (2006). Self and identity processes in school motivation, learning, and achievement. In P. A. Alexander & P. H. Winne (Eds.), *Handbook of educational psychology* (2nd ed., pp. 391–424). Mahwah, NJ: Erlbaum.

Rosenberg. M. (1979). *Conceiving the self.* New York: Basic Books.

Schneider, W., & Nunner-Winkler, G. (1989). Parent interview. In F. E. Weinert & W. Schneider (Eds.), *The Munich Longitudinal Study on the Genesis of Individual Competencies (LOGIC). Report No. 5: Assessment procedures and results of Wave 3* (pp. 26–40). Munich: Max Planck Institute for Psychological Research.

Schneider, W., & Weinert, F. E. (1995). Reference variables. In F. E. Weinert & W. Schneider (Eds.), *The Munich Longitudinal Study on the Genesis of Individual Competencies (LOGIC). Report No. 12: Assessment procedures and results of Wave 9* (pp. 5–19). Munich: Max Planck Institute for Psychological Research.

Schrader, F.-W., Helmke, A., & Heyne, N. (2006). Motivation, personality, and adaptive behavior. In W. Schneider & J. Stefanek (Eds.), *The Munich Longitudinal Study on the Genesis of Individual Competencies (LOGIC). Report No. 14: Assessment procedures and results of Wave 11* (pp. 65–80). Munich: Max Planck Institute for Human Cognitive and Brain Sciences.

Steinberg, L. (1996). *Adolescence* (4th ed.). New York: McGraw-Hill.

Steinberg, L., & Morris, A. S. (2001). Adolescent development. *Annual Review of Psychology, 52,* 83–110.

Tewes, U. (1985). *Hamburg-Wechsler-Intelligenztest für Kinder (HAWIK-R)* [Hamburg-Wechsler Intelligence Test for Children]. Bern: Huber.

Trzesniewski, K. H., Donnellan, M. B., & Robins, R. W. (2003). Stability of self-esteem across the life span. *Journal of Personality and Social Psychology, 84,* 205–220.

Trzesniewski, K. H., Donnellan, M. B., Moffitt, T. E., Robins, R. W., Poulton, R., & Caspi, A. (2006). Low self-esteem during adolescence predicts poor health, criminal behavior, and limited economic prospects during adulthood. *Developmental Psychology, 42,* 381–390.

Wigfield, A., Byrnes, J. P., & Eccles, J. S. (2006). Development during early and middle adolescence. In P. A. Alexander & P. H. Winne (Eds.), *Handbook of educational psychology* (2nd ed., pp. 87–113). Mahwah, NJ: Erlbaum.

8 Doing Experiments and Understanding Science

Development of Scientific Reasoning from Childhood to Adulthood

Merry Bullock, Beate Sodian,
and Susanne Koerber

8.1 INTRODUCTION

In this chapter, we address the development of scientific thinking from middle childhood to early adulthood. The application of the methods and principles of scientific inquiry to reasoning and problem-solving situations is of wide importance for knowledge acquisition in general (Zimmerman, 2007). We adopt a stance similar to that of Kuhn (2002), who broadly defined scientific thinking as *intentional* knowledge seeking that involves the ability to generate, test, and revise theories, and to reflect on the process of knowledge acquisition and change (Kuhn & Franklin, 2006).

In the developmental literature, adolescence has traditionally been considered an important period for the acquisition of scientific thinking skills. Beginning with the seminal work by Inhelder and Piaget (1958), preadolescent children were shown to typically fail to systematically test hypotheses, and to interpret data in a biased way, especially when confronted with multivariate tasks. Since the work of Inhelder and Piaget, numerous other studies have shown a marked improvement throughout adolescence in the ability to generate hypotheses and experimental design, to evaluate evidence, and to draw inferences from data (Kuhn, 2002). In the Piagetian tradition, developmental change was interpreted as a stagelike transition from concrete to formal operational thought. An implication from this interpretation is that a cognitive structure or a coherent set of cognitive abilities underlies the emergence of scientific rationality in laypersons.

However, recent research has questioned this account of universal, stagelike developmental change: On the one hand, early scientific reasoning competencies have been demonstrated in grade school and even preschool children. On the other hand, adolescents and even adults have been shown to be deficient in important ways. It has therefore become difficult to give a coherent description of developmental changes in scientific thinking skills. It is possible that the idea of a coherent conceptual structure underlying scientific reasoning is false and that scientific thinking should better be conceptualized as a set of more or less independent component skills.

It has also become clear from cross-sectional studies that considerable individual differences in scientific reasoning competencies are found in childhood, adolescence, and adulthood, such that it appears misleading to characterize a given age range in terms of deficits or competencies. Because to date no long-term longitudinal research has been conducted on the development of scientific reasoning, we do not know about the stability of individual differences throughout development.

The design of the Munich Longitudinal Study on the Ontogenesis of Individual Competencies (the LOGIC study) allowed us to investigate intraindividual as well as interindividual stability and variation in scientific thinking skills from elementary school age to adulthood, and to assess the role of these skills in predicting performance in complex cognitive tasks of everyday importance that approach the intentional reasoning referred to by Kuhn (2002).

8.1.1 Early Competencies in Scientific Reasoning

Although there was almost no systematic research on scientific reasoning skills in preadolescent children in the 1980s when the LOGIC study started, numerous studies over the last 20 years since then have addressed elementary school (and some even preschool) children's basic scientific thinking skills, including experimentation, evidence evaluation skills, and performance in self-directed experimentation in microgenetic studies. Zimmerman (2007) concluded from a comprehensive review of this literature that children are far more competent than first suspected (p. 213). Most importantly, traditional views about children's inability to conceptually grasp the notion of experimentation have been revised in light of recent findings.

8.1.2 Discrepancies in Scientific Reasoning Competencies

Although elementary and even preschool children's competence seems to have been underestimated for some tasks, this is not true for all scientific reasoning tasks. For example, when interviewed about their explicit, definitional understanding of science (e.g., "What is an experiment?" and "What is the relation between a scientist's ideas and his or her experiments?"), competence appears much later. For example, seventh graders show little understanding of the scientific method (experiments as empirical tests of theoretical ideas), or of the role of theories in deriving hypotheses and experiments. Rather, they, like younger children, articulate an understanding of science in terms of concrete activities (making things work) or in terms of gathering factual knowledge (Carey, Evans, Honda, Jay, & Unger, 1989).

In contrast, when presented with analogous questions embedded in a concrete example of a simple hypothesis, and an experimental idea, even first graders show a basic understanding of hypothesis testing, and differentiate "testing beliefs/ hypotheses" from "producing positive effects." For example, Sodian, Zaitchik, and Carey (1991) presented first and second graders with a story task in which two children held opposing beliefs about the size of a mouse (large versus small). Children were given a choice between two boxes (mouse houses) with different sized openings that contained cheese. In the *feed* condition, children were asked to produce a positive effect by selecting the house that should be used to make sure the mouse could eat the food, regardless of its size. In the *find out* condition, children were asked to choose the house that should be used to determine whether the mouse in the house was large or small. More than half of the first graders and 86% of the second graders correctly differentiated between the *feed* and the *find out* conditions, and were able to justify the choice of a conclusive test in the *find out* condition.

Thus, young children do not always confound hypothesis testing with the production of positive effects. Moreover, they have a basic understanding of how indirect evidence can be brought to bear on a hypothesis—at least in the fairly contrived case of a decision between two mutually exclusive and exhaustive hypotheses. In sum, although many first and second graders were challenged when asked to spontaneously generate a conclusive test, the large majority of the children could recognize one, as demonstrated by Sodian et al. (1991).

8.1.2.1   The Control of Variables Strategy (CVS)

Bullock and Ziegler (1999) reported results from third to sixth graders tested in the LOGIC study on a task requiring the production and recognition of adequate tests for hypotheses about cause–effect relations between variables. The major- ity of third and fourth graders did spontaneously suggest a contrastive test, that is, they varied the focal dimension, suggesting that they understood that testing a hypothesis involves making a critical comparison, rather than just producing a desirable effect. However, very few third and fourth graders, but over 20% of the fifth graders and over 40% of the sixth graders, produced controlled tests, hold- ing the other variable dimensions constant. These findings are consistent with previous research in indicating that preadolescent children do not spontaneously use a *control of variables strategy* (CVS), which is critical for testing for cause– effect relations among two or more variables. However, they also indicate a basic understanding of the notion of "testing" a hypothesis in children around the age of 8 years.

The most important new finding from the Bullock and Ziegler (1999) LOGIC data was, however, children's performance in a "choice" task that required them to evaluate, rather than to generate, tests. More than 30% of the third graders, about 60% of the fourth and fifth graders, and 80% of the sixth graders chose a controlled test, even when they did not produce one. Furthermore, of those who chose controlled tests, more than 50% of the fourth graders, about 80% of the fifth graders, and almost all of the sixth graders justified this choice in terms of controlling variables, indicating some degree of explicit understanding of the CVS.

Similarly, the literature on the effects of training on production of the CVS in elementary school children suggests that children possess at least an implicit metaconceptual understanding of the notion of a controlled test, which supports their fast acquisition of the strategy under training conditions. In an early study by Siegler and Liebert (1975), the majority of fifth graders succeeded in the systematic production of factorial combinations and the isolation and control of variables after instruction. This finding was replicated with the LOGIC sample (Bullock & Ziegler, 1994). In Wave 8, when children were in the fifth grade, half of the sample received a brief training procedure that almost doubled performance on the CVS production task. The gain from this training was not retained when the task was repeated a year later in Wave 9, however. Case (1974) showed that the CVS could even be taught to gifted third graders. More recent research has confirmed that a single session of instruction, as long as it is direct instruction and not self-directed exploration, is sufficient to teach the strategy to elementary school children (Klahr & Nigam, 2004; but see Dean & Kuhn, 2007, for a critical evaluation).

To date, children's explicit knowledge about experimental design has not been studied comprehensively. The research reviewed above suggests that by the fourth grade, many children possess an intuitive understanding of the CVS, but they rarely produce the strategy spontaneously unless specifically trained to do so. A fuller assessment of children's knowledge of experimental design is needed to interpret the knowledge–production gap.

8.1.2.2   Evidence Evaluation

A second component skill of scientific reasoning that has recently been assessed in young children is *evidence evaluation*. Whereas Kuhn, Amsel, and O'Loughlin (1988) found massive tendencies to ignore, distort, or selectively attend to covariation evidence that was inconsistent with the child's own favorite theory in elementary school children (and gradual improvement with age in adolescence), Ruffman, Perner, Olson, and Doherty (1993) showed that children as young as 6 years old understood how perfect or partial covariation evidence supports or undermines a causal belief, as long as there was only one causal factor that covaried with an outcome. Koerber, Sodian, Thoermer, and Nett (2005) gathered additional evidence consistent with Ruffman et al.'s findings. Kindergarteners' performance was, however, much worse when children had to evaluate noncovariation rather than covariation patterns, and when the evidence was inconsistent with a prior belief than when it was neutral with respect to the child's world knowledge. Amsel and Brock (1996) systematically investigated the development of the ability to evaluate covariation data independently of one's prior beliefs: Only college-educated adults tended to conform to the pattern of the "ideal reasoner," making causal judgments based solely on the data and setting aside prior knowledge. In contrast, both second and sixth graders' judgments were heavily biased by prior beliefs.

Thus, the ability to differentiate causal theories from evidence improves with age, and appears to be dependent on educational level. The studies of young children's understanding of covariation data show, however, that the abilities to interpret patterns of covariation and to understand the significance of such data for the evaluation of causal beliefs develop early and guide even preschoolers' reasoning from data. With age and education, people appear to become increasingly able to set aside their theoretical beliefs when reasoning from data. Koslowski (1996) has argued that even in professional scientists' scientific reasoning, there is an interdependence of theory and evidence, and patterns of evidence are necessarily considered in conjunction with information about potential causal mechanisms. Moreover, Koslowski demonstrated the interdependence of theory and evidence in children's and adults' scientific reasoning: Information about mechanism and the plausibility of the covariation evidence influenced causal judgments in all age groups. Thus, some of the shortcomings in children's evidence evaluation (e.g., Kuhn et al., 1988) can also be seen as evidence for a fundamental similarity between children's and professional scientists' reasoning: Both information about covariation and about causal mechanism is incorporated in evidence evaluation. One important difference between children's and scientists' reasoning appears to lie in their metaconceptual awareness of theory and evidence, that is, the ability to recognize theory and evidence as "distinct epistemological categories" (Kuhn & Franklin, 2006, p. 983).

8.1.3   What Develops from Middle Childhood to Adulthood?

Most information-processing analyses converge in arguing that the development of complex strategies, the acquisition of knowledge, and the development of metacognition jointly contribute to cognitive development in adolescence and young adulthood. In scientific reasoning, strategies to reason about causal relations among variables in complex multivariate tasks, and understanding of the nature of scientific knowledge, apart from domain knowledge, have been discussed as major determinants of development (Kuhn & Franklin, 2006).

8.1.3.1   Reasoning Strategies: The Control of Variables Strategy

A single reasoning strategy, the CVS, has been the focus of a large body of research on scientific reasoning. Manipulating the focal variable while holding all other variables constant is certainly necessary for identifying the effect of one individual variable on an outcome, but it is not sufficient to disentangle the complex web of interactions among multiple variables that is characteristic of real-world scientific investigation (Kuhn, Iordanou, Pease, & Wirkala, in press). Both children and adults have difficulty understanding the interaction of multiple variables, and many people just add or average the effects of individual variables (Kuhn & Dean, 2004). Adults do better than children in reasoning with multiple variables, but their performance is far from perfect, and individual differences are substantial. Kuhn and Dean reported that about half of the adults tested in one of their studies performed on the same level as sixth graders, appealing to the effect of either only one or only two of the variables in a multivariate task when making predictions.

Similarly, findings of microgenetic self-directed experimentation studies show that adults start at a higher level and progress further in exploring a micro-world than children. Again, large individual differences were observed in each age group in cross-sectional comparisons (Kuhn, Garcia-Mila, & Andersen, 1995). Developmental and individual differences were attributed to both strategy development and metastrategic awareness, with adults showing a higher ability to monitor and manage their own learning process. Deanna Kuhn and her collaborators (see Kuhn & Franklin, 2006, for a review) argued that the abilities to set aside or "bracket" one's own existing beliefs and to inhibit their influence on the interpretation of new data are key determinants of success in these tasks. Thus, in the LOGIC study, assessment of the CVS was accompanied by tasks measuring the evaluation of evidence and knowledge of a variety of experimental design features.

8.1.3.2 Understanding the Nature of Science

The use of efficient strategies in self-directed experimentation has been linked to both executive functions (e.g., inhibition) and metaconceptual understanding of the nature of science. Laypersons' intuitive epistemologies of science have primarily been explored in the science education literature (Lederman, 1992; McComas, 1998), resulting in a description of both students' and teachers' grasp of the nature of scientific knowledge as deficient, lacking an understanding of the relation between theory and evidence. A similar conclusion was drawn by Kuhn (1991) from studies of laypersons' evidence-based arguments. Even adults often just elaborate their theories when asked to give evidence for a belief, apparently lacking metaconceptual awareness of the theory–evidence distinction. As mentioned earlier, an interview study by Carey et al. (1989) investigating seventh grade students' understanding of the nature of science showed that children mostly conceived of science in terms of concrete activities and the accumulation of factual knowledge. Only rarely did students articulate an understanding of science as a search for explanations or indicate a notion of testing beliefs. A short-term training intervention showed positive effects, but most students only implicitly understood hypothesis testing and the construction of explanations in science.

Subsequent studies by Sodian and colleagues showed that similar effects of a short-term curricular intervention could even be attained in fourth graders (Grygier, 2005; Sodian, Jonen, Thoermer, & Kircher, 2006). Clear effects of long-term constructivist science instruction on students' epistemologies of science were found by Smith, Maclin, Houghton, and Hennessey (2000).

Although the role of theories in the construction of scientific knowledge is not spontaneously articulated by schoolchildren, educated adults also show surprisingly little explicit understanding of the notion of a theory. Thoermer and Sodian (2002) tested science undergraduates' and graduate students' understanding of the nature of science and found little evidence for an explicit awareness of the role of theories in the construction of scientific knowledge, even in PhD students. It may be that an interview requiring participants to respond to fairly abstract questions about concepts like *hypothesis, experiment,* and *theory* may underestimate laypersons' (and even scientists') epistemological understanding, and studies have shown the importance of offering a specific context in a task, especially when testing children. Thus, the strategy followed in the LOGIC study was to develop an interview that was embedded in a story about a fictitious medieval scientist who believed in witchcraft as a cause of disease. This context was designed to highlight the notion of an alternative interpretive framework even for children.

8.1.4 Building a Developmental Picture

Scientific reasoning skills and science understanding are assumed to be important for a wide range of cognitive tasks outside the context of science. A paradigm case is building and understanding arguments about everyday issues such as the causes for unemployment or recidivism in prisoners. Kuhn (1991, 2005) argued that the metaconceptual ability to differentiate theories from evidence underlies both scientific reasoning and argumentation. If this is the case, then scientific reasoning skills should be predictive of skills of argument regardless of content domains. This assumption was tested in the LOGIC study by engaging young adults in a task asking for comparison of models and evidence in discussion of a complex, everyday context.

To briefly summarize, the longitudinal study of scientific reasoning covered in LOGIC from childhood to adulthood had the following major aims:

- To trace the development of a range of scientific reasoning skills from early elementary school through young adulthood;
- To investigate the interrelations among different component skills of scientific reasoning cross-sectionally and longitudinally to address the extent to which scientific reasoning should be conceptualized as a unitary construct;
- To assess the stability of individual differences in scientific reasoning skills across a wide age range;
- To investigate the relation between "doing science" (strategies of experimentation) and a metaconceptual understanding of experiments and theories at different ages (the nature of science); and
- To study the association between scientific reasoning and other cognitive abilities, primarily argumentation skills.

In this chapter, we report data from a subset of the LOGIC tasks addressing scientific reasoning.

8.2 TASKS AND DEVELOPMENTAL PATTERNS

We will first describe the tasks and cross-sectional and longitudinal development for each of three scientific reasoning task domains—Experimentation (Control of Variables), Experimental Design, and the Nature of Science—as well as performance on a task given in Wave 11 that was designed to look at the application of scientific reasoning skills in a more everyday task of "intentional" reasoning about a complex social domain. Next we will look at longitudinal patterns of development and individual differences, including prediction of adult performance and the effects of schooling and IQ differences on performance.

The tasks presented, measurement points, and numbers of subjects at each measurement time are listed in Table 8.1. Because we are primarily concerned with longitudinal results, including consistency, time of mastery measures, and comparison across tasks, we included in our analyses only those participants who had complete data across all measurement points for each task, unless otherwise noted. Overall results for this subsample (which ranged from $n = 132$ to $n = 143$ across tasks) did not differ from the entire sample ($N = 143$ to $N = 193$ per wave) on any of the individual measurements.

8.2.1 EXPERIMENTATION: THE CONTROL OF VARIABLES STRATEGY

Use of the control of variables strategy (CVS) was assessed annually by an Experiment Recognition/Production task. This task (see Bullock & Ziegler, 1999, for task descriptions) yielded measures of whether participants could recognize a controlled experiment when presented a set of possible comparisons and whether they could themselves produce a controlled experiment (an experiment in which one variable was manipulated and all others were held constant). There were 132 participants with complete data for Waves 6 through 11.

TABLE 8.1

Overview of Scientific Reasoning Tasks in the LOGIC Study

	Wave 6	Wave 7	Wave 8	Wave 9	Wave 10	Wave 11	Longitudinal N
CVS strategy use	$N = 190$	$N = 193$	$N = 185$	$N = 170$	$N = 170$	$N = 149$	$N = 132$
Experimental design				$N = 183$	$N = 169$	$N = 143$	$N = 136$
Nature of science			$N = 183$		$N = 171$	$N = 149$	$N = 143$
Argumentation						$N = 143$	

8.2.1.1 Cross-Sectional Results

A difference reported between success at *recognizing* the CVS as the best strategy when asked to choose an adequate experiment (defined as "understanding experimentation"; see Bullock & Ziegler, 1999) and poorer performance in *using* the CVS when asked to design an experiment (defined as "producing an experiment"; see Bullock & Ziegler, 1999) for early LOGIC waves was maintained throughout adolescence. As Figure 8.1 shows, participants performed reliably better in the choice task than in the production task throughout the study (all *p*'s from comparison *t* tests < .001), with the gap narrowing in adolescence and adulthood as performance approached ceiling levels.

As Figure 8.1 shows, although the majority of the participants *chose* the CVS as early as Wave 7 (10 years), this level of performance in the production task was achieved only late in adolescence (Wave 10, 18 years).

8.2.2 EXPERIMENTAL DESIGN: CONTROL GROUP AND CVS SCHEMES

To assess participants' understanding of experimental design, we presented participants with a set of fictitious experiments and asked them to evaluate whether each empirical test was "good" and to identify any design errors. The fictitious experiments each had a specific error in design, as follows:

- Baseline reference (baseline information was unavailable for a pre- and posttest design)
- Variation in focal dimensions (only one value of a factor was tested)
- Control of variables (failure to keep all variables but one constant)
- Control group (intervention given to one group; no comparison control)

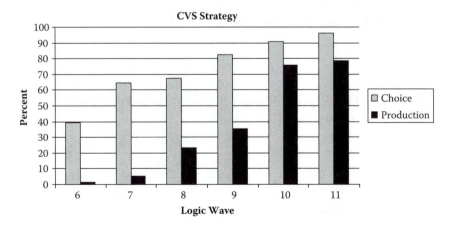

FIGURE 8.1 Performance on control of variables strategy (CVS) use for choice and production tasks.

- Adequate evidence for conclusion (drawing a conclusion based on only partial evidence)
- Construct validity (measurement is not valid for question asked)
- "Law of large numbers" (sample used to ask a question was too small)

As noted above, each design flaw was embedded within a short story. For example, in the "control of variables" story, a doctor tested the effects of music on hospital recovery time by playing "happy" music to patients on the surgery ward and no music to patients on the orthopedics ward and measuring the time to go home, failing to hold all dimensions but music constant. After hearing each story, participants were asked if it was a good experiment and why or why not. If participants identified a design error, they were asked to suggest how the design could be improved. If participants did not identify a design error, they were asked whether the protagonist in the story could then reach a conclusive result and why. Responses were coded as showing understanding if the participant recognized the design error and provided a valid suggestion for improving it. There were 143 participants with complete data across the 3 measurement years (Waves 9 through 11).

8.2.2.1 Cross-Sectional Results

In this chapter, we focus on performance on the three core stories that addressed the logic of experimentation: variation in focal dimension, control of variables, and control group.

Table 8.2 shows performance on each design problem at ages 12, 18 and 23, and Table 8.3 shows the percentage of participants who correctly solved none, one, two, or all three tasks in each wave. Although half of the participants identified all of the features of a good experiment by late adolescence (Wave 10), even adults were not at the ceiling level across all the tasks. There was also considerable variation across tasks, with identifying and fixing a missing control group the most difficult.

TABLE 8.2

Percentage of Participants Who Identified and Articulated Problems with Critical Features of a Good Experiment

| | Age | Experimental Design Feature | | |
		Vary Focal Dimension	Control of Variables	Control Group
Wave 9	12	45	57	34
Wave 10	18	66**	83**	68**
Wave 11	23	94**	89**	69**

** Performance differs from chance by p < .001.

TABLE 8.3
Percentage of Correct Responses on the Design Interview Tasks*

Number of Tasks

	0	1	2	3
Wave 9	20	37	29	14
Wave 10	8	13	29	50
Wave 11	1	8	27	64

* Percentages add to more than 100% because of rounding.

8.2.3 Understanding the Nature of Science

Assessment of participants' understanding of the nature of science included measuring the ability to differentiate theory and evidence, treat theories as interpretive frameworks, and understand that theories determine the interpretation of data, explanation of natural phenomena, and context for scientific investigation.

The Nature of Science (NOS) task was presented as a story and interview about the actions and beliefs of a medieval scientist who wanted to find a cure for a disease and who, like many in his time, believed in witchcraft as a cause of disease. The medieval scientist was contrasted with a contemporary scientist who also wanted to find a cure for the same disease but believed that germs cause the disease.

Participants were asked to respond to a series of questions that addressed five aspects of understanding the nature of science. These were as follows:

- Science is embedded within a larger cultural framework.
- Data are understood within a theoretical framework.
- Explanations are produced within a theoretical framework.
- Concepts may not translate between frameworks.
- Anomalous data will be reinterpreted within a framework.

Responses were coded with a system adapted from Carey et al. (1989) that defines broad levels moving from an understanding of science as a concrete activity or as factual information to an understanding that explicitly acknowledges the notion of interpretive frameworks and the theory-dependent nature of explanations.

For purposes of this study, we coded responses into one of four levels of understanding:

Level 1. Science is equated with finding facts; there is no concept of testing beliefs, and beliefs are not differentiated from states of the world.

Level 2. A transitional level in which there was a weak, not explicitly stated, understanding that science is concerned with generalizable explanations.
Level 3. Science is construed as a search for explanations, and the logic of testing is understood. Explanations are based on simple beliefs that may be implicitly related to a general framework.
Level 4. Science and the production of evidence are based on an explicit understanding of the notion of interpretative frameworks.

There were 143 participants with complete data for the 3 measurement years (Waves 8, 10, and 11).

8.2.3.1   Cross-Sectional Results

The Nature of Science task was administered in Waves 8, 10, and 11. Because the frequency of responding at levels above Level 3 on this task was very low, even in adulthood (the percentage of Level 4 responses was 3% for Wave 8, 7% in Wave 10, and 13% in Wave 11), we combine these responses at Level 3 or higher (in the original coding scale, reported elsewhere, the levels were labeled somewhat differently, with transitional levels given a .5 value). Level 3 reflects an understanding that science is a search for generalizable explanations, and that scientific activities include testing the validity of beliefs.

Figure 8.2 depicts the percentage of participants giving Level 3 or higher responses for each of the five question sets testing five aspects of understanding the nature of science, outlined above. Participants understood the effects of a framework on data and explanations before they were aware of the more general effects of theories on the search for or interpretation of data. Understanding that science is embedded in a cultural framework and distinguishing theory from evidence were not well understood, even by the young adults.

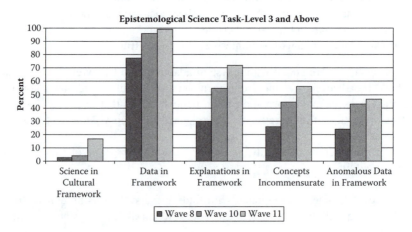

FIGURE 8.2   Epistemological science task: Responses at Level 3 and above.

8.2.4 LONGITUDINAL PATTERNS

Because each of the scientific reasoning tasks was repeated over multiple waves, we could assess the consistency of performance over waves and the timing of task mastery.

We defined *consistency* in terms of the level of responding on one task across multiple waves. Consistent responses were those that were at the same or a higher level than the response in the earlier testing wave. Inconsistent responses were those that were at a lower level than earlier responses. Thus, a participant who scored the lowest (or highest) level across all administrations of a task would be scored as consistent, as would a participant whose response increased from one wave to the next but then stayed the same. Inconsistency responses to a task series were those where a participant decreased in response level from one wave to the next. Across tasks, consistency was acceptable. It ranged from 95% for the Experimental Design task to 87–90% for the Experimentation tasks to 81–86% for the Nature of Science tasks.

We defined a measure of time of mastery for those participants whose responses were consistent for the Experimentation, Experimental Design, and Nature of Science tasks. For the Experimentation task, mastery was defined as CVS use and production. For the Experimental Design task, mastery was defined as correctly identifying and correcting design errors on at least two of the three core problems presented in each wave; and for the Nature of Science task, we defined two mastery measures: NOS-3 reflected Level 3 or higher responses on at least three of the five question sets, and NOS-4 reflected responses at this level on at least four of the five question sets. The time of mastery ranged from early (Wave 8) to late (Wave 11) to never.

Figure 8.3 depicts the developmental course of task mastery of each of the scientific reasoning tasks, and reflects the different levels of mastery obtained by adulthood, in Wave 11. This figure shows that, consistent with the literature, the largest changes in the CVS use (production) and in the understanding of experimental design occur between early and late adolescence—ages 12 and 18 (Waves 9 and 10).

The overall longitudinal picture was confirmed by repeated measure ANOVAs on each of the Experimentation, Experimental Design, and Nature of Science tasks, each of which yielded strong age (wave of testing) effects.

8.2.5 PERFORMANCE IN ADULTHOOD: SCIENTIFIC REASONING AND "INTENTIONAL" REASONING IN AN EVERYDAY TASK

In addition to repeated assessments of the scientific reasoning tasks, participants in Wave 11 were given a supplemental task intended to measure broad "intentional" reasoning about a complex social issue. The intentional reasoning task was adapted from one used by Kuhn (1991) in her studies of complex reasoning. This task required participants to suggest theories and alternate theories for a social issue, and to suggest what information might be used to evaluate them.

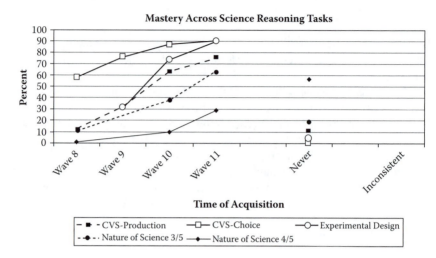

FIGURE 8.3   Developmental changes in mastery of scientific reasoning tasks.

Kuhn found that this was a difficult task even for adults, and that participants often failed to realize that alternative theories could be possible (they seemed to believe that their theory reflected "truth," not possibility).

Specifically, we asked participants to articulate their ideas about what causes prisoners to return to crime after they are released, to indicate the kinds of evidence that would support these ideas, to suggest a test of their ideas, and to indicate what evidence and test would support an alternate explanation to their own.

Responses were coded into three levels of understanding analogous to those used for the Nature of Science task, as follows:

- At Level 1, participants show no differentiation of theory and evidence, and cannot produce evidence or counterevidence for their model. In addition, they hold an "absolutist" view that only one model can be correct.
- Level 2 is a transitional level between 1 and 3 and reflects partial differentiation of theory and evidence. It includes faulty attempts to generate evidence and counterevidence; alternative views are believed to reflect alternate realities.
- At Level 3 and above, participants can distinguish between their views about a phenomenon and evidence for those views; they can generate an alternate view and can propose some evidence that would support their view and an alternate. A conflict between alternate views is acknowledged.

We were interested in how performance on this complex, more everyday task compared to the scientific reasoning tasks, and in whether it was possible to predict this performance from scientific reasoning skills. Table 8.4 shows performance on the Intentional Reasoning task, with performance in the other Wave 11 tasks for comparison purposes. The data in Table 8.4 show that although scientific reasoning strategies (CVS) and knowledge of experimental design were close to the ceiling level by age 23, being able to apply those skills in a complex reasoning task about one's own theories was unlikely, and operating with alternate models by suggesting evidence was very difficult. Across subtests, fewer than half of the participants showed awareness of the theory and cultural embeddedness of their hypotheses, and few of those who did generate alternate hypotheses could suggest evidence to test them.

We looked at concurrent and longitudinal predictors of the Wave 11 Intentional Reasoning task. Table 8.5 shows concurrent correlations with other Wave 11 tasks. Intentional reasoning was related to understanding experimental design and to understanding the nature of science, and was not related to experimentation skills.

We also looked at the relation between intentional reasoning and time of mastery variables, to ask whether early advantages in experimentation skills or understanding experimental design or understanding the nature of science might lead to better intentional reasoning skills. Overall performance on the Intentional Reasoning task was not related to the time of mastery variables for scientific reasoning skills. The one exception was the subtest asking participants to generate evidence for their own theory. This was related to time of mastery for Experimentation and for the more stringent mastery measure (four of five question sets

---

TABLE 8.4
Wave 11 Intentional Reasoning Task and Other Tasks

Wave 11 Tasks

Intentional Reasoning Task	%
Evidence for own model (Level 3 and higher)	45
Evidence against own model	31
Generation of alternate model	47
Evidence supporting alternate model	12
Evidence against alternate model	16

Control of Variables Strategy (CVS) Task	
Production of CVS	79
Choice of CVS	96

Experimental Design Task	
Correct on two thirds of the three tasks	90

Nature of Science Task	
Level 3 or above on at least three or at least four question sets	66/29

TABLE 8.5

Cross-Task Correlations for Wave 11 (N = 131)

	Experimentation CVS Production	Experimentation CVS Choice	Experimental Design	Nature of Science	Intentional Reasoning
CVS production	—	.18*	.18*	.10	.16
CVS choice	.14	—	.53***	.18*	.12
Design	.09	.50***	—	.37**	.29**
Nature of science	.02	.14	.29**	—	.33**
Intentional reasoning	.10	.08	.22*	.27**	—

Note: Correlations with verbal intelligence partialed out are below the diagonal.
* p < .05, ** p < .01, ***<.001.

at Level 3 or higher) for the Nature of Science task. Exploration of this relation showed that very early or very late acquisition of the CVS predicted Level 3 or above evidence generation (75% of those who acquired the CVS from Wave 8 responded at Level 3 or above on the Evidence Generation question, and none responded lower than Level 2; and 75% of those who acquired the CVS only in Wave 11 or not at all responded lower than Level 3). Similarly, all of the participants who showed mastery of the Nature of Science task at the more stringent level (four of five questions at Level 3 or higher) in Wave 8 and 80% who showed mastery in Waves 8 or 10 answered the Evidence Generation question at Level 3 or higher, and there was no difference in response level for those who mastered the Nature of Science task late in Wave 11 or not at all. Thus, earlier acquisition of scientific reasoning skills appears to confer an advantage for the more everyday processes of generating support for what one believes to be true. It does not appear to confer an advantage to the more difficult task of hypothesis generation and possible supporting evidence.

8.2.6 GENERAL DEVELOPMENTAL PATTERNS: LONGITUDINAL RELATIONS AMONG TASKS

A central question in longitudinal studies of cognitive development is the developmental relation between different sets of cognitive skills across time. In the present context, we assessed the relationship between experimentation (CVS choice and production), understanding experimental design, and understanding the nature of science through path model analyses. The first analysis tested the path between experimentation skills (CVS production) and experiment knowledge (experimental design); the second tested the path between experimentation skills and metaconceptual knowledge (Nature of Science).

Figures 8.4 and 8.5 depict the path model results. Each of the path analyses suggests that earlier understanding predicts later production. The path analysis in Figure 8.4 shows a model with good fit ($\chi^2(5) = 5.905$, $p = .316$, ns, RMSEA = .035; CFI = .991, SRMR = .0327) that reveals a relation between CVS use (producing experiments) in Wave 8 and Experimental Design (understanding experiments) in Wave 9, one year later ($r = .36$). In turn, Experimental Design (understanding

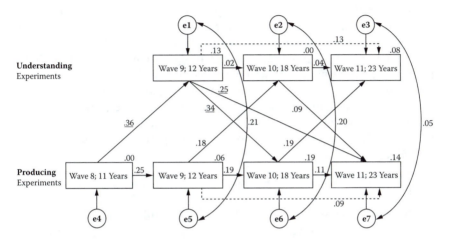

FIGURE 8.4   Path analysis: relations between earlier experimentation skills and experimentation knowledge on later performance.

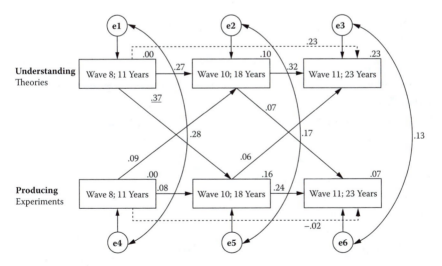

FIGURE 8.5   Path analysis: relations between earlier experimentation skills and metaconceptual knowledge on later performance.

experiments) in Wave 9 predicts CVS use (producing experiments) in Waves 10 (r = .34) and 11 (r = .25). In the later waves (10 and 11), no further predictions could be detected, probably due to ceiling effects.

Figure 8.5 shows that Nature of Science performance (upper path) at age 11 (Wave 8) predicts using the CVS (producing experiments) 7 years later at age 18 (model fit: $\chi^2(2)$ = 2.945, p = .229, ns, RMSEA = .057; CFI = .990, SRMR = .0268).

The contribution of earlier scientific reasoning skills to overall performance in adulthood (tested with a summary score across all tasks in Wave 11) was tested through linear regressions using experimentation skills (CVS production) and understanding experiments (Experimental Design) from Waves 8 through 10. Highlights of the results are presented in Tables 8.6 and 8.7.

These analyses are consistent with our other findings showing that performance in the tasks testing understanding (theories, strategies, and experiments rather than production alone) is a better predictor of later performance, be it the Intentional Reasoning task (see above) or a more general measure of scientific reasoning.

TABLE 8.6
Linear Regression on Wave 11 Scientific Reasoning: Summary Score

Wave	Construct	Beta	Probability
Wave 8	Nature of science	beta = .242	p = .018
	CVS strategy use		ns
	IQ		ns
	Operational level		ns
Wave 9	Experimental design	beta = .250	p = .009
Overall	R^2 adj. = .11		

TABLE 8.7
Linear Regression on Wave 11 Intentional Reasoning Task: Summary Score

Wave	Construct	Beta	Probability
Wave 11	CVS strategy use	beta = .047	ns
Wave 11	Experimental design	beta = .159	$p < .10$
Wave 11	Nature of science	beta = .287	$p < .01$
	Operational level	beta = –.012	ns
	Verbal IQ	beta = .077	ns
			R^2 adj. = .16
Wave 10	Nature of science	beta = .265	p < .01
Wave 10	Verbal IQ	beta = .186	p < .03
			R^2 adj. = .11

8.2.7 INDIVIDUAL DIFFERENCES: THE EFFECTS OF SCHOOLING, IQ, AND OPERATIONAL LEVEL

In the German school system (see Bullock & Schneider, chap. 1, this volume, for a description), children follow different educational tracks beginning in the fifth grade. These tracks are preuniversity (Gymnasium) or vocational. There is a further split in the vocational track to professional trades or semiskilled trades. We could take advantage of this system to ask about the effects of schooling on scientific reasoning.

To some extent, we did not expect school effects: Scientific reasoning *per se* is not taught explicitly in school, so there should not be effects from direct tuition. However, some of the underlying skills—logical reasoning, formal operational skills, and skills of argumentation—may be taught and exercised more in the more rigorous schooling in the higher educational tracks.

To look at the effects of schooling, we compared students in Gymnasium (preuniversity high school) with all other tracks. We conducted repeated measure ANOVAs on each scientific reasoning task. Each of the analyses showed a significant main effect of school type and no interaction with age (wave of measure): $F(1, 128) = 22.9$, $p < .001$, eta^2 = .15 for Experimentation (CVS production) across Waves 8–11; $F(1, 139) = 20.7$, $p < .001$, eta^2 = .13 for Nature of Science; and $F(1, 134) = 12.68$, $p < .001$, eta^2 = .086 for Experimental Design. Figures 8.6, 8.7, and 8.8 show the performance for participants in Gymnasium and other school settings across the three scientific reasoning tasks.

The lack of an interaction between school type and scientific reasoning performance indicates that schooling itself does not lead to differences in performance. For all tasks, early differences (in Wave 8 for the Experiment and Nature of Science tasks, and in Wave 9 for the Experimental Design task) are at about the

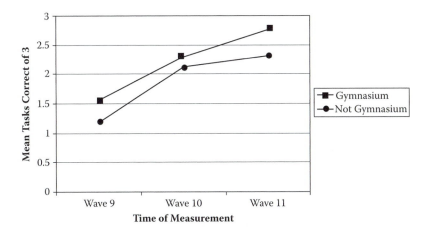

FIGURE 8.6 Educational track and experimental design performance.

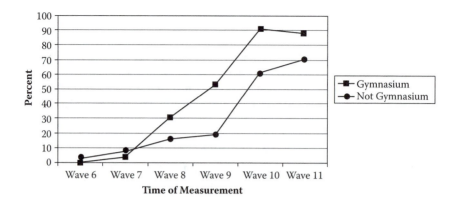

FIGURE 8.7   Educational track and experiment production (control of variables strategy, or CVS) performance.

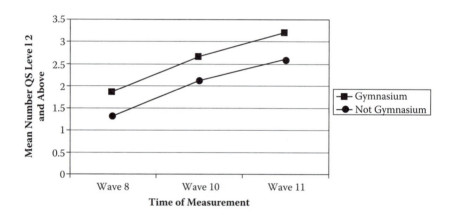

FIGURE 8.8   Educational track and nature of science understanding.

same magnitude as differences in adulthood, 5 or 6 years later. Thus, the type of secondary school that students attended neither enlarged nor reduced the preexisting individual differences.

8.2.8   EFFECTS OF SEX, IQ, AND FORMAL OPERATIONAL LEVEL

We further explored individual differences in the scientific reasoning tasks by looking at the correlations of performance with sex, IQ, and operational level, measured by the Arlin Test of Formal Reasoning (ATFR), a paper-and-pencil measure of formal operations (see Schneider, Stefanek, & Niklas, chap. 2, this volume, for a description), on developmental changes in each of the scientific reasoning tasks. There were no sex effects on any of the scientific reasoning variables, although there were sex effects in performance on the Arlin test, with boys performing better. With the exception of experimentation performance in Waves 6 and 7 (where there were floor effects), IQ was positively related to each measure, in a range from .16 to .42. Operational level was also related to scientific reasoning performance, and it remained significant after IQ was partialed out for experiment choice performance in Waves 7, 8, and 9, and experiment production performance in Waves 9 and 10. It was related to Experimental Design performance in Waves 9 and 10, and to understanding the Nature of Science in Wave 10 and, to a lesser extent, Wave 11. Operational level was also related to the time of mastery for both Experimentation and Experimental Design, but not to the Nature of Science task.

8.3 DISCUSSION

The broad range of tasks addressed in this report of the LOGIC study of the development of scientific reasoning allows us to address each of the goals outlined in the introduction. In this section, we will review developmental changes in scientific reasoning strategies and understanding of the Nature of Science from third grade to young adulthood. We will discuss the findings with respect to developmental changes, intertask relations (is scientific reasoning a unitary competence?), and individual differences. We will address the significance of scientific reasoning skills for real-world competencies.

Many studies have addressed the control of variables strategy. The main novel finding of the present study was the dissociation between the recognition and the production of a controlled experiment. Whereas the production of a controlled test was mastered only in adolescence, most elementary school children consistently preferred a controlled over a confounded experiment, and were able to give a valid reason for their choice. The LOGIC results are consistent with other recent findings showing a beginning understanding of hypothesis testing in elementary school. Thus, developmental change between childhood and adolescence appears less fundamental than was traditionally assumed. Neither new capacities for logical reasoning nor a fundamental restructuring of the knowledge base has to be assumed to explain developmental progress between childhood and adolescence.

Adolescents, however, are able to access their strategy knowledge with less contextual support than children. Why do adolescents need less contextual support? Certainly, a number of factors contribute to developmental change, such as better allocation of working memory resources, and increasingly flexible and explicit access to previously tacit knowledge. One of the questions guiding our study was whether the development of explicit metaconceptual knowledge about the nature of science is important for spontaneous production of the CVS, in the sense that it will help participants to efficiently cope with processing demands and improve executive control. Metaconceptual knowledge about experimental design and about interpretive frameworks was assessed independently of the CVS task with the Nature of Science task. Both tasks showed a protracted development over the course of the study. Although most adults (and about 70% of the adolescents) attained an articulated understanding of the most important features of experimental design, only about two thirds of the adults showed an explicit understanding of an alternative interpretive framework. This is consistent with research on epistemological beliefs in general (e.g., Kuhn, Cheney, & Weinstock, 2000) and epistemologies of science (Thoermer & Sodian, 2002) in indicating that adults are far from the ceiling in attaining a mature epistemological stance. The abilities to put oneself into the perspective of a medieval person who believed in witchcraft and to derive predictions that are consistent with such a framework are available earlier than understanding the implications of some critical features of the alternative framework, such as its resistance to change.

These differences may be characterized as a difference between *taking* multiple perspectives and *operating with* multiple perspectives. Consistent with this interpretation, some children, and most adolescents and adults, showed some ability to work within an alternative interpretive framework (see Bullock & Sodian, 2003), but a consistent metaconceptual understanding of the alternative theory was much harder at each age level. This difference was also reflected in adults' performance on the everyday argumentation task, where it was easier to suggest evidence and alternative evidence for one's own model than for a hypothetical, alternative model.

It is important to note that although there is marked developmental change in adolescence in both scientific reasoning and understanding the nature of science, even adolescents and young adults do not conform to the stereotype of the ideal reasoner. It appears that the different abilities develop over a protracted period of time from middle childhood to adulthood.

The view of a stagelike development of a unitary ability to reason scientifically is inconsistent with the cross-sectional findings and with results on intraindividual variability in task performance. Intertask correlations were moderate in size (between $r = .3$ and $.4$ at all ages) but do not offer support for a single construct. Rather, they suggest that scientific reasoning skills form as a set of interrelated cognitive components, rather than one underlying cognitive ability. Results from the path analyses conducted to further investigate developmental pathways between science understanding and strategy production are consistent with this interpretation. They do not support the view of a unidirectional relation between science understanding and strategy production, with understanding being a necessary or even a necessary and sufficient condition for production. Rather, the relationship between understanding experimental design and producing a good experiment appears to be bidirectional, with early strategy production predicting later strategy understanding and early strategy understanding predicting later strategy acquisition. The use of intentional knowledge-seeking strategies may initially be driven by a beginning metaconceptual understanding of hypothesis testing, which will in turn be enhanced by successful strategy use, thus contributing to reflective awareness and the acquisition of an increasingly sophisticated understanding of hypothesis testing.

Our findings indicate that a focus on experimental design may be too narrow to fully understand the relation between strategy development and understanding of the nature of science. Early theory understanding proved to be a remarkably good predictor of later strategy production, indicating that a broader understanding of the theory–evidence relation may be important for strategy development. Additional support for this view comes from a series of curricular intervention studies in which fourth graders were given tasks to introduce them to the construction of scientific knowledge. The curriculum had both short-term and long-term effects on the production of the CVS, although this strategy was not explicitly taught as part of the curriculum (Grygier, 2005; Sodian et al., 2006).

An important focus of the present longitudinal study was on interindividual differences. Although cross-sectional research indicates that there are considerable individual differences in scientific reasoning abilities at different ages, to date no long-term longitudinal data on the stability and the correlates of such differences have been reported. Our data showed that about 30% of the participants were precocious and produced the CVS in the Experimentation task, even in elementary school. Consistency was relatively high: At least 75% of the children who produced the strategy early (in Wave 8) maintained it over the course of the study. The children who used the CVS in the third, fourth, or fifth grade performed at a level that was reached by the other participants only at age 18. Individual differences in performance existed before students entered different educational tracks, and schooling did not have an effect on them. Rather, there was a close association between IQ and experiment production, such that age differences between elementary school and adolescence were no longer significant when IQ was entered as a covariate. This was the case only for the experiment production task, not for the Experimental Design task, where both IQ and age yielded significant effects. In a sense, these findings appear to support Jean Piaget's view that scientific reasoning skills, such as control of variables, are "pure" indicators of intellectual maturity. However, these indicators are not sufficient for capturing reasoning in context. Performance on the complex argumentation task in early adulthood was not related to CVS performance either concurrently or longitudinally. Participants who mastered the CVS strategy in elementary school were not significantly better than those who acquired the strategy later on in this study. In contrast, measures of understanding experimental design and understanding the nature of science were significantly correlated with performance on the intentional reasoning task. Thus, it appears that complex cognitive abilities of real-world importance may be more closely associated with understanding what science is about and how to do science than with the acquisition of experimentation strategies.

8.4 IMPLICATIONS FOR THE FUTURE

The results from this study lead to strong suggestions for science education. First, they suggest that science education should begin early in elementary school, and this education should include lessons that incorporate information on the nature of science as well as traditional science content matter. Second, they suggest that understanding *about* science is important for the development of scientific reasoning and for the application of scientific reasoning to everyday, intentional knowledge. Third, they suggest that individual differences are present early and are not easily affected by differential educational experiences. This suggests both that scientific precocity should be recognized and fostered early and that strong science curricula even for those not "good" at science are important to assure that science literacy becomes available to all.

REFERENCES

Amsel, E., & Brock, S. (1996). The development of evidence evaluation skills. *Cognitive Development, 11*, 523–550.

Bullock, M., & Sodian, B. (2003). Entwicklung des wissenschaftlichen Denkens [Development of scientific thinking]. In W. Schneider & M. Knopf (Eds.), *Entwicklung, Lehren und Lernen* (pp. 75–92). Göttingen, Germany: Hogrefe.

Bullock, M., & Ziegler, A. (1994). Scientific thinking. In F. E. Weinert & W. Schneider (Eds.), *The Munich Longitudinal Study on the Genesis of Individual Competencies (LOGIC). Report No. 11: Assessment procedures and results of wave eight* (pp. 56–76). Munich: Max Planck Institute for Psychological Research.

Bullock, M., & Ziegler, A. (1999). Scientific reasoning: Developmental and individual differences. In F. E. Weinert & W. Schneider (Eds.), *Individual development from 3 to 12: Findings from the Munich Longitudinal Study* (pp. 38–54). Cambridge: Cambridge University Press.

Carey, S., Evans, R., Honda, M., Jay, E., & Unger, C. (1989). An experiment is when you try it and see if it works: A study of junior high school students' understanding of the construction of scientific knowledge. *International Journal of Science Education, 11*, 514–529.

Case, R. (1974). Structures and strictures: Some functional limitations on the course of cognitive growth. *Cognitive Psychology, 6*, 544–573.

Dean, D., Jr., & Kuhn, D. (2007). Direct instruction vs. discovery: The long view. *Science Education, 91*, 384–397.

Grygier, P. (2005). Wissenschaftsverständnis—Schon in der Grundschule? [Understanding of science: Already available in elementary school?]. In D. Cech & H. Giest (Eds.), *Sachunterricht in Praxis und Forschung. Probleme und Perspektiven des Sachunterrichts* (Vol. 15, pp. 177–189). Bad Heilbrunn, Germany: Klinkhardt.

Inhelder, B., & Piaget, J. (1958). *The growth of logical thinking from childhood to adolescence.* New York: Basic Books.

Klahr, D., & Nigam, M. (2004). The equivalence of learning paths in early science instruction: Effects of direct instruction and discovery learning. *Psychological Science, 15*, 661–667.

Koerber, S., Sodian, B., Thoermer, C., & Nett, U. (2005). Scientific reasoning in young children: Preschoolers' ability to evaluate covariation evidence. *Swiss Journal of Psychology, 64*(3), 141–152.

Koslowski, B. (1996). *Theory and evidence: The development of scientific reasoning.* Cambridge, MA: MIT Press.

Kuhn, D. (1991). *The skills of argument.* New York: Cambridge University Press.

Kuhn, D. (2002). What is scientific thinking and how does it develop? In U. Goswami (Ed.), *Handbook of childhood cognitive development* (pp. 371–393). Oxford: Blackwell.

Kuhn, D. (2005). *Education for thinking.* Cambridge, MA: Harvard University Press.

Kuhn, D. (2007). Reasoning about multiple variables: Control of variables is not the only challenge. *Science Education, 91*(5), 710–716.

Kuhn, D., Amsel, E., & O'Loughlin, M. (1988). *The development of scientific thinking skills.* Orlando, FL: Academic Press.

Kuhn, D., Cheney, R., & Weinstock, M. (2000). The development of epistemological understanding. *Cognitive Development, 15,* 309–328.

Kuhn, D., & Dean, D. (2004). Connecting scientific reasoning and causal inference. *Journal of Cognition and Development, 5,* 261–288.

Kuhn, D., & Franklin, S. (2006). The second decade. What develops (and how). In D. Kuhn & R. S. Siegler (Vol. Eds.), *Handbook of child psychology. Vol. 2: Cognition, perception and language* (6th ed., pp. 953–993). Hoboken, NJ: Wiley.

Kuhn, D., Garcia-Mila, Z., & Andersen, C. (1995). Strategies of knowledge acquisition. *Monograph of the Society for Research on Child Development, 60,* 1–127.

Kuhn, D., Iordanou, K., Pease, M., & Wirkala, C. (In press). Beyond control of variables: What needs to develop to achieve skilled scientific thinking. *Cognitive Development.*

Lederman, N. G. (1992). Students' and teachers' conceptions of the nature of science: A review of the research. *Journal of Research in Science Teaching, 29,* 331–359.

McComas, W. F. (Ed.). (1998). *The nature of science in science education.* Dordrecht, the Netherlands: Kluwer.

Ruffman, T., Perner, J., Olson, D. R., & Doherty, M. (1993). Reflecting on scientific thinking: Children's understanding of the hypothesis-evidence relation. *Child Development, 64,* 1617–1636.

Siegler, R. A., & Liebert, R. M. (1975). Acquisition of formal scientific reasoning by 10- and 13-year-olds: Designing a factorial experiment. *Developmental Psychology, 11,* 401–412.

Smith, C. L., Maclin, D., Houghton, C., & Hennessey, M. G. (2000). Sixth-grade students' epistemologies of science: The impact of school science experiences on epistemological development. *Cognition & Instruction, 18*(3), 349–422.

Sodian, B., Jonen, A., Thoermer, C., & Kircher, E. (2006). Die Natur der Naturwissenschaften verstehen. Implementierung wissenschaftstheoretischen Unterrichts in der Grundschule [The nature of scientific understanding: Implementing instruction on the philosophy of science in elementary school curriculum]. In M. Prenzel & L. Allolio-Näcke (Eds.), *Untersuchungen zur Bildungsqualität von Schule— Abschlussbericht des DFG-Schwerpunktprogramms* (pp. 147–160). Münster, Germany: Waxmann.

Sodian, B., Zaitchik, D., & Carey, S. (1991). Young children's differentiation of hypothetical beliefs from evidence. *Child Development, 62,* 753–766.

Thoermer, C., & Sodian, B. (2002). Science undergraduates' and graduates' epistemologies of science: The notion of interpretive frameworks. *New Ideas in Psychology, 26,* 263–283.

Zimmerman, C. (2007). The development of scientific thinking skills in elementary and middle school. *Developmental Review, 27*(2), 172–223.

9 The Development of Reading and Spelling

Relevant Precursors, Developmental Changes, and Individual Differences

Wolfgang Schneider

9.1 INTRODUCTION

From the very beginning of the Munich Longitudinal Study on the Ontogenesis of Individual Competencies (the LOGIC study), one goal was to assess relevant precursors of reading and spelling when children were about to enter the last year of kindergarten, and to evaluate the impact of these predictor variables for reading and spelling development over the subsequent years in school.

At the time that the LOGIC study began in 1984 (when the children were 3–4 years old and just entering kindergarten), our understanding of important precursors to reading and spelling was underdeveloped compared with the current state of the literature close to 30 years later. The literature on reading and spelling published through the mid-1980s (i.e., the time when decisions about measurement and assessment in the LOGIC study had to be made) revealed numerous studies with a variety of predictor variables for reading and spelling that did not yield consistent findings. According to an inventory published by Schneider and Edelstein (1990), the majority of the longitudinal studies on reading and spelling carried out before 1985 (about 30) were conducted in Europe. By and large, this first generation of longitudinal studies on the prediction of reading and spelling suffered because the selection of predictor measures was not guided by theoretical considerations. Rather, a vast array of mostly psychometric measures were used that in most cases were not proximal to reading and spelling (e.g., motor skills, general cognitive ability, and behavioral-emotional functioning; for reviews, see Horn & Packard, 1985; Tramontana, Hooper, & Selzer, 1988). Interestingly enough, many of these variables predicted later reading performance surprisingly well. However, their differential validity was rather low in that the precursor variables predicted developmental changes in math and other subject matters taught in school as well as literacy.

A second generation of longitudinal studies on the prediction of reading and spelling began to be published just at the start of the LOGIC study. This second generation did base its selection of precursor variables on theoretical assumptions (e.g., Bradley & Bryant, 1985; Juel, 1988; Lundberg, Frost, & Petersen, 1988; Skowronek & Marx, 1989; Stanovich, Cunningham, & Feeman, 1984). The number of relevant studies increased quickly during the 1990s and beyond. In an update of the 1990 inventory, Schneider and Stengard (2000) identified 144 longitudinal studies on reading and spelling in Europe, and estimated that the true number of relevant studies carried out on this issue internationally was considerably higher.

Overall, the second generation of longitudinal studies identified three relevant predictor domains within a broad theoretical frame labeled *phonological information processing* (see Wagner & Torgesen, 1987). A first predictor domain is *phonological awareness*, that is, the ability to reflect on and to manipulate the phonemic segments of speech, which was a very good predictor of children's later reading and spelling performance (see Tunmer & Nesdale, 1985; Wagner & Torgesen, 1987). According to Skowronek and Marx (1989), phonological awareness can be distinguished in a broad sense to refer to larger language units such as words, syllables, and rhymes, and in a more narrow sense that refers to small units such as phonemes and distinguishing sounds within words. Skowronek and Marx assumed that both components are relevant for subsequent reading and spelling performance in school. Although phonological awareness in the broad sense is acquired naturally during the course of the kindergarten period, phonological awareness in the narrow sense usually develops at the beginning of the first grade, when children learn to read and write. One controversial issue discussed in the literature concerned whether phonological awareness in the narrow sense can be acquired without knowledge of the alphabetic code (see, for example, Morais and colleagues: e.g., Morais, 1991; Bradley & Bryant, 1985; Lundberg, 1991).

A second relevant predictor domain is *phonological working memory* (see Brady, 1991; Gathercole & Baddeley, 1993; Wagner, 1988), which refers to children's ability to temporarily maintain phonological information in memory. Efficient recoding in working memory would aid beginning readers who face a challenging task when confronted with a new long word. They not only have to retrieve the sounds of the letters but also have to store initial sounds while continuing the recoding process. Finally, the whole sequence of sounds has to be kept active in working memory when the decoding process starts, that is, when children try to make sense of the sound sequence, blend the sounds together, and identify the word.

A third relevant phonological information-processing component is *verbal information-processing speed*, in particular the speed with which children can approach their semantic lexicon. It has been repeatedly shown that dyslexic children are slower than control groups when asked to label picture items in confrontation naming tasks (see Wimmer, Mayringer, & Landerl, 2000).

In addition to specifying a coherent set of phonological predictor variables, there was also broad agreement in the newer literature that *early literacy*, that is, insight into the alphabetic system (e.g., letter knowledge) acquired before entering school, is another important predictor of reading and spelling (see Lundberg, 1991; Skowronek & Marx, 1989). Letters can serve as an effective system representing the phonemic structure of words. Another early literacy skill, print awareness, may also be an indirect precursor of reading skills.

9.1.1 MAJOR GOALS OF THE LOGIC STUDY

Using the theoretically based, well-defined proposed precursors to reading reported in the second generation of longitudinal studies, the LOGIC assessments were designed to address a number of issues, including the following:

1. Do predictor variables such as phonological awareness, phonological working memory, verbal information-processing speed, and early literacy influence the acquisition of both reading and spelling in comparable ways? Given that most longitudinal studies on reading and spelling were based on English (which has an irregular orthography), we were especially interested in asking whether the results would replicate with children learning to read German (a regular orthographic system) and whether results would generalize to spelling in German (an irregular orthographic system). We were also interested in asking whether indicators representing phonological awareness in the broad and narrow senses would be important for predicting reading and spelling development in school.

2. Are there interrelationships among the different sets of independent predictor variables (e.g., IQ, memory capacity, phonological awareness, verbal information-processing speed, and early literacy) for predicting reading and spelling in school? From a methodological point of view, structural equation modeling procedures (causal models) using latent variables are necessary to test structural similarities and dissimilarities in the pattern of interrelationships.

3. Do short-term precursor variables have a long-lasting impact on the acquisition of literacy? There is little literature on this question. Most longitudinal studies that were available at the onset of the LOGIC study focused on the transition from kindergarten to elementary school. The longtime course of the LOGIC study allowed us to ask whether individual differences in predictor variables early on have direct effects on all subsequent assessments of literacy, or whether their direct influence is restricted to the beginning stages of reading and spelling, with initial competencies in reading and spelling causally affecting the further course of literacy development.

4. A final issue concerned the impact of early individual differences in reading and spelling on later developmental trends. We were interested in whether early differences prove stable over time, or whether the early acquisition process is dynamic, characterized by low test–retest stabili-

ties, followed by higher stability in later periods of skill development. Specifically, we wanted to explore whether early problems with the acquisition of literacy were maintained throughout the course of childhood and adolescence, and whether those children scoring at the bottom quartile of the achievement distribution at the beginning of schooling continued to perform poorly in subsequent years.

9.2   DESCRIPTION OF SAMPLE AND TEST INSTRUMENTS

A total of 210 children were initially recruited for the LOGIC study. For various reasons, 22 children were not promoted to elementary school together with the rest of the sample but stayed in kindergarten for one more year. Reading and spelling data for these participants are not considered in our analyses. Complete data sets from 163 children were available for the analyses dealing with spelling performance across the first 5 years of school, that is, up to Grade 5. Due to organizational problems, not all of the children participated in the decoding and reading comprehension tests provided in Grade 2. Data on the elementary school reading tests are available for only 121 children.

Design: Participants were given the phonological information-processing tasks at the age of 6 during the last year of kindergarten. Reading tests were given in Grade 2 and at the age of 23. Tests of spelling skill were given in Grades 2, 3, 4, and 5, and later again at the ages of 18 and 23. The main reason why spelling was investigated more intensively than reading was that spelling problems occur more frequently than reading problems in the German orthography, and because spelling problems lead to more negative consequences than reading problems, as far as progress in school is concerned.

9.2.1   Predictor Variables Assessed During
the Last Year of Kindergarten
9.2.1.1   Phonological Awareness

Four different measures were used to measure phonological awareness. First, a German version of Bradley and Bryant's (1985) phonological oddity task was used to assess children's understanding of *rhyming*. In this task, children were instructed that they would hear four words from a tape recorder, and that one of the four words would not sound like the others. In the middle-sound oddity condition, the target word always shared the last phone with the other three words but differed regarding the middle sound. In the end-sound oddity condition, the target word always shared the same middle phone as the other three words but differed concerning the end sound. Finally, in the first-sound condition, children had to detect the one out of four words with a first sound differing from that of the three other words. Correct answers were given one point. There was a total of 27 trials, yielding a maximum score of 27.

The second subtest assessing children's phonological awareness was adapted from the Bielefeld Longitudinal Study on Early Risk Identification (Skowronek

& Marx, 1989). This test consisted of 10 word pairs. For each pair, children had to indicate whether the items sounded alike. Again, correct responses were given one point, yielding a maximum score of 10.

A *syllable segmentation task* was also adapted from the Bielefeld Longitudinal Study (Skowronek & Marx, 1989). In this task, children were instructed that they would participate in a word repetition game. When presenting the practice items, the experimenters segmented the words into syllables and clapped their hands. Children were instructed to clap their hands when repeating the words. The number of correct word segmentations was used as the dependent variable in this task (max. = 10).

The *sound-to-word-matching task* was also taken from the Bielefeld study (see Skowronek & Marx, 1989). Children were told that they would hear a number of words, and that they had to listen very carefully. They first would have to repeat each word and then indicate if a specific sound pronounced by the experimenter was in that particular word. As an example, the experimenter presented the word *Auge* (eye) and asked subjects if they could hear an *au* in it. The number of correct responses was recorded (max. = 10).

9.2.1.2 PHONOLOGICAL RECODING IN LEXICAL ACCESS (INFORMATION-PROCESSING SPEED)

Two rapid-naming tasks also taken from the Bielefeld study were used to measure phonological recoding in lexical assess. In the first, *rapid color naming of noncolored objects*, eight sets of black-and-white drawings of four different objects were presented and labeled by the experimenter. The children were asked to name the correct colors of these objects as quickly as possible.

In the second rapid-color-naming task (*rapid color naming of objects with incongruent colors*), the same stimulus materials were used. The only difference was that all objects had wrong colors in this task. The children were instructed to give the correct colors of the objects as quickly as possible. Total time needed to complete the tasks and the number of errors were taken as dependent measures in both rapid-naming tasks.

9.2.1.3 Working Memory Capacity

Two verbal memory span tests were used to assess phonetic recoding in working memory. A German version of the Case, Kurland, and Goldberg (1982) *word span task* tapped children's short-term memory for words. The set sizes varied between three and seven 1-syllable words. Beginning with sets of three words, two trials were given for each set size. Children were instructed to first listen to the entire set, then to repeat the words they heard. Scores were taken from the maximum number of words repeated in the correct order. The word span measure was given in Waves 1, 3, 5, and 8.

A *sentence span* or *listening span measure* was adapted from Daneman and Blennerhassett (1984). Seventy-five sentences (at maximum), ranging in length from three to seven words, were read to each child. Sentences were grouped in five sets each of one, two, three, four, and five sentences. Children were presented the one-sentence sets first, followed by the two-sentence sets, and so on. With the exception of the one-sentence sets, sentences within each set were read in quick succession. Children were asked to repeat the sentences in each set verbatim. Testing terminated when the child failed to recall all five sentences at a particular level. The total number of sentences recalled correctly was chosen as the dependent variable. This task was given in Waves 3 to 5, 7, 10, and 11.

9.2.1.4 Additional Measures Assessed in Kindergarten

In addition to the three components of phonological processing, two further constructs that had been referred to as important predictors of reading skill in the literature were also included in our battery of predictors. The first component, as emphasized by Lomax and McGee (1987) and Share, Jorm, Maclean, and Matthews (1984), refers to *early literacy* or young children's concepts about print. We included three variables tapping this construct in the collection of predictor measures.

The first measure, a *letter-naming task*, assessed children's grapheme–phoneme correspondence knowledge. The number of letters correctly identified was chosen as the dependent variable. The second task (*sign knowledge* or *logo task*) was originally developed by Brügelmann (1986) and later modified by the Bielefeld group (Skowronek & Marx, 1989). The logo task tapped children's knowledge of letters and words that are hidden in familiar settings. Typical examples are traffic signs (e.g., the STOP sign) and trademarks. In some trials, only the original letters were given without any graphic context. In others, only the graphic context was given and the letters were omitted. We used the number of correct responses in trials focusing on the letters (without graphic context) as the dependent variable in the present analysis. The third measure tapping early literacy was *name writing*. Children were asked to write down a word they already knew on a sheet of paper. Those children who were able to write down at least one word were told that the experimenter wanted them to write down another 12 words. The number of words correctly spelled was used as the dependent variable.

The list of predictor variables was completed by tests of *verbal intelligence*. Three verbal subtests (i.e., general knowledge, vocabulary, and general understanding) from the Hannover-Wechsler Intelligence Test for Preschool Children (HAWIVA; Eggert, 1978) were chosen to represent the verbal intelligence construct. The HAWIVA was administered twice, when children were 4 and 5 years old. Combined scores of the three verbal subtests were computed on each occasion and used to represent verbal intelligence in the present study.

With the exception of the verbal intelligence measures and the indicator of reading speed, all predictor variables were assessed during the last kindergarten year.

9.2.2   CRITERION MEASURES ASSESSED IN SCHOOL AND BEYOND

9.2.2.1   Reading Speed and Comprehension

A task assessing early *word and nonword decoding speed* was adapted from Rott and Zielinski (1986) and presented in Grade 2. The items (four-letter words and pseudowords) were presented on a computer screen. An internal timing device measured children's responses from the moment of presentation on the screen. A total of 30 words and 30 nonwords were provided. Mean decoding speed was calculated separately for both types of words. The decoding speed tasks were given at the beginning and end of the second grade.

A 30-item test developed by Näslund (1990) was used to measure reading comprehension and word knowledge within the context of single sentences and longer text (short stories), and was given in Grade 2. A total of 18 multiple-choice items tapped *word knowledge*. They included finding synonyms and antonyms within the context of a sentence. The text *comprehension* part consisted of five short stories followed by two or three multiple-choice questions. This task was designed to test children's understanding of text, deducing answers from inferences based only on information in the stories.

In preparing the last wave of the LOGIC study, it was decided to include measures of reading speed and reading comprehension. A test later published by Schneider, Schlagmüller, and Ennemoser (2007) was based on a Norwegian essay about the importance of bread and brussels sprouts for daily life. Participants were instructed to read the text as quickly and accurately as possible within a time frame of 4 minutes. They were also told that they would find three words in parentheses after a number of sentences, and that their task was to underline the word that completed the particular sentence adequately. After 4 minutes of reading, participants were asked to mark the last line that they had read. The number of words (out of a total of 1,847) read within 4 minutes was used to assess reading speed. Reading comprehension was inferred from the number of correct word selections.

Two tests taken from the Organization for Economic Cooperation and Development (OECD) Programme for International Student Assessment (PISA) 2000 study were also presented in Wave 11 to assess young adults' reading comprehension. A text on "Origins of the Moon" was part of the German contribution to reading comprehension in PISA 2000 (see Artelt, Brunner, Schneider, Prenzel, & Neubrand, 2003; Artelt, Schiefele, & Schneider, 2001). Participants had to read a text about the origins of the moon and to memorize the content as well as possible. After 8 minutes of reading time, participants were given 13 questions referring to the content of the text, and several shorter items that assessed the domain knowledge as well as their interest in the domain covered by the text, yielding a maximum score of 48.

The second PISA text concerned a story ("Amanda and the Duchess") that was included in a field trial but not considered for the main PISA 2000 study. This narrative text is about a meeting between Amanda, a young saleslady, and a duchess. Participants read the study and were then asked to answer five questions about the story, two in multiple-choice format and three using an open format. Correct answers to four of the questions were given one point, and answers to the fifth item were given three points, yielding a maximum score of seven points.

9.2.2.2 Spelling Tasks

The two *spelling tests* given in the second grade (word dictations) consisted of two partially overlapping versions, one presented at the beginning of the second grade and the other shortly before the end of the second grade. Each test included about 20 target words that were taken from different sources and were judged to be particularly suited to assess spelling competence in the second grade. The spelling tests provided in grades 3, 4, and 5 (i.e., Waves 6, 7, and 8) were more comprehensive (60 words, 81 words, and 88 words, respectively), and were given as sentence dictations. About two thirds of the material consisted of familiar words taken from the official vocabulary list for third and fourth graders distributed by the Bavarian Ministry of Education. It was assumed that these words were already practiced in the classroom and thus could be mastered by the majority of children. The remaining items were less familiar and consisted of irregular words.

In Waves 10 and 11, a subtest ("Moselfahrt") taken from a standardized test of spelling skills (Rechtschreibungstest, or RT; Jaeger et al., 1974) was used. In this test, a narrative text is read to the participants. Responses are given in a fill-in-the-blank test. An answer sheet provided to participants included parts of the text with empty spaces for a total of 65 target words that participants were to write in. Test norms were available for older children (from age 13 onward), adolescents, and adults. For this test and all other spelling measures included in the LOGIC study, the number of correct items was chosen as the dependent variable.

9.3 MAJOR FINDINGS

9.3.1 RELATIONSHIPS AMONG KINDERGARTEN PREDICTORS AND READING AND SPELLING IN SCHOOL

A detailed account on the means, standard deviations, and ranges of the various predictor and criterion variables can be found in an earlier publication on reading and spelling development of the LOGIC sample (see Schneider & Näslund, 1999, pp. 132ff). A summary of intercorrelations among the various predictor variables are shown in Table 9.1, indicating moderate to strong interrelationships among the various phonological information-processing variables, early literacy, and IQ.

Relationships among the various criterion measures tapping reading and spelling performance in elementary school are depicted in Table 9.2. It can be seen from this table that reading speed assessed in grade 2 was rather stable over a little less than one year, and that it was moderately related to reading comprehension measured in the same grade. There was also a substantial correlation between reading speed and spelling in the early school grades. Interestingly, the

TABLE 9.1

Intercorrelations Among Various Predictor Variables (Kindergarten Period)

	2	3	4	5	6	7	8	9	10	11	12
1. Rhyming (total number correct, first sound), Wave 3	.286	.349	-.193	-.185	.046	.250	.378	.445	.214	.287	.205
2. Rhyming (total number correct, middle sound), Wave 3	—	.664	-.246	-.209	.178	.332	.144	.202	.256	.307	.243
3. Rhyming (total number correct, end sound), Wave 3		—	-.373	-.314	.199	.504	.153	.296	.303	.369	.294
4. Color naming, noncolored objects (time), Wave 3			—	.597	-.074	-.237	-.099	-.284	-.186	-.269	-.150
5. Color naming, incorrectly colored objects (time), Wave 3				—	-.042	-.259	-.134	-.225	-.272	-.166	-.265
6. Syllable segmentation (corr.), Wave 3					—	.239	.098	.200	.172	.142	.092
7. Sound-to-word matching (corr.), Wave 3						—	.074	.239	.244	.276	.343
8. Logos correctly identified, Wave 3							—	.365	.140	.106	.112
9. Letter knowledge (max. 26), Wave 3								—	.202	.185	.325
10. Serial word span, Wave 3									—	.358	.217
11. Listening span (total number of correct sentences), Wave 3										—	.296
12. Verbal IQ, Wave 2											—

TABLE 9.2

Intercorrelations Among Various Criterion Variables (Elementary School)

	2	3	4	5	6	7	8
1. Reading speed (at the beginning of the second grade)	.72	-.54	-.49	-.31	-.39	-.43	-.43
2. Reading speed (at the end of the second grade)	—	-.57	-.49	-.63	-.60	-.49	-.43
3. Reading comprehension (at the beginning of the second grade)		—	.79	.46	.55	.59	.54
4. Reading comprehension (at the end of the second grade)			—	.35	.36	.42	.43
5. Spelling (at the end of the second grade)				—	.81	.74	.59
6. Spelling (at the end of the third grade)					—	.87	.79
7. Spelling (at the end of the fourth grade)						—	.83
8. Spelling (at the end of the fifth grade)							—

relationship calculated for reading speed at the end of the second grade and spelling performance at the end of the second and third grades was much stronger than that obtained between reading speed at the beginning of the second grade and the two spelling indicators (–.63 and –.60 versus –.31 and –.39, respectively). This relationship tended to be higher than that between reading comprehension and spelling in grades 2 and 3 (coefficients ranging between .35 and .55). In fact, the correlation between reading speed at the end of Grade 2 and spelling was significantly higher than that for reading comprehension at the end of Grade 2 and spelling, a somewhat unexpected result.

Given that most predictor variables assessed during the last year of kindergarten were substantially correlated with the criterion variables measured in elementary school, we explored their potential in predicting reading and spelling in school. We were interested in the extent to which the battery of predictor variables would account for the variance in both reading and spelling criterion variables.

Table 9.3 summarizes the results of two stepwise regression analyses addressing reading as a function of criterion measure (reading speed and reading com-

TABLE 9.3
Results of Stepwise Regression Analyses Using Spelling at the End of Grade 2 and Grade 3 as Criterion Variables

Predictor	R^2	ΔR^2
End of Grade 2		
Nonverbal IQ	.11	
Rapid naming	.21	.10
Letter knowledge	.26	.05
Sound-to-word matching	.29	.03
Sound blending	.32	.03
Sign knowledge	.34	.02
Listening span	.35	.01
Word writing	.36	.01
End of Grade 3		
Nonverbal IQ	.13	
Rapid naming	.40	.04
Letter knowledge	.29	.16
Sound-to-word matching	.44	.02
Nonword repetition	.67	.10
Sign knowledge (logos)	.46	.02
Listening span	.36	.07
Word writing	.42	.02

prehension). Overall, the battery of predictor variables only accounted for modest amounts of variance (about 27 to 35%) explained in the reading speed and reading comprehension variables. The regression analyses shown in Table 9.3 also indicate that different kindergarten predictors contributed to the explanation of individual differences in reading speed and reading comprehension, and that prediction patterns were not stable over time. Overall, IQ was more important for the prediction of reading comprehension than for predicting reading speed. At the end of Grade 2, rhyming skills and information-processing speed contributed significantly to the prediction of both reading speed and reading comprehension. In addition to these predictors, letter knowledge and listening span also turned out to be important for the prediction of reading speed, particularly at the beginning of Grade 2.

Results of the stepwise regression analyses using spelling at the end of Grade 2 and at the end of Grade 3 as criterion variables are depicted in Table 9.3. As can be seen, about 36% of the variance in the spelling variable could be explained by the end of Grade 2, and even more variance (47%) by the end of Grade 3. Regression analyses carried out for the subsequent years revealed that the impact of the kindergarten predictor variables decreased after Grade 3, which is not surprising given the long time interval between predictor and criterion assessments.

Interestingly, the set of variables accounting for the prediction of spelling was not that different from the set accounting for the reading measures. Again, letter knowledge played an important role, followed by rapid naming, various phonological awareness indicators, and listening span. In comparison, however, these variables were more powerful predictors of spelling than of reading. Almost 50% of the variance in spelling assessed at the end of Grade 3 could be predicted by measures assessed 3 years earlier at the end of kindergarten.

9.3.2 Findings from Structural Equation Modeling

As noted above, one important issue was to explore the interrelationships among the various sets of independent variables (e.g., IQ, memory capacity, phonological awareness, verbal information-processing speed, and early literacy) in predicting reading and spelling in school. Consequently, structural equation modeling (SEM) procedures using a latent variable causal modeling approach (LISREL; see Jöreskog & Sörbom, 1989) were used to develop and test adequate structural models. Given that these modeling approaches have been described in more detail elsewhere (see Schneider & Näslund, 1992, 1999), results will be only briefly summarized.

For predicting reading comprehension at the end of Grade 2, IQ and phonological awareness showed both direct and indirect effects. In comparison, the contribution of working memory was indirect only in that this variable significantly affected both early literacy (e.g., letter knowledge) and reading speed, which in turn had direct effects on the reading comprehension variable. In total, about 47% of the variance in reading comprehension could be explained by this structural model, which fit the data well. The amount of variance in the reading comprehension criterion explained by the causal modeling procedure was clearly larger than that explained by the stepwise regression analyses based on manifest variables.

Figures 9.1 and 9.2 show two causal models estimated to predict spelling performance at two different time points (i.e., at the end of Grade 2 and at the end of Grade 5). Figure 9.1 shows that spelling assessed at the end of Grade 2 was directly affected by phonological awareness, information-processing speed, and early literacy assessed at the end of kindergarten, which in turn were predicted

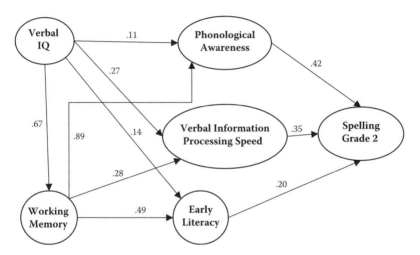

FIGURE 9.1   Causal model predicting spelling performance at the end of Grade 2.

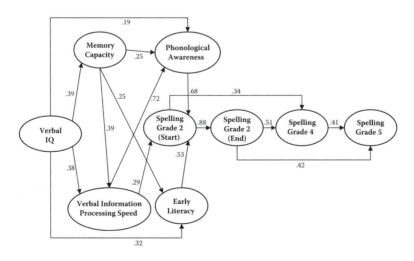

FIGURE 9.2   Causal model predicting spelling performance at different time points (i.e., at the beginning of Grade 2 and at the end of Grades 2, 4, and 5).

by IQ and working memory assessed somewhat earlier during the kindergarten years. The total amount of variance explained in the spelling criterion was 62%, and it would appear that the preschool predictors have a long-lasting impact on the development of literacy. However, this impression changed when the perspective was broadened in a later SEM analysis, and other spelling measures assessed at different points in time were additionally included in the model (see Figure 9.2). One of the most obvious insights from this additional analysis was that although the kindergarten predictor measures had a strong impact on spelling assessed at the beginning of Grade 2, they did not predict any further. That is, from Grade 2 onward, individual differences in spelling assessed at an earlier time point substantially predicted spelling assessed at a later time point, with individual differences in kindergarten predictors playing no additional role. Obviously, the model depicted in Figure 9.1 suffers from a *specification error*, meaning that theoretically important variables such as spelling at the beginning of Grade 2 were not included in the model. Overall, almost 70% in the spelling variance at the end of Grade 5 could be explained by the model depicted in Figure 9.2, which also fit the data very well.

9.3.3 THE IMPACT OF INDIVIDUAL DIFFERENCES IN CHILDHOOD READING AND SPELLING ON LATER SKILL DEVELOPMENT

We already clarified the fact that our kindergarten precursor variables did not have long-lasting influences on the development of reading and spelling in school. However, what still remains to be explored is whether individual differences in early reading and spelling skills predicted reading and spelling performance at subsequent occasions. We address this issue separately for reading and spelling, given that spelling was more intensively studied in the LOGIC study than reading.

9.3.3.1 Relationships Between Early and Late Reading Skills

Reading and literacy precursor variables were assessed in the LOGIC study intensely until the second grade, and then not again until Wave 11, when participants were about 23 years of age. At that time, both reading speed and comprehension were assessed.

In a first step of data analysis, we calculated intercorrelations among verbal IQ, reading speed, and reading comprehension variables for both measurement points. As can be seen from Table 9.4 (upper part), correlations were moderately high to high for the IQ and reading measures assessed in Grade 2. The same was also true for intercorrelations among verbal IQ, reading speed, and reading comprehension assessed in young adulthood (see Table 9.4, lower part). We did encounter some problems with the adult measurement. The distribution of sum scores for the "Amanda and the Duchess" story was highly skewed, suggesting ceiling effects in the data (mean score: 4.80; $SD = 1.76$; range 0–7). Although findings for the second text comprehension measure taken from the PISA items ("Origins of the

TABLE 9.4

Intercorrelations Among Verbal IQ, Reading Speed, and Reading Comprehension Assessed in Grade 2 and Young Adulthood

Grade 2	(2)	(3)	(4)
1. Verbal IQ	.350	.410	
2. Reading speed		.610	
3. Reading comprehension			
Young Adulthood			
1. Verbal IQ	.453	.349	.570
2. Reading speed	—	.370	.317
3. Reading comprehension ("Amanda and the Duchess")		—	.357
4. Reading comprehension ("Origins of the Moon")			—

Moon") also suggested that the test was rather easy for young adults, there was no evidence of a ceiling effect (mean score: 34.53; SD = 8.07; range: 11–48). The same was true for the reading speed and comprehension test ("Bread and Brussels Sprouts"), where scores for reading comprehension and reading speed were normally distributed.

When test–retest correlations were calculated separately for reading speed and reading comprehension, stabilities turned out to be moderately high (with coefficients ranging between .38 and .42). This seems remarkable given that the time interval between the two measurement points comprised more than 15 years.

9.3.3.2 Relationships Between Early and Late Spelling Skills

In addition to its relative importance in the German school system for educational success, spelling is more difficult than reading in the German orthography, reflected by the fact that the number of phoneme–grapheme (sound–letter) correspondence rules broadly exceeds the number of grapheme–phoneme correspondence rules. Thus, the German orthography is regular, as far as reading is concerned, and highly irregular, as far as spelling is concerned. As a consequence, most dyslexic German children can read fairly well but suffer from serious and persistent spelling problems.

As can be seen from Table 9.5, intercorrelations among early and late spelling skills were substantial. Individual stabilities in spelling skills could be demonstrated from the age of 8 (Wave 5) onward. The test–retest stability between the ages of 8 and 18 was .57, and a stability score of .74 was found for the interval between the ages of 10 and 18. Given the substantial correlation of .82 between

TABLE 9.5
Intercorrelations Among Early and Late Spelling Skills (Between Ages 8 and 23)

Age (in years)	10	18	23
8	.74	.57	.50
10		.74	.69
18			.82

spelling skills at the ages of 18 and 23, it seems clear that the rank order in spelling competencies did not change much between adolescence and early adulthood. Interestingly, the long-term stabilities obtained for spelling were at least as high as those obtained for the various intelligence components assessed in the LOGIC study (see Schneider, Stefanek, & Niklas, chap. 2, this volume).

Moreover, spelling skills did not improve significantly between adolescence and young adulthood. A repeated analysis of variance using Sex as the independent factor and Measurement as the dependent factor revealed a significant effect of Sex, $F(1, 146) = 5.80$, $p < .05$, but no effect of time, and no interaction. Females outperformed males on both occasions, and both sexes gained an average of about one word (out of a total of 66) from age 18 to age 23. Obviously, peak performance was already reached in late adolescence for most participants.

Findings from a stepwise regression analysis on spelling at the age of 23 that included spelling at the age of 10, verbal IQ (assessed in grade 3), chronological age, and the first year of schooling as independent variables further confirmed the impression of high individual stabilities over time in this literacy skill (see Table 9.6). Spelling assessed at the age of 10 accounted for most of the variance explained in spelling assessed at the age of 23, followed by the year of schooling, IQ, and age. In total, 60% of the variance in the criterion variable could be explained by this set of predictors. It seems interesting that the variable indicating timing of the first year of schooling showed a reliable effect. This means that

TABLE 9.6
Prediction of Spelling at the Age of 23

Predictor	Beta	p
Spelling (grade 4)	.68	.0001
Hamburg-Wechsler Intelligence Scale for School Children (HAWIK-R; grade 3)	.25	.001
Age	.21	.01
Year of school enrollment	.39	.001

those participants who had entered school one year later than the other participants performed comparably worse than the rest of the sample when tested in
young adulthood.

Finally, given that a rather dated spelling test (Moselfahrt) was used to assess
spelling skills in young adulthood, it was possible to compare achievement levels
across a time period of almost 40 years. Overall, our LOGIC sample produced
about twice as many errors in the test than the standardization sample tested
in 1968. Accordingly, about 60% of the participants in the LOGIC study would
have been classified as dyslexic (percentile 15 and less) according to the original
test norms. This finding suggests that spelling skills in German students have
decreased over the past few decades.

9.4   DISCUSSION

9.4.1   THE IMPACT OF KINDERGARTEN PREDICTOR
VARIABLES ON THE ACQUISITION OF LITERACY

One of the specific features of the LOGIC study was that precursors of reading
and spelling development were assessed simultaneously, and that a rather large
set of kindergarten predictors was used to describe and explain individual differences in the acquisition of literacy. The most relevant findings concerning the
early school period were already summarized by Schneider and Näslund (1992,
1999). Results of their causal modeling analyses, for example, clarified the role of
working memory as a predictor of reading versus spelling development in German-speaking children. At the time of data collection, it seemed unclear to which
degree working memory and phonological awareness contributed to the acquisition of literacy. Whereas some researchers claimed that phonological awareness
is the driving force (e.g., Goswami & Bryant, 1990), others believed in the causal
predominance of working memory in the reading acquisition process. The causal
modeling results obtained for the LOGIC sample supports the position that working memory plays a part, but an indirect one. They further indicated that the
direction of the memory contribution varies with the outcome measure. That is,
children's working memory capacity contributes very strongly to phonological
awareness, verbal information-processing speed, and early literacy, which in turn
all predict individual differences in the early stages of the spelling process. However, when reading comprehension was used as the outcome measure, working
memory continued to make an indirect contribution through recoding and early
literacy, but independently from phonological awareness.

In his thoughtful comments on these findings, Peter Bryant (1999) speculated
about the reason for this discrepancy, noting that letter–sound relationships may
pose greater demands on memory in spelling than in reading. In his view, young
children are more familiar with sounds than with letters. Accordingly, it may
impose a far greater burden on children for them to start with a sound and have
to remember the appropriate letter than to start with a letter (spelling) and have
to remember the appropriate sound (reading). In our view, there may be another

factor involved. As noted above, the German orthography is rather easy (regular) as far as reading is concerned, and very difficult (irregular) in the case of spelling. Thus, this specific feature of the German orthography seems to add to the importance of both working memory and phonological awareness in predicting spelling achievement. In a recent longitudinal study covering 8 school years, Landerl and Wimmer (2008) were able to show that phonological awareness was the strongest predictor for spelling, whereas rapid naming was the best predictor of reading fluency at the end of school. Again, phonological awareness was more important for predicting spelling outcomes than reading. Of course, this pattern of findings replicated for the German orthography (see Wimmer, Landerl, & Schneider, 1994) may not transfer to irregular orthographies such as that of English, given that memory capacity and phonological skills may both be needed to acquire both reading and spelling competencies in school.

9.4.2 STABILITY OF SPELLING DIFFERENCES OVER TIME

A second major outcome of the causal modeling procedures carried out by Schneider and Näslund (1999) was that the impact of the phonological processing variables (i.e., phonological awareness, working memory, and verbal information-processing speed) and early literacy was particularly important for the initial stages of the spelling acquisition process, that is, for progress in spelling observed during Grade 1. There were no signs of any long-term effects of early experience in phonology on the acquisition of spelling skills assessed after Grade 2. Given the enormous individual stability in spelling development over time, spelling achievement assessed in a previous grade strongly predicted spelling skills observed at a later measurement point, leaving no substantial amounts of unexplained variance to be accounted for by additional variables. It seems remarkable that long-term stabilities obtained for spelling were comparable to stability coefficients typically found for psychometric intelligence. Although the LOGIC participants experienced rather different educational settings after elementary school (at the end of Grade 4), these differences did not change the rank order of spelling skills tested through early adulthood. This is not to say that there were no schooling differences. A detailed assessment of developmental changes in spelling as a function of educational context (low versus high educational track) revealed that spelling differences between students in the high versus low educational track were already apparent in elementary school and further increased during the initial stages of secondary school until the age of 11 (Schneider & Stefanek, 2004). From Grade 6 onward, mean performance differences between the two groups remained constant over time.

9.4.2.1   Sex Differences

One of the core assumptions related to the assessment of reading and spelling skills and relevant precursor variables is that of consistent sex differences in favor of girls. When this issue was analyzed using our LOGIC data after 5 years of schooling, the message was rather mixed (see Schneider & Näslund, 1999). Although girls tended to be better on several measures of phonological processing, the mean difference was always small. Also, no significant sex differences were found for reading speed or reading comprehension at the end of Grade 2. The analyses conducted for spelling showed a somewhat different picture. Although there were no sex differences in the mean number of words correctly spelled at the two testing points in Grade 2, more pronounced performance differences between girls and boys were found from Grade 3 onward. Although these differences were all significant, they did not indicate substantial effects. The spelling advantage of females continued to be significant at the ages of 18 and 23, probably due to girls' comparably better school adjustment and more positive learning motivation. Taken together, these findings confirm the view that performance differences between males and females increase with age and amount of schooling.

9.4.3 STABILITY OF READING COMPETENCIES OVER TIME

In retrospect, one of the regrettable decisions made during the course of the LOGIC study was to discontinue the assessment of reading development after Grade 2. This decision was made for personnel reasons (Jan Näslund, one of the driving forces behind the reading concept, left the project at that point in time) and logistical reasons (persistent demands on research time in the LOGIC study). After the second grade, we agreed to focus on spelling development because spelling seemed more interesting for the prediction of academic success. At that time (i.e., in the early 1990s), we could not predict the impact of the PISA 2000 study and its focus on adolescents' reading comprehension on German educational policy. After the publication of the first results of the PISA study in 2001 and subsequent secondary analyses (e.g., Artelt et al., 2001), research on reading comprehension exploded in German-speaking countries. Needless to say, it would have been nice to present LOGIC data describing the natural course of reading development from the beginning of school until adolescence.

Although this problem was impossible to cure, we decided to use various measures of reading competency (i.e., reading speed and reading comprehension) as criterion variables in early adulthood. Overall, the correlations found between reading speed and comprehension at grade 2 and reading speed and comprehension in young adulthood were moderately high, ranging between .38 and .42, showing remarkable stability given a time lag of about 15 years. Although we can only speculate about across-age reading correlations for shorter time intervals such as those calculated for the spelling variables (see above), there is reason to assume that short-term stability assessed for the reading variables would not differ much from that assessed for spelling. In both cases, individual differences were rather stable after grade 2. Of course, this does not mean that educational context is not important for the acquisition of literacy. On the contrary, we found impressive gains in reading and spelling skills for most children during the course of elementary school. However, individual differences among students established early in the process were only minimally affected by subsequent pedagogical interventions.

REFERENCES

Artelt, C., Brunner, M., Schneider, W., Prenzel, M., & Neubrand, J. (2003). Literacy oder Lehrplanvalidität? Ländervergleiche auf der Basis lehrplanoptimierter PISA-Tests [Literacy or curriculum validity? Comparisons among German states based on curriculum-corrected PISA tests]. In J. Baumert, C. Artelt, E. Klieme, J. Neubrand, M. Prenzel, U. Schiefele, et al. (Eds.), *PISA 2000: Ein differenzierter Blick auf die Länder der Bundesrepublik Deutschland* (pp. 77–108). Opladen, Germany: Leske + Budrich.

Artelt, C., Schiefele, U., & Schneider, W. (2001). Predictors of reading literacy. *European Journal of Psychology of Education, 16*, 363–384.

Bradley, L., & Bryant, P. E. (1985). *Rhyme and reason in reading and spelling.* Ann Arbor: University of Michigan Press.

Brady, S. A. (1991). The role of working memory in reading disability. In S. A. Brady & D. P. Shankweiler (Eds.), *Phonological processes in literacy: A tribute to Isabelle Y. Liberman* (pp. 129–151). Hillsdale, NJ: Erlbaum.

Brügelmann, H. (1986). *Lese- und Schreibaufgaben für Schulanfänger* [Reading and spelling tasks for first graders]. Bremen, Germany: Universität Bremen, Studiengang Primarstufe.

Bryant, P. (1999). Comment: Sounds logic. In F. E. Weinert & W. Schneider (Eds.), *Individual development from 3 to 12: Findings from the Munich Longitudinal Study* (pp. 148–153). Cambridge: Cambridge University Press.

Case, R., Kurland, D. M., & Goldberg, J. (1982). Operational efficiency and the growth of short-term memory span. *Journal of Experimental Child Psychology, 33,* 386–404.

Daneman, M., & Blennerhassett, A. (1984). How to assess the listening comprehension skills of prereaders. *Journal of Educational Psychology, 76,* 1372–1381.

Eggert, D. (1978). *Hannover-Wechsler-Intelligenztest für das Vorschulalter* [Hannover-Wechsler Intelligence Scale for Preschool Children (German version of the WPPSI)]. Bern, Switzerland: Huber-Verlag.

Gathercole, S., & Baddeley, A. (1993). *Working memory and language processing.* Hove, UK: Erlbaum.

Goswami, U., & Bryant, P. (1990). *Phonological skill and learning to read.* Hove, UK: Erlbaum.

Horn, W. F., & Packard, T. (1985). Early identification of learning problems: A meta-analysis. *Journal of Educational Psychology, 77,* 597–607.

Jaeger, A. O., Althoff, K., Greif, S., Henning, G., Hess, R., & Roeber, J. (1974). *RT— Rechtschreibungstest* [Spelling test RT]. Göttingen, Germany: Hogrefe.

Jöreskog, K. G., & Sörbom, D. (1989). *LISREL VII: Analysis of linear structural relationship (user's guide).* Mooresville, IN: Scientific Software.

Juel, C. (1988). Learning to read and write: A longitudinal study of 54 children from first through fourth grades. *Journal of Educational Psychology, 80,* 437–447.

Landerl, K., & Wimmer, H. (2008). Development of word fluency and spelling in a consistent orthography: An 8-year follow-up. *Journal of Educational Psychology, 100,* 150–161.

Lomax, R. G., & McGee, L. M. (1987). Young children's concepts about print and reading: Toward a model of word-reading acquisition. *Reading Research Quarterly, 22*, 237–256.

Lundberg, I. (1991). Phonemic awareness can be developed without reading instruction. In S. A. Brady & D. P. Shankweiler (Eds.), *Phonological processes in literacy: A tribute to Isabelle Y. Liberman* (pp. 47–53). Hillsdale, NJ: Erlbaum.

Lundberg, I., Frost, J., & Petersen, O. P. (1988). Effects of an extensive program for stimulating phonological awareness in preschool children. *Reading Research Quarterly, 23*, 263–284.

Morais, J. (1991). Constraints on the development of phonemic awareness. In S. A. Brady & D. P. Shankweiler (Eds.), *Phonological processes in literacy: A tribute to Isabelle Y. Liberman* (pp. 5–27). Hillsdale, NJ: Erlbaum.

Näslund, J. (1990). The interrelationships among preschool predictors of reading acquisition for German children. *Reading & Writing: An Interdisciplinary Journal, 2*, 327–380.

Rott, C., & Zielinski, W. (1986). Entwicklung der Lesefertigkeit in der Grundschule [The development of reading skills in elementary school]. *Zeitschrift für Entwicklungspsychologie und Pädagogische Psychologie, 18*, 165–175.

Schneider, W., & Edelstein, W. (1990). *Inventory of European longitudinal studies in behavioral and medical sciences.* Munich: Max Planck Institute for Psychological Research.

Schneider, W., & Näslund, J. C. (1992). Cognitive prerequisites of reading and spelling: A longitudinal approach. In A. Demetriou, M. Shayer, & A. Efklides (Eds.), *Neo-Piagetian theories of cognitive development: Implications and applications for education* (pp. 256–274). London: Routledge.

Schneider, W., & Näslund, J. C. (1999). The impact of early phonological processing skills on reading and spelling in school: Evidence from the Munich Longitudinal Study. In F. E. Weinert & W. Schneider (Eds.), *Individual development from 3 to 12: Findings from the Munich Longitudinal Study* (pp. 126–147). Cambridge: Cambridge University Press.

Schneider, W., Schlagmüller, M., & Ennemoser, M. (2007). *Lesegeschwindigkeits- und -verständnistest für die Klassenstufen 6–12* [Reading speed and reading comprehension test for grades 6–12]. Göttingen, Germany: Hogrefe.

Schneider, W., & Stefanek, J. (2004). Entwicklungsveränderungen allgemeiner kognitiver Fähigkeiten und schulbezogener Fertigkeiten im Kindes- und Jugendalter—Evidenz für einen Schereneffekt? [Developmental changes in general cognitive abilities and achievement-related skills over the course of childhood and adolescence: Is there evidence for an increasing achievement gap?]. *Zeitschrift für Entwicklungspsychologie und Pädagogische Psychologie, 36*, 147–149.

Schneider, W., & Stengard, C. (2000). *Inventory of European longitudinal studies on reading and spelling.* Luxembourg: Office for Official Publications of the European Communities.

Share, D. L., Jorm, A. F., Maclean, R., & Matthews, R. (1984). Sources of individual differences in reading acquisition. *Journal of Educational Psychology, 76*, 1309–1324.

Skowronek, H., & Marx, H. (1989). The Bielefeld longitudinal study on early identification of risks in learning to write and read: Theoretical background and first results. In M. Brambring, F. Lösel, & H. Skowronek (Eds.), *Children at risk: Assessment, longitudinal research, and intervention* (pp. 268–294). New York: de Gruyter.

Stanovich, K., Cunningham, A. E., & Feeman, D. J. (1984). Intelligence, cognitive skills, and early reading progress. *Reading Research Quarterly, 19*, 278–303.

Tramontana, M., Hooper, S., & Selzer, S. (1988). Research on the preschool prediction of later academic achievement: A review. *Developmental Review, 8*, 89–146.

Tunmer, W. E., & Nesdale, A. R. (1985). Phonemic segmentation skill and beginning reading. *Journal of Educational Psychology, 77*, 417–427.

Wagner, R. K. (1988). Causal relations between the development of phonological processing abilities and the acquisition of reading skills: A meta-analysis. *Merrill-Palmer Quarterly, 34*, 261–279.

Wagner, R. K., & Torgesen, J. K. (1987). The nature of phonological processing and its causal role in the acquisition of reading skills. *Psychological Bulletin, 101*, 192–212.

Wimmer, H., Landerl, K., & Schneider, W. (1994). The role of rhyme awareness in learning to read a regular orthography. *British Journal of Developmental Psychology, 12*, 469–484.

Wimmer, H., Mayringer, H., & Landerl, K. (2000). The double-deficit hypothesis and difficulties in learning to read a regular orthography. *Journal of Educational Psychology, 92*, 668–680.

10 The Development of Mathematical Competencies

Sources of Individual Differences and Their Developmental Trajectories

Elsbeth Stern

10.1 INTRODUCTION

Children's ease in learning to count in the low-number range and to model changes in set size by addition and subtraction contrasts sharply with the well-documented difficulties many children have when learning mathematics in school. What are the reasons for this discrepancy?

Results from infant research have provided abundant evidence for the modularized bases of mathematical competencies. Transfer of mathematical language to situations in the perceivable world is facilitated by intuitive, universal mathematical knowledge. A set of objects or events may be quantified by counting, and an increase or decrease in set size can be modeled by addition and subtraction. In the course of cultural development, complex mathematical concepts that have been crucial for technological and scientific progress have been elaborated from simple mathematical principles, often combined with certain means of visual-graphical representation. Despite the overwhelming importance of mathematics to modern society, the vast majority of people nonetheless find it challenging to acquire mathematical competencies. At all age levels, it is a particular challenge for students to solve complex problems embedded in new contexts, for which they have no ready solution.

In this chapter, I will describe individual differences in mathematical competencies from immediately before the LOGIC participants entered school (age 6) to adulthood (age 23). In the first part of the chapter, I will address the kind of competencies children acquire before they eventually approach an advanced level of mathematical understanding based on problems presented to the participants in the LOGIC study. The second part of the chapter will address the development of individual differences. Questions will include the age at which individual differences become stable and the impact of sex and general cognitive capabilities on mathematics achievement.

10.2 UNIVERSAL TRANSITIONS IN MATHEMATICS: FROM INTUITIVE QUANTIFICATION TO SYMBOL-BASED REASONING

If young children are shown two sets of objects, one with three objects and one with four, they already know which set contains more objects. Similarly, when young children are asked to compare a set with 10 objects to one with 40 objects, it will be obvious to them which set contains more objects. On the other hand, if asked to compare a randomly organized set of 103 objects with a randomly organized set of 104 objects, even adults are unlikely to spontaneously tell which set is larger. Mastering this task requires access to culturally based counting tools, whereas the first two tasks can be solved on a perceptual basis available to all normally developing human beings (Baroody & Lai, 2007). Results from infant research have suggested competencies both for quantitatively comparing small quantities and for estimating large quantities. There is evidence that the small-set and large-set quantitative systems initially work independently of each other, but become integrated as a uniform system of quantitative reasoning through the use of number symbols (Feigenson, Dehaene, & Spelke, 2004).

All cultures, even preliterate ones, have number words. However, having specific symbols for numbers is not present among all cultures, even those with script. The Arabic place-value number system, which is now common in most parts of the world, was developed only about 1,000 years ago. Our present decimal system was possible only after the number zero had made its way from India via the Arabic countries to Europe. Even the most intelligent inhabitant of the Roman world would not have been able to solve the problem CIV / XXVI = __, whereas today an average elementary school child will easily find an answer for 104 / 26 = ____. The Roman number system, although appropriate for quantification, only allowed restricted computation. It was superseded by the Arabic system centuries ago. It was the Arabic number system that opened the pathway to advanced academic mathematics. The core contents of the mathematics curriculum in secondary higher education, such as calculus, were developed less than 3 centuries ago. It thus comes as no surprise that teachers are challenged by the fact that young people in modern schools have to acquire knowledge within a few years that has developed over centuries by genius minds with tremendous effort.

There is a long tradition in mathematics education that proscribes practicing problems followed by feedback as the most effective way of learning mathematics. Only recently, this approach has been complemented by debates about what kinds of problems are most helpful at what age levels, how practice problems should be organized, and what degree of teacher support should be provided at what level of competence. Following constructivist models of learning, it is now widely accepted that students benefit from working on problems for which they have no ready solution, but for which they have to construct a new strategy out of already available elements of knowledge. Even if students do not ultimately solve a problem, trying to find their own solution in working on the problem allows them to activate already available knowledge and to build on it. Teachers thus have an opportunity to involve students in deliberate cognitive activities that help them to extend and restructure their already available knowledge.

The findings from the LOGIC study support this constructivist approach. Staub and Stern (2002) showed that there were higher achievement gains in word problem solving for students who attended classrooms with teachers who held a more constructivist view of learning mathematics. Teacher's views of learning were assessed with a questionnaire from Fennema, Carpenter, and Loef (1990) that contained 48 statements about children's best way of learning word problems. Teachers expressed their degree of agreement with the statement made in the item on a Likert scale. Half of the items expressed a more constructivist view, such as "Children learn math best by figuring out for themselves the ways to find answers to simple word problems" or "Children should have many informal experiences solving simple word problems before they are expected to memorize number facts." The other half of the items expressed a more direct transmission view, such as "An effective teacher demonstrates the right way to do a word problem" or "Time should be spent practicing computational procedures before children are expected to understand the procedures." Hierarchical linear model analyses showed a remarkable impact of teachers on students' achievement trajectories—teachers' attitudes accounted for more than 25% of the between-classroom variance in achievement growth in mathematics.

During childhood, mathematical cognition undergoes a number of transitions before students are ready to understand advanced mathematical concepts. Most importantly, children must become aware of the dual function of mathematical language: Mathematical symbols can be used as instruments of reasoning for describing real-world situations (signifier function), and they can be used as objects of reasoning because they possess a meaning in themselves. For instance, in its signifier function, the number 9 is a symbol that refers to a set of nine objects. In its signifier function, 9 may mean *root of 81* or *square of 3*. This distinction is compatible with the distinction made by Geary (2005) between primary and secondary cognitive abilities. Related to the field of mathematics, *primary cognitive abilities* refer to the counting function of numbers. Learning to count is biologically prepared and does not need professional support. In contrast, secondary cognitive abilities required for academic learning are based on cultural transformations and therefore require schooling. Learning the signifier function of numbers (as tools) is based on primary abilities, whereas understanding the signifier function is based on secondary cognitive abilities. Thus, mathematical symbols both represent parts of the perceivable world and themselves become objects of reasoning, allowing the construction of concepts that have no direct relation to the perceivable world. For example, *infinity* is a genuine mathematical concept that contrasts our experience with the material world, where everything is limited. Despite its high degree of abstractness, elementary school children already understand the concept of infinity because they can reenact that numbers can be indefinitely increased by just adding 1 to a newly generated number. Because data sampling for the LOGIC study started before the participants entered school, the transition from primary to secondary mathematical abilities took place within this time period. A question of interest is the extent to which individual differences in academic mathematical competencies can be traced back to basic aspects of mathematical understanding measured before children entered school. In this chapter, I will ask how measures of mathematical competence collected over the course of preschool and school mathematics tasks predict later mathematical competencies at age 18 and at age 23.

10.3 DEVELOPMENT TESTS OF MATHEMATICAL COMPETENCIES BETWEEN AGE 6 AND AGE 12

LOGIC participants were presented with tasks measuring mathematical competencies during the entire period of data collection. All tasks measured more general mathematical reasoning rather than direct outcomes of school instruction. We chose one measure to represent children's mathematical knowledge at each of four ages during the LOGIC study—6, 8, 10, and 12 years—to compare with later mathematical competencies in late adolescence and adulthood. They are described in the following sections.

10.3.1 NUMBER SENSE AT THE AGE OF 6

Around their fourth birthday, children increasingly focus on the exact number of objects or events when faced with quantitative problems. Hannula and Lehtinen (2005) showed that an early spontaneous focus on numerosity was a good predictor for mathematical skills in early school grades. Two tasks given to children in the LOGIC study before entering school measured similar abilities: a number conservation task and an estimation of quantities task. The first task requires the children to understand that the quantity of objects rather than their spatial spread is decisive for answering questions referring to a quantitative comparison ("more" or "less" questions). The second task requires children to estimate the quantity of sets of objects without counting. Estimating quantities, therefore, might be a first step toward an advanced number concept. Each task is illustrated in Figure 10.1. The tasks were presented when LOGIC participants were 5 to 6 years old, which was in the year before they entered school. At this time, 56% of the children mastered the number invariance task reliably. The mean number of estimated objects was 5.2.

10.3.2 UNDERSTANDING QUANTITATIVE COMPARISONS AT AGE 8

Although most children are able to add and to subtract numbers before they enter school, their limited arithmetic understanding becomes apparent when they are

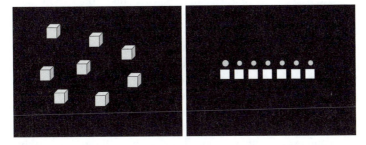

FIGURE 10.1   Material for measuring early number sense: the number estimation task (left) and number invariance task (right).

asked to solve arithmetic word problems. Whereas about 90% of 6-year-old children solve exchange problems such as "Mary had 8 marbles. Then she gave John 3 marbles. How many marbles does Mary have now?" only 20% of the same children can solve the comparison problem "Mary has 8 marbles. She has 3 more marbles than John. How many marbles does John have?" (Stern & Lehrndorfer, 1992). The discrepancy between solution rates for problems with an isomorphic structure is highlighted by the following example. Eighty percent of preschoolers solve the following problem: "5 birds are hungry. They find 3 worms. How many birds won't get a worm?" However, if the problem ends with the comparison question "How many more birds than worms are there?" the solution rate drops below 30% even for children through grade 3.

Children's inability to solve problems dealing with comparisons of sets is because they require a more sophisticated understanding of numbers that goes beyond their counting function (Stern, 1993). In the sentence "John has 5 more marbles than Peter," the information does not refer to a concrete, existing set but rather describes the *relation* between two sets. To solve comparison problems, children need to construct a mental representation abstracted from the concrete objects of the situation described. If they are unable to associate the number 5 with anything but five objects, they will fail to understand the sentence. However, if they can represent 5 as a section of a number line representing the relation between two numbers (e.g., between 0 and 5, between 2 and 7, or between 4 and 9), they will be able to understand comparison tasks.

There is wide variation in the extent to which children are exposed to such problems in school, as shown by comparisons between mathematics textbooks for elementary school children of different nations. Although quantitative comparison problems such as "John and Peter have 12 marbles altogether. John has 2 marbles less than Peter. How many marbles does Peter have?" appear quite frequently in Japanese textbooks, they are rarely found in U.S. textbooks (Fuson, Stigler, & Bartsch, 1988). Comparisons between Eastern European countries (the former Soviet Union, Slovakia, and the former East Germany [GDR]) and the former West Germany revealed similar results (Stern, 2005). Fewer than 4% of the word problems in the textbooks used in the classrooms of the LOGIC participants dealt with quantitative comparisons. Classroom observation revealed that a large amount of time was spent on training number facts in multiplication and on written subtraction and division. LOGIC participants did not have many opportunities in school for extending their number understanding through practicing problems based on quantitative comparisons. Many children were nevertheless able to solve such kinds of problems, even complex ones.

At the age of 8, when most of the LOGIC participants were in grade 2, they were presented 10 comparison word problems that varied in difficulty. The easiest problems were simple comparisons, such as "John has 5 rabbits. Peter has 3 rabbits more than John. How many rabbits does Peter have?" The most difficult problem was a multistep problem: "John has 5 rabbits. He has 3 rabbits more than Peter. Susanne has 6 rabbits. She has 2 rabbits less than Cordula. How many rabbits do Peter and Cordula have altogether?" There was broad individual variation: Solution rates ranged from .06 to .82, with a mean rate of .52 ($SD = .23$).

10.3.3 Beyond Dividing Cakes and Repeated Addition: Advanced Understanding of Division and Multiplication at Age 10

Similar to word problems requiring addition and subtraction of numbers, word problems that require multiplication or division can be based on different situational models (Greer, 1992). Several studies have shown that it is relatively easy to understand multiplication as repeated addition ("3 boys had 4 marbles each. How many marbles did they have altogether?") and to understand division as equal sharing ("12 cookies were divided equally among 3 girls. How many did each get?"). In contrast, the literature shows that situations that are based on quantitative measures ("In a photograph, a car is 4 cm long. If the photograph is enlarged by a factor of 2, how long will the car be?") or that require an understanding of the Cartesian product (e.g., "Mary has 4 pairs of trousers and 3 T-shirts. How many outfits can she create?") present severe difficulties. Solution rates for word problems with the same underlying equation vary between about 90% for problems that can be understood as repeated addition and 10% for mathematically isomorphic problems that require an understanding of the Cartesian product (for 10 year olds; Greer, 1992).

At the age of 10, when most of the LOGIC participants were in grade 4, they were presented with 10 written word problems dealing with the multiplication and division of two or more numbers. Three of these problems dealt with the Cartesian product. The mean solution rate was .43 ($SD = .19$).

10.3.4 A New View to Numbers: Proportional Reasoning and Understanding Fractions at Age 12

Understanding rational numbers such as fractions requires moving beyond principles that underlie the understanding of natural numbers. Although every natural number has a next larger successor, this is not true for rational numbers. For example, although there is a referent for *the next number after one*, there is no referent for *the next number after one half.* There is a smallest natural number but no smallest rational number, and although all natural numbers that lie between two numbers can be enumerated, this does not hold for rational numbers. Natural numbers get their meaning by denominating sets of objects, whereas rational numbers get their meaning by purely symbolic manipulations. Adolescents' difficulties with understanding proportions, decimal numbers, and fractions are well documented. The most frequent mistake made is that larger numerals are considered to refer to larger values than smaller numerals. Thus, because nine is larger than eight, children have difficulties with understanding that 7/8 is larger than 7/9.

LOGIC participants were presented with classical proportional reasoning tasks, among them mixing juice. They had to compare which of two beverages made from glasses of raspberry juice and glasses of water would taste more intensive. Depending on the numbers chosen, children can use different kinds of strategies to find the right answer (Stern, 1999). At the age of 12, when most of the children were in grade 6, they used three strategies: A *bidimensional comparison strategy* is based on a comparison between water and juice in each beverage. These children chose the glass where the amount of raspberry juice exceeded the amount of water. If this was the case for both glasses, they guessed. The *bidimensional strategy with quantification* was to subtract the amount of juice from the amount of water for each glass. These children chose the glass with the smaller difference as the one with the more intensive taste. The *ratio strategy* based the decision on division. The inappropriate bidimensional strategy with quantification often supplies the correct results. Only the use of particular numbers makes evident whether a child uses the inappropriate subtraction method or whether he or she derived an answer from the ratio strategy. For instance, having one glass with three parts of raspberry and four parts of water, and having a glass with seven parts of raspberry and nine parts of water, would lead to the wrong answer if the child chooses the one with the smaller difference.

Children were presented with 12 proportional reasoning problems that were embedded in different context stories, such as testing the taste of raspberry juice, estimating the weight of pieces of cheese differing in size, or collecting money for a good purpose. For half of the problems, subtracting the numbers would result in the wrong answer. Thus, the test should indicate whether children use a ratio strategy.

Results revealed a mean solution rate of .53 (*SD* = .24). Only 4% of the students performed 100% correct, and 30% were correct at least in one of the six problems that required the ratio strategy. These results suggest that most of the students were not fully capable of proportional reasoning. Rather, the bidimensional strategy with quantification was the prevailing strategy.

10.4 PREDICTING LATER
MATHEMATICAL PERFORMANCE

10.4.1 THE IMPACT OF INTELLIGENCE AND PRIOR KNOWLEDGE ON ADVANCED MATHEMATICAL COMPETENCIES AT THE AGE OF 18

In the follow-up study conducted with LOGIC participants when they were about 18 years old, mathematical competencies were tested by tasks from the Third International Mathematics and Science Study (TIMSS; Baumert et al., 1997) solved under time pressure. Though these tasks mainly target content usually taught in grade 8, solutions are not trivial, even for participants with more sophisticated mathematical competencies. This is illustrated by the following example: "Which x value fulfills the equation $x^2 - 14x + 49 = 0$: A) 7 and 0, B) 7, C) -14, D) 7 and -7, or E) 14 and 0?" The number of tasks presented was so large that even mathematics experts could not have solved them within the time limit. The mean number of problems solved was 4.5, with a standard deviation of 2.1.

We used the LOGIC data to help ask how these achievement differences in algebra might be explained. For the analyses that follow, we used children's performance in the LOGIC mathematics tasks described above as well as IQ scores collected annually throughout the LOGIC study. A subsample of the LOGIC sample—58 participants, all of them students in upper secondary school (Gymnasium)—was considered. We may assume that if correlations for this subsample are significant in spite of its restricted variance, they indicate substantial influences.

Table 10.1 shows the Spearman correlations between mathematics performance at age 18 with intelligence and mathematics performance at earlier age levels. The highest coefficient turned out to be the one between achievement in comparison problems at age 8 and mathematics achievement at age 18, whereas there is no correlation between intelligence in the earlier age and mathematics achievement at age 18 (for the complete sample, the correlation is $r = .38$, $p < .01$).

TABLE 10.1
Spearman Correlations Between Achievement in Mathematics Measured at Age 18 (Grade 11) and Measures of Intelligence and Prior Knowledge in Mathematics at Different Ages

Age	Mathematics	Intelligence
6	.32**	.03
8	.62**	.04
10	.41**	.40**
12	.50**	.41**
18		.38**

**$p < .01$.

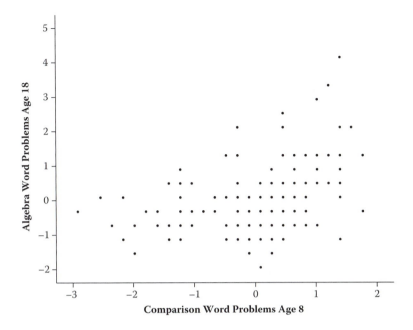

FIGURE 10.2   Stability of mathematical achievement (z scores at both measurement points) during a period of 10 years.

Moreover, mathematics achievement at age 18 and the IQ at the same age level are not as highly correlated as mathematics achievement at age 18 and achievement in solving word problems at age 8. The scatterplot depicted in Figure 10.2 shows that this correlation is not based on outliers. At the same time, it also indicates that all participants who do not contribute to stability show a similar development—a finding of high importance in understanding the development of mathematical competencies. The upper left half of the scatterplot is empty, which means that no child who failed to show average or above-average achievement in solving comparison problems at age 8 was good or excellent in mathematics performance at age 18. The lower left half, on the contrary, is occupied by several subjects whose achievement had been above average at age 8, when most participants were in grade 2, but had in later years dropped to average or even below average. The data show that early mathematical understanding as shown by the ability to solve demanding word problems is a necessary but by no means sufficient prerequisite for later mathematical competencies.

The results show that even in a domain like mathematics that is closely related to intelligence, high achievement crucially depends on prior knowledge. Knowing, as early as at age 8 (which is grade 2), that numbers can be used not only for modeling the size and transformation of sets but also for representing relations between sets seems to be a necessary, though not sufficient, prerequisite for higher mathematics achievement in upper secondary school. As yet, however,

German curricula for elementary school hardly ever include demanding word problems that involve a comparison of sets.

10.4.2 THE EXPLANATION OF ACHIEVEMENT DIFFERENCES
IN MATHEMATICAL REASONING AT THE AGE OF 23

At the final LOGIC measurement point, when participants were 23 years of age, all participants had been out of high school for at least 4 years. Some of these were working and some were in university, but most had not had subsequent mathematics instruction. Under these conditions, it would not have made sense to administer achievement tests focusing on academic mathematics. Rather, we presented participants with a standardized test of mathematical reasoning. Six numerical subtests of the Berliner Intelligenz Struktur Test (Jäger, Süß, & Beauducel, 1997) were administered as speed tests (time limits between 1 and 4 minutes). These subtests were selected because the mathematical knowledge required for solving the problems was taught in all types of schools and all participants would have been exposed to it during their secondary school education. The test consisted of six subtests:

> Word Problems: Participants had to solve five word problems with different degrees of difficulty. One example was "Which number has to be added to the number 12 for the proportion between the sum of these two numbers and 15 to be the same as the proportion between 30 and 25?"
>
> Number Series: In these tasks, nine rows with 6 to 7 numbers were presented, requiring participants to supplement the subsequent number according to an underlying principle they had to figure out. For example, "5 10 20 10 20 40 30 __?"
>
> Computing with Large Numbers: A computing task with large numbers was presented. The participants had to select the appropriate answer in a multiple-choice format. For example:
> 56324186 − 52418218 = ?
> a) 3643074 b) 4094032 c) 3905968 d) 4742404 e) 3126068
>
> Computing with Small Numbers: A list of 130 one- or two-digit numbers was presented. The task for the participant was to cross out all numbers that were bigger by three than the preceding number. The achievement score was determined by subtracting the number of correctly crossed-out numbers from the number of incorrectly crossed-out numbers.
>
> Memorizing Numbers: Participants were given one minute to memorize nine 4-digit numbers. Afterward, they were presented with 66 numbers, among them the nine numbers that had to be memorized. These numbers had to be crossed out. The achievement score was determined by subtracting the number of correctly crossed-out numbers from the number of incorrectly crossed-out numbers.

Number Combinations: Within a given time limit, participants had to find out as many numbers as possible that would fit the following equation: _____ × _____ + _____ = 60.

The standardized test allowed a comparison between the LOGIC sample scores and test norms. The overall score of the LOGIC sample was slightly higher ($d = .18$) than the norm sample mean. This result corresponds to other findings that have shown that the LOGIC sample was modestly positively skewed.

The test data showed good internal consistency: With one exception, the correlations among subtests were significant and varied between $r = .32$ and $r = .58$, indicating that mathematical reasoning at the age of 23 can be seen as a unified construct. The largest correlation was between number series and word problems ($r = .58$). There were no significant correlations between Memorizing Numbers and the other tests.

Table 10.2 shows the correlations between mathematical reasoning at age 23 and measures of mathematical competencies at earlier ages without and with partialing out intelligence.

The correlation of $r = .43$ between early number sense at age 6 and mathematical reasoning at age 23 suggests that individual differences in mathematics are, to a considerable extent, determined by factors that took effect before children entered school. These relationships are further depicted in Figures 10.3a and 10.3b, which show scatterplots for performance at age 23 and ages 6 and 12. The void upper left field is common to each. Almost none of the students who scored below average at age 6 or at age 12 caught up later on. On the other hand, there were several children who scored above average on mathematical achievement measures at age 6, but dropped off afterward, as shown in Figure 10.3a. As shown in Figure 10.3b, with increasing age there were fewer students who were above average at an earlier age but dropped off later.

TABLE 10.2
Correlation Between Mathematical Reasoning at Age 23 and Earlier Measures

Measure of Mathematical Ability and Age Level of Administering	Without Partialing Out Intelligence	Intelligence Partialed Out
Number sense (age 6)	.43**	.34**
Comparison word problems (age 8)	.44**	.32**
Mathematical word problems (age 10)	.49**	.35**
Proportional reasoning age (age 12)	.51**	.32**
Algebra problems (age 18)	.56**	.41**

** $p < .01$.

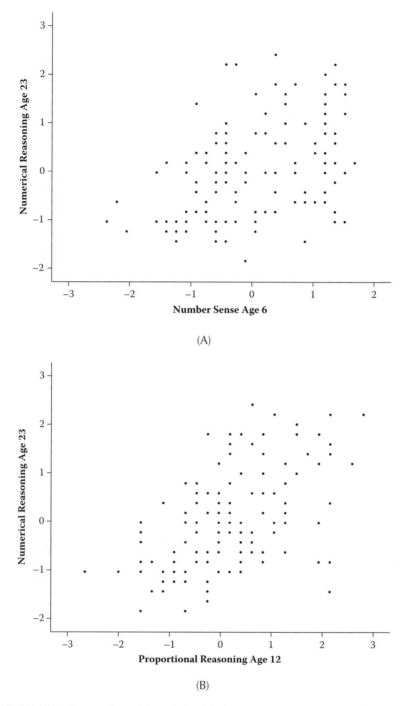

FIGURE 10.3   Scatterplots of the relationship between mathematical reasoning at the age of 23 and earlier mathematical competencies (*z* scores at all measurement points).

It is most remarkable that all correlations between mathematical reasoning at the age of 23 and mathematical achievement measures from earlier ages remained significant after the intelligence score from the respective age was partialed out. This result clearly suggests that the source of individual differences in mathematics goes beyond the general intelligence level and already emerges before the start of systematic instruction.

10.4.3   MATHEMATICAL COMPETENCIES IN FEMALE STUDENTS: THE LEAKY PIPELINE

A large number of studies have shown that males outperform females in many aspects of mathematics (see Hyde [2005] for a review). Females are particularly underrepresented in the upper quartile of mathematical performance. Earlier analyses of the LOGIC data confirmed these findings (Stern, 1998). Significant sex differences in favor of males were found at all age levels, with an effect size varying between $eta^2 = .03$ and $.09$. Many studies also report that females are particularly underrepresented in the upper achievement levels, a trend also found in the LOGIC data, where females were underrepresented in the upper achievement quarter at all ages; this trend increased with age. There was not an analogous bias for general intelligence scores.

Table 10.3 depicts the percentage of females in the top quartile of the achievement distribution. Were there equal numbers of females and males in this category? Even before children entered school, females were underrepresented in the top quartile of mathematics achievement. Around the age of 10, there are twice as many male top achievers as female. Comparisons between females who stayed in the top quartile and those who decreased in performance did not reveal any differences with respect to general intelligence. Analogously, there were no differences between male and female top achievers with respect to general intelligence or with regard to visual spatial abilities.

Despite the preponderance of males at the higher achievement level, there was at least one female among the top 5% at every age level. These results are in accord with other findings suggesting that there are talented female students at

---

TABLE 10.3

Adjusted Percentage of Female Students in the Top Quartile of the Achievement Distribution

Measure	%
Number sense (age 6)	43
Comparison word problems (age 8)	39
Mathematical word problems (age 10)	32
Proportional reasoning age (12)	33
Algebra problems (age 18)	23
Mathematical reasoning (age 23)	27

all age levels (Lubinski & Benbow, 2006) and correspond to discussions of gender imbalances in the fields of science and mathematics (Spelke, 2005): There is no evidence for sex differences in the intrinsic aptitudes necessary for advanced competencies in these fields. This does not, of course, necessarily imply that the lower proportion of females can be entirely traced back to environmental differences in gender-specific socialization. Rather, Spelke concluded, "We must look beyond cognitive ability to other aspects of human biology and society for insights into this phenomenon" (p. 956).

10.4.4 DEVELOPMENT OF MATHEMATICAL COMPETENCIES WITHIN A TRACKING SYSTEM: THE INTERACTION BETWEEN PRECONDITIONS AND LEARNING ENVIRONMENT

After finishing 4 years of elementary school (e.g., around age 10), German students are assigned to different school types based on their grades in the core elementary school subjects. At the time of the LOGIC study, the state of Bavaria offered two main school tracks for students (special education tracks will not be discussed here): Gymnasium as the upper track and Hauptschule or Realschule as the lower track. Gymnasium lasts for the next 9 years and is considered as preuniversity education. The Hauptschule or Realschule track splits further after grade 6 into a middle track (Realschule) and the lowest track (Hauptschule). After grade 4, about 48% of the LOGIC participants were recommended for the Gymnasium, which is above the average for the state.

Table 10.4 depicts the amount of achievement variance accounted for by the two school tracks students started to attend around the age of 10. Long before children joined the separate school tracks, they differed in their mean achievement level. Nonetheless, the differences were relatively small at all age levels, given that the tracking system is entirely based on the idea of different types of giftedness. At the age of 23, only 15% of achievement differences in mathematics can be traced back to the school tracks. The highest amount of explained variance by school track was found when children were about 9 years old, which was some

---

TABLE 10.4
Effect Sizes *d* and Percentage of Explained Variance by School Track (Gymnasium Versus No Gymnasium)

Mathematical Achievement Measures	D	Eta² × 100
Number sense (age 6)	48	10
Comparison word problems (age 8)	68	14
Mathematical word problems (age 10)	49	10
Proportional reasoning (age 12)	78	23
Algebra problems (age 18)	76	18
Mathematical reasoning (age 23)	64	15

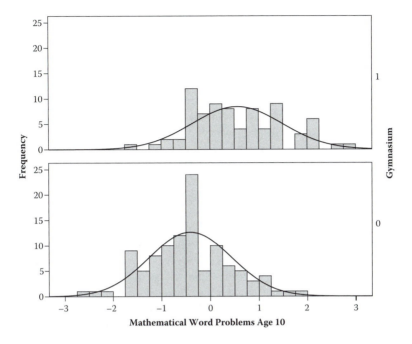

FIGURE 10.4   Distribution of the achievement in mathematical word problem solving (z values) immediately before the separation into the school tracks (gymnasium or no gymnasium) was realized.

months before the final decision was made. Nonetheless, even at this age level, there was a remarkable achievement overlap between students who were supposed to attend the Gymnasium as compared to those who were not. Figure 10.4 depicts the distribution of achievement in mathematical word problem solving at the age of 10 for those students subsequently assigned to the Gymnasium and those who were not. By comparison, the variance found in IQ tests traced to school tracking was 28% on average, clearly higher than for mathematics. Although there is no evidence for an increase in the IQ gap as a result of tracking (Schneider & Stefanek, 2004), intelligence seems to determine selection processes to a larger extent than achievement in mathematics does.

10.5   CONCLUSIONS

The most remarkable result of the longitudinal analyses was the high stability of interindividual differences from the very beginning of data collection. This was found not only for mathematics but also for other content areas investigated in the LOGIC sample. The results presented in this chapter reveal different trajectories of mathematical competencies starting to emerge even before children enter school. These differences are hardly affected in the subsequent years of formal instruction at school. It goes without saying that there is universal growth in mathematical competencies from professional classroom instruction. However, at the same time, the results of the LOGIC study reveal that differential effects of schooling seem to be relatively temporary and instable. Even quite strong "interventions" such as assignment to different school tracks have a relatively modest impact on the development of individual differences. A reason for this may be the quite uniform and restricted curriculum and classroom practice usual in Germany in the time period the LOGIC data were collected. The content as well as the presentation and practice in mathematics were generally specified, and even creative teachers had only few opportunities to translate innovative ideas of teaching into classroom practice. This was also evident in the study by Staub and Stern (2002), which demonstrated significant but limited effects of constructivist beliefs held by the teachers on students' achievement gains. Since the late 1980s and the 1990s, the time period the LOGIC participants had been in school, the German educational system has undergone tremendous challenges, particularly after the results of international comparison studies like PISA or TIMMS (Baumert, Artelt, Klieme, & Stanat, 2002) showed quite dramatic deficits in German school education. Since that time, innovative and creative ideas of designing learning environments, particularly in mathematics, have had a much better chance of implementation in the classroom. This may also affect trajectories of individual differences.

REFERENCES

Baroody, A. J., & Lai, M-L. (2007). Preschoolers' understanding of the addition-subtraction inverse principle: A Taiwanese sample. *Mathematical Thinking and Learning, 9,* 131–171.

Baumert, J., Artelt, C., Klieme, E., & Stanat, P. (2002). PISA—Programme for International Student Assessment: Zielsetzung, theoretische Konzeption und Entwicklung von Meßverfahren. In F. E. Weinert (Ed.), *Leistungsmessungen in Schulen* (2nd ed., pp. 285–310). Weinheim, Germany: Beltz.

Baumert, J., Lehmann, R., Lehrke, M., Schmitz, B., Clausen, M., Hosenfeld, I., et al. (1997). *TIMMS—Mathematisch-naturwissenschaftlicher Unterricht im internationalen Vergleich: Deskriptive Befunde* [TIMMS: Mathematical-scientific lessons in international comparison: Descriptive findings]. Opladen, Germany: Leske + Budrich.

Feigenson, L., Dehaene, S., & Spelke, E. S. (2004). Core systems of number. *Trends in Cognitive Sciences, 8,* 307–314.

Fennema, E., Carpenter, T. P., & Loef, M. (1990). *Teacher belief scale: Cognitively guided instruction project.* Madison: University of Wisconsin.

Fuson, K., Stigler, J. W., & Bartsch, K. (1988). Grade placement of addition and subtraction topics in Japan, mainland China, the Soviet Union, Taiwan, and the United States. *Journal for Research in Mathematics Education, 19,* 449–456.

Geary, D. C. (2005). Folk knowledge and academic learning. In B. J. Ellis & D. F. Bjorklund (Eds.), *Origins of the social mind* (pp. 493–519). New York: Guilford.

Greer, B. (1992). Multiplication and division as models of situations. In D. A. Grouws *(Ed.),* Handbook of research on mathematics teaching and learning (pp. 276–295). New York: Macmillan.

Hannula, M. M., & Lehtinen, E. (2005). Spontaneous focusing on numerosity and mathematical skills of young children. *Learning and Instruction, 15*(3), 237–256.

Hyde, J. S. (2005). The gender similarities hypothesis. *American Psychologist, 60*(6), 581–592.

Jäger, A. O., Süß, H-M., & Beauducel, A. (1997). *Berliner Intelligenzstruktur-Test.* Göttingen, Germany: Hogrefe.

Lubinski, D., & Benbow, C. (2006). Study of Mathematically Precocious Youth (SMPY) after 35 years: Uncovering antecedents for the development of math-science expertise. *Perspectives of Psychological Science, 1,* 316–343.

Schneider, W., & Stefanek, J. (2004). Entwicklungsveränderungen allgemeiner kognitiver Fähigkeiten und schulbezogener Fertigkeiten: Evidenz für einen Schereneffekt? [Developmental changes in cognitive abilities and school-related skills in children and adolescents: Evidence for a widening gap?]. *Zeitschrift für Entwicklungspsychologie und Pädagogische Psychologie, 36,* 147–159.

Spelke, E. (2005). Sex differences in intrinsic aptitude for science and mathematics? *American Psychologist, 60,* 950–958.

Staub, F., & Stern, E. (2002). The nature of teachers' pedagogical content beliefs matters for students' achievement gains: Quasi-experimental evidence from elementary mathematics. *Journal of Educational Psychology, 93,* 144–155.

Stern, E. (1993). What makes certain arithmetic word problems involving the comparison of sets so hard for children? *Journal of Educational Psychology, 85,* 7–23.

Stern, E. (1998). *Die Entwicklung des mathematischen Verständnisses im Kindesalter* [The development of mathematical understanding in childhood]. Lengerich, Germany: Pabst.

Stern, E. (1999). Development of mathematical competencies. In F. E. Weinert & W. Schneider (Eds.), *Individual development from 3–12: Findings from the Munich Longitudinal Study* (pp. 154–170). Cambridge: Cambridge University Press.

Stern, E. (2005). Knowledge restructuring as a powerful mechanism of cognitive development: How to lay an early foundation for conceptual understanding in formal domains. In P. D. Tomlinson, J. Dockrell, & P. Winne (Eds.), *Pedagogy: Teaching for learning* (British Journal of Educational Psychology Monograph Series 2, No. 3; pp. 153–169). Leicester: British Psychological Society.

Stern, E., & Lehrndorfer, A. (1992). The role of situational context in solving word problems. *Cognitive Development, 7,* 259–268.

11 Epilogue

Problems and Potentials of the Munich Longitudinal Study

Wolfgang Schneider and Merry Bullock

11.1 INTRODUCTION

Now, more than 25 years after the onset of the Munich Longitudinal Study (the LOGIC study) and several years after the last wave of data collection, the time is appropriate to reflect on what we did and what we are learning from this comprehensive enterprise. Why did we do all this? Were the initial goals of such a long-term project on human development and its implementation based on careful planning? Did we know from the very beginning what the ultimate focus and scope of the study would be? Yes and no. When Franz Weinert began his new job as a founding director of the Max Planck Institute for Psychological Research in 1982, he was already thinking about a unique longitudinal study covering the domains of cognitive and social-personality development with a strong focus on the genesis of individual differences, and with links to school achievement. Although he was never explicit about his staff recruitment strategy, his selection of (then) young collaborators created a research unit representing expertise from different developmental areas.

Undoubtedly, the plans for LOGIC were also stimulated by the opportunity to establish an ambitious longitudinal project that, at that time, could not be carried out within a German university setting, mainly because of cost issues. It was well-known in the early 1980s that the enormous costs associated with conducting longitudinal studies over an extended period of time and the difficulties in enduring funding for such projects represented one of the major reasons for the overall lack of longitudinal work, despite the fact that calls for such studies were frequent in the literature (see Harway, Mednick, & Mednick, 1984; Schneider, 1989). Given the traditional research orientation of Max Planck institutes and their comparably privileged funding situation at that time, the cost issue was not a barrier for Franz Weinert and his team.

When data collection for the LOGIC study began in 1984, the scientists involved in the project had identified the domains of interest. Thus, most (but not all) of the topics discussed in the different chapters of this volume were already identified as research areas at the beginning of the LOGIC study. In addition, the project team also agreed to study development from early to late childhood, beginning with 3- to 4-year-olds who had just entered preschool and ending with 12 year olds at the end of childhood. They also agreed to focus on individual patterns of competencies, studying interindividual differences in intraindividual changes (for more details, see Weinert, Schneider, Stefanek, & Weber, 1999).

The team members also agreed on logistics. The study was organized according to a fixed and rapid time schedule, with three assessment periods per school year that then were aggregated and labeled as a *measurement wave*. Of course, this decision put a lot of pressure on the LOGIC team, primarily because we could not stop time. One of the consequences of this dense time schedule that caused challenges not fully anticipated by the LOGIC research team was that it was usually necessary to plan a future assessment before evaluating the full implications of completed assessments. This turned out to be especially painful in the case of unanticipated ceiling effects. Although the team used parallel pilot testing as much as possible, fine-tuning assessments were sometimes not possible because of the need to develop measures, standardize procedures, and train testers without pause. Pressures were incessant, taking many forms beyond those mentioned in publications. As Block and Block (2006) nicely put it when reflecting on their own 30-year longitudinal enterprise, "Doing a longitudinal study means wrapping an albatross around one's neck, placing a monkey on one's back, mounting a tiger, and grabbing a bear by its tail" (p. 321).

11.2   SAMPLE AND DESIGN ISSUES

As is true for most longitudinal approaches, problems related to sample characteristics, the choice of relevant content areas, and the assessment schedule cannot be easily corrected. Although we escaped most of the problems cited in the literature (such as high dropout rates and a very mobile sample), some of our early decisions had long-term and unanticipated consequences. For instance, when we established participant recruitment strategies, we thought it theoretically and practically important to distinguish subsamples of *urban* (from Munich) and *rural* (from more rural parts of Bavaria) when assessing individual changes in cognitive and social domains over time. Given that we were all newcomers to the Munich area in the early 1980s, we thought it sufficient to visit villages about 30–40 km away from the city to recruit a truly "rural" subsample. It did not take us long to discover that we were wrong in this respect: Our "rural" sample was actually comparable to the urban subsample in many more respects than we liked it to be. In fact, only a very small percentage of our "rural" participants came from farmer families. Most parents were commuters, and the mean socioeconomic status (SES, or income and educational level) was roughly comparable across the two subsamples. Later on, we occasionally referred to the two subsamples as "urban" and "suburban" (see Weinert, Schneider, et al., 1999), but used this distinction only rarely in the further course of the study. Logistically, however, the practical consequences of this early decision were enormous, at least during the preschool and kindergarten years. We had to travel long distances to complete our assessments in the "rural" kindergartens, and later on had to reimburse parents and children from these areas large sums for transportation to get to the testing sessions in the Max Planck Institute in Munich.

Another issue relevant to long-term longitudinal studies is the selection and timing of assessment of core variables that are expected to prove fruitful over the course of the study. Overall, we were reasonably successful in this regard. As the chapters in this book attest, the theoretical constructs and topics we selected in the 1980s are still relevant today, and for most cases, even the assessment procedures we first used more than 20 years ago are still current. However, some decisions made early on in the LOGIC study seem regrettable in hindsight, especially given that LOGIC continued beyond its planned end in late childhood to trace our participants into early adulthood. For example, we assessed the development of motor skills very carefully and continuously from age 4 to age 12 (and also at age 23), but omitted this construct at the first follow-up (i.e., age 18) mainly due to organizational constraints. This was unfortunate because interesting changes observed between the ages of 12 and 23 could not be analyzed in detail, and speculations about the type of growth curves could not be validated based on the available data (see Ahnert, Schneider & Bös, chap. 3, this volume).

Similarly, we later regretted the fact that we stopped analyzing the development of reading skills at the end of grade 2, when children were about 8 years old. At that time, a postdoctoral colleague, Jan Näslund, who was mainly responsible for the assessment of reading in our group, left the institute. We decided to focus instead on spelling development, given that spelling proficiency is more important than reading skills for children's academic achievement in German schools (which is certainly not true for the rest of the world). However, when Germany later became involved in the Organization for Economic Cooperation and Development (OECD) funded Programme for International Student Assessment (PISA) study, which had a focus on 15 year olds, the issue of reading comprehension became much more popular, and many educators and politicians asked for information on longitudinal changes in this domain, which we could not offer. Although we did include reading skill in the assessment battery used at the last measurement point, this did not allow us to reconstruct the developmental function and relevant individual differences in this variable over time (see Schneider, Stefanek, & Niklas, chap. 2, this volume).

Despite these and similar problems, however, we learned a lot about developmental changes and individual differences in these changes in the various domains under study, as documented by the variety of findings described in the chapters of this volume. The most notable findings are summarized below.

11.3   NEW INSIGHTS

One of the topics of high interest was generalizations about development across different domains. One way we addressed that was by considering the developmental functions—a topic addressed in many chapters of this book. As already noted by Weinert, Bullock, and Schneider (1999), developmental functions can be described according to several dimensions: their trajectory (continuous and noncontinuous), their rate (fast versus slow), and their specificity in relation to the development of other behaviors in the same person. Measurements taken over several waves provided data to assess developmental functions in general, and also to address the stability of developmental functions at the individual level. Stability and change were research issues repeatedly addressed in LOGIC. In the following, we briefly discuss the most remarkable findings concerning these issues, first for the cognitive domain, and then for the domains of personal and social development.

11.3.1 COGNITIVE DEVELOPMENT

Most developmental functions in the cognitive domain appear to suggest continuous, more or less linear change, at least for the time period between young childhood and early adolescence. This characterizes the development of both verbal and nonverbal intelligence, and also characterizes most memory measures assessed in the LOGIC study, in particular, memory capacity and memory for text. The typical shape of the developmental functions showed a rather steep increase in slope over the age period from 4 to 12 and a flattening curve between the ages of 12 and 23, accompanied by substantial test–retest correlations (individual stabilities). The strong individual stabilities indicated that most participants developed the cognitive ability under study at about the same pace, maintaining their relative rank ordering within their reference group, regardless of the shape of the respective developmental function.

It seems important to note here that the issues of continuity or discontinuity of a growth function and its individual stability over time are conceptually independent. That is, the shape of a mean growth curve does not necessarily imply information about individual stability of the developmental function (see Appelbaum & McCall, 1983). We were reminded of this truism when analyzing developmental trends in the development of strategic memory (see Sodian & Schneider, 1999). Although the mean growth curves suggested a linear age trend for two strategies of sorting and clustering, an inspection of individual stabilities revealed that only a minority of participants showed the gradual developmental pattern indicated by the mean growth curve. In contrast, about 80% of the LOGIC children acquired the organizational strategy very rapidly, but at different time points. Thus, developmental changes in strategic memory followed a nonlinear pattern (see Schneider, Knopf, & Sodian, chap. 4, this volume). These findings illustrate that it is important to check both mean growth curve changes and interindividual stabilities in intraindividual change when deriving conclusions about the type of the growth curve function inherent in the data.

Our findings on moral motivation development provide a similar example. Here, the steady mean increase in moral motivation observed from early childhood to early adulthood suggested stability in this trend, that is, similar changes for all participants. However, a closer inspection of data on the individual level showed that there was little overall stability, confirming the assumption that participants followed quite different developmental trajectories, including patterns that showed decreases in moral development between childhood and early adulthood (see Nunner-Winkler, chap. 5, this volume). Accordingly, mean developmental trends in moral motivation did not mirror the variety of intraindividual change patterns.

In the area of memory development, another interesting and unexpected finding concerned the interrelationship among the three components of verbal memory assessed in the LOGIC study (i.e., memory capacity, strategic memory, and memory for texts). Although we did not have very clear expectations about changes in this interrelationship over the course of time, we assumed that intercorrelations should be rather strong in early childhood and decrease over time, mainly because the impact of individual differences in strategy use, metacognitive knowledge, and domain-specific knowledge should determine individual differences in verbal memory performance at later assessment periods. Our analyses showed that we were wrong in this respect: Intercorrelations among the three verbal memory components were only moderate at the beginning of the study and did not change much over time. Interestingly, the size of intercorrelations among the three components was comparable to their correlations with verbal intelligence. Thus, the new insight from these analyses was that it may not be appropriate to use the term *verbal memory* as a single construct, given that it cannot be conceived of as a unitary psychological function.

We also gained insights concerning the development of nonverbal and verbal intelligence. Our multilevel change analyses revealed substantial influences of individual difference variables such as sex, SES, and age group in the early measurement waves of the LOGIC study, but not in subsequent waves. In our view, the new insight derived from this pattern of results is that important individual differences in intellectual functioning are already established before children enter preschool. In accord with classic American longitudinal studies (e.g., Sontag, Baker, & Nelson, 1958), substantial interindividual stability in intraindividual changes was found for our psychometric IQ measures. Also, the finding that correlations between the verbal and nonverbal IQ components were moderately high from the very beginning and did not change much over time was in line with outcomes of previous longitudinal studies (see Gardner & Clark, 1992). The new aspect of LOGIC was that individual stabilities in Piagetian-type measures such as the Arlin Test of Formal Reasoning were as high as those obtained for the psychometric IQ components from the advanced elementary school years onward. Analyses of growth curve patterns (raw scores) revealed nonlinear trends, with a rather steep slope obtained from early to late childhood, and flattening thereafter. Whereas no significant developmental changes in verbal IQ were found between late adolescence and early adulthood, the increase in nonverbal IQ found for the period from age 18 to age 23 was small but statistically significant (see Schneider et al., chap. 2, this volume, for details). Overall, the developmental trend data obtained for the IQ measures are similar to those found for the various memory components in showing that participants were already very close to their personal peak performance by late adolescence.

One unexpected finding relating to both memory and intelligence development was an unexpected age difference within the sample. Because the age of our participants spanned about a year, we performed analyses using a median-split procedure to assess the impact of differences in chronological age on various aspects of cognitive development. We hypothesized that the mean age difference of about 3–4 months observed in the LOGIC sample might influence results in the early periods of the study but should disappear as a function of time. Surprisingly, this was not the case. We found a rather stable IQ difference between the two subsamples, varying between 5 and 10 points, throughout the course of the study. Moreover, systematic age group differences in memory performance were observed from the very beginning onward, with the advantages found for the older subsample persisting until young adulthood. Similar performance differences also concerned math, spelling, and logical reasoning (see also Weinert, Bullock & Schneider, 1999). The consistency of these age group differences across a wide variety of cognitive tasks and time points was unexpected. Given that we cannot exclude a sampling problem in our study, this issue should be addressed in future longitudinal studies assessing cognitive development across childhood and adolescence.

As already noted above, one major goal of the LOGIC study was to explore the importance of early individual differences in cognitive variables for subsequent performance in school and beyond. In particular, we were interested in the predictability of scientific reasoning, reading, spelling, and math from precursor variables assessed during the preschool and kindergarten periods. The basic assumption was that more specific kindergarten measures such as number invariance, number estimation, counting (in the case of math), letter knowledge, phonological awareness, verbal memory capacity, and speed in accessing the semantic lexicon (in the case of reading and spelling) should be more powerful predictors of subsequent math and literacy development in school than general intelligence. The findings for the school period summarized in previous chapters by Bullock and Ziegler (1999), Schneider and Näslund (1999), and Stern (1999) all provided evidence for the predictive power of those preschool, kindergarten, and early school measures for later assessment of school measures, regardless of the domain under study. Although the impact of general intelligence could not be ignored, it did not exceed that of the more specific predictors. These findings also showed, however, that the relative impact of these specific predictors was restricted to the early phase of elementary school. Subsequent assessments clearly demonstrated the increasing importance of domain-specific knowledge for performance development during the school years.

The contributions in this volume by Bullock, Sodian, and Koerber (chap. 8), Schneider (chap. 9), and Stern (chap. 10) all showed that the relative importance of general and domain-specific predictors could be generalized to the periods of adolescence and young adulthood. In particular, the test–retest correlations obtained for time intervals of 10 years and more seemed impressive, indicating high individual stability over time. Interestingly, these stability scores remained pretty much the same after individual differences in intelligence were controlled for. As noted by Stern (chap. 10, this volume) for mathematics, such a finding suggests that the source of individual differences in mathematics goes beyond general intelligence and already emerges before formal instruction in school begins.

This leads to a final interesting aspect of this research: The moderately high to high individual stabilities found from the onset of schooling seem to indicate that differences in instruction (classroom settings) did not affect the rank orders found for memory, math, reading, and spelling performance across the course of the LOGIC study (see also Schneider, Knopf, & Stefanek, 2002; Schneider & Stefanek, 2004). Although there was plenty of evidence that our LOGIC participants considerably benefited from classroom instruction in math, reading, and spelling, there were almost no differential effects of schooling. For instance, the rank order regarding spelling performance obtained at the age of 23 was rather similar to that obtained at the beginning of spelling instruction at the end of Grade 2. This seems surprising given that in the German school system, children are assigned to different educational tracks (high, middle, and low) at the end of Grade 4, very early in the schooling process. It should be noted that there are other German longitudinal studies that do not replicate these findings for the domain of math, demonstrating larger gains for those students allocated to the high educational track (see Becker, Lüdtke, Trautwein, & Baumert, 2006). However, the findings of the LOGIC study do seem consistent with those of previous studies on the impact of educational context on achievement carried out in both Germany (see the review by Helmke & Weinert, 1997) and the United States (e.g., the review by Fraser, Walberg, Welch, & Hattie, 1987).

11.3.2 SELF-CONFIDENCE AND PERSONALITY DEVELOPMENT

As noted by Weinert, Bullock & Schneider (1999), we continued the traditional distinction between cognitive and social-personality functioning for the LOGIC study, given that different models and methodologies have been used throughout the history of psychology to study these areas. Although most modern textbooks agree that the theoretical base for such a distinction is weak, it still exerts an influence on contemporary psychological concepts. In the LOGIC study, the concepts of self-concept and personality were assessed by two different research teams. Whereas Andreas Helmke and Friedrich Schrader focused on developmental changes in self-concept and self-confidence over time, Jens Asendorpf, Marcel van Aken, and Jaap Denissen concentrated on aspects of personality compatible with the "Big Five" approach and closely linked to the concepts of ego control and ego resiliency initially developed and longitudinally explored by Jack and Jeanne Block (1980, 2006).

What are the major findings regarding the development of self-confidence and personality over time? The constructs of self-concept and self-confidence investigated by Helmke and Schrader (Helmke, 1999; Schrader & Helmke, chap. 7, this volume) are theoretically linked to aspects of cognitive development, driven by

intellectual and physical development and also influenced by socialization processes. It was shown for the early period of the LOGIC study (that is, for the time
period between ages 5 and 12) that the developmental function of the self-concept
of ability was characterized by a negative slope, indicating that initial overestima-
tions of one's own competence were followed by more realistic assessments, and
that the more realistic assessments were more closely linked to academic achievement (see Helmke & Weinert, 1999). Individual stability in this construct was
moderately high from the very beginning of the study. Subsequent assessments in
late childhood, early adolescence, and early adulthood did not confirm the popular
assumption that adolescence and early adulthood are periods of instability or even
crisis. Consistent with findings reported by Block and Robins (1993) and the statistical meta-analysis by Trzesniewski, Donnellan, and Robins (2003), such instability could not be confirmed by the data from the LOGIC study.

Mainly based on questionnaire data, Schrader and Helmke (chap. 7, this volume) found higher self-confidence for males than for females in both adolescence
and young adulthood. This finding is basically consistent with that of Block and
Block (1980, 2006), who found no sex differences in self-esteem of their longitudinal sample at age 14, but significant differences in favor of males at the
ages of 18 and 23, and also divergent trends for the two sexes: Whereas mean
self-esteem of the male participants in the Block and Block longitudinal study
increased steadily over time, the mean self-esteem of females decreased over the
three measurement points. Similar trends were not reported in the Schrader and
Helmke chapter (chap. 7, this volume), which may be due to different assessment
procedures (Q-sort versus questionnaire data), national differences, or both.

As to stability over time, findings indicated moderately high stability in self-
confidence from adolescence to young adulthood, indicating some variability in
developmental changes. Interestingly, although the number of critical life events
experienced during childhood and adolescence did not predict individual differences in adults' self-confidence, the impact of specific critical incidents such as
parents' divorce on adult self-confidence was significant even after individual differences in adolescent self-confidence were taken into account. A further step
from the results reported in this volume would be to combine analyses from
Schrader and Helmke (chap. 7, this volume) and Asendorpf et al. (chap. 6, this
volume) to examine whether there is support for the assumption first made by
Block, Block, and Gjerde (1986) that boys of parents undergoing divorce were
already relatively undercontrolled *before* the critical life event took place—that
is, a finding previously said to be a consequence of divorce existed prior to the
fact of divorce. Given that only about 10% of the LOGIC participants referred to
parental divorce as a critical life event, however, this subsample may be too small
for further analyses.

The study of personality development turned out to be particularly reinforcing. When Jens Asendorpf started his research on shyness in the context of the
LOGIC study, his work was largely exploratory and not governed by strong developmental hypotheses. This work gained a sharp theoretical focus through a continuous, long interplay of exploratory data analysis, interpretation, formalization,

and inductive reasoning (see Asendorpf, 1999). Asendorpf developed a complex social-personality development model that stimulated a new phase of empirical research in subsequent stages of the LOGIC study (see Asendorpf et al., chap. 6, this volume). Asendorpf et al. explored interindividual differences in developmental changes in core internalizing and externalizing behavioral tendencies such as ego control (undercontrolling versus overcontrolling) and ego resiliency, with a focus on changes from adolescence to young adulthood. Their analyses of long-term effects of early personality differences were based on a person-centered approach, thereby reducing broad personality patterns to a few personality types. Given that the variable-centered research on the Big Five factors of personality did not yet exist when the LOGIC study started in 1984, such a measure was not an option initially, even though it was adopted by Asendorpf and his colleagues in later assessments. One specific advantage of selecting ego control and ego resiliency as core personality dimensions was that findings could be directly compared with other long-term and comprehensive studies such as the Block and Block Longitudinal Study and the Dunedin Longitudinal Study based on a representative New Zealand birth cohort (e.g., Caspi & Silva, 1995). One of the main issues investigated by Asendorpf and colleagues concerned the question of to what extent developmental outcomes assessed later in life can be predicted by data on personality dimensions gathered early in a child's life. The existing database was not consistent, particularly as far as the stability of individual personality traits was concerned. For instance, whereas statistical meta-analyses indicated moderate stability over time, with stability being comparably low during early as well as middle childhood and subsequently increasing as a function of age (e.g., Roberts & DelVecchio, 1996), the available longitudinal evidence suggested stability from early childhood onward (e.g., Caspi & Silva). Overall, the data presented by Asendorpf and his colleagues confirmed previous longitudinal evidence in that personality traits showed an impressive stability over a time period of almost 20 years. Their findings seem to deviate from those of the Block and Block Longitudinal Study in that high individual stability over time was found for both sexes, regardless of personality type. As noted by Block and Block (2006), such a pattern was also typical for ego control and also for their male participants with respect to ego resiliency, but was not found for their females in the case of ego resiliency for the transition from adolescence to adulthood.

Overall, one of the most remarkable and striking aspects of the research reported in this volume is that individual differences in most domains turned out to be so strong and persistent. We did expect such outcomes for most cognitive domains, but not necessarily for areas such as motor development, self-concept, and personality development. As noted above, high group stability over time does not imply that this corresponds to high individual stability, or that valid predictions can be made for specific members of the group. For instance, the only outstanding athlete in the LOGIC sample (a decathlete) could not be identified as particularly talented based on his results in the various motor tasks presented throughout the LOGIC study. Also, eight presumably hyperactive children, who at the beginning of the first grade were at risk of being sent to a special school for behaviorally disordered children (which we prevented), did not show notable behavioral problems in later stages of the LOGIC study. In fact, they completed school without any further problems, and one of them was the first participant of the LOGIC sample to finish university studies (in engineering), at the age of 22.

11.4 CONCLUSIONS

Conducting a long-term longitudinal study represents a large and difficult task, requiring substantial time and money. In many cases, the true merits of such an enterprise become evident only after many years, given that it takes a while before findings seem interesting enough for publication. In the case of the LOGIC study, we were fortunate enough to generate publishable data from an early point in time onward. The list of LOGIC publications contains more than 150 items (see the Bibliography), indicating a long period of productive research. However, as already noted by Weinert, Bullock & Schneider (1999), not all of the ambitious goals formulated at the beginning of the LOGIC study could actually be reached. For instance, there are only a small number of cross-domain analyses, illustrating the fact that most LOGIC researchers decided to focus on their domains of interest and expertise.

We doubt that the LOGIC team will be able to provide a comprehensive analysis of the goldmine of data collected over a time period of about 20 years. Thus, a last phase of the LOGIC study is to make the data set available for other researchers. The process of creating a comprehensive database is well underway. Plans are in place to transfer the LOGIC data resource to the Zentrum für Psychologische Information und Dokumentation (Center for Psychological Information and Documentation) at the University of Trier, Germany, where it will be available for external access by the end of 2009.

REFERENCES

Appelbaum, M. I., & McCall, R. B. (1983). Design and analysis in developmental psychology. In P. M. Mussen (Ed.), *Handbook of child psychology* (Vol. I, pp. 415–476). New York: Wiley. *Individual development from 3 to 12: Findings from the Munich Longitudinal Study* (pp. 227–242). Cambridge: Cambridge University Press.

Asendorph, J. B. (1999). Social-personality development. In F. E. Weinert & W. Schneider (Eds.), *Individual development from 3 to 12: Findings of a logitudinal study* (pp. 227–242). New York: Cambridge University Press.

Becker, M., Lüdtke, O., Trautwein, U., & Baumert, J. (2006). Leistungszuwachs in Mathematik: Evidenz für einen Schereneffekt im mehrgliedrigen Schulsystem? [Achievement gains in mathematics: Evidence for differential achievement trajectories in a tracked school system?]. *Zeitschrift für Pädagogische Psychologie, 20*, 233–242.

Block, J. H., & Block, J. (1980). The role of ego-control and ego-resiliency in the organization of behavior. In W. A. Collins (Ed.), *The Minnesota Symposia on Child Psychology* (Vol. 13, pp. 39–101). Hillsdale, NJ: Erlbaum.

Block, J., & Block, J. H. (2006). Venturing a 30-year longitudinal study. *American Psychologist, 61*, 315–327.

Block, J. H., Block, J., & Gjerde, P. F. (1986). The personality of children prior to divorce: A prospective study. *Child Development, 54*, 401–408.

Block, J., & Robins, R. W. (1993). A longitudinal study of consistency and change in self-esteem from early adolescence to early adulthood. *Child Development, 64*, 909–923.

Bullock, M., & Ziegler, A. (1999). Scientific reasoning: Developmental and individual differences. In F. E. Weinert & W. Schneider (Eds.), *Individual development from 3 to 12: Findings from the Munich Longitudinal Study* (pp. 38–54). Cambridge: Cambridge University Press.

Caspi, A., & Silva, P. A. (1995). Temperamental qualities at age predict personality traits in young adulthood: Longitudinal evidence from a birth cohort. *Child Development, 66*, 486–498.

Fraser, B. J., Walberg, H. J., Welch, W. W., & Hattie, J. A. (1987). Syntheses of educational productivity research. *International Journal of Educational Research, 11*, 145–152.

Gardner, M. K., & Clark, E. (1992). The psychometric properties of intellectual development in childhood and adolescence. In R. J. Sternberg & C. A. Berg (Eds.), *Intellectual development* (pp. 16–43). Cambridge: Cambridge University Press.

Harway, M., Mednick, S. A., & Mednick, B. (1984). Research strategies: Methodological and practical problems. In S. A. Mednick, M. Harway, & K. M. Finello (Eds.), *Handbook of longitudinal research. Vol. 1: Birth and childhood cohorts*. New York: Praeger.

Helmke, A. (1999). From optimism to realism? Development of children's academic self-concept from kindergarten to grade 6. In F. E. Weinert & W. Schneider (Eds.), *Individual development from 3 to 12: Findings from the Munich Longitudinal Study* (pp. 198–221). Cambridge: Cambridge University Press.

Helmke, A., & Weinert, F. E. (1997). Bedingungsfaktoren schulischer Leistung [Determinants of school achievement]. In F. E. Weinert (Ed.), *Psychologie des Unterrichts und der Schule* (Enzyklopädie der Psychologie, Serie Pädagogische Psychologie, Vol. 3, pp. 171–176). Göttingen, Germany: Hogrefe.

Helmke, A., & Weinert, F. E. (1999). Schooling and the development of achievement differences. In F. E. Weinert & W. Schneider (Eds.), *Individual development from 3 to 12: Findings from the Munich Longitudinal Study* (pp. 176–192). Cambridge: Cambridge University Press.

Roberts, B. W., & DelVecchio, W. F. (1996). The rank-order consistency of personality traits from childhood to old age: A quantitative review of longitudinal studies. *Psychological Bulletin, 126*, 3–25.

Schneider, W. (1989). Problems of longitudinal studies with children: Practical, conceptual, and methodological issues. In M. Brambring, F. Lösel, & H. Skowronek (Eds.), *Children at risk: Assessment, longitudinal research, and intervention* (pp. 313–335). New York: de Gruyter.

Schneider, W., Knopf, M., & Stefanek, J. (2002). The development of verbal memory in childhood and adolescence: Findings from the Munich Longitudinal Study. *Journal of Educational Psychology, 94*, 751–761.

Schneider, W., & Näslund, J. (1999). The early prediction of reading and spelling: Problems and perspectives. In F. E. Weinert & W. Schneider (Eds.), *Individual development from 3 to 12: Findings from the Munich Longitudinal Study* (pp. 126–147). Cambridge: Cambridge University Press.

Schneider, W., & Stefanek, J. (2004). Entwicklungsveränderungen allgemeiner kognitiver Fähigkeiten und schulbezogener Fertigkeiten: Evidenz für einen Schereneffekt? [Developmental changes in cognitive abilities and school-related skills in children and adolescents: Evidence for a widening gap?] *Zeitschrift für Entwicklungspsychologie und Pädagogische Psychologie, 36,* 147–159.

Sodian, B., & Schneider, W. (1999). Memory strategy development: Gradual increase, sudden insight, or roller-coaster? In F. E. Weinert & W. Schneider (Eds.), *Individual development from 3 to 12: Findings from the Munich Longitudinal Study* (pp. 61–77). Cambridge: Cambridge University Press.

Sontag, L. W., Baker, C. T., & Nelson, V. L. (1958). Mental growth and personality development: A longitudinal study. *Monographs of the Society for Research in Child Development, 23* (Serial No. 68).

Stern, E. (1999). Development of mathematical competencies. In F. E. Weinert & W. Schneider (Eds.), *Individual development from 3 to 12: Findings from the Munich Longitudinal Study* (pp. 154–170). Cambridge: Cambridge University Press.

Trzesniewski, K. H., Donnellan, M. B., & Robins, R. W. (2003). Stability of self-esteem across the life span. *Journal of Personality and Social Psychology, 84,* 205–220.

Weinert, F. E., Bullock, M., & Schneider, W. (1999). Universal, differential, and individual aspects of child development from 3 to 12: What can we learn from a comprehensive longitudinal study? In F. E. Weinert & W. Schneider (1999), *Individual development from 3 to 12: Findings from the Munich longitudinal study* (pp. 324–350). Cambridge: Cambridge University Press.

Bibliography of Publications Stemming from the LOGIC Project

1. BOOKS AND GENERAL REPORTS

Schneider, W. (Ed.). 2008). *Entwicklung von der frühen Kindheit bis zum frühen Erwachsenenalter: Befunde der Münchner Längsschnittstudie LOGIK* [Development from early childhood to young adulthood: Findings from the Munich Longitudinal Study LOGIC]. Weinheim, Germany: Beltz.

Schneider, W., & Knopf, M. (Eds.). (2003). *Entwicklung, Lehren und Lernen—Zum Gedenken an Franz E. Weinert* [Development: Teaching and learning—in memory of Franz Weinert]. Göttingen, Germany: Hogrefe.

Weinert, F. E. (1991). Die Entwicklung kognitiver, motivationaler und sozialer Kompetenzen zwischen dem 4. und 8. Lebensjahr [The development of cognitive, motivational and social competencies between ages 4 and 8]. In D. Frey (Ed.), *Bericht über den 37. Kongreß der Deutschen Gesellschaft für Psychologie in Kiel 1990* (Vol. 2, pp. 650–653). Göttingen, Germany: Verlag für Psychologie.

Weinert, F. E. (Ed.). (1998). *Entwicklung im Kindesalter* [Development in childhood]. Weinheim, Germany: Beltz.

Weinert, F. E., & Helmke, A. (Eds.). (1997). *Entwicklung im Grundschulalter* [Development in grade school]. Weinheim, Germany: Psychologie Verlags Union.

Weinert, F. E., & Schneider, W. (Eds.). (1999). *Individual development from 3 to 12: Findings of a longitudinal study*. New York: Cambridge University Press.

2. JOURNAL ARTICLES AND BOOK CHAPTERS

Ahnert, J & Schneider, W. (2007). Zur Entwicklung und Stabilität motorischer Fähigkeiten im Vorschul- bis ins früheErwachsenenalter – Befunde der Munchner Längsschnittstudie LOGIK [The development and stability of motor skills from preschool until early adulthood – Findings from the Munich Longtitudinal Study LOGIC]. *Zeitschrift fur Entwicklungspsychologie und Padagogische Psychologie, 39*, 12–24.

Ahnert, J & Schneider, W. & Bös, K. (2008). Entwicklung motorischer Fähigkeiten vom Vorschul- bis ins früheErwachsenenalter [The development of motor skills from early childhood until early adulthood]. In W. Schneider (Ed.), *Entwicklung von der Kindheit bis zum Erwachsenenalter* [Development from childhood to adulthood] (pp. 23–42). Weinheim, Germany: Beltz.

Asendorpf, J. B. (1989). Individual, differential, and aggregate stability of social competence. In B. H. Schneider, G. Attili, J. Nadel, & R. Weissberg (Eds.), *Social competence in developmental perspective* (pp. 71–86). Dordrecht, the Netherlands: Kluwer.

Asendorpf, J. B. (1989). *Soziale Gehemmtheit und ihre Entwicklung* [The development of social inhibition]. Berlin: Springer.

Asendorpf, J. B. (1990). Beyond social withdrawal: Shyness, unsociability, and peer avoidance. *Human Development, 33,* 250–259.

Asendorpf, J. B. (1990). Development of inhibition during childhood: Evidence for situational specificity and a two-factor model. *Developmental Psychology, 26,* 721–730.

Asendorpf, J. B. (1990). The expression of shyness and embarrassment. In W. R. Crozier (Ed.), *Shyness and embarrassment: Perspectives from social psychology* (pp. 87–118). Cambridge, MA: Cambridge University Press.

Asendorpf, J. B. (1990). Soziale Bedingungen früher Persönlichkeitsformung [The social conditions of early personality development]. *Unterrichtswissenschaft, 3,* 249–258.

Asendorpf, J. B. (1991). Development of inhibited children's coping with unfamiliarity. *Child Development, 62,* 1460–1474.

Asendorpf, J. B. (1992). Beyond stability: Predicting interindividual differences in intraindividual change. *European Journal of Personality, 6,* 103–117.

Asendorpf, J. B. (1992). A Brunswikean approach to trait continuity: Application to shyness. *Journal of Personality, 60,* 53–77.

Asendorpf, J. B. (1992). Continuity and stability of personality traits and personality patterns. In J. B. Asendorpf & J. Valsiner (Eds.), *Stability and change in development: A study of methodological reasoning* (pp. 116–142). Newbury Park, CA: Sage.

Asendorpf, J. B. (1993). Abnormal shyness in children. *Journal of Child Psychology & Psychiatry & Allied Disciplines, 34,* 1069–1081.

Asendorpf, J. B. (1993). Beyond temperament: A two-factorial coping model of the development of inhibition during childhood. In K. H. Rubin & J. B. Asendorpf (Eds.), *Social withdrawal, inhibition and shyness in childhood* (pp. 265–289). Hillsdale, NJ: Erlbaum.

Asendorpf, J. B. (1993). Social inhibition: A general developmental perspective. In H. C. Traue & J. W. Pennebaker (Eds.), *Emotion, inhibition, and health* (pp. 80–99). Seattle, WA: Hogrefe & Huber.

Asendorpf, J. B. (1994). The malleability of behavioral inhibition: A study of individual developmental functions. *Developmental Psychology, 30,* 912–919.

Asendorpf, J. B. (1994). Zwei Formen von Schüchternheit [Two forms of shyness]. *Grundschule, 4,* 20–22.

Asendorpf, J. B. (1998). Die Entwicklung sozialer Kompetenzen, Motive und Verhaltensweisen [The development of social competencies, motives and behaviors]. In F. E. Weinert (Ed.), *Entwicklung im Kindesalter* (pp. 153–176). Weinheim, Germany: Beltz.

Asendorpf, J. B. (1999). Social-personality development. In F. E. Weinert & W. Schneider (Eds.), *Individual development from 3 to 12: Findings of a longitudinal study* (pp. 227–242). New York: Cambridge University Press.

Asendorpf, J. B. (2002). Die Persönlichkeit als Lawine: Wann und warum sich Persönlichkeitsunterschiede stabilisieren [Personality as an avalanche: When and why personality differences become stable]. In G. Jüttemann & H. Thomae (Eds.), *Persönlichkeit und Entwicklung* (pp. 46–72). Weinheim, Germany: Beltz.

Asendorpf, J. B. (2003). Head-to-head comparison of the predictive validity of personality types and dimensions. *European Journal of Personality, 17,* 327–346.

Asendorpf, J. B., & Denissen, J. J. A. (2006). Predictive validity of personality types versus personality dimensions from early childhood to adulthood: Implications for the distinction between core and surface traits. *Merrill-Palmer Quarterly, 52*, 486–513.

Asendorpf, J. B., Denissen, J. J. A., & van Aken, M. A. G. (2008). Der lange Schatten der frühen Persönlichkeit [The long shadow of early personality]. In W. Schneider (Ed.), *Entwicklung von der frühen Kindheit bis zum frühen Erwachsenenalter: Befunde der Münchner Längsschnittstudie LOGIK* (pp. 124–140). Weinheim, Germany: Beltz.

Asendorpf, J. B., Denissen, J. J. A., & van Aken, M. A. G. (2008). Inhibited and aggressive preschool children at 23 years of age: Personality and social transitions into adulthood. *Developmental Psychology 44*, 997–1011.

Asendorpf, J. B., Denissen, J. J. A., & van Aken, M. A. G. (In press). Personality trajectories from early childhood through emerging adulthood. In W. Schneider & M. Bullock (Eds.), *Human development from early childhood to early adulthood.* Mahwah, NJ: Erlbaum.

Asendorpf, J. B., & Nunner-Winkler, G. (1992). Children's moral motive strength and temperamental inhibition reduce their immoral behavior in real moral conflicts. *Child Development, 63*, 1223–1235.

Asendorpf, J. B., & van Aken, M. A. G. (1991). Correlates of the temporal consistency of personality patterns in childhood. *Journal of Personality, 59*, 689–703.

Asendorpf, J. B., & van Aken, M. A. G. (1994). Traits and relationship status: Stranger versus peer group inhibition and test intelligence versus peer group competence as early predictors of later self-esteem. *Child Development, 65*, 1786–1798.

Asendorpf, J. B., & van Aken, M. A. G. (1999). Resilient, overcontrolled, and undercontrolled personality prototypes in childhood: Replicability, predictive power, and the trait-type issue. *Journal of Personality and Social Psychology, 77*(4), 815–832.

Asendorpf, J. B., & van Aken, M. A. G. (2003). Die Persönlichkeit als Lawine: Konsequenzen früher Persönlichkeitsunterschiede auf die weitere Entwicklung [Personality as an avalanche: Effects of early personality differences on later development]. In W. Schneider & M. Knopf (Eds.), *Entwicklung, Lehren und Lernen: Zum Gedenken an Franz Emanuel Weinert* (pp. 109–124). Göttingen, Germany: Hogrefe.

Asendorpf, J. B., & van Aken, M. A. G. (2003). Personality-relationship transaction in adolescence: Core versus surface personality characteristics. *Journal of Personality, 71*, 629–666.

Asendorpf, J. B., & van Aken, M. A. G. (2003). Validity of Big Five personality judgments in childhood: A 9 year longitudinal study. *European Journal of Personality, 17*, 1–17.

Asendorpf, J. B., & Weinert, F. E. (1990). Stability of patterns and patterns of stability in personality development. In D. Magnusson & L. R. Bergman (Eds.), *Data quality in longitudinal research* (pp. 181–197). Cambridge: Cambridge University Press.

Bullock, M. (1991). Scientific reasoning in elementary school: Developmental and individual differences. Paper presented at the Symposium on Scientific Thinking, SRCD, Seattle, WA (Paper 12/1991). Munich: Max-Planck-Institut für psychologische Forschung.

Bullock, M. (1992). Are grade schoolers really so bad at testing hypotheses? A replication (Paper 2/1992). Munich: Max-Planck-Institut für psychologische Forschung.

Bullock, M. (1992). Die Entwicklung des Experimentierens [The development of experimentation] (Paper 12/1992). Munich: Max-Planck-Institut für psychologische Forschung.

Bullock, M. (1993). Scientific thinking: Are school children really so bad? (Paper 8/1993). Munich: Max-Planck-Institut für psychologische Forschung.

Bullock, M., & Sodian, B. (2003). Entwicklung des wissenschaftlichen Denkens [The development of scientific reasoning]. In W. Schneider & M. Knopf (Eds.), *Entwicklung, Lehren und Lernen: Zum Gedenken an Franz Emanuel Weinert* (pp. 75–92). Göttingen, Germany: Hogrefe.

Bullock, M., & Ziegler, A. (1997). Entwicklung der Intelligenz und des Denkens: Ergebnisse aus dem SCHOLASTIK-Projekt [The development of intelligence and thinking: Results from the SCHOLASTIC project]. In F. E. Weinert & A. Helmke (Eds.), *Entwicklung im Grundschulalter* (pp. 27–35). Weinheim, Germany: Psychologie Verlags Union.

Bullock, M., & Ziegler, A. (1999). Scientific reasoning: Development and individual differences. In F. E. Weinert & W. Schneider (Eds.), *Individual development from 3 to 12: Findings of a longitudinal study* (pp. 38–54). New York: Cambridge University Press.

Denissen, J. J. A., Asendorpf, J. B., & van Aken, M. A. G. (2008). Childhood personality predicts long-term trajectories of shyness and aggressiveness in the context of demographic transitions in emerging adulthood. *Journal of Personality, 76*(1) , 67–100.

Helmke, A. (1991). Entwicklung des Fähigkeitsselbstbildes vom Kindergarten bis zur dritten Klasse [Development of the self-concept of ability from kindergarten to third grade]. In R. Pekrun & H. Fend (Eds.), *Schule und Persönlichkeitsentwicklung. Ein Resumee der Längsschnittforschung* (pp. 83–99). Stuttgart, Germany: Enke.

Helmke, A. (1992). *Selbstvertrauen und schulische Leistungen* [Self-confidence and school achievement]. Göttingen, Germany: Hogrefe.

Helmke, A. (1993). Die Entwicklung der Lernfreude vom Kindergarten bis zur 5. Klassenstufe [The development of learning motivation from kindergarten to 5th grade]. *Zeitschrift für Pädagogische Psychologie, 7,* 77–86.

Helmke, A. (1997). Das Stereotyp des schlechten Schülers: Ergebnisse aus dem SCHOLASTIK-Projekt [The stereotype of the poor student: Results from the SCHOLASTIC project]. In F. E. Weinert & A. Helmke (Eds.), *Entwicklung im Grundschulalter* (pp. 269–279). Weinheim, Germany: Psychologie Verlags Union.

Helmke, A. (1997). Educational research on classroom instruction and its effects: Shortcomings, dead ends, and future perspective. In W. Bunder & K. H. Rebel (Eds.), *Teacher education: Theoretical requirements and professional reality.* Kiel, Germany: IPN-Materialienreihe.

Helmke, A. (1997). Entwicklung lern- und leistungsbezogener Motive und Einstellungen: Ergebnisse aus dem SCHOLASTIK-Projekt [Development of learning and achievement related motivation and attitudes: Results from the SCHOLASTIC project]. In F. E. Weinert & A. Helmke (Eds.), *Entwicklung im Grundschulalter* (pp. 59–76). Weinheim, Germany: Psychologie Verlags Union.

Helmke, A. (1997). Individuelle Bedingungsfaktoren der Schulleistung: Ergebnisse aus dem SCHOLASTIK-Projekt [Individual differences in school achievement: Results from the SCHOLASTIC project]. In F. E. Weinert & A. Helmke (Eds.), *Entwicklung im Grundschulalter* (pp. 203–216). Weinheim, Germany: Psychologie Verlags Union.

Helmke, A. (1997). Sackgassen und Perspektiven der empirischen Forschung zu den Wirkungen des Unterrichts [Facts and perspectives from research on instructional effectiveness]. *Pädagogisches Handeln, 1,* 57–70.

Helmke, A. (1998). Vom Optimisten zum Realisten? Zur Entwicklung des Fähigkeitsselbst-
bilds vom Kindergarten bis zur 6. Klassenstufe [From optimism to realism? Development of the self-concept of ability from kindergarten to 6th grade]. In F. E. Weinert
(Ed.), *Entwicklung im Kindesalter* (pp. 115–132). Weinheim, Germany: Beltz.

Helmke, A. (1999). From optimism to realism? Development of children's academic self-
concept from kindergarten to grade 6. In F. E. Weinert & W. Schneider (Eds.), *Individual development from 3 to 12: Findings of the Munich Longitudinal Study* (pp.
198–221). New York: Cambridge University Press.

Helmke, A., & Mückusch, C. (1994). Handlungs- und Lageorientierung bei Grundschülern [Action and state orientation in grade school children]. *Zeitschrift für Pädagogische Psychologie, 8*, 63–72.

Helmke, A., & Renkl, A. (1992). Das Münchner Aufmerksamkeitsinventar (MAI): Ein
Instrument zur systematischen Verhaltensbeobachtung der Schüleraufmerksamkeit
im Unterricht [The Munich Attention Inventory (MAI): An instrument for systematic behavioral observation of students' attention during instruction]. *Diagnostica,
38*, 130–141.

Helmke, A., & Renkl, A. (1993). The Munich Attention Inventory (MAI): An instrument
for the systematic observation of students' attentional behavior during instruction.
German Journal of Psychology, 17, 48–49.

Helmke, A., & Renkl, A. (1993). Unaufmerksamkeit in Grundschulklassen: Problem der
Klasse oder des Lehrers? [Lack of attention in grade school classes: class problems
or teacher problems?]. *Zeitschrift für Entwicklungspsychologie und Pädagogische
Psychologie, 25*, 185–205.

Helmke, A., & Rheinberg, F. (1996). Anstrengungsvermeidung—Morphologie eines Kon-
struktes [Avoidance of effort: Morphology of a construct]. In C. Spiel, U. Kast-
ner-Koller, & P. Deimann (Eds.), *Entwicklung und Sozialisation* (pp. 207–224).
Münster, Germany: Waxmann.

Helmke, A., & van Aken, M. A. G. (1995). The causal ordering of academic achievement
and self concept of ability during elementary school: A longitudinal study. *Journal
of Educational Psychology, 87*, 624–637.

Helmke, A., & Weinert, F. E. (1997). Unterrichtsqualität und Leistungsentwicklung:
Ergebnisse aus dem SCHOLASTIK-Projekt [Instructional quality and the develop-
ment of achievement: Results from the SCHOLASTIC project]. In F. E. Weinert
& A. Helmke (Eds.), *Entwicklung im Grundschulalter* (pp. 241–251). Weinheim,
Germany: Psychologie Verlags Union.

Helmke, A., & Weinert, F. E. (1999). Schooling and the development of achievement
differences. In F. E. Weinert & W. Schneider (Eds.), *Individual development from 3
to 12: Findings of a longitudinal study* (pp. 176–192). New York: Cambridge University Press.

Knopf, M. (1995). Eine Längsschnittstudie zur Entwicklung interindividueller und
intraindividueller Gedächtnisunterschiede im Kindesalter [A longitudinal study of
the development of interindividual and intraindividual memory differences in child-
hood]. In H-P. Langfeldt & R. Lutz (Eds.), *Sein, Sollen und Handeln. Beiträge zur
Pädagogischen Psychologie und ihren Grundlagen* (pp. 75–89). Göttingen, Germany: Hogrefe.

Knopf, M. (1999). The development of memory for texts. In F. E. Weinert & W. Schneider
(Eds.), *Individual development from 3 to 12: Findings of a longitudinal study* (pp.
106–122). New York: Cambridge University Press.

Knopf, M., & Schneider, W. (1998). Die Entwicklung des kindlichen Denkens und die Verbesserung der Lern- und Gedächtniskompetenzen [The development of children's thinking and improvements of their learning and memory competencies]. In F. E. Weinert (Ed.), *Entwicklung im Kindesalter* (pp. 75–94). Weinheim, Germany: Beltz.

Knopf, M., Schneider, W., Sodian, B. & Kolling, T. (2008). Die Entwicklung des Gedächtnisses vom Kindergartenalter bis ins frühe Erwachsenenalter [Memory development from early childhood to early adulthood]. In W. Schneider (Ed.), *Entiwicklung von der Kindheit bis zum Erwachsenenalter* [Development from childhood to adulthood] (pp. 85–102). Weinheim, Germany: Beltz.

Langeheine, R., Stern, E., & van de Pol, F. (1994). State mastery learning: Dynamic models for longitudinal data. *Applied Psychological Measurement, 18,* 277–291.

Meier, G. (1993). *Persönlichkeit und soziales Verhalten von Kindern im Alltag* [Children's everyday personality and social behavior]. Hamburg: Kovac.

Näslund, J. C. (1990). The interrelationship among preschool predictors of reading acquisition for German children. *Reading and Writing: An Interdisciplinary Journal, 2,* 327–360.

Näslund, J. C. (1993). Predicting reading: Acquisition in high and low IQ groups. In R. M. Joshi & C. K. Leong (Eds.), *Reading disabilities: Diagnosis and component processes* (pp. 279–293). Dordrecht, the Netherlands: Kluwer.

Näslund, J. C., & Schneider, W. (1991). Longitudinal effects of verbal ability, memory capacity, phonological awareness, and decoding speed on reading comprehension. *European Journal of the Psychology of Education, 6,* 375–392.

Näslund, J. C., & Schneider, W. (1993). Emerging literacy from kindergarten to second grade: Evidence from the Munich longitudinal study on the genesis of individual competencies. In H. Grimm & H. Skowronek (Eds.), *Language acquisition problems and reading disorders: Aspects of diagnosis and intervention* (pp. 295–318). Berlin: de Gruyter.

Neyer, F. J., Schäfer, M., & Asendorpf, J. (1998). Bindung, Gehemmtheit, soziale Netzwerke und die Entwicklung sozialer Beziehungen im Kindergarten [Attachment, inhibition, social networks and the development of social relationships in preschool]. *Zeitschrift für Entwicklungspsychologie und Pädagogische Psychologie, 30*(2), 70–79.

Nunner-Winkler, G. (1989). Wissen und Wollen. Ein Beitrag zur frühkindlichen Moralentwicklung [Knowing and wanting: On moral development in early childhood]. In A. Honneth, T. McCarthy, C. Offe, & A. Wellmer (Eds.), *Zwischenbetrachtungen. Im Prozeß der Aufklärung* (pp. 574–600). Frankfurt am Main: Suhrkamp.

Nunner-Winkler, G. (1990). Zur frühkindlichen Moralentwicklung [On early moral development]. In H. Dettenborn & G. Prillwitz (Eds.), *Psychologie und moralisches Handeln. Tagungsbericht* (pp. 41–44). Berlin: Humboldt-Universität.

Nunner-Winkler, G. (1992). Die Genese moralischer Motivation [The origins of moral motivation]. In *Friedrich Jahresheft 1992* (No. 10, Verantwortung, pp. 10–13). Velbert, Germany: Erhard Friedrich.

Nunner-Winkler, G. (1992). Frühe moralische Weisheit? Zur Kritik an der Theorie von den zwei Moralen [Early moral wisdom? A critique of dual morality theories]. In W. Herzog & E. Violi (Eds.), *Beschreiblich weiblich. Aspekte feministischer Wissenschaft und Wissenschaftskritik* (pp. 71–90). Zürich: Rüegger.

Nunner-Winkler. G. (1992). Vom Selbst zum Miteinander. Soziales Lernen im Kindesalter [From alone to in a group: Social learning in childhood]. *Welt des Kindes, 4,* 11–15.

Nunner-Winkler, G. (1992). Zur frühkindlichen Moralentwicklung [On moral development in early childhood]. In W. Althof & F. Oser (Eds.), *Moralische Selbstbestimmung. Modelle der Entwicklung und Erziehung im Wertebereich* (pp. 193–196). Stuttgart, Germany: KlettCotta.

Nunner-Winkler, G. (1992). Zur moralischen Sozialisation [On moral socialization]. *Kölner Zeitschrift für Soziologie und Sozialpsychologie, 44,* 252–272. Shortened version (1993) in *Forum für interdisziplinäre Forschung* [Forum for interdisciplinary research], *11,* 105–120. Reprint of an edited version (1993) in H. Huber (Ed.), *Sittliche Bildung. Ethik in Erziehung und Unterricht* [Moral education: Ethics in education and teaching] (pp. 105–127). Asendorf, Germany: MUT-Verlag.

Nunner-Winkler, G. (1993). Die Entwicklung moralischer Motivation [The development of moral motivation]. In W. Edelstein, G. Nunner-Winkler, & G. Noam (Eds.), *Moral und Person* (pp. 278–303). Frankfurt am Main: Suhrkamp. English Version (1993) in G. Noam & T. Wren (Eds.), *The moral self* (pp. 269–291). Cambridge, MA: MIT Press. Abbreviated version (1994) in *Moral Education Forum, 19,* 8–20.

Nunner-Winkler. G. (1996). Moralische Entwicklung und die These von den Zwei Moralen [Moral development and the hypothesis of two types of morality]. In W. Stark, T. Fitzner, K. Giebeler, & C. Schubert (Eds.), *Moralisches Lernen in Schule, Betrieb und Gesellschaft. Internationaler Kongreß der Ev. Akademie Bad Boll* (Protokolldienst 7/96, pp. 53–62). Bad Boll, Germany: Evangelische Akademie.

Nunner-Winkler, G. (1996). Moralisches Wissen—moralische Motivation—moralisches Handeln. Entwicklungen in der Kindheit [Moral knowledge, moral motivation, moral action: Development in childhood]. In M. S. Honig, H. R. Leu, & U. Nissen (Eds.), *Kinder und Kindheit. Soziokulturelle Muster, sozialisationstheoretische Perspektiven* (pp. 129–173). Munich: Juventa.

Nunner-Winkler, G. (1998). The development of moral understanding and moral motivation. *International Journal of Educational Research, 27,* 587–603.

Nunner-Winkler, G. (1998). Zum Verständnis von Moral: Entwicklungen in der Kindheit [Understanding morality: Development in childhood]. In F. E. Weinert (Ed.), *Entwicklung im Kindesalter* (pp. 133–152). Weinheim, Germany: Beltz.

Nunner-Winkler, G. (1999). Development of moral understanding and moral motivation. In F. E. Weinert & W. Schneider (Eds.), *Individual development from 3 to 12: Findings of a longitudinal study* (pp. 253–290). New York: Cambridge University Press.

Nunner-Winkler, G. (1999). Zum frühkindlichen Moralverständnis [On moral understanding in early childhood]. In Sachverständigenkomission Zehnter Kinder- und Jugendbericht (Ed.), *Kindliche Entwicklungspotentiale. Normalität, Abweichung und ihre Ursachen* (Materialien zum Zehnten Kinder- und Jugendbericht, Vol. 1, pp. 53–151). Munich: DJI Verlag.

Nunner-Winkler, G. (2000). Nicht mal der liebe Gott darf andere schlagen [Even God can't hit others]. *Psychologie heute, 27*(12), 48–53.

Nunner-Winkler, G. (2003). Moralentwicklung im Verlauf des Lebens [Moral development across the life span]. In W. Schneider & M. Knopf (Eds.), *Entwicklung, Lehren und Lernen: Zum Gedenken an Franz Emanuel Weinert* (pp. 125–145). Göttingen, Germany: Hogrefe.

Nunner-Winkler, G. (2004). Sociohistoric changes in the structure of moral motivation. In D. K. Lapsley & D. Narvaez (Eds.), *Moral development, self, and identity* (pp. 299–333). Mahwah, NJ: Erlbaum.

Nunner-Winkler, G. (2004). Weibliche Moral: Geschlechterdifferenzen im Moralverständnis? [Female morality: Sex differences in moral understanding?] In R. Becker & B. Kortendiek (Eds.), *Handbuch Frauen- und Geschlechterforschung. Theorie, Methoden*, Empirie (pp. 78–84). Wiesbaden, Germany: Verlag für Sozialwissenschaften.

Nunner-Winkler, G. (2004). Wertbindungen und Identität [Values and identity] . In H. Poser & B. B. Reuer (Eds.), *Bildung Identität Religion. Fragen zum Wesen des Menschen* (pp. 77–98). Berlin: Weidler Buchverlag. (Originally published in 2002 as Identität und Moral [Identity and morality]. In J. Straub & J. Renn [Eds.], Transitorische Identität. Frankfurt am Main: Campus.)

Nunner-Winkler, G. (2005). Soziohistorischer Wandel in der Struktur moralischer Motivation [Sociohistorical changes in the structure of moral motivation]. In J. Berger (Ed.), *Zerreißt das soziale Band? Beiträge zu einer aktuellen gesellschaftspolitischen Debatte* (pp. 77–117). Frankfurt: Campus Verlag.

Nunner-Winkler, G. (2005). Strategischer Einsatz von Moral [Strategic uses of morality]. In R. Reichenbach & H. Breit (Eds.), *Skandal und politische Bildung. Aspekte zu einer Theorie des politischen Gefühls* (pp. 141–158). Berlin: Logos Verlag.

Nunner-Winkler, G. (2005). Zum Verständnis von Moral—Entwicklungen in der Kindheit [Understanding moral development in childhood]. In D. Horster & J. Oelkers (Eds.), *Pädagogik und Ethik* (pp. 173–192). Wiesbaden, Germany: VS Verlag für Sozialwissenschaften. (Originally published in 1998 as Chap. 7 in F. E. Weinert [Ed.], Entwicklung im Kindesalter. Weinheim, Germany: Beltz, 1998.)

Nunner-Winkler, G. (2006). Die Effektivität und Effizienz von Lernprozessen und die Grenzen von institutionalisiertem ethischen Lernen. L'efficacité des processus d'apprentissage et les limites d'instruction éthique institutionalisée [Effectiveness and efficiency in learning processes and the limits of institutionalized ethical learning]. In A. Hügli & U. Thurnherr (Eds.), *Ethik und Bildung* (pp. 155–205). Frankfurt am Main: Peter Lang.

Nunner-Winkler, G. (2006). Freiwillige Selbstbindung aus Einsicht—ein moderner Modus moralischer Motivation [Insight and self-awareness: A modern form of moral motivation]. In H. F. Klemme, M. Kühn, & D. Schönecker (Eds.), *Moralische Motivation. Kant und die Alternativen*. Hamburg: Felix Meiner Verlag.

Nunner-Winkler, G. (2006). Moralbezogene Emotionen und Motive moralischen Handelns [Moral emotions and motives for moral action]. In N. Scarano & M. Suárez (Eds.), *Ernst Tugendhats Ethik. Einwände und Erwiderungen* (pp. 60–76). Munich: C. H. Beck.

Nunner-Winkler, G. (2006). Zur Entwicklung des Moralverständnisses in Kindheit und Jugend [The development of moral understanding in childhood and youth]. *Renovatio*, 62(1/2), 6–17.

Nunner-Winkler, G. (2007). Development of moral motivation from childhood to early adulthood. *Journal of Moral Education*, 36(4), 399–414.

Nunner-Winkler, G. (2007). Frühe emotionale Bindungen und Selbstbindung an Moral [Early emotional relations and commitment of the self to morality?]. In C. Hopf & G. Nunner-Winkler (Eds.), *Frühe Bindungen und moralische Entwicklung*. Weinheim, Germany: Juventa Verlag.

Nunner-Winkler, G. (2008). Zur Entwicklung moralischer Motivation [The development of moral motivation]. In W. Schneider (Ed.), *Entwicklung von der Kindheit bis zum Erwachsenenalter* [Development from childhood to adulthood] (pp. 103–123). Weinheim, Germany: Beltz.

Nunner-Winkler, G., & Sodian, B. (1988). Children's understanding of moral emotions. *Child Development*, 59, 1323–1338.

Renkl, A., & Helmke, A. (1992). Discriminant effects of performance-oriented and structure-oriented tasks in elementary math instruction. *Contemporary Educational Psychology, 17,* 47–55.

Renkl, A., & Helmke, A. (1993). Prinzip und Nutzen der Generalisierungstheorie am Beispiel einer längsschnittlichen Analyse des Aufmerksamkeitsverhaltens von Grundschülern [Principles and uses of generalization theory with examples from a longitudinal analysis of attention in grade school children]. *Empirische Pädagogik, 7,* 63–85.

Renkl, A., Helmke, A., & Schrader, F-W. (1997). Schulleistung und Fähigkeitsselbstbild—Universelle Beziehungen oder kontextspezifische Zusammenhänge? Ergebnisse aus dem SCHOLASTIK-Projekt [School achievement and the self-concept of ability: Universal or context specific relations? Results from the SCHOLASTIC project]. In F. E. Weinert & A. Helmke (Eds.), *Entwicklung im Grundschulalter* (pp. 373–383). Weinheim, Germany: Psychologie Verlags Union.

Renkl, A., & Stern, E. (1994). Die Bedeutung von kognitiven Eingangsvoraussetzungen und Lernaufgaben für das Lösen von einfachen und komplexen Textaufgaben [The meaning of cognitive entry characteristics and task demands for solving simple and complex story problems]. *Zeitschrift für Pädagogische Psychologie, 8,* 27–39.

Rubin, K. H., & Asendorpf, J. B. (Eds.). (1993). *Social withdrawal, inhibition and shyness in childhood.* Hillsdale, NJ: Erlbaum.

Schneider, W. (1989). Frühe Vorhersage von Lese-/Rechtschreibleistungen: Der Ansatz des Münchner Längsschnittprojekts (LOGIK) [Early prediction of reading and spelling: Contributions from the Munich Longitudinal Study LOGIC]. In H. Balhorn & H. Brügelmann (Eds.), *Jeder spricht anders—Normen und Vielfalt in Sprache und Schrift* (pp. 190–193). Konstanz, Germany: Faude.

Schneider, W. (1989). Problems of longitudinal studies with young children: Practical, conceptual, and methodological issues. In M. Brambring, F. Lösel, & H. Skowronek (Eds.), *Children at risk: Assessment, longitudinal research, and intervention* (pp. 313–335). New York: de Gruyter.

Schneider, W. (1993). The longitudinal study of motor development: Methodological issues. In A. F. Kalverboer, B. Hopkins, & R. Geuze (Eds.), *Motor development in early and later childhood: Longitudinal approaches* (pp. 318–342). Cambridge: Cambridge University Press.

Schneider, W. (1994). Geschlechtsunterschiede beim Schriftspracherwerb: Befunde aus den Münchner Längsschnittstudien LOGIK und SCHOLASTIK [Sex differences in the development of spelling: Findings from the Munich longitudinal studies LOGIC and SCHOLASTIC]. In S. Richter & H. Brügelmann (Eds.), *Mädchen lernen anders lernen Jungen. Geschlechtsspezifische Unterschiede beim Schriftspracherwerb* (pp. 71–82). Bottighofen, Switzerland: Libelle.

Schneider, W. (1997). Erwerb des Lesens und des Rechtschreibens. Ergebnisse aus dem SCHOLASTIK-Projekt [The development of reading and spelling: Results from the SCHOLASTIC project]. In F. E. Weinert & A. Helmke (Eds.), *Entwicklung im Grundschulalter* (pp. 113–130). Weinheim, Germany: Psychologie Verlags Union.

Schneider, W. (2008). Entwicklung und Erfassung der Rechtschreibkompetenz im Jugend- und Erwachsenenalter [Development and measurement of spelling competencies in youth and young adulthood]. In W. Schneider, H. Marx, & M. Hasselhorn (Eds.), *Diagnostik von Rechtschreibleistungen und -kompetenz* (Tests und Trends N.F., Vol. 6, pp. 145–158). Göttingen, Germany: Hogrefe.

Schneider, W. (2008). Die Entwicklung der Intelligenz und des Denvermönogens in Kindheit, Jugend- und Erwachsenenalter [The development of intelligence and thinking in childhood, adolescence, and adulthood]. In W. Schneider (Ed.), *Entiwicklung von der Kindheit bis zum Erwachsenenalter* [Development from childhood to adulthood] (pp. 43–66). Weinheim, Germany: Beltz.

Schneider, W. (2008). Entwicklung der Schriftsprachkompetenz vom frühen Kindes- bis zum frühen Erwachsenenalter [Literacy development from early childhood to early adulthood]. In W. Schneider (Ed.), *Entiwicklung von der Kindheit bis zum Erwachsenenalter* [Development from childhood to adulthood] (pp. 43–66). Weinheim, Germany: Beltz.

Schneider, W. & Bullock, M. (2008). Die Längsschnittstudie LOGIK: Versuch einer zusammenfassedden Würdigung [The longitudianl sudy LOGIK: Final comments]. In W. Schneider (Ed.), *Entiwicklung von der Kindheit bis zum Erwachsenenalter* [Development from childhood to adulthood] (pp. 203–218). Weinheim, Germany: Beltz.

Schneider, W., Bullock, M., & Sodian, B. (1998). Die Entwicklung des Denkens und der Intelligenzunterschiede zwischen Kindern [The development of reasoning and intelligence differences in children]. In F. E. Weinert (Ed.), *Entwicklung im Kindesalter* (pp. 53–74). Weinheim, Germany: Beltz.

Schneider, W., Hasselhorn, M., & Körkel, J. (2003). Entwicklung des Gedächtnisses und Metagedächtnisses im Kindes- und Jugendalter [The development of memory and metamemory in children and adolescents]. In W. Schneider & M. Knopf (Eds.), *Entwicklung, Lehren und Lernen. Zum Gedächtnis an Franz Emanuel Weinert* (pp. 15–34). Göttingen, Germany: Hogrefe.

Schneider, W., Knopf, M., & Stefanek, J. (2002). The development of verbal memory in childhood and adolescence: Findings from the Munich longitudinal study. *Journal of Educational Psychology, 94*, 751–761.

Schneider, W., & Näslund, J. C. (1992). Cognitive prerequisites of reading and spelling: A longitudinal approach. In A. Demetriou, M. Shayer, & A. Efklides (Eds.), *Neo-Piagetian theories of cognitive development* (pp. 256–274). London: Routledge.

Schneider, W., & Näslund, J. C. (1993). The impact of early metalinguistic competencies and memory capacity on reading and spelling in elementary school: Results of the Munich longitudinal study on the genesis of individual competencies. *European Journal of Psychology of Education, 8*(3), 273–287.

Schneider, W., & Näslund, J. C. (1999). The impact of early phonological processing skills on reading and spelling in school: Evidence for the Munich Longitudinal Study. In F. E. Weinert & W. Schneider (Eds.), *Individual development from 3 to 12: Findings of a longitudinal study* (pp. 126–147). New York: Cambridge University Press.

Schneider, W., Perner, J., Bullock, M., Stefanek, J., & Ziegler, A. (1999). The development of intelligence and thinking. In F. E. Weinert & W. Schneider (Eds.), *Individual development from 3 to 12: Findings of a longitudinal study* (pp. 9–28). New York: Cambridge University Press.

Schneider, W., & Sodian, B. (1990). Gedächtnisentwicklung im Vorschulalter: "Theoriewandel" im kindlichen Verständnis des Lernens und Erinnerns? [Memory development in preschool: "Theory change" in children's understanding of learning and memory?]. In M. Knopf & W. Schneider (Eds.), *Entwicklung. Allgemeine Verläufe—Individuelle Unterschiede—Pädagogische Konsequenzen. Festschrift zum 60. Geburtstag von Franz Emanuel Weinert* (pp. 45–64). Göttingen, Germany: Hogrefe.

Schneider, W., & Sodian, B. (1991). A longitudinal study of young children's memory behavior and performance in a sort–recall task. *Journal of Experimental Child Psychology, 51*, 14–29.

Schneider, W., & Sodian, B. (1997). Memory strategy development: Lessons from longitudinal research. *Developmental Review, 17*, 442–461.

Schneider, W., & Stefanek, J. (2004). Entwicklungsveränderungen allgemeiner kognitiver Fähigkeiten und schulbezogener Fertigkeiten im Kindes- und Jugendalter: Evidenz für einen Schereneffekt? [Developmental changes in general cognitive abilities and academic skills in childhood and adolescence: Evidence for a ceiling effect?] *Zeitschrift für Entwicklungspsychologie und Pädagogische Psychologie, 36*(3), 147–159.

Schneider, W., & Stefanek, J. (2007). Entwicklung der Rechtschreibleistung vom frühen Schul- bis zum frühen Erwachsenenalter: Längsschnittliche Befunde der Münchner LOGIK-Studie [Development of spelling achievement from early schooling to early adulthood: Longitudinal findings of the Munich Longitudinal Study]. *Zeitschrift für Pädagogische Psychologie, 21*, 77–82.

Schneider, W., Stefanek, J., & Dotzler, H. (1997). Erwerb des Lesens und des Rechtschreibens: Ergebnisse aus dem SCHOLASTIK-Projekt [The acquisition of reading and spelling: Results from the SCHOLASTIC project]. In F. E. Weinert & A. Helmke (Eds.), *Entwicklung im Grundschulalter* (pp. 113–129). Weinheim, Germany: Psychologie Verlags Union.

Schneider, W. & Weber, A. (2008). Die Längsschnittstudie LOGIK: Einführung und Überblick [The lonitudianl study LOGIK: Introduction and overview]. In W. Schneider (Ed.), *Entiwicklung von der Kindheit bis zum Erwachsenenalter* [Development from childhood to adulthood] (pp. 10–22). Weinheim, Germany: Beltz.

Schneider, W., & Weinert, F. E. (1989). Universal trends and individual differences in memory development. In A. de Ribeaupierre (Ed.), *Transition mechanisms in child development: The longitudinal perspective* (pp. 68–106). Cambridge, MA: Cambridge University Press.

Schneider, W., & Weinert, F. E. (1995). Memory development during early and middle childhood: Findings of the Munich Longitudinal Study (LOGIC). In F. E. Weinert & W. Schneider (Eds.), *Memory performance and competencies. Issues in growth and development* (pp. 263–279). Mahwah, NJ: Erlbaum.

Schrader, F. -W. & Helmke, A. (2008). Selbstvertrauen beim Übergng vom Jugend- zum Erwachsenenalter [Self confidence development from adolescence to adulthood]. In W. Schneider (Ed.), *Entiwicklung von der Kindheit bis zum Erwachsenenalter* [Development from childhood to adulthood] (pp. 141–166). Weinheim, Germany: Beltz.

Schrader, F-W., Helmke, A., & Dotzler, H. (1997). Zielkonflikte in der Grundschule: Ergebnisse aus dem SCHOLASTIK-Projekt [Goal conflicts in elementary school: Results from the SCHOLASTIC project]. In F. E. Weinert & A. Helmke (Eds.), *Entwicklung im Grundschulalter* (pp. 299–316). Weinheim, Germany: Psychologie Verlags Union.

Sodian, B., Bullock, M. & Koerber, S. (2008). Wissenschaftiliches Denken und Argumentieren [Scientific thinking and argumentation]. In W. Schneider (Ed.), *Entiwicklung von der Kindheit bis zum Erwachsenenalter* [Development from childhood to adulthood] (pp. 67–84). Weinheim, Germany: Beltz.

Sodian, B., & Schneider, W. (1999). Memory strategy development: Gradual increase, sudden insight or roller coaster? In F. E. Weinert & W. Schneider (Eds.), *Individual development from 3 to 12: Findings of a longitudinal study* (pp. 61–77). New York: Cambridge University Press.

Stern, E. (1993). What makes certain arithmetic word problems involving the comparison of sets so hard for children? *Journal of Educational Psychology, 85,* 7–23.

Stern, E. (1994). Die Bewältigung neuer Anforderungen: Eine allgemeine oder eine inhaltsspezifische Intelligenzleistung? [Meeting new challenges: General or content-specific intelligence performance?]. In D. Bartussek & M. Amelang (Eds.), *Fortschritte der differentiellen Psychologie und psychologischen Diagnostik* (pp. 333–344). Göttingen, Germany: Hogrefe.

Stern, E. (1995). Keiner wie der andere? Zum Umgang mit Leistungsunterschieden im Grundschulalter [No one like the others? On performance differences in grade school]. *Grundschulmagazin, 11,* 37–40.

Stern, E. (1997). Early training: Who, what, when, why, and how? In M. Beishuizen, K. P. E. Gravemeijer, & E. C. D. M. van Lieshout (Eds.), *The role of contexts and models in the development of mathematical strategies and procedures* (pp. 239–253). Utrecht, the Netherlands: CD Press.

Stern, E. (1997). Erwerb mathematischer Kompetenzen: Ergebnisse aus dem SCHO-LASTIK-Projekt [The development of mathematics competencies: Results from the SCHOLASTIC project]. In F. E. Weinert & A. Helmke (Eds.), *Entwicklung im Grundschulalter* (pp. 157–170). Weinheim, Germany: Psychologie Verlags Union.

Stern, E. (1999). Development of mathematical competencies. In F. E. Weinert & W. Schneider (Eds.), *Individual development from 3 to 12: Findings of a longitudinal study* (pp. 154–170). New York: Cambridge University Press.

Stern, E. (2003). Früh übt sich: Neuere Ergebnisse aus der LOGIK-Studie zum Lösen mathematischer Textaufgaben in der Grundschule [Early works out: Newer results from the LOGIC study on solving mathematical text problems in grade school]. In A. Fritz, G. Ricken, & S. Schmidt (Eds.), *Rechenschwäche. Lernwege, Schwierigkeiten und Hilfen bei Dyskalkulie* (pp. 116–130). Weinheim, Germany: Beltz.

Stern, E. (2003). Lernen ist der mächtigste Mechanismus der kognitiven Entwicklung: Der Erwerb mathematischer Kompetenzen [Learning is the magical mechanism for cognitive development: The acquisition of mathematical competencies]. In W. Schneider & M. Knopf (Eds.), *Entwicklung, Lehren und Lernen: Zum Gedenken an Franz Emanuel Weinert* (pp. 207–217). Göttingen, Germany: Hogrefe.

Stern, E., (2008). Verpasste Chancen? Was wir aus der LOGIK-Studie über den Mathematikunterricht lernen können [Missed chances? What does the LOGIC study tell us about math instruction]. In W. Schneider (Ed.), *Entiwicklung von der Kindheit bis zum Erwachsenenalter* [Development from childhood to adulthood] (pp. 187–201). Weinheim, Germany: Beltz.

Stern, E., & Mevarech, Z. (1996). Understanding of successive divisions in different contexts. *Journal of Experimental Child Psychology, 1,* 153–172.

Stern, E., Weinert, F. E., & Schneider, W. (1994). Jenseits des Intelligenzquotienten— die Entwicklung von Fähigkeitsunterschieden in der Kindheit [Beyond the IQ: The development of ability differences in childhood]. In Max-Planck-Gesellschaft (Eds.), *Jahrbuch 1994* (pp. 614–617). Göttingen, Germany: Vandenhoeck & Ruprecht.

Sturaro, C., Denissen, J. J. A., van Aken, M. A. G., & Asendorpf, J. B. (2008). Person–environment transactions during emerging adulthood: The interplay between personality characteristics and social relationships. *European Psychologist, 13*(1), 1–11.

van Aken, M. A. G., & Asendorpf, J. B. (1996). Continuity of the prototypes of social competence and shyness over the life span and across life transitions. *Journal of Adult Development, 15,* 205–216.

van Aken, M. A. G., & Asendorpf, J. B. (1997). Support by parents, classmates, friends, and siblings in preadolescence: Covariation and compensation across relationships. *Journal of Social and Personal Relationships, 14,* 79–93.

van Aken, M. A. G., & Asendorpf, J. B. (1999). A person-centered approach to development: The temporal consistency of personality and self-concept. In F. E. Weinert & W. Schneider (Eds.), *Individual development from 3 to 12: Findings of a longitudinal study* (pp. 301–319). New York: Cambridge University Press.

van Aken, M. A. G., Asendorpf, J. B., & Wilpers, S. (1996). Das soziale Unterstützungsnetzwerk von Kindern [Children's social support networks]. *Psychologie in Erziehung und Unterricht, 43,* 114–126.

van Aken, M. A. G., Helmke, A., & Schneider, W. (1997). Selbstkonzept und Leistung—Dynamik ihres Zusammenspiels: Ergebnisse aus dem SCHOLASTIK-Projekt [Self-concept, achievement and their interaction: Results from the SCHOLASTIC project]. In F. E. Weinert & A. Helmke (Eds.), *Entwicklung im Grundschulalter* (pp. 341–350). Weinheim, Germany: Psychologie Verlags Union.

Weber, A. (1992). Aggressivität, soziale Gehemmtheit und Erinnerung: Behaltensunterschiede für persönlichkeitsbezogene Ereignisse [Aggression, social inhibition and memory: Behavioral differences in autobiographical memory] (Paper 5/1992). Munich: Max-Planck-Institut für psychologische Forschung.

Weber, A. (1993). *Autobiographische Erinnerung und Persönlichkeit* [Autobiographical memory and personality]. Frankfurt am Main: Lang.

Weber, A. (1993). Die Teilnahme an einer psychologischen Untersuchung. Zum autobiographischen Gedächtnis von Kindern [Participation in a psychological study: Autobiographical memory in children] (Paper 11/1993). Munich: Max-Planck-Institut für psychologische Forschung.

Weber, A., & Stefanek, J. (1998). Überblick über die Längsschnittstudie LOGIK [Overview of the LOGIC study]. In F. E. Weinert (Ed.), *Entwicklung im Grundschulalter* (pp. 37–52). Weinheim, Germany: Beltz.

Weber, A., & Strube, G. (1999). Memory for events experienced and events observed. In F. E. Weinert & W. Schneider (Eds.), *Individual development from 3 to 12: Findings of a longitudinal study* (pp. 78–93). New York: Cambridge University Press.

Weinert, F. E. (1995). Die Entwicklung des menschlichen Gedächtnisses im Kindesalter: Differentialpsychologische Perspektive [The development of human memory in childhood: A perspective from differential psychology]. In D. Dörner & E. van der Meer (Eds.), *Das Gedächtnis* (pp. 415–432). Göttingen, Germany: Hogrefe.

Weinert, F. E. (1995). Kognitive Entwicklung im Kindesalter: Universelle Veränderungen oder individueller Kompetenzerwerb? [Cognitive development in childhood: Universal changes or individual acquisition of competencies?]. In K. Pawlik (Ed.), *Bericht über den 39. Kongreß der Deutschen Gesellschaft für Psychologie in Hamburg 1994* (pp. 742–747). Göttingen, Germany: Verlag für Psychologie.

Weinert, F. E. (1998). Das LOGIK-Projekt: Rückblicke, Einblicke und Ausblicke [The LOGIC project: Looking back, looking now, and looking into the future]. In F. E. Weinert (Ed.), *Entwicklung im Kindesalter* (pp. 177–196). Weinheim, Germany: Beltz.

Weinert, F. E. (1998). Überblick über die psychische Entwicklung im Kindesalter [Overview of psychological development in childhood]. In F. E. Weinert (Ed.), *Entwicklung im Kindesalter* (pp. 1–36). Weinheim, Germany: Beltz.

Weinert, F. E., Bullock, M., & Schneider, W. (1999). Universal, differential and individual aspects of child development from 3 to 12: What can we learn from a comprehensive longitudinal study? In F. E. Weinert & W. Schneider (Eds.), *Individual development from 3 to 12: Findings of a longitudinal study* (pp. 324–350). New York: Cambridge University Press.

Weinert, F. E., & Hany, E. A. (2002). Stabilität und Variabilität der Intelligenz [Intelligence, stability, and variability]. In G. Jüttemann & H. Thomae (Eds.), *Persönlichkeit und Entwicklung* (pp. 73–98). Weinheim, Germany: Beltz.

Weinert, F. E., & Helmke, A. (1993). Wie bereichsspezifisch verläuft die kognitive Entwicklung? [How domain specific is cognitive development?]. In R. Duit & W. Gräber (Eds.), *Kognitive Entwicklung und Lernen der Naturwissenschaften. Tagungsband zum 20. IPN-Symposium aus Anlaß des 60. Geburtstages von Prof. Dr. Heinrich Stork* (pp. 27–45). Kiel, Germany: Institut für die Pädagogik der Naturwissenschaften (IPN).

Weinert, F. E., & Helmke, A. (1995). Interclassroom differences in instructional quality and interindividual differences in cognitive development. *Educational Psychologist, 30,* 15–20.

Weinert, F. E., & Helmke, A. (1995). Learning from wise mother nature or big brother instructor: The wrong choice as seen from an educational perspective. *Educational Psychologist, 30,* 135–142.

Weinert, F. E., & Helmke, A. (1996). Der gute Lehrer: Person, Funktion oder Fiktion? [The good teacher: Function or fiction?]. In A. Leschinsky (Ed.), *Die Institutionalisierung von Lehren und Lernen. Beiträge zu einer Theorie der Schule* (pp. 223–233). Weinheim, Germany: Beltz.

Weinert, F. E., & Helmke, A. (1998). The neglected role of individual differences in theoretical models of cognitive development. *Learning and Instruction, 8*(4, Special Issue), 309–323.

Weinert, F. E., Helmke, A., & Schneider, W. (1989). Individual differences in learning performance and in school achievement: Plausible parallels and unexplained discrepancies. In H. Mandl, E. de Corte, N. Bennett, & H. F. Friedrich (Eds.), *Learning and instruction* (pp. 461–479). Oxford: Pergamon Press.

Weinert, F. E., & Lingelbach, H. (1995). Teaching expertise: Theoretical conceptualizations, empirical findings, and some consequences for teacher training. In R. Hoz & M. Silberstein (Eds.), *Partnerships of schools and institutions of higher education in teacher development* (pp. 293–302). Beer-Sheva, Israel: Ben Gurion University of the Negev Press.

Weinert, F. E., & Schneider, W. (1993). Cognitive, social, and emotional development. In D. Magnusson & P. Casaer (Eds.), *Longitudinal research on individual development: Present status and future perspectives* (pp. 75–94). Cambridge: Cambridge University Press.

Weinert, F. E., Schneider, W., Asendorpf, J. B., Bullock, M., Helmke, A., Knopf, M., et al. (1991). Intra- und interindividuelle Unterschiede in der psychischen Entwicklung von Kindern [Intra- and interindividual difference in children's psychological development]. In Max-Planck-Gesellschaft (Eds.), *Jahrbuch 1991* (pp. 518–522). Göttingen, Germany: Vandenhoeck & Ruprecht.

Weinert, F. E., Schneider, W., Stefanek, J., & Weber, A. (1999). Introduction and overview. In F. E. Weinert & W. Schneider (Eds.), *Individual development from 3 to 12: Findings of a longitudinal study* (pp. 1–8). New York: Cambridge University Press.

Weinert, F. E., & Stefanek, J. (1997). Entwicklung vor, während und nach der Grund-schulzeit: Ergebnisse aus dem SCHOLASTIK-Projekt [Development before, during and after elementary school: Results from the SCHOLASTIK project]. In F. E. Weinert & A. Helmke (Eds.), *Entwicklung im Grundschulalter* (pp. 423–451). Weinheim, Germany: Psychologie Verlags Union.

Wimmer, H., Landerl, K., & Schneider, W. (1994). The role of rhyme awareness in learning to read regular orthography. *British Journal of Developmental Psychology, 12,* 469–484.

3. TECHNICAL REPORTS ON THE LOGIC STUDY

Schneider, W., & Stefanek, J. (Eds.). (2006). *The Munich Longitudinal Study on the Genesis of Individual Competencies (LOGIC): Report No. 14. Assessment procedures and results of wave eleven.* Munich: Max Planck Institute for Psychological Research.

Weinert, F. E., & Schneider, W. (Eds.). (1986). *First report on the Munich Longitudinal Study on the Genesis of Individual Competencies (LOGIC).* Munich: Max Planck Institute for Psychological Research.

Weinert, F. E., & Schneider, W. (Eds.). (1987). *The Munich Longitudinal Study on the Genesis of Individual Competencies (LOGIC): Report No. 2. Documentation of assessment procedures used in waves one to three.* Munich: Max Planck Institute for Psychological Research.

Weinert, F. E., & Schneider, W. (Eds.). (1987). *The Munich Longitudinal Study on the Genesis of Individual Competencies (LOGIC): Report No. 3. Results of wave one.* Munich: Max Planck Institute for Psychological Research.

Weinert, F. E., & Schneider, W. (Eds.). (1988). *The Munich Longitudinal Study on the Genesis of Individual Competencies (LOGIC): Report No. 4. Results of wave two.* Munich: Max Planck Institute for Psychological Research.

Weinert, F. E., & Schneider, W. (Eds.). (1989). *The Munich Longitudinal Study on the Genesis of Individual Competencies (LOGIC): Report No. 5. Results of wave three.* Munich: Max Planck Institute for Psychological Research.

Weinert, F. E., & Schneider, W. (Eds.). (1989). *The Munich Longitudinal Study on the Genesis of Individual Competencies (LOGIC): Report No. 6. Psychological development in the preschool years: Longitudinal results of waves one to three.* Munich: Max Planck Institute for Psychological Research.

Weinert, F. E., & Schneider, W. (Eds.). (1991). *The Munich Longitudinal Study on the Genesis of Individual Competencies (LOGIC): Report No. 7. Assessment procedures and results of wave four.* Munich: Max Planck Institute for Psychological Research.

Weinert, F. E., & Schneider, W. (Eds.). (1992). *The Munich Longitudinal Study on the Genesis of Individual Competencies (LOGIC): Report No. 8. Assessment procedures and results of wave five.* Munich: Max Planck Institute for Psychological Research.

Weinert, F. E., & Schneider, W. (Eds.). (1993). *The Munich Longitudinal Study on the Genesis of Individual Competencies (LOGIC): Report No. 9. Assessment procedures and results of wave six.* Munich: Max Planck Institute for Psychological Research.

Weinert, F. E., & Schneider, W. (Eds.). (1993). *The Munich Longitudinal Study on the Genesis of Individual Competencies (LOGIC): Report No. 10. Assessment procedures and results of wave seven.* Munich: Max Planck Institute for Psychological Research.

Weinert, F. E., & Schneider, W. (Eds.). (1994). *The Munich Longitudinal Study on the Genesis of Individual Competencies (LOGIC): Report No. 11. Assessment procedures and results of wave eight.* Munich: Max Planck Institute for Psychological Research.

Weinert, F. E., & Schneider, W. (Eds.). (1995). *The Munich Longitudinal Study on the Genesis of Individual Competencies (LOGIC): Report No. 12. Assessment procedures and results of wave nine.* Munich: Max Planck Institute for Psychological Research.

Weinert, F. E., & Schneider, W. (Eds.). (2000). *The Munich Longitudinal Study on the Genesis of Individual Competencies (LOGIC): Report No. 13. Assessment procedures and results of wave ten.* Munich: Max Planck Institute for Psychological Research.

Author Index

Subject Index

A

Academic performance, *see* Educational achievement
Adolescence; *see also* Self-esteem
  identity crisis, 145
  and moral motivation, 108
  peer acceptance, 149
  personality, 119, 120
  and self-concept, 146
  and well-being, 149
Adulthood
  emerging, 120
  scientific reasoning in, 185–188
  verbal intelligence test, 14
Aggression, 132–133, 139
  and externalizing, 120, 122
  and gender, 132
  observations of, 126
  and part-time work, 136, 139
  by personality type, 125
  self-judgments of, 133
Amsterdam Growth Study, 36
Arlin Test of Formal Reasoning (ATFR), 15–16, 192, 243
ATFR, *see* Arlin Test of Formal Reasoning (ATFR)

B

Berkeley Growth Study, 9
Berkeley Guidance Study, 120
Berliner Intelligenz Struktur Test, 230
Bielefeld Longitudinal Study, 202, 203
Block and Block Longitudinal Study, 120, 247

C

California Child Q-set (CCQ), 121, 122
CFT, *see* Culture Fair Intelligence Test (CFT)
Clinical method, 10
CMMS, *see* Columbia Mental Maturity Scale (CMMS)
Cognitive development, 10–12, 242–245
  in mathematics, 223
  and motor development, 38–39, 44–46, 54–55
  Piaget's stages, 11

primary and secondary abilities, 223
and psychometric measures, 29
variability, 14
Columbia Mental Maturity Scale (CMMS), 15
Culture Fair Intelligence Test (CFT), 15, 16

D

Dunedin Longitudinal Study, 120, 137, 247

E

Early childhood
  intelligence, 15
  motor abilities in, 46
  motor tests for, 40, 42
Early literacy, 200, 204; *see also* Reading; Spelling
  assessment variables, 204
Educational achievement
  and classroom setting, 245
  and domain-specific knowledge, 244
  and personality, 134–135, 136, 139–140
  predicting, 2, 11, 244
  prerequisites, 148
  and self-esteem, 148
Emerging adulthood, 120

F

Fels Longitudinal Study, 120

G

Gender
  identification, 112
  and mathematical competencies, 233–234
  and moral motivation, 94, 109–110, 112
  and moral stability, 112–114
  and motor abilities, 37, 39, 55, 56
  role stereotypes, 56, 110–111
German school system, 4

H

Hamburg-Wechsler Intelligence Scale (HAWIE), 14, 16